MILITARY
MOTORCYCLES
OF THE WORLD

MILITARY MOTORCYCLES
OF THE WORLD

- A complete reference guide to 100 years of military motorcycles, from their first use in World War I to the specialized types of today

- Featuring over 160 machines with 550 historical and modern photographs

PAT WARE

LORENZ BOOKS

This edition is published by
Lorenz Books, an imprint of
Anness Publishing Ltd
www.lorenzbooks.com
info@anness.com

© Anness Publishing Ltd 2022

Publisher: Joanna Lorenz
Editorial Director: Helen Sudell
Senior Editor: Felicity Forster
Designer: Nigel Pell
Production Director: Ben Worley

A CIP catalogue record is available for this title at
the British Library

PUBLISHER'S NOTES
Although the advice and information in
this book are believed to be accurate at the
time of going to press, neither the authors
nor the publisher can accept any legal
responsibility or liability for any errors or
omissions that may be made.
    The nationality of each motorcycle
is identified in the relevant specification
box by the national flag that was in
use at the time of service.

PAGE 1: **Harley-Davidson, WL.**
PAGE 2: **BMW R-35, 350cc, single cylinder.**
PAGE 3: **Harley-Davidson, WLA.**

Contents

Introduction

The history of the military motorcycle dates back to the very beginning of military mechanization, and to the earliest days of the development of motorcycles. Soon after the close of the 19th century, Britain, Germany, and Austria had all started to acquire motorcycles for military use. By the time of World War I, other nations had also purchased their first military motorcycles as the machine began to be seen as a possible replacement for the horse.

However, clearly the military motorcycle could also be used in other roles. Back then, the "weapon of mass destruction" was the machine-gun. In Britain and Germany, in particular, tacticians realized that relatively small groups of soldiers could lay down withering barrages of fire using their weapons. What is more, the introduction of the motorcycle sidecar combination meant that machine-guns could become mobile. While it was not possible to fire on the move, at least not without considerable risk to other riders, firing parties could move rapidly from one position to another – what is known in military parlance as "shoot and scoot".

Not only did the motorcycle become technically more reliable during World War I, but also proved to be of tactical and logistical value. By the 1920s, the military motorcycle was a standard item in the inventory of most armies.

There had been experiments with armoured sidecars during World War I, and several nations also attempted to produce small armoured reconnaissance, and even offensive vehicles, using solo and combination motorcycles during the 1930s. Similarly, the addition of tracks to a motorcycle might

ABOVE: **A line-up of sidecar-equipped Harley-Davidsons of the US Motorcycle Corps photographed at Fort Brown, Brownsville, Texas. The machines have the standard civilian sidecar.**

improve cross-country capability but did little for cornering performance and the general dynamics involved in balancing a fast-moving machine on two wheels.

In the years leading up to World War II, the Nazi government purchased thousands of motorcycles for military use. Amongst the combatant nations in the conflict, the *Wehrmacht* used more motorcycles for service with combat troops. Germany was also alone in commissioning large numbers of specialized military motorcycles as opposed to simply adapting existing civilian models. Indeed, the big BMW and Zündapp sidecar outfits of the *Kradschützen* probably remain the high point in the development of the military motorcycle.

Although Britain had experimented with machine-gun sidecars in the early stages of the war, the arrival of the US-built Jeep saw Allied use of the motorcycle reduced to the messenger role from around 1942.

The late 1940s and the decades which followed, saw the military motorcycle being used in a relatively minor role, relegated to traffic control and convoy escort duties. Notwithstanding some experiments with automatic transmission, those machines purchased were frequently derived directly from civilian types. Indeed, so few military motorcycles were being procured across the world during

the 1960s and 1970s, that the Japanese "invasion" of the motorcycle market had little effect.

During the 1980s and 1990s, military motorcycles were lightweight multi-terrain machines which could be used by reconnaissance troops or despatch riders. Others were stripped-down utility versions of the big civilian touring machines which could be used for convoy escort and military police work.

It is only in the last decade or so, that the military motorcycle market has been rejuvenated by experience gained in the so-called "asymmetric" conflicts in Iraq and Afghanistan.

Here, quad bikes and enduro-type off-road machines have proved enormously valuable in moving lightly equipped troops across difficult terrain. Perhaps the increases in size and weight of vehicles such as the HMMWV, and even the Land Rover, mean that Special Forces and clandestine units really need a new "Jeep" – and the quad bike and trailer is almost a Jeep. Finally, a recent joint UK/US project has seen the emergence of the first practical diesel-powered motorcycle.

This book details the fascinating story of the use of the military motorcycle over more than 100 years.

ABOVE: **The *Wehrmacht* was an enthusiastic user of motorcycles of all sizes during the late 1930s and throughout World War II.** LEFT: **The multi-terrain Armstrong, later Harley-Davidson, MT350 and MT500 are typical of current military motorcycles.**

The History of the Military Motorcycle

The development of the military motorcycle has followed the same path as the civilian machines.

Little more than pedal bicycles with a motor, early motorcycles had either a V-belt or chain to transmit power to the rear wheel. Frequently, the pedals remained in place, providing a means of starting the engine and assisting the power unit to drag machine and rider up an incline.

For more than seven decades, motorcycle frames were still recognizably derived from bicycle practice, with engine and transmission placed below the rider. Machines were two-speed at first but were soon followed by three- and four-speed. V-belt drive disappeared, and some machines were fitted with shaft drive.

Most engines were air-cooled with up to four cylinders. A few manufacturers retained water-cooling for the cylinders, a practice which came to the forefront in the 1970s when Japanese manufacturers began producing high-powered liquid-cooled engines.

The front forks were provided with suspension from the earliest days, but it was not until the 1950s that rear suspension became a standard fitment.

It would be fair to say that by the end of the 1950s, all of the elements of the modern motorcycle were in place. Developments since then have seen incredible increases in engine power and machine performance and reliability.

LEFT: **Exhaustion enables a man to sleep anywhere. This World War II Canadian despatch rider has managed to use his Norton 16H as a makeshift bunk.**

ABOVE: **The Harley-Davidson military Model J with the standard factory sidecar was widely used by US and Allied forces during World War I.**

The role of the military motorcycle

Before the advent of reliable radio communications and encryption techniques, the physical – or "ear-to-ear" – delivery of messages, orders, despatches, etc was a vital military function. At first runners were used for this purpose and, in time, horses supplanted the runners – Robert Browning's poem tells how the "good news" was brought from the Belgian city of Ghent to Aix by three riders, while in the previous century, Paul Revere's historic overnight ride from Boston to Lexington in 1775 told the rebels of the movements of the British Army.

As the motorcycle started to replace the horse during World War I, it seemed obvious that the horse-mounted despatch rider could simply be replaced by one riding a motorcycle. Given a degree of mechanical reliability, the mount would not succumb to fatigue – the rider was another matter altogether – and the motorcycle was able to negotiate cratered ground that would have caused the horse to throw its rider.

While despatch riding almost certainly was the first role for the military motorcycle and, nearly a century

ABOVE: **During World War II, the British Army tended to restrict motorcycles to the liaison and despatch role.** FAR LEFT: **The German Zündapp company produced the K500W from 1933 until 1940 and, although it was basically a civilian machine, it was widely used by the *Wehrmacht*.** LEFT: **The *Wehrmacht* was not always the epitome of mechanization – here Nazi infantrymen carry a pigeon basket on a lightweight motorcycle.**

LEFT: **The Armstrong-designed Rotax-engined MT350 was first supplied to the British Army in 1985; the larger-engined MT500 followed in 1993 and both were also produced by Harley-Davidson.**
BELOW: **Motorcycles have always been popular with military display teams. These US soldiers are demonstrating riding and shooting prowess on Harley-Davidson Electra-Glides of the late 1990s.**

later, remains a significant aspect of the use of these machines, it was not the only role.

The motorcycle also allowed reconnaissance and scouting units to penetrate into enemy territory. The first US soldier into Germany during World War I – Corporal Roy Holtz of Chippewa Falls, Wisconsin – was taking his captain on a reconnaissance mission in northern Belgium. The pair, riding a Harley-Davidson motorcycle, became lost and ended up asking for directions at a farmhouse, which they then discovered was being used as a German Army billet. Both were taken prisoner only to be released a couple of days later when the armistice was declared.

Attempts were also made to use motorcycles as a kind of mechanical cavalry and during World War I, the British, US and German armies all experimented with mounting a machine-gun on to a motorcycle, either using a specially adapted sidecar or by fitting the gun directly on to the handlebars. It was impossible to fire the thing on the move, at least with any hope of hitting anything, but nevertheless, motorcycles continued to carry machine-guns throughout World War II. In the mid-1950s, the French even tried to mount a recoilless anti-tank weapon on a scooter. The German heavy motorcycles of World War II were also designed to act as artillery tractors or to tow light trailers.

Medical evacuation was a particular problem during World War I and many motorcycles were fitted with ambulance or stretcher-carrier sidecars. While a bumpy ride on a primitive motorcycle across the rutted and shell-holed ground would not have been the first choice of any seriously wounded man, the alternative was probably to be left in a shell hole to die.

During World War II, ultra-light motorcycles were developed by Britain, America and Italy that could be air-dropped by parachute alongside airborne troops. Although the machines were slow and uncomfortable, they did at least provide instant mobility in the field. Other behind-the-lines roles included convoy escort duties, traffic control and military police work.

Today, no-one would dream of using a motorcycle combination as a regular means of transporting the wounded and, while guns might not be mounted on to motorcycles, there is every reason to believe that the quad bike lends itself well to such a role. The modern army has significantly fewer motorcycles, but in many other respects, surprisingly little has changed. The motorcycle continues to be used for despatch and courier duties, convoy escort work, traffic control, rescue missions behind enemy lines, reconnaissance, and in military police units. The mobility of the motorcycle remains its primary military advantage.

The motorcycle pioneers

There is a saying that "when the time comes to railroad, everybody railroads" and in the latter years of the 19th century there were sufficient attempts being made to build a powered bicycle to suggest that here was an idea whose time had come. The earliest machines were steam powered but, aside from the obvious safety issues for anyone sitting astride a firebox and a tank full of boiling water, there were practical considerations such as the problems of carrying, or finding, sufficient fuel and water for a journey of more than 24km/15 miles.

Steam-powered motorcycles never really became a practical proposition but the way forward came in the form of the internal combustion engine. In 1885, two German engineers, Gottlieb Daimler and Paul Maybach, fitted a 270cc four-stroke petrol engine into a largely wooden two-wheeled chassis that

ABOVE: **Although women had yet to be granted the right to vote, during World War I the shortage of men frequently found women doing what had traditionally been men's work. These uniformed women of a voluntary AID detachment are mounted on a selection of essentially civilian outfits.** RIGHT: **A US infantryman attends to his Indian Powerplus, a model introduced in 1917. Indian, Excelsior and Harley-Davidson quickly established themselves as the leading manufacturers in the USA.**

they called *Einspur* or *Reitwagen*, depending on your source. Despite its small stabilizer wheels, many consider this to be the world's first proper motorcycle.

In 1894, the Germans Hildebrand & Wolfmüller produced the first commercial motorcycle, a 1,488cc twin-cylinder machine which used rubber belt drive and was capable of 40kph/25mph. Only a few hundred were built and it was not a commercial success.

However, while the German engineers had proved that the manufacture of such a device was possible, it took a pair of Frenchmen, Count Albert de Dion and Georges Bouton to kick-start the motorcycle industry. In 1897, De Dion-Bouton offered their own engine for general sale. Initially with a capacity of 270cc but soon uprated to 500cc, the engine was licensed and copied across the world.

Meanwhile, the pedal cycle industry was in full swing in the years leading up to the turn of the 20th century and, by 1885, the frame and wheel layout devised by John Kemp Starley for his Rover "safety cycle" had become the norm. With its low centre of gravity, chain transmission and equal-sized wheels, the design lent itself well to being motorized, and the subsequent availability of reliable engines, persuaded many cycle builders to offer motorized versions of their products. Despite experiments that placed the engine over the rear wheel, behind the saddle, and even on a small trailer which pushed the machine along, it was clear that the best place for the engine was between the frame down-tube and the seat-tube, close to the ground. Thus was established the standard motorcycle layout.

As engines became more powerful, the design started to move away from its bicycle origins and features such as sprung forks and multi-speed transmissions started to appear. The number of manufacturers increased rapidly, and many of the companies that would be the big names

ABOVE: **The motorcycle is a Triumph Model H, but clearly safety was not a primary concern during these early years.**

of the industry for the next half century appeared in the years leading up to World War I.

The British company Scott produced their first motorcycle in 1898 and went into full production in 1908. Triumph and Ariel were both established in 1902, Velocette in 1904, and BSA in 1906. In France, Clement and René Gillet started motorcycle production in 1897 and 1898, respectively, and Peugeot began working on motorcycles in 1899. Terrot was established in 1901. The German company NSU made its first motorcycle in 1901, and Wanderer in 1902. Over in the USA, Carl Oscar Hedstrom and George I.M. Hendee had founded the Hendee Manufacturing Company in 1900. Their aim was to produce a "motor-driven bicycle for the everyday use of the general public". Within a year, they had produced the Single, a 1.75hp machine with a top speed of 40kph/25mph. By 1914, Hendee's Indian motorcycle had become the best-selling motorcycle in the world. Harley-Davidson, soon to take this title from Indian, first appeared in 1903.

By 1914, more than 720 motorcycle manufacturers had been established worldwide, albeit more than a few failed within a year or two of starting operations. But, when Europe went to war that year, for many soldiers it was astride a motorcycle.

ABOVE: **Motorcycles were quickly adopted for military use and were frequently seen as a direct replacement for the horse.**

ABOVE: **Sidecars were used to mount machine-guns and also to carry parts and ammunition. Some were fitted as stretcher carriers.**

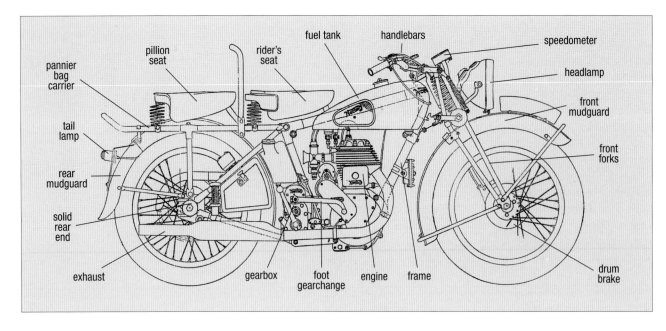

The anatomy of a motorcycle

In the early days, there was little consensus on how the various components of the motorcycle should be assembled with designers disagreeing over the details of engines, suspension, brakes and transmission.

Frame

Early motorcycles were constructed on a diamond-shaped tubular backbone frame similar to that used for pedal cycles. Until well into the 1950s, it was common to employ a single down-tube, but as the machines got heavier and engines got larger, paired wishbone shaped down-tubes of the duplex frame were required to provide a wider engine support.

External pressed-steel perimeter frames appeared during the 1930s, with the frame wrapping around the outside of the machine. In recent years this style has returned, now using square-section steel or aluminium tubing. Some modern machines use the frame tubes as an oil, or even fuel, reservoir.

Engine

Many of the pioneering manufacturers used proprietary engines – for example, the products of JAP, MAG, Villiers and Sachs.

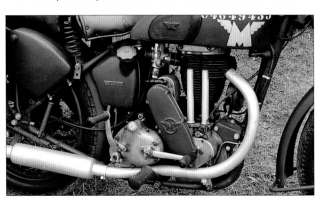

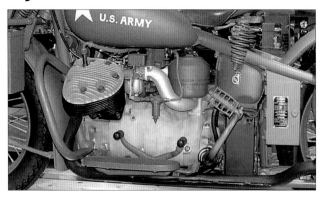

Side-valve or inlet-over-exhaust valve layout was common at first but by the early 1950s almost all machines were fitted with overhead valves. Two-strokes started to appear in the 1930s, and were particularly championed by DKW. Diesel power is extremely rare in motorcycles since the power characteristics of the engine do not really suit the performance required from a motorcycle.

Pre-war engines with a capacity up to 500cc were frequently of single-cylinder design but even from the early days, twin-cylinder arrangements were not uncommon, including V, horizontally opposed, side-by-side (parallel), and in-line configurations, while Ariel became famous for their four-cylinder square layout. Puch devised an unusual split-piston two-stroke using two pistons running in parallel cylinder bores, but sharing a combustion chamber, spark plug and cylinder head; one piston controlled the inlet ports, the other the exhaust. Modern motorcycles tend to be multi-cylinder design.

TOP, ABOVE AND LEFT: **Although there was plenty of room for eccentricity in design during the early years, a standardized motorcycle layout quickly emerged, and while the US favoured big V-twin engines (above), the single or twin-cylinder design (left) was more usual in Europe.**

Magneto ignition was common until the 1940s, but this was gradually replaced by the familiar battery and coil arrangement, and then by solid-state electronic systems.

Virtually all machines built before the 1980s were air-cooled, but water-cooling has become far more common.

Transmission

While the very earliest machines used a form of direct drive, a multi-speed gearbox is essential to exploit the torque and power characteristics of the engine. Initially installed separately, the gearbox was usually connected to the engine by an exposed primary chain. So-called "unitary construction" became more common from the 1930s, whereby the gear train is incorporated in the engine castings.

Some early motorcycles had the gearbox in the rear hub, and some manufacturers have even experimented with automatic or stepless belt drive.

Final drive

The final drive connects the gearbox to the rear wheel. Many early machines used belt drive, either a flat leather belt, or a fabricated belt made from separate links. The big German BMW and Zündapp machines were notable for their use of shaft drive – in modern versions the shaft runs inside an oil bath in one of the rear fork legs, but on older machines the shaft was exposed. However, roller chains remain by far the most common form of drive.

MIDDLE AND ABOVE: **Most motorcycles manufactured before 1945 had a rigid, unsprung rear end (middle). The standard rear end these days consists of a swing arm suspended on a telescopic unit (above).**

ABOVE AND ABOVE RIGHT: **The girder parallelogram forks (left) remained the standard design until the end of World War II, when the telescopic pattern (right) began to be fitted.**

Front forks and suspension

The earliest front suspension consisted of parallelogram forks, with tubular girder or pressed-steel fork blades secured by short pivoting links to a pair of yokes at the steering head. The forks were cushioned against movement using one, or a pair of friction-damped coil springs between the top and bottom yokes or, less frequently, using a horizontal leaf spring. On leading link forks, the pivot points are at the bottom of the forks, with the centre of the wheel placed forward of the steering axis, but Indian and early BMW machines used a trailing link which placed the axle behind the steering axis.

These designs gradually gave way to the modern telescopic forks whereby the coil spring and damping mechanism are contained in a telescopic strut filled with hydraulic fluid.

Rear forks and suspension

Early motorcycles had no rear suspension at all, relying on a sprung saddle to insulate the rider from road shocks. From about the mid-1940s it became common to provide cushioned rear forks, most commonly using a trailing arm or hinged subframe suspended on a friction-damped coil spring; compressed rubber blocks or leaf springs have also been used. Plunger-type suspension was also common for a period, notably used by BMW and Ariel, where the forks remained fixed but the rear axle was allowed to move on coil-sprung vertical plungers.

Modern machines tend to use a trailing swing arm, often single-sided, suspended on a coil spring, which is damped by a sealed hydraulic shock absorber.

Brakes

It was not unusual at first to provide brakes only on the rear axle, frequently using a block acting directly on to the rim or on to either the belt-drive pulley or a dummy rim. Early front brakes were sometimes of the caliper design.

Since the 1920s, it has been standard practice to fit brakes at front and rear, at first using mechanically operated expanding shoes inside a drum, this gradually giving way to hydraulic operation. Modern practice is to use hydraulic disc brakes, front and rear.

A standardized layout emerges

These days, all motorcycles conform to a standardized layout – the engine nestles in the frame beneath the tank and drives the rear wheel via a clutch, unit-constructed gearbox, with final drive by chain or propeller shaft. The front and rear forks are both provided with damped suspension in the interests of road-holding and rider comfort. As regards controls, forward motion is controlled by a right-hand twist grip, and the gear change is operated via a foot pedal on the right side; a second pedal, on the left, is used to apply the rear

brake. A hand lever on the right operates the front brake, a similar lever on the left operates the clutch.

It wasn't always thus. It took until 1914 for the standardized layout of frame, engine and transmission to appear – and by this time, the motorcycle had acquired its own set of design rules and had lost its early resemblance to the bicycle.

Notwithstanding the handful of brave manufacturers who chose to place the engine over the rear wheel, or even ahead of the front forks where it drove the front wheel, there was an early consensus on fitting the power unit low down in the frame, just above what would have been the bottom bracket on a conventional pedal cycle frame. Not only did this give the optimum centre of gravity, but it also made it relatively easy to get drive to the rear wheel. And the obvious place for the fuel tank was above the engine, although there were still those who chose to fit the tank behind the engine.

Virtually all early machines were started by pedalling, and were fitted with standard cycle-type pedals for this purpose. This tended to dictate the frame geometry and ergonomics and, for this reason – plus the fact that most pioneering motorcycle manufacturers had graduated from pedal cycles – early machines strongly resemble pedal cycles. Inertia kick starters were quick to appear and pedals had disappeared completely by around 1915. Indian tried to introduce electric start before World War I but the system was unreliable and almost bankrupted the company.

ABOVE: **Although it dates from the inter-war years, this Harley-Davidson clearly shows the standardized motorcycle layout which quickly emerged.** LEFT: **As with this early Triumph, some manufacturers continued to use belt drive even after the virtues of the roller chain had been well proven.**

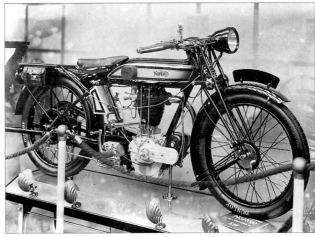

Electric start became the norm in the 1970s and 1980s as Japanese imports stormed the world markets.

Some early pioneers used a two- or even three-speed epicyclic gearbox, placing this in the rear hub, following the style of the pedal cycle; this also allowed the clutch to be fitted in the hub. Pioneered by Triumph on their 500cc Model H, the most logical position for the gearbox was behind the engine, with the clutch placed between the engine and gearbox, and this was quickly adopted by all manufacturers. So-called unitary construction techniques subsequently incorporated the gearbox into the crankcase casting.

While the use of a rear brake was almost universal, it was some time before all manufacturers also fitted brakes for the front wheel, and many riders still believed that the use of a front brake was dangerous. Rim brakes gave way to drum brakes, and then to the universal adoption of disc brakes; similarly, mechanical operation by rod or cable eventually yielded to hydraulics, meaning that it was no longer necessary to provide huge brake levers in order to get sufficient leverage to stop a heavy machine.

The standard layout described had become pretty much universal on all motorcycles by the outbreak of World War I but, curiously, it was decades before there was any agreement on where the brake, clutch and gear-change controls should be placed. Specifically, there were differences between machines produced in Europe and the USA, and this must have led to more than a few accidents or near-misses as riders rode on unfamiliar machines during the two wars. Harley-Davidson, for example, used a left-hand throttle and hand gear-change on the war-time WLA, and continued to offer a hand gear-change right up to 1972/73. These days, only motor scooters, with their rear engines and lack of foot controls, seem to vary from this standard layout.

ABOVE: **Although broadly conforming to the norm, this early Norton has the magneto carried ahead of the frame down-tube, a position favoured by more than one British manufacturer.**
ABOVE LEFT: **The distinctive gear change lever on the Harley-Davidson was always mounted on the left-hand side of the fuel tank.** LEFT: **The British Matchless G3L of 1941 was one of the first military motorcycles to adopt telescopic front forks.**

Expanding military usage

During the opening years of the 20th century, motorcycles began to improve significantly in reliability and, as the design of the machines also started to settle down, the number of motorcycle manufacturers expanded rapidly. The military started to take an interest in these new machines and the manufacturers began to vie with one another for military contracts. By 1905 it was obvious that there was a real role for the military motorcycle and, in Britain, companies such as Scott, Triumph and BSA had started to supply motorcycles to the Army, with purchases often being under the control of individual commanding officers. In Germany, it was a similar story, where the first German military motorcycles had entered service as early as 1901.

Among civilians, the popularity of the motorcycle was progressing in leaps and bounds. By 1913, there were 100,000 motorcycles registered in Britain, and by 1914, many of the major European and American manufacturers had already been established – Triumph, BSA, AJS, Norton, Indian, Harley-Davidson, Puch, Peugeot and NSU were in business before 1914, and all would go on to have a major influence on the industry over the next 50 years. All of these companies would also become major suppliers to the world's armed forces.

When World War I broke out in 1914, the demand for motorcycles took another unprecedented leap forward. Thousands of civilian machines were requisitioned and pressed into service alongside those that had been supplied direct to the military. However, while the war may have been a catalyst for production, it did little for innovation. The armed forces may have purchased thousands of motorcycles but they tended to favour reliability over innovation, effectively forcing the manufacturers to be conservative. At the same time, the civilian market shrank and many small companies did not make it through the war years.

By the end of the war, the German *Reichswehr* had an inventory of 5,400 motorcycles, mostly civilian types that had received little more militarization than a coat of matt paint and

ABOVE: **Germany was quick to see the advantages of the motorcycle in military terms and, by 1914, had almost 5,400 motorcycles available.** LEFT: **Early motorcycles were not necessarily reliable, as this Highlander would certainly attest.**

LEFT: **The 2.75hp machine produced by the British manufacturer Douglas was widely adopted by the British Army, with more than 13,000 in service by 1918. Douglas retained the V-belt drive and exposed flywheel into the post-war years.** BELOW LEFT: **The water-cooled Scott 3.25hp was used by the British Army as a machine-gun carrier. The machines operated in threes, one with a tripod-mounted gun, one with just the tripod, and one carrying parts and/or personnel.**

a pillion seat. But this number paled into insignificance against the British Army's 1918 total of 48,000 machines from more than 50 different manufacturers – a fact which can hardly have helped the problems of maintaining adequate stocks of spare parts.

France had been one of the first nations to embrace mechanization of its army and, although the nation's army did not employ large numbers of motorcycles during World War I, companies such as René Gillet, Peugeot, Griffon and Terrot had started supplying military motorcycles from the

turn of the century. In Belgium, the armaments company FN produced their first motorcycles in 1902, and their products were supplied to a number of the Western Allies during the conflict, including Australia.

The US Army was slower to embrace the new developments and did not start buying motorcycles until about 1913. Nevertheless, something like 15,000 Harley-Davidsons and 18,000 (Hendee) Indians were supplied during World War I, with other machines coming from Excelsior and Cleveland, as well as from British manufacturers such as Rover and Triumph.

Italy started to procure military motorcycles in 1914, and the nation had something like 6,500 machines in service by the time the conflict came to an end.

By 1918, all of the major combatants had acquired large stocks of motorcycles and, at the end of the conflict, thousands of surplus motorcycles were put up for sale across Europe and America, with ex-servicemen among the eager buyers. Those manufacturers who were still in business returned to producing purely civilian machines, some with little more than modified pre-war models. But, for many, the war had been invaluable in improving the breed and the new machines were considerably more reliable than their pre-war counterparts.

The motorcycle had finally come of age and technological progress in the post-war period was rapid, with features such as chain drive, electric lighting, and front and rear brakes becoming the norm. New manufacturers would continue to spring up over the coming decades and many of the early pioneers were seen to fail, but this was a period of exciting technological progress, with specialized heavyweight military machines starting to appear in the decade before World War II.

ABOVE: **Typical of civilian motorcycles of the period, the Triumph Model H, which was nicknamed "Trusty" for its reliability, was widely used by the British Army.**

Civilian motorcycles go to war

The earliest military motorcycles were basic civilian machines. Most armies had not started to evolve any motor vehicle policy and there was little attempt made at standardization. With the outbreak of World War I, it was soon apparent that there was a shortage of motorcycles and many were requisitioned. Others entered service and remained privately owned, effectively "loaned" to the army by their civilian volunteer riders. Militarization, such as it was, generally consisted of little more than fitting leather panniers and a rear rack, and painting the machine with the typical overall matt grey or green finish that was supposed to hide its outline from the all-seeing field glasses of the enemy.

At the time it must have seemed that issues such as reliability and performance were largely a matter of chance and, until the outbreak of World War I, the military usage of motorcycles was such that there had been little opportunity for any specialized requirements to emerge. Civilian motorcycles were widely available and it should

ABOVE: **Aside from the inevitable, although not necessarily universal, coat of matt green paint, early military motorcycles were rarely different to their civilian counterparts.**
RIGHT: **Posing in front of the Austin armoured cars that were supplied to the Imperial Army during World War I, these Russian soldiers are equipped with two bicycles and three civilian motorcycles of indeterminate origin.**

be no surprise that it was these which the world's armies started to buy from around the turn of the century. However, when World War I led to huge increases in the numbers of motorcycles required, the sheer diversity of types which entered in service began to present something of a logistical nightmare that was never really resolved.

In Britain, the Government banned the sale of motorcycles to civilians in 1916, diverting many of those who had been making motorcycles to the production of other war supplies. But this had no effect on the types of machine available and orders continued to be placed with the remaining manufacturers for the duration of the conflict for what were essentially civilian machines. By 1918, some 48,000 motorcycles remained in service with the British Army, drawn from a list of manufacturers that reads like a roll-call of the early industry: Ariel, BSA, Clyno, Douglas, James, Norton, Rover, Rudge, Scott, Sunbeam, Triumph, and others now long-forgotten. However, the majority of the machines came from just two manufacturers. Triumph supplied 30,000 examples of the 550cc Model H – known as the "Trusty" – while Douglas provided 25,000 examples of their 348cc Model V. Both had started life as civilian machines. The

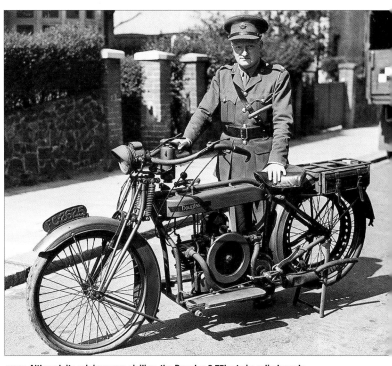

ABOVE: **Although its origins were civilian, the Douglas 2.75hp twin-cylinder solo machine was the closest thing to a standardized military motorcycle in the British Army, second only to the Triumph Model H in numbers. A larger 4hp model was used for sidecar duties.**

Douglas was a pre-war design, with a somewhat antiquated V-belt drive and two-speed gearbox, while the more modern Triumph had been launched in 1915.

The German and Austrian armies used rather less motorcycles than Britain but, having realized the importance of reliability, had early on decided to choose only those machines which could be shown to be capable of withstanding the rigours of a service life. As early as 1899, the German Imperial Army had established the *Inspektion de Verkehrstrüppen* to test prototype military vehicles, including motorcycles. The products of NSU – known at the time as Neckarsulm – and Triumph were among the first motorcycles to be considered suitable for military use. NSU supplied three different militarized civilian models, the lightweight 190cc Pony, and two types of V-twin, a 499cc machine rated at 3.5hp, and a big 995cc model rated at 7–9hp, while Triumph (TWN) supplied their 489cc JAP-engined 4.25hp machine. Puch and Wanderer were also important suppliers, and many civilian machines, of various makes, were also requisitioned.

The US Army deployed domestic motorcycles from Hendee (Indian), Harley-Davidson, Excelsior and Cleveland, alongside requisitioned machines and the products of a number of the British motorcycle factories.

It was not until the post-World War I years that the specialized military motorcycle started to emerge.

LEFT: **Harley-Davidson started supplying motorcycles to the US Army in 1916. Photographed in France in 1919, this essentially civilian V-twin Model J is typical of the machines produced by the company during World War I.**

Horse power gives way to horsepower

At the turn of the last century, the motorcycle was still in its infancy and many of the machines being produced were primitive, unreliable and difficult to ride. And yet by 1914, when the opposing armies of Britain and Germany faced each other across the flat lands that lay between France and Belgium, motorcycles had become relatively commonplace. Many soldiers had ridden such machines in civilian life and it must have seemed perfectly logical that the motorcycle would begin to replace the horse in the military world in the same way that it been replacing the horse elsewhere. While the motorcycle could not pull a heavy field piece, replace a cavalry mount or transport large numbers of men and supplies, the inherent flexibility and mobility of the machine allowed it to be adopted for a variety of military roles.

When World War I broke out, it had been just 15 years since Vickers & Maxim Limited had demonstrated a single-cylinder motor quadricycle adapted to carry a crew of two and an air-cooled Maxim machine-gun to the British War Office. None was purchased, but conventional military motorcycles followed soon after. The German Army's first military motorcycles were purchased in 1904 and the US government bought Indian Powerplus machines as early as 1913. By 1916, the first Harley-Davidsons were being used to pursue Francisco "Pancho" Villa – into Mexico, where legend has it that Villa's men were mounted on Indian motorcycles. However, even at this stage, not everyone believed that the motorcycle was necessarily the way forward.

ABOVE: **An early civilian specification Triumph Model H, in front of armoured cars of the Royal Naval Air Service.** BELOW: **The single-cylinder BSA Model H was typical of the solo machines used during World War I; the British Army had more than 500 in service by the end of the conflict.**

Looking back, many now consider World War I to be the first mechanized conflict, but in the early years, the opposing sides were still continuing to rely on mounted despatch riders and runners to convey messages. However,

ABOVE: **Sidecars were frequently seen as a means of providing transportation for officers in the field.** LEFT: **BSA began motorcycle production in 1911 and their belt-drive Model H, dating from 1914, was widely supplied to the Allies during World War I.**

as the conflict wore on, the ground conditions deteriorated to such a point that the motorcycle appeared to offer the most effective means of transporting messages. The British Signals Corps' despatch riders adopted motorcycles in place of horses, sometimes getting the best of both worlds by attaching baskets for carrier pigeons to the machines, bringing the pigeons closer to the front to reduce the transit time for the message.

Frequently, motorcycles were the only vehicles able to negotiate the terrible conditions, and sidecar outfits were adapted to provide a means of evacuating the wounded from the trenches to the casualty clearing stations. A sidecar outfit also provided a flexible form of transport, allowing equipment and ammunition to be brought up to the front line across ground which heavier transport was unable to negotiate.

The motorcycle also provided a means of mobilizing machine-guns and both sides experimented with machine-gun sidecars, usually with some sort of simple armoured screen for the gunner. It must have been immediately obvious that there was no prospect of firing accurately on the move but at least the motorcycle allowed the gunner to move rapidly from one location to another using the technique that is now called "shoot and scoot".

By the end of the war, it was obvious that there had been a change. The military motorcycle became the

preferred choice over the horse or mule for the transport of personnel and light supplies, as well as providing the perfect mount for couriers and despatch riders.

ABOVE: **This motorcycle is a Harley-Davidson under control of the American Red Cross, but the sidecars are on the left, suggesting that the machine is to be used in Britain.**

23

War production

In 1914, there were 200 motorcycle manufacturers in Britain and, for the first years of the war, business continued much as before – if they were lucky, some of them received the bonus of some nice big military contracts. Then, in late 1916, the British Government banned the sale of motorcycles to civilians, an act which helped those manufacturers whose products were approved but pushed many companies into bankruptcy.

Like much of the British engineering sector, the unlucky motorcycle manufacturers were forced to turn to other defence work. A few were allowed to continue to produce motorcycles which were considered useful to the military alongside other government work. For example, BSA and Royal Enfield resumed the mass production of guns and parts for guns, although both were also allowed to continue to manufacture motorcycles. For BSA, this led to considerable expansion and, although there was no further land available at the company's Small Heath works, the demand for motorcycles from Britain, France and Russia was such that a new production facility was constructed at Redditch, which placed the company in a very strong position when the war was over.

At Triumph's nearby Coventry factory, some 30,000 examples of the chain-drive Model H were supplied to the Allied forces – 20,000 of which went to the British Army. Demand for the machine was such that Triumph profited considerably from the war and it is interesting to note that at the end of the war, Colonel Claude Vivian Holbrook who had been responsible for motorcycle procurement for the War Office joined Triumph as general manager.

Douglas produced 25,000 machines during the war years, putting them just behind Triumph as the second-largest manufacturer, and Phelon & Moore – later trading as Panther –

were in third place with something like 3,500 machines produced, their 3.5hp machine having become the standard mount for the Royal Flying Corps.

Alongside the manufacture of a single military model, Matchless turned to the production of aircraft parts. Sunbeam turned out radiators for motor vehicles and aircraft as well as motorcycles, many of which went to the French. Rudge was forced to discontinue the production of motorcycles in 1916 and concentrate on munitions and aircraft wheels. Ariel, James, Norton and Rover continued to supply motorcycles, many of

ABOVE: **To accommodate the demand for all of the company's products, BSA built a new factory at Redditch, England, which placed the company in a very strong position after the war.** RIGHT: **New BSA motorcycles awaiting despatch to France.**

LEFT: **Photographed in BSA's new Redditch facility, the overhead line-shafting and belt-drive machinery arranged in serried ranks is typical of machine shops of the period. The lack of guarding is surprising to modern eyes.** BELOW: **Employee welfare became increasingly important during the war years and companies such as BSA started to provide medical, canteen and social facilities. Women also began to become increasingly important in the workplace.**

which were destined for Russia but, unable to complete the deliveries because of the 1917 Revolution, the machines remained stockpiled at the ports.

For other companies, things were different and while some were able to resume motorcycle manufacture in 1919, others disappeared.

In Germany, NSU concentrated on the manufacture of munitions but still found time to produce the majority of the motorcycles used by the Imperial German Army, and their 3.5hp machine became the most widely used German military motorcycle. The largest Austrian company, Puch, produced only small numbers of machines between 1914 and 1918 but went on to become a major motorcycle supplier in the immediate post-war years.

In a reverse of the situation in Europe, Harley-Davidson production was initially affected by the war in Europe to the extent that certain imported components became unavailable and the cost of iron and steel, rubber and other raw materials rose in response to increased demand – the consequent increase in the price of their products affected sales adversely. The US Army began buying military motorcycles in 1916, and Indian devoted almost their entire production facility to the war effort, choosing deliberately to stop selling to civilians. While Indian offered 20,000 machines to the US Government in 1916, with a similar figure for 1917, Harley supplied just 7,000 in each of the two years. In 1918, Harley started to construct a new factory and when the war was over, was in a strong position to take Indian's number one sales spot.

By the time the war was over, the US motorcycle industry had supplied almost 60,000 motorcycles to the war effort, 41,000 of which came from Indian.

By 1918, military contracts had been cancelled or scaled down but, development had been put on hold during the conflict, and many British and European motorcycle manufacturers were hardly in a position to put new models on to a market that would soon be awash with surplus machines. It was to be some years before the industry recovered.

Dressing the part

During the first two years of World War I, more than three million men volunteered to serve in the British Armed Forces. Many of the motorcycle despatch riders who signed up to the Signals Corps during this period were what these days we would term enthusiasts, men who had enjoyed motorcycling during the pre-war years and who joined up willingly in the belief that they would be able to serve their country while also riding a motorbike at the same time. These men required no training, but the rates of attrition on the Western Front meant that this situation could not continue.

In 1916, Britain introduced conscription and many of the men who followed had little idea of how to ride a motorcycle and needed training in how to handle their machines, how to find their way and how to undertake simple maintenance. Military training centres were established for this purpose but the combination of relatively untrained riders and fragile machines was not a good one.

ABOVE: **Crash helmets did not exist during World War I. This man, balancing a pigeon basket on his sidecar, is using his steel helmet as protection.** ABOVE LEFT: **A British officer attired in leather boots, pith helmet and a cartridge bandolier.**

While it is easy to relate to the need for training – and at the same time to underestimate the importance of the standardization in the layout of the motorcycle's controls which had yet to take place – it is just as easy to underestimate the hardships which these early riders endured. Dirt roads kicked up clouds of filthy dust during the summer and turned to seas of mud in the winter. The widespread use of sharp stone road dressings led to frequent punctures, while wet or icy cobbles or granite setts, such as were common in France and Belgium, presented their own set of hazards.

Riding a motorcycle was a dirty business. The total-loss lubrication systems that were the order of the day meant that the machine was inevitably covered in a film of oil and dust that was guaranteed to make any clothing filthy. Primitive suspension systems, combined with high-pressure tyres gave a hard bumpy ride which shook the machines apart and necessitated frequent rest stops during which the rider would have to check that his machine was fit to continue. It was not uncommon for the rider to be expected to mend a puncture by the roadside, or to refit a drive chain or belt, or clean a spark plug fouled by dirty fuel.

But, perhaps most important, purpose-designed protective clothing was non existent. In cold weather the early motorcyclist would dress in layers of thick clothing, his hands would be encased in stiff gloves and, for his feet, there was nothing more than horse-riding or working boots.

LEFT: **World War I re-enactors dress in the correct uniform of the day. Riding breeches and boots are not really the thing for riding motorcycles.**

LEFT: **It is hard to imagine that the typical peaked cap would remain in place at any speed.** ABOVE: **US infantrymen wearing the regulation puttees and steel helmets; the bag on the man's chest almost certainly contains a gas mask.**

Military despatch riders were required to ride in uniform, and a military greatcoat, flapping in the wind, was not exactly the best way to keep warm and dry. The British Army issued motorcyclists with high boots or leather gaiters to replace the standard puttees, and a special mackintosh for winter use, but nevertheless, many men resorted to stuffing newspaper or rags under their clothing to provide an extra layer of insulation; but it must have been desperately uncomfortable.

Although the Germans had a crude protective hat for motorcyclists, and the French seemed keen on riding a motorcycle wearing the standard military protective steel helmet, proper crash helmets did not exist and it is equally common to see photographs of men riding these early machines with their head protected only by a cloth cap or peaked military hat. Hinged glass flying goggles were generally used to keep dust, and the ever-present flies of the Western Front, out of the eyes.

In wet weather, oilskins or a cape might be worn in an attempt to keep dry. Spare parts and tools were often carried in a backpack and spare inner tubes could be worn around the shoulders or wrapped around the handlebars.

But hardship breeds camaraderie and these early despatch riders considered themselves to be a very special breed, united by their own particular brand of hell and a breed that was apart from the common foot soldier.

LEFT: **In 1933, the German Army developed a special motorcyclist's coat – the *Kradmantel*. It remained in widespread use until the end of World War II.** BELOW: **British despatch riders of World War II wearing the regulation uniform for the role.**

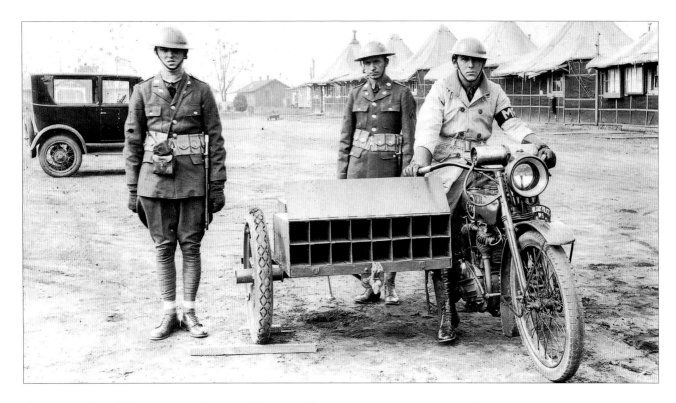

Specialist roles for the motorcycle

The majority of the motorcycles deployed by the Allies and the Central Powers in World War I were of civilian origin. In the case of despatch riders and messengers these motorcycles were used in the same way that they would have been used in civvy street, but there also evolved specialized roles which had no civilian equivalent.

The combat role is a good case in point. Back in those early days there must have been a tendency to view the motorcycle and rider as a mechanized cavalryman and this suggested that the motorcycle could be assigned a front-line role. Conversely, the role of evacuating the wounded, was almost certainly forced on to the motorcycle by virtue of the condition of the ground around the front line, where it was simply impossible to make any progress in a conventional motor ambulance.

Motorcycle-mounted machine-guns

The machine-gun was the "weapon of mass destruction" of the late 19th and early 20th centuries. The Maxim gun was the first machine-gun to use the recoil energy to eject each spent cartridge and insert the next, making it far more efficient than previous hand-cranked multi-barrel weapons. It was first used by Britain's colonial forces in the First Matabele War (1893–94) where, in one engagement, 50 soldiers are said to have fought off 5,000 warriors with just four Maxim guns. With a high rate of cyclical fire, a single machine-gun could cover a broad sweep of territory, indiscriminately cutting down any soldier foolish enough to venture into the field of fire and, by the first year of World War I, both sides were deploying improved machine-guns with terrifying rates of fire.

ABOVE: **A Harley-Davidson Model FUS fitted with a special ammunition sidecar during World War I. Unusually, the rider is a military policeman.**

The Imperial German Army had integrated the weapon fully into its organization structure and in the first year of the war, had something like 12,000 machine-guns; by 1916, motorcycles were attached to all machine-gun sections. Although the standard German Maxim-derived gun weighed 19kg/43lb and was too heavy to be manhandled or used by an individual, it was sufficiently compact to mount on a motorcycle sidecar, sometimes with a simple armoured shield, and required only three men to form an efficient crew. Two or three mobile machine-gun teams could quickly move from one location to another, carrying guns, crews, ammunition and spares on their motorcycles. The Germans even mounted machine-guns on solo motorcycles.

In Britain, too, the War Department had been thinking of mounting machine-guns on sidecars since the turn of the century, and in the USA, Harley-Davidson supplied machine-gun sidecars from 1916.

During World War I, British machine-gun motorcycles operated in teams of three, in support of infantry advances or attacking isolated enemy positions. Although the gun was mounted in such a way that it could be fired on the move, it must have become obvious almost immediately that this was a non-starter. Trying to control a machine-gun from a bucking sidecar would, in many cases, have presented what these days we would describe as a "friendly fire" incident, with equal hazards experienced by both sides. However, one contemporary popular source described

ABOVE: **Although, as seen below, there were specialist pigeon loft sidecars, these men have strapped the pigeon basket to their backs and are riding solo machines.**
LEFT: **A special driven sidecar was developed for the Belgian Army and was used with FN, Gillet-Herstal and Sarolea motorcycles.**

the result as an "efficient little engine of war, large numbers of which are used on active service (where) they are in great demand for scouting and reconnoitring purposes where rapidity of movement is so essential".

Despite their shortcomings, both sides persevered with motorcycle-mounted machine-guns to the end of the conflict.

Motorcycle stretcher bearers

During the five years of total warfare, the toll of dead and wounded was on a scale that hitherto would have been unbelievable. The Allies lost more than 5 million men in action, with a further 12.88 million wounded; the armies of the Central Powers lost more than 3.38 million men, with 9 million wounded.

On the Allied side, this represents an injury rate of 8,241 men a day and the task of evacuating these men from the front line, assessing their injuries and assigning them for further

treatment was formidable. While there was often no alternative to carrying the wounded from the trenches to a relatively safe rear area, equally, the motorcycle was often the only practicable means of getting the man to the next link in the chain which might eventually see him repatriated to the UK.

All of the combatants used motorcycles in this role, sometimes, as in the case of the British Sunbeam, using a purpose-made sidecar, at other times simply making do with strapping the stretcher to the sidecar chassis.

Other roles

During the early days, motorcycle sidecar outfits were also used to carry pigeon lofts and baskets and, when pigeons gave way to up-to-date wireless equipment. Sidecars were also used to accommodate the relatively bulky accumulators, chargers, aerial masts, and transmitters and receivers.

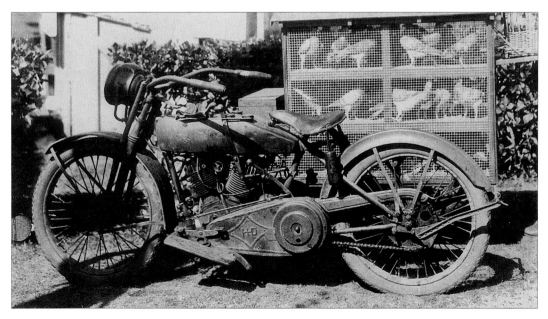

LEFT: **Photographed in June 1930, this Harley-Davidson outfit has been equipped with a pigeon loft sidecar. Pigeons were still used for communication into World War II.**

Motorcycle stretcher bearers

As well as lending itself to mounting a machine-gun, during World War I, the relative mobility of the motorcycle across the cratered ground of the ebbing and flowing front line led to the machines being used for other roles. Most significant of these was the use of the sidecar as a stretcher carrier.

In all conflicts it had been the practice of the Royal Army Medical Corps (RAMC) to establish a chain of medical establishments stretching from the front-line positions back to hospitals in the United Kingdom or, for example, India. The first step involved regimental stretcher bearers – during World War I these were not RAMC men but were often regimental bandsmen who had received some rudimentary first aid training – taking the wounded man to a Regimental Aid Post (RAP), a small, often temporary position near the front line where some treatment could be delivered. From here, RAMC Field Ambulance stretcher bearers would collect those wounded that required further treatment and deliver them to the Field Ambulance Advanced Dressing Stations (ADS), if further evacuation were needed, the casualty would be moved to a Clearing Hospital, later called a Casualty Clearing Station, and then, by rail and ship back to Britain.

At first, horse ambulances, and then motor ambulances, were employed to move the wounded from the Aid Posts to the Dressing Stations but, in the absence of good roads, the motorcycle sidecar provided an excellent, if somewhat uncomfortable, alternative. If the evacuation was taking place close to the front, the machines were driven by men but,

ABOVE: **During World War I Sunbeam produced a special softly sprung sidecar for the medical evacuation role.** BELOW: **Motorcycles were widely used as stretcher carriers but, as this open double-decker shows, not every injured man had the benefit of even the most basic weather protection.**

in the relative safety of the behind-the-lines areas, it was not uncommon for the riders to be women volunteers – and more than a few lost their lives when shelling went astray.

These were not sophisticated machines and any ride for a wounded man must have involved considerable discomfort. In its crudest form, the ambulance consisted of little more than a stretcher strapped across the sidecar

LEFT: **Clearly the man's injuries are not life threatening and he is almost certainly on his way from the front-line Dressing Station to a medical facility somewhere behind the lines. The sidecar offers very little protection but at least his feet are covered and one must hope that he is strapped in.**

chassis, with a blanket or canvas cover used to keep the injured man warm. Even the better ambulances included no more than a folding cover to protect the occupant from the elements. Weight was always an issue in developing more comfortable alternatives and although the British company Watsonian started building completely covered sidecar ambulances with special springs in 1916, and both Harley-Davidson and the US-based Flxible Sidecar Company built purpose-made ambulance sidecars for the US Army, the motorcycle ambulance was at best a necessary evil. Similar equipment was deployed by the French, German and Belgian armies.

The practice remained widespread during World War I and the US Army certainly continued to equip its medical service with motorcycle sidecars during the 1920s but the more mobile nature of the conflict during World War II, and the use of Jeep stretcher-bearers and other four-wheel drive vehicles, had rendered the motorcycle stretcher bearer almost, but not quite obsolete by 1940. The US Army was using a scooter sidecar combination, equipped with an almost coffin like lidded rectangular box, to move patients around the site of an Army hospital in Northern Ireland in 1943. The inclusion of emergency lights suggest that it was used to get casualties from incoming medevac flights into the emergency rooms.

LEFT: **Motorcycles were still being used for medical evacuation during World War II but almost certainly only during airborne operations when conventional ambulances were not available. The two-wheeled stretcher carrier would not normally have been towed – even behind a four-wheeled vehicle.**

Armoured and machine-gun motorcycles

In 1899 Frederick R. Simms designed the "motor scout" for Vickers, Son & Maxim. It was little more than a motorized quadricycle on which was mounted a water-cooled Maxim machine-gun but it seemed to offer mobility for the machine-gun. Contemporary photographs show an incongruously bowler-hatted rider crouched behind a small armoured screen and, while there was almost certainly never any question of firing on the move, the machine would have permitted motorcycle troops to move with relative speed from one firing point to another, as well as allowing multiple machine-guns to act in concert, laying down interlocking fields of fire.

The machine was demonstrated to the War Office, but no decisions were made regarding series production.

However, while the "motor scout" might not have been quite the right machine for the job, the notion of mounting a machine-gun behind a small armoured screen on a motorcycle was clearly an idea whose time had come. Just months into World War I, British Army Order 480, dated November 12, 1914, approved the creation of Motor Machine Gun (MMG) batteries, attached to the Royal Field Artillery. By September 1915, there were 18 MMG battalions in France, mounted for the most part on Clyno and Scott motorcycles – although Matchless, Premier, Zenith and Enfield machines were also used – carrying a water-cooled Vickers machine-gun on a special sidecar. There was no protection for the rider but the gunner was provided with a small armoured screen. The machines were operated in threes, one equipped with a gun, one carrying a spare tripod position, and a third with ammunition and spares.

Collectively, these units were known as the Motor Machine Gun Service (MMGS) and special efforts were made to enlist men known to be interested in motorcycling – the Coventry office of the enthusiasts' magazine *Motor Cycle* was even designated as a recruiting office. However, it soon became obvious that to be fully effective, machine-guns needed to be used in larger units and, in October 1915, the MMGS was incorporated into the newly formed Machine Gun Corps (MGC) which had infantry, cavalry and motor branches. Each motor battery of the MGC included 18 sidecar combinations, carrying

ABOVE: **Mounting a water-cooled Vickers machine-gun behind an armoured shield, the British Clyno/Vickers outfit was widely used by the Machine Gun Corps. The gun could also be dismounted and used on its tripod from a ground position.**
RIGHT: **By September 1915, there were 18 Motor Machine Gun Battalions in France, mounted for the most part on Clyno (as shown) and Scott motorcycles – although Matchless, Premier, Zenith and Enfield motorcycles were also used.**

six Vickers machine-guns with ammunition and spare equipment; eight motorcycles without sidecars; two or three wagons or cars; and a sidecar combination for the commanding officer.

This approach was not unique to the British Army and in 1915 the *Reichswehr* also started to mount rear-facing machine-guns on to the sidecars of NSU 7hp motorcycles; once again, the gunner had a small armoured screen which gave a measure of protection. And in the USA, during 1916, Harley-Davidson supplied the US Army with a number of sidecar-equipped Model J outfits, which allowed tripod-mounting of a machine-gun behind a folding armoured shield; unlike the British and German machines, there was a seat for the gunner, and a small degree of armoured protection was provided for the rider in the form of leg shields. Excelsior machines were similarly used, equipped with the Flxible sidecar.

The end of World War I did not quite spell the end of the road for the armoured motorcycle and throughout the 1920s and 1930s, various experiments were carried out in an attempt to provide cheap, mobile armoured vehicles for snipers.

For example, in 1932, a Harley-Davidson VSC/LC sidecar outfit was supplied to the Swedish company Landsverk for conversion to an armoured machine-gun mount for the Danish Army. This time, both gunner and rider were enclosed by an armoured hull; the gunner faced to the rear and fired a machine-gun through an armoured screen, or dismounted to use the gun from in front of the machine in the anti-aircraft role. The weight can have done little for the machine's performance and the experiment, known as the Landsverk 210, was abandoned.

ABOVE: **The water-cooled Vickers was not the only gun mounted on a motorcycle; this photograph shows a drum-fed Lewis machine-gun.**

The Italian Army specified the Moto-Guzzi GT17, also dating from 1932, with forward-facing armoured protection for the rider and a machine-gun mount and, although it was not equipped with a gun, in one of its incarnations, Mercier's curious half-tracked motorcycle of 1936 was provided with a curved armoured screen to protect the rider. The following year, Venezuela and Argentina both purchased a number of Belgian FN M86 combination outfits that were fitted with armoured screens and sidecars, and the Danish Army also deployed Nimbus sidecar machines which were equipped with Madsen machine-guns on a special military sidecar.

Eventually it was realized that the motorcycle's strengths lay elsewhere and, the only use of armoured machines during World War II seems to have been the 1942 Moto-Guzzi *Triace*, examples of which mounted a rear-facing heavy machine-gun behind an armoured shield.

ABOVE: **By the end of World War I, the British Army had almost 1,800 Clynos in service, many of which were used as machine-gun carriers.** LEFT: **The gun was rarely fired from the sidecar but, of course, the motorcycle provided excellent mobility, allowing the crew to adopt the modern "shoot and scoot" tactic.**

Peacetime returns

In 1918, all outstanding British and US military motorcycle contracts were cancelled as, of course, were those in Germany and Austria. However, there is little doubt that the military use of motorcycles during World War I had helped to further the motorcycle industry, both in the UK and in the USA. Innovation may have taken a back seat, but the machines became more reliable, and the manufacturers learned how to increase productivity to meet the military demands for their products – BSA, for example, had opened a huge new four-storey factory in 1915 to cope with the Army's demands.

Many returning soldiers had been exposed to motorcycles for the first time during their military service and became potential customers when peace returned. At the same time, the real increases in productivity allowed post-war civilian prices to be lowered.

Civilian production in post-war Britain resumed almost immediately, although the strike in Glasgow during 1919 supporting a reduced 40-hour working week in many industries, including iron and steel, had a serious effect on production, affecting most manufacturers. However, there was considerable pent-up consumer demand and, in 1919, the first national exhibition of motorcycles was held at Olympia in London, with 112 manufacturers showing their products, and with more than one appearing for the first time. The number of motorcycle manufacturers in Britain continued to grow steadily and, in the three years following the end of the war, about 100 new manufacturers joined the industry. The machines themselves became increasingly sophisticated and, by 1920, there were more than a quarter of a million motorcycles registered in Britain. Motorcycle production hit an all-time high in Britain in 1929, when some 147,000 machines were produced.

Despite the burgeoning civilian market, the British Army was happy to continue to operate surplus machines from the war years. In fact, it was to be a further decade before the British

TOP: **The US Army's motorcycle dump in France, 1918. The machines are awaiting disposal.** ABOVE: **There is more than one military use for a motorcycle.**

Army took further significant interest in acquiring, or even testing, new motorcycles.

In the USA the story was somewhat different perhaps due, in part, to competition from Henry Ford's Model T which had appeared in 1908 and which was selling half a million units a year by 1915. There had been 200 US-based motorcycle manufacturers when the US Expeditionary Force left for Europe in 1917 but, within two years of the end of the war, this number had been reduced to less than 40. The largest of these were Excelsior, Harley-Davidson and Indian, all of which had invested heavily in their production facilities during 1917 and 1918. However, Indian had relied too heavily on military contracts and, when these came to an end, the company was unable to fund the recovery of its civilian markets. Harley-Davidson was in considerably better shape, having

LEFT: **Although the belt-drive machines are decidedly antique in appearance, these Belgian motorcyclists date from the immediate post-war years.**

never really abandoned civilian production, and sales during the 1919 model year – the first with no military contracts – totalled around 24,000. In 1918, Harley-Davidson had also borrowed $3 million and started the construction of a new manufacturing facility and, although Excelsior managed to sell 100,000 machines during 1919, Harley-Davidson had become the largest motorcycle manufacturer in the world by 1920. By the end of the decade, the big three US motorcycle companies comprised the entire US motorcycle industry.

Elsewhere in Europe, it was to be a decade or so before new manufacturers started to enter the industry but it is certainly worth recording that 1919 was the year that BMW started to look at the motorcycle industry. Forbidden by the Treaty of Versailles to manufacture aircraft, BMW's head designer Max Fritz, considered producing motorcycle and motorcar engines to sustain the company. It took him just four weeks to complete the drawings for the now-famous "Boxer" engine and a production example was installed in a motorcycle just two years later, albeit not under the BMW name.

ABOVE: **The machine is an Indian of the early 1920s, and the riders are clearly in uniform, but the reason for the front-wheel disc is not known. Note the semi-elliptical multi-leaf suspension on the front forks.**
RIGHT: **The German Army of the inter-war years purchased thousands of motorcycles, with dozens of different, mostly civilian style, models. There was a total of one million such machines in military service by 1937.**

The Great Depression

While the 1920s were a time of increasing civilian sales, the Great Depression of the early 1930s told a different story altogether. Britain and the USA were the worst affected, with too many companies chasing too few customers, but the global nature of the Depression meant that export sales were hit equally hard. The British government introduced a tax on large engines, forcing domestic manufacturers to concentrate on small and inexpensive models and by 1932–33, as conditions started to improve, many manufacturers had closed their doors for good. By the end of the Depression in the USA, the only manufacturers to survive were Harley-Davidson and Indian, Excelsior having finally called in the receivers in 1931. However, during this period the design of motorcycle continued to improve and evolve even if military and civilian sales were slow.

The British Army had made few new purchases since 1918 but, by the end of the 1920s, those World War I machines which remained in service were becoming outdated and the War Office started to draw up a set of requirements for the perfect military motorcycle. The newly established Mechanical Warfare Experimental Establishment (MWEE) was set the task of examining every motorcycle available at the time. During 1929, examples of 350cc production machines were purchased from seven British manufacturers – AJS, BSA, Douglas, Francis Barnett, Matchless, New Hudson and OEC – with the notion that they would be put through a series

ABOVE: **For many manufacturers, the 1930s was a time of dwindling sales and many of the smaller companies, particularly those that persevered with labour-intensive construction methods, failed to survive.**
RIGHT: **This method of assembling motorcycles on static benches was not particularly efficient since it would have required two or three men to lift the completed motorcycle.**

ABOVE: **By 1924, there were 500,000 motorcycles registered in Britain and although it was hardly typical of what was available during the Depression, the British manufacturer BSA had started to produce the 770cc V-twin Model G14 in 1921. Available in solo and sidecar combination form, it was popular with ex-servicemen.** RIGHT: **In Germany during the 1930s, light motorcycles, with engines under 350cc, were typically produced by BMW, DKW, NSU and TWN (Triumph).**

of comparative trials. At the end of the trials, the Matchless T/4, AJS M6 and Douglas L29 were considered to be suitable for further testing but eventually it was concluded that no civilian machine would be suitable and that MWEE should design a purpose-made military motorcycle. The only useful outcome of the trials was probably the standardization of the layout of motorcycle controls.

There never was a purpose-designed British military motorcycle but BSA's 500cc, so-called WD Twin, was procured in large numbers from around 1934.

Elsewhere, the closing of the 1920s and the early years of the new decade were a period of expansion, with new manufacturers springing up across the world. In the Soviet Union, the Izhevsk Steel Plant launched five new motorcycles in 1928, with lighter Soviet machines beginning to appear in 1930. With restricted domestic potential, the machines found a ready use with the Red Army.

The Polish CWS state workshops started manufacturing motorcycles in 1930, the M-III of 1933 being particularly suited to military use. In the newly created Czechoslovakia, there were eventually something like 120 motorcycle manufacturers, and companies such as CZ, Jawa, Ogar, Praga, and Itar & Walter supplied both military and civilian machines. Japan copied the big Harley-Davidson V-twin to produce the Sankyo *Shinagawa* Rikuo 97 in 1937. The Italian Moto-Guzzi, Gilera and Benelli companies were all established during the mid-1930s and their products were widely used by the Italian Army. In France, Peugeot, Gnome & Rhône, René Gillet, Mercier, and Terrot supplied heavy motorcycles to the French Army, while the Belgian FN, and Gillet-Herstal companies pioneered the driven-wheel sidecar outfits which were later to be used so successfully by the *Wehrmacht*. The Swedish company Husqvarna had started supplying the Swedish Army from the early 1920s.

In Germany, the motorcycle industry had been well established by 1920. Victoria had started motorcycle

production in 1899, and NSU in 1901; Zündapp, Ardie and DKW had been building motorcycles since 1919. Newcomer, BMW produced the first motorcycle under its own name in 1923. As the Third Reich increased the production of consumer goods as a way of improving the average German's standard of living, motorcycle production increased year on year. More than 200,000 motorcycles were produced between 1934 and 1939, and many of these civilian machines eventually found their way into military service.

The USA was keen to never again become involved in a European conflict, and had imposed its isolationist strategy. Although, for a period, there was a plan to issue every newly graduated GI with a motorcycle, the Great Depression brought such notions to an abrupt end. Civilian motorcycle sales declined sharply during the inter-war years – in 1929 for example just 96,400 motorcycles were sold in the USA – and although both Indian and Harley-Davidson machines were purchased by the US Army, it was in small numbers, and export orders to both sides in the Spanish Civil War and to China made little difference. However, everything changed in 1939.

ABOVE: **After 1931, Harley-Davidson and Indian became the only surviving volume motorcycle manufacturers in the USA, with Harley being the larger. These lads are mounted on a Harley-Davidson Model JD.**

Increasing sophistication and reliability

During the inter-war period, motorcycle development progressed in leaps and bounds, and the 1920s and 1930s might be considered by many as the golden age of motorcycling as the machines became faster and more reliable. Although rear suspension did not become a standard feature until the post-war period, engines became more powerful and side valves began to be replaced by overhead valves. Lubrication was hugely improved as engine-driven pumps, in combination with a proper sump, ousted the early hand pumps and total-loss systems that had been common in the early days. Belt drive disappeared completely and the old two- and three-speed gearboxes with clumsy hand change levers started to be replaced by four-speed units, often with a slick foot-pedal operation. Brakes were universally fitted to both front and rear wheels and had been improved beyond measure.

ABOVE LEFT AND ABOVE: **During the late 1920s, J.S. Ramussen's DKW Zschopauer Motorenwerke had become the largest motorcycle manufacturer in the world. In 1927, the company exhibited this DKW motorcycle at London's Motorcycle Show at Olympia.**

New manufacturers continued to emerge, some of them offering ever-more sophisticated machinery, and the mid-to-late 1930s saw some of the most innovative designs in motorcycling, albeit many of these were more expensive. At the same time, in Britain and Europe, the motorcycle continued to be seen as an inexpensive alternative to public transport or a step up from the pedal cycle and many manufacturers also exploited this utilitarian trend.

DKW was established in Germany in 1919, specializing in two-strokes, Horex produced its first motorcycle in 1923, and

LEFT: **As this photograph shows, Adolf Hitler very much believed that both military and sporting success might help the German nation to regain its pride. The motorcycle is a racing BMW.**

A factory to assemble Triumph motorcycles in Germany was established in 1903. During the inter-war years the machines were badged as TWN (Triumph Werke Nürnberg). Shown is a 350cc model of 1935.

Maico was established in 1935. Two names which were later to be associated with powerful and sophisticated military motorcycles – Zündapp and BMW – were established in 1921 and 1923, respectively. In Italy, Benelli started production in 1917 and soon made a name for itself with fast road-going and racing machines, notably incorporating water cooling. Moto-Guzzi was created in 1921 and, within two years, was producing racing machines using overhead camshafts. Jawa started production of a sophisticated shaft-driven 500cc machine in Czechoslovakia in 1929; CZ following in 1932 with a range of lightweight machines with tiny engines and pressed-steel frames. The French Motobécane company started producing motorcycles in 1923, producing a high-quality in-line four-cylinder machine with a unit gearbox and shaft drive, later becoming France's largest manufacturer.

In Britain, well-established marques such as BSA, Matchless, Ariel and Triumph dominated the market, but it seemed that there was always room for a newcomer. For example the advanced JAP-engined HRDs first appearing in 1924, and the high-quality Vincent, with its unique rear suspension, was first marketed in 1928.

While the civilian motorcycle became increasingly powerful and sophisticated during these inter-war years, there remained a steady market for more utilitarian military machines. It may be true that the military were never afraid to try something new – witness the curious three-wheeled and tracked machines that the War Office in Britain thoroughly tested in the late 1920s – but the machines that were purchased in quantity tended to be very conventional. One exception to this rule was the concept of the driven sidecar wheel, which was developed in Belgium as a means of providing a heavy military motorcycle which could travel literally anywhere. The Belgian FN, Gillet and Sarolea companies all produced such machines during 1937/38 and, of course, the concept was subsequently adopted enthusiastically by the *Wehrmacht* during World War II.

Although steady from the mid-1920s, European military procurement of motorcycles started to gather pace as many nations embarked on rearmament programmes.

In the USA, the combination of the low-priced utilitarian Ford Model T followed by the Great Depression had a serious impact on motorcycle sales. Excelsior and Henderson both closed in 1931, leaving just Harley-Davidson and Indian. Both companies continued to produce high-quality well-built machines but they did not sell in large numbers on the domestic market and high tariffs prevented them reaching the European markets. Only the US police services remained loyal to the big US machines during this period – as even the military reduced expenditure on motorcycles. It was probably sport which helped to save the US motorcycle industry as the machines became a favourite of enthusiasts and amateur racers during the 1930s.

THE HISTORY OF THE MILITARY MOTORCYCLE

Tracked motorcycles

During World War I, four-wheel drive vehicles were something of a rarity, and motorcycles were employed for their ability to make headway on unmade roads and across ground that was pockmarked with craters from the incessant shelling. Nevertheless, the damage to the ground was often so severe that even a motorcycle was unable to make progress and, in the same way that automotive engineers began to experiment with four- and six-wheel drive and with the use of half-track systems in the years following World War I, so motorcycles also came under the spotlight.

One of the first attempts at improving the traction of the motorcycle came in 1923, when the US Army tested an Indian Chief, which had been fitted with a Chase track system. The rear wheel was pushed further back by the use of a sub-frame and a chain was used to drive a cleated canvas track wrapped around the rear wheel, with an idler wheel to control tension and to extend the length of the track in contact with the ground. The system had been used on Dodge and Ford vehicles the year before, but had proved unsuitable for military use.

During the 1920s, the British Army believed that the 6x4 drive-line layout offered almost as good a performance as the 4x4 (or 6x6) without the mechanical complexity. Mechanics of the Royal Army Service Corps (RASC) attempted to produce what might be described as a 3x2 motorcycle by adapting a Triumph Model P to mount a bogie at the rear which carried a pair of in-line wheels. The first wheel was chain-driven by a sprocket; on the other side of this wheel,

TOP, ABOVE AND BELOW: **Following the modification of a Triumph Model P by RASC mechanics, the British company OEC produced three versions of this unlikely three-wheeled motorcycle which was described as a "tractor". A flexible track could be wrapped around the rear wheels, both of which were driven, to improve traction.**

a pulley was fitted which drove the second wheel by means of a substantial V belt. If extra traction was required, a track could be fitted around these wheels. The prototype was submitted for trials during 1926 and apparently performed well across soft ground, and reasonably well on tarmac. There was a tendency for the rearmost wheel to lift as the bogie responded to power, and cornering on tarmac must have been interesting, but the machine was considered to have sufficient potential for further development and the project was passed to OEC in 1928.

OEC was selected to continue the development work since it had a reputation as a manufacturer of "custom" motorcycles and during 1927/28 three further prototypes were produced which OEC confusingly described as a "caterpillar tractor". Two of the machines were powered by a 350cc Blackburne engine, the third used a 490cc JAP; all three employed a variation of the in-line bogie at the rear which had been devised by the RASC. The trials were eventually abandoned with the War Office concluding that the added complexity did not outweigh the increase in off-road performance.

In 1936, the Swiss (or French) Mercier company built a prototype of a JAP-engined half-tracked motorcycle – or *moto-chenille* – in which the track was fitted at the front. The engine was mounted ahead over the handlebars and the four-wheel bogie was driven via an exposed chain. It was tested by the French Army and then by the British War Office in 1939 but was considered to be slow, unwieldy, uncomfortable and unsafe. Surprisingly, the machine still exists.

The only successful tracked motorcycle design was the German *Kettenkrad* but so little of the machine was derived from the motorcycle that it probably does not really count.

Finally, although not tracked, it is worth mentioning the Rokon motorcycle developed by Californian inventor Charles Fehn. Fehn set out to build the ultimate off-road lightweight motorcycle and, by combining full-time two-wheel drive, with an automatic transmission and high-flotation hollow wheels, the Rokon delivers unrivalled performance across virtually every type of terrain.

ABOVE: **Built by NSU, the German *Kettenkrad* is probably the world's only successful tracked motorcycle, albeit much of the technology is derived from the *Wehrmacht*'s conventional half-tracked vehicles.**
LEFT: **The Rokon motorcycle, developed by Charles Fehn, includes two-wheel drive and automatic transmission.**

ABOVE: **Although this photograph of massed infantry motorcyclists might suggest otherwise, the British tended to confine the motorcycle to the messenger role during World War II.**

ABOVE AND BELOW: **Nazi Germany saw the motorcycle, particularly when combined with a military sidecar, as a legitimate tool of the Blitzkrieg tactic and even mounted machine-guns on sidecars, a carry over from World War I.**

Deployment of the motorcycle in World War II

Huge numbers of motorcycles were constructed and deployed by the opposing nations during World War II (1939–45). Total Allied production amounted to something like 530,000 machines during this period; of these, 425,000 were built in the UK, with the majority of the remainder coming from Indian and Harley-Davidson in the USA. During those same years Germany – including Austria – produced 305,640 machines, of which some 80,000 were supplied to civilians, although many were subsequently requisitioned by the military. The Germans also used captured and requisitioned machines produced in France and Belgium. Thousands more motorcycles were produced in Italy and Japan.

Clearly, for all sides of what was the first fully mechanized conflict, motorcycles were an important element and the machines were deployed across all the combat theatres as well as being widely used for domestic duties. Typical roles for the motorcycle included despatch riding, personnel transport, and reconnaissance; motorcycles were also used by military police units, and in traffic control and convoy escort duties.

Despatch riding had been the first significant military use for the motorcycle during World War I, and motorcycles had been used to carry vital messages, orders, maps and documents between often geographically separated locations. Despite the widespread growth in radio and electronic signals traffic, despatch riding remained a vital role during World War II and still remains the most important role for the military motorcycle.

The relative mobility of the motorcycle compared to the primitive motor trucks of the period had ensured that the transportation of personnel in the field was also a significant role during World War I. Two decades later, Allied officers were more likely to be found riding in a staff car behind the lines and, if the going got rough, the vehicle of choice was almost certainly going to be a Jeep. Nevertheless, the Germans often favoured the motorcycle combination as a form of personnel carrier, and even among the Allies the sidecar still had its uses both for transporting personnel and moving vital cargo where other transport might, perhaps, be unable to proceed.

ABOVE: **Although the riders are in typical British tropical uniform, the motorcycles are strictly civilian overhead valve Triumphs, probably the T80 Tigers which remained in production until 1939.**
LEFT: **A British despatch rider posing in front of a Vickers medium tank.**

weave around and move ahead of a column of vehicles, keeping the road clear and ensuring that stragglers did not become separated from the main body of the convoy. And by riding ahead of the convoy, opposing or cross traffic could be held up as necessary to allow a convoy to pass through a major intersection as a unit.

Military police and border guards were frequently motorcycle mounted, patrolling bases and off-limits areas to ensure that night-time and security restrictions were observed. The US Navy used motorcycles for shore patrols in the same way.

The German and Soviet armies were alone in making widespread use of motorcycles as a fighting part of a combat unit; these roles are dealt with separately. The Allies also assigned motorcycles to both infantry and armour divisions – a US division during World War II, for example, might have had 200 motorcycles available, but they were used exclusively in an administrative or reconnaissance role.

Unlike the previous conflict, motorcycles were no longer used as stretcher carriers, although the *Wehrmacht* certainly mounted medical staff on motorcycle combinations, nor were they used to mount radios or carry pigeons.

The motorcycle was also the ideal mount for reconnaissance forces. The small size and relative unobtrusiveness of a solo motorcycle will often allow it to approach closer to enemy positions than a larger armoured vehicle, while the speed and manoeuvrability of the machine also allows a quick retreat should this be necessary. Motorcycle reconnaissance units were typically used to report on the condition of roads, to locate and report on the strength of enemy units, and to call in the accuracy of artillery fire.

Behind the lines, motorcycles were widely deployed for traffic control and convoy escort duties. A number of motorcycles accompanying a typical convoy were able to

ABOVE: **Mounted on Victoria KR6 heavy sidecar combinations, these German motorcycle troops – *Kradschützen* – are masked against the dust.**
RIGHT: **The Norton Big Four, complete with a driven sidecar wheel, was a British Army experiment with a heavy motorcycle in the German style. It was not a success and was replaced by the American Jeep.**

Motorcycles in combat

The Germans employed their elite motorcycle troops – the so-called *Kradschützen* – with great effect during the Blitzkrieg campaigns of the early years of World War II, where they could be considered as mechanized cavalry, forming part of the highly mobile and hard-hitting spearhead units. Even the reconnaissance *Abteilung* (battalion) included motorcycle-mounted combat troops who were willing and able to fight should the opportunity or need arise.

The Germans were almost alone in their widespread use of motorcycle combat troops. The Red Army used small numbers of motorcycles as part of their hybrid cavalry-mechanized groups, neither the British nor the US armies chose to copy this tactic, preferring instead to restrict motorcycles to the reconnaissance, despatch rider and administrative roles – although it must be pointed out that motorcycles did feature in a number of airborne operations. It was not always thus.

In the inter-war years, the strategic planners of the US Marine Corps saw little future for the military motorcycle, preferring to concentrate on the use of "cross-country cars" for reconnaissance duties and arguing that the motorcycle had a limited range and was restricted to "fairly good roads".

On the other hand, the US Army envisaged motorcycle-mounted troops speeding out in front of advancing columns of armour and reporting on the enemy's strengths and positions. As late as 1941, for example, the US 2nd Cavalry Division was equipped with horses, scout cars, Jeeps and motorcycles. Sadly, a man mounted on a solo motorcycle can do little to defend himself – he generally needs both hands to control the machine and has little opportunity to fire at a pursuer or at enemy units upon which he may have stumbled. Nevertheless, US Signal Corps photographs from the late 1930s show US infantrymen

ABOVE: **Clearly, a motorcycle, in this case a BSA M20, can provide a useful vantage point even if this is not quite what was meant by motorcycle reconnaissance.**

in training, wearing full-face masks against the clouds of dust thrown up by their own machines, they can be seen hurling their big Harley-Davidson or Indian motorcycles on to the ground and crouching behind them with carbines raised. Other training shots show columns of motorcycles operating alongside Jeeps and armoured scout cars but, in practice, the US Army motorcyclist was rarely part of a front-line combat unit.

In Britain, too, the years before the widespread appearance of the Jeep saw the War Office continuing to develop the combat role of the motorcycle combination by mounting a

LEFT: **The Germans were almost alone in their widespread use of motorcycles for combat troops – these *Kradschützen* head-up a convoy of military vehicles in what is almost certainly an exhibition of power and authority.**

machine-gun on a special sidecar. More than 4,700 Norton Big Four sidecar outfits were procured between 1938 and 1942 and one of its envisaged roles was to provide an all-terrain mount for both reconnaissance and combat units. The sidecar body could also be removed and replaced by a tripod-mounted mortar. The Jeep put an end to these ideas and the motorcycle was generally relegated to behind-the-lines roles.

The French and Belgian armies had also come round to the idea that motorcycle troops could replace cavalry units during the inter-war years but neither nation had any opportunity to put these ideas into practice.

The Italian Army toyed with mounting machine-guns on the distinctive motor tricycles produced by Gilera, Moto-Guzzi and Benelli but they were almost certainly never in widespread use with combat troops. It was a similar story in Japan where machine-guns were frequently mounted on motorcycles but rarely used as a combat tactic.

In common with the Germans, although on a much smaller scale, the Soviets considered motorcycle troops to be a vital component of combat units and included motorcycle battalions in the Red Army Order of Battle even as late as mid-1944. For example, during the latter stages of the fighting on the Eastern Front, the 30th Motorcycle Regiment had been used as part of

ABOVE LEFT: **The Germans also used motorcycle combinations to provide transport for the lower ranks of officers.**
ABOVE: **British motorcycle outriders accompanying a mixed convoy of vehicles. Note the Jeep behind the Bren carrier.** RIGHT: **Motorcycle riders were easily thrown from their mounts or even decapitated by a wire stretched across the road at a strategic height. Like Jeeps, motorcycles were frequently fitted with some means of deflecting and breaking the wire.**

the Soviet mixed cavalry-mechanized group. The tactic involved using the armoured and motorized formations of the mechanized corps to provide the main combat power, while the horse-mounted elements provided flexibility for fighting in difficult terrain such as large forests, or waterlogged ground.

LEFT: **The US Army developed this technique for using motorcycles as cover for infantrymen but it is doubtful that the tactic was ever used in anger. If nothing else, a motorcycle would have been very vulnerable to enemy fire, leaving the rider stranded.**

Kradschützen – elite motorcycle troops

In mechanizing their army, the German High Command placed considerable importance on the rapid mobility of the motorcycle. The so-called *Kradschützen*, or motorcycle infantrymen – often called *Kradmelder* (despatch riders) – were a vital part of the German Blitzkrieg tactic and were considered to be elite troops. Using the principle of "fire and movement", and exploiting the superiority in speed and movement available from the motorcycle, their role was to surprise and outflank the enemy far ahead of their own armoured forces.

The German *Reichswehr* had formed its first motorcycle infantry company in 1929, and further motorcycle infantry units were formed during 1934/35, mainly by restructuring former cavalry regiments. Although their equipment and weapons were light, and the lightly modified and requisitioned civilian motorcycles of the period were often lacking in reliability, these units were very effective in combat, proving their worth during the campaigns in France and Poland.

However, the shortcomings of these essentially civilian machines became all too obvious, and it was clear that a

ABOVE: **Heavy motorcycle combinations were produced for the** *Wehrmacht* **by Zündapp and BMW, both companies also producing a version with a driven wheel to the sidecar.** ABOVE RIGHT: **Dating from 1937, the single-cylinder BMW R-35 was widely used for training, despatch and liaison duties.** RIGHT: **The horizontally opposed engine has become something of a BMW trademark and, although lacking sidecar drive, the 750cc R-12 was typical of the German heavy motorcycle of World War II.**

purpose-designed military motorcycle was the only way forward. The *Wehrmacht* had already been purchasing the Zündapp KS600-W heavy combination outfit since 1938, eventually acquiring some 18,000 of these machines, but the big Zündapp was also to provide the basis for a new, powerful and specialized military machine with all-wheel drive.

Development work on the Zündapp KS750, and the similar BMW R-75, started in April 1940, with the first machines introduced in mid-1941 during the North African campaign. Both machines were designed to be able to transport three men together with their equipment, and could also double as a prime mover for airborne light artillery or tow a light trailer. The notion of driving the sidecar wheel had been developed in France and Belgium where various manufacturers had been producing such machines since the mid-1930s – but by combining this with other features, Zündapp and BMW produced a state-of-the-art heavy military motorcycle, albeit at a cost which exceeded that of the *Kübelwagen*.

With their sidecar-wheel drive, low-ratio cross-country gears, and reverse – both machines even featured a lockable differential – these machines provided a cross-country performance that often exceeded that of the US-built Jeep.

An *Einheits* (standard) design of single-seat sidecar was used, with stowage for a spare wheel, ammunition and fuel, and with provision for a radio; a light mortar was also occasionally carried. A pintle mount was often fitted on the nose of the sidecar, allowing an MG-34 or MG-42 machine-gun to be fired on the move.

More than 35,000 of these heavy motorcycles were constructed by the two companies between 1941 and 1944 but, for the motorcycles which had performed so well in Africa and on the Western Front, it was a very different story when Germany turned to the East.

On June 22, 1941, Germany launched "Operation Barbarossa", the invasion of the Soviet Union where they faced not only the might of the Red Army but the appalling conditions of the Russian winter. With the autumn rains, the roads turned into impassable bogs and the land became a sea of apparently bottomless oozing mud. When a motorcycle could be persuaded to move, more often than not it was defeated by the liquid mud which was ingested by the intake system. Motorized forces were reduced to travelling less than 16km/10 miles a day. The arrival of winter heralded plumetting temperatures – at minus 40°C (-40°F), the engine and transmission oil virtually froze solid. Some lucky soldiers benefited from the special foot and hand warming systems that were fitted to their motorcycles; others simply froze to death.

BMW sent engineers to the Front to see, first hand, how the motorcycles fared, but there was little that could be done. The German war machine ground to a halt at Stalingrad and never recovered – even the elite *Kradschützen* were simply overwhelmed by the Russian winter.

ABOVE: **Both BMW and Zündapp adopted the pressed-steel external frame. Wearing the *Kradmantel*, this German soldier seems to have attracted something of a crowd of onlookers around his mud-encrusted machine.** BELOW: **German *Kradschützen* at rest: the motorcycles that can be identified appear to be BMW R-12s. The helmets and rifles suggest that the troops are waiting for orders to deploy.**

Motorcycle design during World War II

By 1939, motorcycle design was well into what might be termed its second phase. A specific design language had started to emerge and, although the machines no longer resembled pedal cycles, the high-tech revolution started by the Japanese was still some years into the future. Where the 1930s had been a time of innovation, the war brought this to an end, and the emphasis was placed firmly on volume production. In Britain and the USA particularly, the manufacturers produced what were essentially militarized pre-war civilian machines throughout the long years of the conflict and, despite some British and US experiments in this direction, only in Germany was there any serious attempt made to produce a purpose-designed military motorcycle.

Regardless of origin, military motorcycles can be considered to fall broadly into three categories – nicely summed up by the always-orderly Germans, following one of the Schell rationalization programmes, as "lightweight", "medium weight" and "heavy weight". Machines in the upper end of the medium-weight category and heavy-weight machines were equally suitable for solo or sidecar use although, with the notable exception of Germany, sidecars were generally less favoured than had been the case during World War I.

Lightweight machines, some of which were specifically designed for use by airborne troops, were powered by a single-cylinder engine of less than 250cc, either of the two-stroke or four-stroke type. Most British motorcycles, and the more numerous of the German models, fell into the medium-weight category, these employing an engine of between 250cc and 500cc, and again generally of single-cylinder design. Motorcycles in the third category, typically produced by Germany and the USA, were powered by an engine of more than 500cc, often of twin-cylinder design. The Germans invariably used the horizontally opposed "boxer" layout, while the US-built Indian and Harley-Davidson companies favoured the V-twin.

ABOVE: **Germany annexed Austria in 1938 and used large numbers of Puch motorcycles throughout World War II, as well as Austrian-built trucks.**
BELOW: **It was not only the rigours of combat that shortened the life of the motorcycle – competitive use away from the front line also caused damage.**

Side-valve engines still tended to predominate, although most manufacturers were well aware of the performance advantages of overhead valves, and even overhead camshafts. Most machines continued to use magneto ignition although there were advantages to the use of the battery-and-coil system. Notwithstanding Indian's early experiments with electric starting, which had almost bankrupted the company, inertia kick starting remained the norm.

Japanese and Soviet designers tended to follow US practice but Italy produced the most exotic designs of the conflict. For example, Moto-Guzzi, uniquely, stuck with their pre-war exposed

ABOVE: **Although the weight and unfamiliar controls counted against it, RAF motorcyclists found the Indian 741B motorcycle to be reliable and comfortable.**

flywheel and single horizontal cylinder engine, and Benelli used overhead camshafts. Alone among the European armies, Italy also favoured a widespread use of three-wheeled motor tricycles, as did the Japanese in the Far East.

Except for the very smallest airborne lightweight motorcycles, a multi-speed transmission was the norm. A handful of ultra-lightweights might have used a two-speed transmission, but for most there was a proper three or four-speed gearbox. British motorcycles tended to favour a foot change for the gearbox but the Germans and the Americans were just as likely to employ a tank-mounted hand-change lever. Belt drive had been discontinued back in World War I and final drive was normally by means of a roller chain, although BMW and Zündapp, particularly, tended to favour shaft drive for their purpose-designed military machines.

Sidecar wheel drive had been pioneered in the UK for trials racing in the 1930s, and the concept was subsequently adopted for specialized military machines produced by Belgian motorcycle manufacturers FN, Sarolea and Gillet-Herstal at the end of the 1930s. In Germany, Zündapp, and then BMW,

produced heavy military motorcycles from 1940 that incorporated drive to the sidecar wheel as well as having low-ratio gears to aid cross-country work.

There was little innovation in suspension design. From the earliest days of motorcycle design, front suspension had quickly become a standard feature, almost invariably by means of friction-damped coil springs and girder parallelogram forks and this remained the norm. There were a few exceptions to this, with some BMWs and Zündapps and Britain's Matchless G3L notably using telescopic forks. It was still unusual for the rear forks to be sprung.

As shortages of materials, notably rubber and aluminium, became apparent, manufacturers were forced to adopt substitutes. In Britain and the USA, for example, rubber was in short supply due to Japanese action in the Far East, and this led to the adoption of canvas handlebar grips and cast-steel footrests rather than the previous rubber-cushioned type; unnecessary rubber items such as knee pads were eliminated. Aluminium was essential for aircraft production and items such as primary chain cases, and even crankcases, which had previously been cast in aluminium, were often remanufactured in steel or cast iron.

Motorcycles remained in production by all of the major combatants throughout the conflict but there is no doubt that their role became less significant, and certainly more mundane, after the appearance of lightweight all-terrain vehicles such as the US-built Jeep and the German *Kübelwagen.*

BELOW: **During World War II, advances in technology took second place to reliability but even so, the life of a motorcycle on the front line was often very short. These Italian outriders are mounted on typical lightweight machines of the period.**

Heavy motorcycles of World War II

During World War II, the heaviest military motorcycles were those fitted with an engine larger than 500cc, together with drive to the sidecar wheel. This excludes virtually all of the British motorcycles of the period since most were fitted with engines of 350cc or just under 500cc and few were used with sidecars at all. It also eliminates all of the US-built Harley-Davidsons and Indians which, although they were almost universally powered by large engines, were never provided with sidecar wheel drive. So, the category really only includes the British Norton 633cc Big Four and the big Zündapp and BMW sidecar outfits favoured by combat units of the *Wehrmacht*.

It is probably no coincidence that the Norton Big Four falls into the same category as the Zündapps and BMWs since it was almost certainly inspired by the same big Belgian outfits as the German machines.

ABOVE: **The side-valve BMW R-12 was typical of German heavy motorcycles until the production of more capable machines with sidecar drive in 1940.**

ABOVE: **The use of selectable sidecar wheel drive, and even limited-slip differentials, gave the later German outfits a formidable off-road performance.** LEFT: **While the heavy German motorcycles were frequently used in combat, lighter machines, like this 200cc pressed-frame DKW, were used in their thousands behind the lines.**

The Belgian FN company had produced its first 3x2 sidecar outfit, the M12-SM, in 1937, and the British War Department would certainly have known of its existence. In 1938, a second Belgian company, Gillet-Herstal, also produced a similar heavy motorcycle with selectable drive to the sidecar wheel and in 1939, at the request of the Belgian company, one of these outfits was pitched head-to-head with the then-new Norton Big Four at the British Mechanical Warfare Engineering Establishment (MWEE).

The Norton Big Four was a development of the company's 16H which had first been trialled with sidecar wheel drive in 1938. Although it is said to have been inspired partly by a competition trials outfit, it is inconceivable that the design was not also influenced by the developments in Belgium. The engine was a huge 633cc single-cylinder unit in combination with a four-speed forward and reverse gearbox, and drive to the sidecar wheel was via a dog clutch. Performance was said to be excellent across country and the machine was intended to be used by combat troops, with a machine-gun mounted on the sidecar in the style of the German Blitzkrieg units. Following the trials, the Gillet-Herstal machine was not felt to offer any particular advantages and the Norton Big Four was approved for production, with some 4,737 examples produced during the period 1938 to 1942. It was never really used as intended and many examples were disposed of on the civilian market after the appearance of the Jeep in 1941, albeit with the sidecar drive disconnected.

Meanwhile, the *Wehrmacht* had almost certainly appropriated FN, Sarolea and Gillet-Herstal 3x2 motorcycles from the Belgian Army after 1940 and would have been well aware of the advantages of such a system. When the rigours of service in the Western Desert exposed the weaknesses of existing German motorcycle outfits, both BMW and Zündapp were asked to design powerful military motorcycles that could withstand the desert conditions. Features of the resulting BMW R-75 and Zündapp KS750 combination outfits included the elimination of the troublesome roller chain in favour of shaft drive, a forward

ABOVE: **Although it lacked rear suspension, the Zündapp KS750 was possibly the most advanced motorcycle used by any of the combatants during World War II. Features included telescopic front suspension, overhead-valve engine, shaft drive, forward/reverse gearbox and sidecar drive.**

and reverse gearbox with a low-ratio crawler gear for off-road use, permanent sidecar wheel drive, manual differential lock, hydraulic brakes on the sidecar and rear wheel, and high-efficiency air filters. Production started in 1941. BMW's R-75, first produced in 1940, shared many of these features and, with its three-speed plus overdrive main gearbox and two-speed auxiliary gearbox, also offered almost a full set of low-ratio gears. Curiously, neither machine featured rear suspension, although both had telescopic front forks. These were not cheap machines, with the price said to be higher than that of the VW *Kübelwagen*, and production of both was eventually cancelled in 1944 after 18,635 KS750s and 16,510 R-75s had been manufactured.

As for the US "heavies", it is not quite fair to eliminate them entirely since there were trials of the Harley-Davidson XA with a driven sidecar, as well as possibly a prototype WLA with a driven sidecar wheel intended for the Soviet Army, but there was no production of either.

Lightweight motorcycles of World War II

With the amount of attention that is directed at the US-built Harley-Davidsons and Indians, and the big German motorcycles of World War II, there is an understandable tendency to believe that these heavy machines were typical of motorcycles in military use. In fact, both sides used large numbers of relatively lightweight machines, typically for liaison duties and in the airborne role.

The big Zündapp and BMW sidecar machines were not produced in massive numbers and there were many, many more lightweight machines in *Wehrmacht* service. In fact, the only German motorcycle to remain in production for the entire duration of the war was the small DKW RT-125, essentially a pre-war civilian machine powered by a single-cylinder two-stroke engine and fit only for light duties; unladen weight was 91kg/200lb. DKW also produced an even smaller machine, the 98cc RT-3 that was widely used by *Wehrmacht*.

Similar lightweight machines were produced by Ardie, in the form of the RBZ200 and the VF125, at 197cc and 125cc, respectively, and by Phänomen whose 124cc AHOI entered service in 1938. Even Zündapp produced a lightweight 125cc machine, the DBK-200 Derby of 1935, which was used by the *Wehrmacht*. Other lightweight commercial machines came from the Czech Ogar, Jawa and CZ factories, none of them with engines larger than 350cc.

British motorcycles of World War II tended to be 250cc or 350cc side-valve machines, but these were certainly not the whole story. Even if you disregard the specialist lightweight airborne machines, which are dealt with separately, the British Army employed a total of more than 14,500 lightweights produced by James and Royal Enfield.

Nicknamed the "Clockwork Mouse", the 125cc James ML was first manufactured in 1943 and, with folding handlebars and footrests, it was originally intended for use by airborne and assault units, although it was subsequently widely used by

ABOVE: **Lightweight motorcycles were popular in Germany and were produced by Ardie, DKW, Phänomen, and NSU.** BELOW: **Lightweight civilian machines, often unmodified, were frequently used for training purposes.**

ABOVE AND BELOW: **The James ML "Clockwork Mouse" was intended for use by airborne and assault units and featured folding handlebars and footrests.**

to European eyes, it was an almost conventional lightweight motorcycle. Procured in limited numbers for use by airborne troops during 1943, it was a militarized version of the company's Powercycle and was powered by a 194cc two-stroke engine with belt drive to the rear wheel via a twin pulley arrangement that gave the rider a choice of two gears; top speed was 50kph/30mph. The weight was quoted at 75kg/165lb.

The US Army also procured examples of the Indian Aerocycle, which was designated "extra light solo motorcycle M1 – standard". It was standardized in December 1944 and, again, was intended largely for use by airborne troops. The engine was a single-cylinder 221cc unit that gave a top speed of 73kph/45mph, and the machine was also said to be suitable for off-road use. With a total unladen weight of 114kg/250lb it was around half the weight of a standard US Army Harley-Davidson or Indian machine and could be lightened further by removing the battery – the ignition was a magneto design – lights and generator. This brought the weight down 114kg/250lb but nevertheless it did not compare well to, for example, the British James ML or Royal Enfield WD/RE.

Lightweight motorcycles, including mopeds and scooters, were also widely used by all nations in the post-war years.

Commandos and ground forces. Powered by a small single-cylinder Villiers engine installed in a lightweight tubular frame, it was not dissimilar to the lightweight DKWs, and weighed in at just 72kg/157lb. The Royal Enfield WD/RE of 1942 – better known as the "Flying Flea" – was based on a lightweight pre-war civilian motorcycle, which, in turn, is said to have been derived from the German-built DKW RT-98. With a 125cc single-cylinder engine, it was similar to the James ML but at 62kg/137lb it had a 9kg/20lb weight advantage, and tended to be favoured for use by airborne assault troops where it was air-dropped in a special protective cradle.

Even the USA had a choice of lightweight machines at their disposal. The Simplex Servi-Cycle was described by the Ordnance Corps as a "motor-driven bicycle" although,

ABOVE: **Indian produced this "extra light" solo machine, described as the Aerocycle Model 144, or 148, according to the date of manufacture. It was also intended for airborne use.**
RIGHT: **German *Hitler-Jugend* demonstrate an unusual use for a lightweight motorcycle at a training camp in the late 1930s.**

Folding and airborne motorcycles

The emergence of airborne troops that could be inserted behind enemy lines by either parachute or glider also demanded a new approach to the design of equipment. The troops could not be heavily equipped, but needed sufficient in terms of firepower and mobility to complete their allotted tasks. Foot power was all very well, but there were limits to how far troops could travel under their own power. In Britain, Jeeps were adapted for airborne use but were restricted to glider delivery while, at the other end of the scale, folding airborne bicycles were produced both in Britain and the USA.

However, motorcycles seemed to offer a good compromise. Providing it was protected by a suitable enclosure or container,

ABOVE: **British paratroopers loading a Jeep and motorcycles into an early type Airspeed Horsa assault glider.** ABOVE LEFT: **The US Cushman Autoglide 53 was designed for air-dropping.**

even a standard lightweight civilian motorcycle could be air-dropped alongside paratroops, and could provide some mobility in the early hours or days of an airborne assault. British airborne doctrine held that if key individuals in an operation were mobilized it would speed the movement of messages between elements of, what could often be a widely dispersed, airborne operation.

Produced from 1942, the British Royal Enfield WD/RE "Flying Flea" and the James ML were both lightweight, expendable – for

ABOVE: **The British James ML was sufficiently lightweight to permit easy manhandling.** RIGHT: **The Excelsior Welbike was also light enough to be easily lifted into an aircraft.**

which read "low-cost" – machines considered to be suitable for air-dropping in a specially designed cradle, or for being carried in a glider. Both of these were lightweight civilian machines that had been adapted for a military role, but the Excelsior Welbike was designed from the start as a lightweight airborne machine.

The Welbike was designed to provide a simple, lightweight expendable motorcycle that could be reduced in size to fit into a standard air-drop container. Powered by a 98cc two-stroke Villiers engine, the prototype was produced by J. R. V. Dolphin at Welwyn – hence the name – with development work taking place at the Airborne Forces Experimental Establishment (AFEE). It was designed around a tubular space frame that allowed the handlebars and saddle to be folded or collapsed to reduce the overall height and, with small wheels and compact automotive layout, could be stowed inside a cylindrical container. The container, incidentally could also be fitted with wheels to provide a useful trailer when the motorcycle was unpacked and made ready for use. Excelsior started production of the machine in late 1942, with almost 4,000 examples built. The Welbike was deployed during airborne and assault landings at Anzio and Normandy.

Even smaller than the Welbike was the Volugrafo Aeromoto, a tiny 123cc airborne motorcycle produced in Italy from 1942. A rudimentary seat was provided on top of the fuel tank, and with its rectangular duplex frame, folding seat and handlebars, and 715mm/28in wheelbase, it could hardly be considered to be a "real" motorcycle at all, although it was capable of 50kph/30mph. There was no suspension, and the wheels were twinned, front and rear, to help support the weight of a fully kitted airborne soldier. Less than 2,000 were built and it was also used by the *Wehrmacht*.

The US Army had its own airborne machines, in the form of the Cushman Autoglide 53. Resembling an overgrown child's scooter, with balloon tyres providing its only suspension, it was

ABOVE: **The British Excelsior Welbike was designed to fold, thus allowing it to be stowed into a cylindrical air-drop container. It needed push starting and lacked gears but was a useful mode of transport for airborne troops.**

powered by a 246cc single-cylinder engine. Parachute lifting rings were fitted front and rear, which would suggest that the Americans considered a protective cradle or container to be unnecessary. A total of 4,734 examples were completed over a two-year period and it was classified as "limited standard", but photographs of the machine in action are rare.

Although the French used a licence-built Vespa scooter – the ACMA TAP150 – in the airborne role in the mid-1950s, these machines generally disappeared in the post-war years as the advent of larger transport aircraft made them redundant.

LEFT: **It was not only lightweight motorcycles which could be carried in aircraft. Here, *Fallschirmjäger* load a heavy motorcycle combination into a Junkers Ju52.**

The German *Kettenkraftrad* SdKfz 2

The development of the curious *Kettenkraftrad* SdKfz 2 – more usually shortened to *Kettenkrad* and meaning, simply, "half-track motorcycle" – was originated in 1938, by the German Air Force. It was designed by NSU together with input from the German Defence Ministry Office Group 6

(*Wäffenprüfamt 6*) for Development and Testing of Army Weapons and was intended to be used as a light artillery prime mover for the newly formed paratroop (*Fallschirmjäger*) units. It would typically have been required to tow the 7.5cm *Gebrigskanone* 15/28 gun, 2cm FlaK 30 and 38 anti-aircraft guns, or 3.7cm

ABOVE: **The NSU *Kettenkrad* consisted of the front end of a motorcycle attached to a box-like hull which was carried on a standard German half-track system. It was used as a gun tractor and personnel carrier and had seats for two men facing to the rear.** LEFT: **Perhaps the only successful tracked motorcycle, and despite a heavy maintenance requirement, the *Kettenkrad* is popular with military-vehicle enthusiasts.**

Pak 36 anti-tank gun, all of which were suitable for air-transportation but which were too heavy for man-handling.

The basic design for the *Kettenkrad* was derived from the *Motorkarette* – a four-wheeled/half-tracked load-carrying vehicle that had been designed for the Austrian Army by Heinrich Ernst Kniepkamp. A prolific engineer, by the end of the war Kniepkamp had patented around 50 individual designs covering various aspects of track-laying vehicles.

With the *Kettenkrad*, Kniepkamp effectively took the *Motorkarette* design a stage further by marrying a small, box-like steel hull supported on steel tracks to the front end of a motorcycle. Early prototypes had a motorcycle-type spoked front wheel but, on production models, a steel disc wheel was adopted which was presumably stronger and easier to manufacture. The front forks were originally adapted from those used on the NSU 601 OS(L) motorcycle but they proved unequal to the rigours of off-road performance and, in 1942, were replaced by a wholly new pattern incorporating a hydraulic damper. The reverse gear was also a weak point as well as the differential brakes, the latter tended to become contaminated with oil. The brakes were mechanically operated.

Power came from a centrally mounted 1,488cc Opel four-cylinder petrol engine – taken from the company's Olympia motor car – which was connected to a six-speed gearbox (3F1Rx2) located under the driver's saddle. Although the engine output was a modest 37bhp, the vehicle was capable of a speed of 73kph/45mph on the road, while also offering formidable off-road capabilities.

The track system shared some design principles with the other World War II German half-tracks and, like these, the front wheel also provided the initial steering input, with the differential braking system automatically coming into action once the handlebars were turned beyond a certain angle.

The driver sat in the normal motorcycle position, and there was a transverse rear-facing seat for two behind the engine compartment. A small, amphibious, trailer was also designed for use with the vehicle.

Production started in 1939 at NSU's Neckarsülm factory, with the first vehicles delivered during 1940/41; Stoewer also contributed production from 1943. Once production was underway, a larger vehicle was prototyped which would provide seating for a driver plus five men, enabling it to also act as a personnel carrier; the extended track length required five pairs of wheels as opposed to the four pairs of the standard machine. Powered by either the six-cylinder engine of the Opel Kapitän or a Stump K20 engine, ten prototypes were produced of this so-called HK-102 *Grosses Kettenkraftrad*, but there was no series production.

A total of 8,345 vehicles had been constructed by the end of the war and the vehicle remained in production until 1948, marketed as a light agricultural tractor, with perhaps 500–550 more being produced.

Variants

NSU HK-100 Series

SdKfz 2	Half-track, motorcycle, $^1/_2$ ton, tractor; HK-100, HK-101
SdKfz 2	Half-track, motorcycle, $^1/_2$ ton, crane; HK-101
SdKfz 2/1	Half-track, motorcycle, $^1/_2$ ton, field telephone cable layer; HK-101
SdKfz 2/2	Half-track, motorcycle, $^1/_2$ ton, heavy field telephone cable layer; HK-101

ABOVE: **The combination of tracks at the rear, and a high power-to-weight ratio, gave the machine a formidable off-road performance.**

Motor tricycles

Tricycles, and even quadricycle machines, were relatively common in the very early years before the motorcycle evolved into its definitive form. Indeed, the British Army had toyed with the AC Auto Carrier tricycle back around the turn of the century. However, the tricycle had disappeared by about 1910 and it was not until the early 1930s that such machines started to reappear. Indian and Harley-Davidson produced motor tricycles in 1932 and 1933 respectively and both machines were provided with a special towbar to provide a convenient means for the automotive service

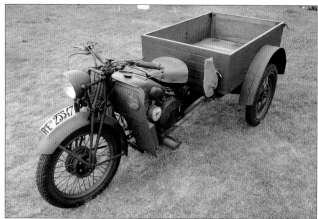

TOP AND ABOVE: **During the late 1930s and in World War II, Italian motorcycle manufacturers produced three-wheeled versions of standard machines. The Moto-Guzzi *Trialce* was typical of the type.** LEFT: **Wrecked Japanese *Sanrinsha* motor tricycle, probably produced by Kurogane.**

station to collect and deliver customers' cars without requiring a second driver. Harley-Davidson named theirs Servi-Car, Indian chose the name Dispatch-Tow and, although a handful of Servi-Cars entered military service, neither machine was procured in any quantity.

In Italy and Japan it was a different story and the motorized tricycle was commonly used as a commercial load carrier. Both countries produced military versions of the standard civilian machines for use during World War II.

In 1932, Moto-Guzzi introduced a tricycle version of the company's GT17 motorcycle known as the *Mototriciclo Militare 32*. Typical of the design of such machines, a motorcycle front end, in this case with a front fork assembly which incorporated both compression and rebound springs, was married to a rear sub-frame mounting a two-wheeled driven axle. Power was provided by the same 500cc engine as was used for the

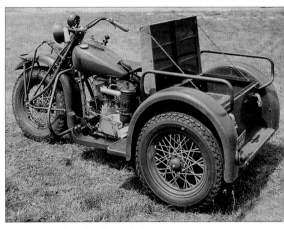

ABOVE AND LEFT: **The Indian Motocycle Company produced this tricycle for the US Army in 1940, based on the Chief model; a total of just 16 was purchased.**

motorcycle driving the axle through a four-speed gearbox and exposed chain, but the gear ratios would almost certainly have been reduced to handle the increased weight. The standard body was an open load-carrying box, with a 500kg/1,102lb payload, but there were also fighting variants which mounted a machine-gun in the rear. When the GT17 was replaced by the *Alce*, the three-wheeled variant was known as the *Trialce*, and in 1942, a contro folding variant was produced called the *Smontabile*. The heavier Moto-Guzzi 500U (*Unificato*) of 1942 was similar but was capable of carrying 1,000kg/1,100lb.

Benelli produced a similar device based on their 500cc motorcycle in 1942. As well as being used as a general load carrier, it was also employed as a communications vehicle and as a tractor for the Italian 47mm anti-tank gun.

Between 1943 and 1963, Gilera also supplied their 500cc *Mercurio* heavy motor tricycle to the Italian Army. Shaft-driven, and with a payload of 1,300kg/2,850lb, this was the largest machine of its type, and was produced with both drop-side cargo and tipper bodies.

The pinnacle of the development of three-wheeled load carriers was probably the Moto-Guzzi *Mulo Meccanico*, a hybrid motorcycle-derived 3x3 load carrier designed in 1959/60. With demountable tracks for the rear wheels, user-adjustable rear axle width, six-speed gearbox, and lockable differentials, it was perfect for the narrow passes of the Italian Alps.

Alongside many others, the Japanese Kurogane company supplied a 3x2 motor tricycle to the Imperial Japanese Army for use both as a personnel carrier and with a 240kg/500lb cargo box. Similar machines were supplied by other companies including Iwasaki and Toyo Kogyo.

The US Army trialled experimental motor tricycles produced by GM-Delco, Harley-Davidson, Indian, and Crosley between 1938 and 1940 but the development of the Jeep appears to have brought these developments to an end. However, the US Army did purchase small numbers of load-carrying three-wheeled scooters for use around bases during World War II. The most numerous of these was the Cushman Model 39 Package Kar, but the Custer light delivery vehicle was similar.

Unlike the Italian and Japanese tricycles, these machines both had a rear-mounted engine driving and steering through a single rear wheel, while the load-carrying box was fitted at the front, supported on a pair of small wheels.

Subsequent lightweight load carriers, including devices such as the DAF Pony which evolved into the the US Army's Mechanical Mule, the British Hunting-Percival Harrier, and of course, recent quad bikes, have tended to be four wheelers.

ABOVE: **Dating from 1959, the Moto-Guzzi *Mulo Meccanico* was probably the pinnacle of motor tricycle design. Powered by a 745cc V-twin engine, it featured drive to all three wheels, extensible rear track and could be fitted with a track system over the rear wheels.**

The Jeep enters service

In 1940, Harley-Davidson produced 15 pre-production examples of what was described as a "field car" for the US Army. The three-seat machine employed the front end of a motorcycle and was clearly derived from Harley's GA Servi-Car, although the rear locker was replaced by a rear-facing bench seat. It was powered by the company's 999cc "knucklehead" engine driving the rear wheels through a three-speed gearbox and propeller shaft. Apparently lacking sufficient power during trials, one of these machines was modified by boring the engine out to 1,130cc.

The trials came to naught and the field car disappeared, little more than a margin note in the development of the military motorcycle. Had it entered production, the little field car might have served in the same kind of roles as the German-built Zündapp and BMW 3x2 motorcycle outfits. In the light of other events taking place in 1940, it is not difficult to understand why this did not happen.

On June 14, 1940, William F. Beasley, Chief Engineer of the US Ordnance Department, drew up the basic requirements for what was to become the Jeep. His free-hand sketch showed a small four-wheeled utility vehicle with cut-away door openings, open sides, a canvas top, and a machine-gun mount. In mid-July, 135 US motor manufacturers were approached to bid for the development and eventual production of this machine –

TOP: **Jeeps were light enough to be carried by glider and were more versatile than the motorcycle.** ABOVE RIGHT: **When the Jeep appeared in 1941, it was used for most of the roles which had previously been assigned to the motorcycle.** RIGHT: **A superbly restored World War II Jeep finished in Royal Airforce markings, displayed at the War and Peace Show, Beltring, Kent.**

LEFT: **The large American motorcycle, typified here by the Harley-Davidson WLA, cost the US Government an average of $380 – although a Jeep cost around $1,000 it was a far more useful vehicle.**
BELOW: **Almost 650,000 Jeeps were produced during World War II, and was used by all of the Allies in every theatre of operation. By comparison, Britain and the USA produced something like 550,000 motorcycles during the same period.**

just two responded. American Bantam had a prototype running by September 23. Willys-Overland was a little slower, their prototype, based partly on the work done by Bantam, being delivered to Camp Holabird, Maryland, on November 13. The mighty Ford Motor Company, having been coerced, submitted a prototype ten days later.

Each of the three companies received a contract to construct 1,500 examples of their particular take on Beasley's vehicle. With the manufacturing work underway, elements of the Willys and Ford vehicles were combined to produce a standardized design. Bantam received no more contracts and Willys and Ford built some 640,000 examples of the standardized Jeep between 1941 and 1945.

At 1,575mm/62in, the Jeep was just 254mm/10in wider than Harley's field car. Granted, it weighed almost twice as much – 1,115kg/2,460lb against some 635kg/1,400lb – but it was still light enough to be man-handled when necessary and, it had room for four men, could mount a machine gun or anti-tank rifle, carry stretchers and tow a field gun. But perhaps most importantly, it had four-wheel drive and could go almost anywhere that a tracked vehicle – or a motorcycle – could go.

The Jeep spelled the end of the field car project. It also brought a fundamental change to the way that the US Army – and to some extent, all of the Allies – used the motorcycle. It would be fair to say that from about mid-1942, motorcycles were largely superseded by the ubiquitous Jeep. For example, US Army standing orders had initially decreed that motorcycles be attached to each armoured division, but this practice came to an end in March 1942 when the vehicle type was removed from the Tables of Organization and Equipment (TOE), having been replaced by the Jeep. Of course, this does not mean that armoured units did not use motorcycles; it simply means they were not authorized. Similarly, motorcycles were not listed for

US Army field Military Police (MP) units for the years 1943–45, although camp and station MP units were authorized a maximum of 16 motorcycles – or Jeeps.

The motorcycle remained useful in the airborne role, and for despatch riders, traffic control and convoy escort work but it was never used by the Allies as a combat vehicle in the way that the Germans used their big Zündapp and BMW machines.

The Jeep also effectively ended any further development of the specialized military motorcycle. In the immediate post-war years, the Allies continued to use wartime machines in a restricted range of roles and, when new machines were eventually procured, they were invariably of civilian origin.

Willys did not know how right they were when they coined the slogan, "The sun never sets on the mighty Jeep".

Reaping the whirlwind

During the early years of World War II, German bombers conducted a campaign of attrition against Britain's manufacturing capabilities. Factories, docks and ports were all considered legitimate targets and the strategic bombing carried out by the *Luftwaffe* between September 1940 and May 1941 took its toll on major manufacturing

ABOVE: **The city of Coventry was devastated by German air raids during the night of November 14, 1940. The Triumph motorcycle factory was all but totally destroyed.** BELOW: **During the later years of the war, the Allies exploited their air superiority to hit back at the German war machine.**

centres, particularly in London and the West Midlands. Between November 1940 and February 1941, the campaign was widened to include other important industrial and port cities including Coventry, Southampton, Birmingham, Liverpool, Bristol, Swindon, Plymouth, Cardiff, Manchester, Sheffield, Portsmouth and Avonmouth (Bristol).

The German bombing raids spelled disaster for many companies who were never able to recover from the loss of plant, tools and equipment.

One of the worst raids of 1940 took place on the night of November 14 when the *Luftwaffe* devastated the West Midlands city of Coventry. The *Luftwaffe* was using a new navigation technique called *X-Gerät* in which a radio beam led the pathfinder squadron *Kampfgeschwader 100* to the target. The job of the pathfinders was to drop incendiary bombs which would start fires, these, in turn, guiding the bombers of *Luftflotte 3*. More than 500 bombers took part in the raid, dropping 30,000 incendiary bombs and 500 tons of high explosive on the city. Reports later estimated that 4,330 homes were destroyed and 75 per cent of the city's factories were affected.

Coventry was home to Daimler, Armstrong Whitworth, Courtaulds, GEC, Dunlop, Alvis, and of course Triumph motorcycles. Triumph's Priory Street works was so badly damaged that the company was forced to move production to a temporary location in Warwick, while a new factory on the Birmingham–Coventry road outside Meriden was built. Staff salvaged what they could from the ruins, including tools and usable parts, but the first batch of 50 3TW "twins" was destroyed, effectively bringing this model to an untimely end and, although Triumph struggled on in what remained usable at the Priory Street works, it was not really until June 1941 that full-scale production resumed. The bombing also destroyed all of Triumph's technical records, drawings and designs.

Less than a week later, on November 19, 1940, BSA's Small Heath factory was also directly hit by German bombers. A large section of the original 1915 workshop in Armoury Road was destroyed, killing 53 nightshift workers. Two nights later, a second raid almost completely destroyed the old 1863 structure. BSA lost 1,600 machine tools in these two raids, badly affecting the company's manufacturing ability.

However, by 1944, the tide had turned and strategic bombing action by the RAF and the USAF was systematically destroying Germany's industrial base. The German tank, truck and armaments industries became primary targets and, while motorcycle plants were not deliberately attacked, the bombing forced many factories to be relocated. At this stage in the war, there was no possibility of constructing new facilities and the only way to continue with production was for the manufacturers who were within range of the Allied bombers to disperse undamaged machines and production lines to existing sites elsewhere. This had the effect of displacing other activities that were taking place. For example, BMW was forced to turn over most of its München plant to producing aircraft engines, effectively ending motorcycle production there. Both NSU and Zündapp, with plants located in Neckarsulm and Stuttgart respectively, also reduced the number of motorcycles produced in order to concentrate on other armaments. In Austria, Steyr ceased the production of motorcycles in favour of trucks. Other plants were unable to continue as a direct result of Allied action – the Ardie plant at Nürnberg was destroyed, as was the small engine producing plant of Fichtel & Sachs at Hamburg.

By 1944, the effects of the bombing raids combined with a savage standardization programme of military motor vehicles meant that Auto-Union DKW had become the only German motorcycle manufacturer producing any volume. The company's Zschopau factory continued to produce 125cc and 350cc machines for as long as the raw materials were available but, by March 1945, the shortages were so acute that all motor vehicle production in Germany effectively came to an end. How the mighty had fallen – in 1939, German motorcycle production had topped 200,000 units. By 1944 the effects of bombing, shortages of materials and components, and plant dispersal had reduced this figure to little more than 30,000.

ABOVE AND LEFT: **The Allies used a target prioritization system to attack German centres of production, often forcing factories to relocate. Motorcycle factories were not specifically targeted but, by the end of the war, the Ardie plant had been destroyed. DKW was the only motorcycle manufacturer to remain in production.**

Military motorcycles in France

The French Army started buying trucks and motorcars and, in smaller quantities, motorcycles before the turn of the 19th century. Peugeot, René Gillet, and Werner had all started producing motorcycles in France before 1900, followed by Terrot and Griffon in 1901 and 1902, respectively. Although Terrot grew to become the largest motorcycle manufacturer in France, and supplied large numbers of machines to the French Army, the domestic industry was not generally ever able to meet the demand for military motorcycles.

Werner closed in 1908, and most of the French motorcycles deployed during World War I and in the inter-war years, came from Terrot and René Gillet, both of them having acquired a reputation for producing reliable, robust machines. The René Gillet machine of 1916 was often fitted with an ambulance or machine-gun sidecar.

ABOVE: **French motorcycle outriders accompany a Panhard-powered Citroën-Kégresse half-track armoured car of 1929. The exposed flywheel of the lead motorcycle suggests a Motobécane B4 or B44 of the early 1930s.**

Mechanization continued slowly in the immediate post-war years, but the French Army continued to purchase motorcycles from the domestic suppliers, albeit in small numbers. The products of René Gillet and Terrot continued to feature heavily and although Griffon had closed in the late 1920s, new manufacturers, such as Gnome & Rhône (1919), Motobécane (1923) and Monet Goyon (1917), had also been established.

The 750cc René Gillet Model G, introduced in 1926, and the later G1, was among the most widely used, for both solo and specialized sidecar work, right up until the outbreak of World War II. Newcomers Gnome & Rhône produced two heavy machines that were widely used by the French as well as

ABOVE: **Monet-Goyon's L5 model, and the subsequent L5A1, was a standard production machine widely used in solo and sidecar form by the French Army and the *Gendarmerie* (police).** LEFT: **The French company Monet-Goyon produced high-quality motorcycles in the British style between 1917 and 1957.**

LEFT: **By the mid-1960s, Peugeot was the only surviving French motorcycle manufacturer. The little SX8T *Armée* was a military version of a standard civilian lightweight two-stroke multi-terrain motorcycle, with some 75 machines procured for trials by the French Army during 1977. Production started in earnest the following year and, although it remained in service for some 20 years it was always felt to be underpowered. The SX8T has subsequently become popular with collectors looking for a low-priced ex-military machine.**

being requisitioned by, and perhaps even produced for, the *Wehrmacht* after 1940. The first of these was the 750cc *Armée* of 1935, but in 1938 this was replaced by the 800cc AX2 which featured shaft drive, four-speed forward and reverse gearbox, and driven sidecar wheel. Gnome & Rhône's 500cc D5A was also widely used, as was the Terrot 500cc RDA, both machines dating from 1938.

The Simca-SEVITAME Type B *Armée* of 1938/39 – the acronym stands for *Société d'Etude des Véhicules Issus de la Technique Automobile Moderne et Economique* – is worth describing if only for its technical innovation. Designed by Marcel Violet, the engine was a 330cc in-line twin-cylinder unit installed with the crankshaft at the top and the cylinders facing down; cooling was achieved by means of some 12 litres/2.65 gallons of oil. Final drive was by exposed shaft and a small propeller could be attached to the shaft to allow the motorcycle to be used as an outboard to power a boat. The fuel tank formed the rear mudguard. Few had been manufactured by the time France fell to Germany in 1940.

Sadly the domestic motorcycle industry remained unable to supply the Army's needs even up to World War II, and, in 1939, the French Army had ordered 5,000 Indian Chiefs from the USA. Although the machines had been manufactured by March 1940, the fall of France in May meant that there was not sufficient time to make delivery and the machines were diverted to Britain. Similarly, a number of motorcycles ordered from Ariel and Velocette during 1939/40 were also diverted to the British Army.

The French motorcycle industry never really recovered from World War II. René Gillet closed in 1957 as did Koehler

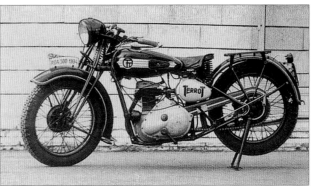

ABOVE: **At one time, Terrot was the largest motorcycle manufacturer in France, and the company's 500cc RDA, dating from 1938, was typical of the larger French motorcycles of the pre-war period. The factory's Dijon location put it out of reach of the occupying Germans but production was halted in 1944.**

and Monet-Goyon; Gnome & Rhône survived until 1959 and Terrot staggered on against falling sales until the early 1960s. Only Peugeot has survived to the present day.

As with most Western armies, the military motorcycle fell from favour during the 1960s but, during the previous decade the French Army had procured various domestic machines, including the 170cc Peugeot 176TC4 and the earlier 176D4, the 200cc Gnome & Rhône LX200, and the 500cc Terrot RGST. By 1960, with very little domestic motorcycle industry remaining, the government purchased a number of 250cc BMW R-27TS machines, followed, in 1966, by the Triumph T20WD, a derivative of the Tiger Cub. In 1978, the tiny Peugeot SX8 and SX8T *Armée* was procured for off-road use, and although it saw 20 years of service, it was always felt to lack sufficient power.

LEFT: **Belgian Army motorcycle troops with radio equipped sidecars. In the late 1930s, the Belgian manufacturers FN, Sarolea and Gillet-Herstal all produced heavy motorcycle combination outfits that included selectable drive to the sidecar wheel.**
BELOW LEFT AND BELOW: **Sarolea produced motorcycles from 1898 to 1957, including many military machines. This is the side-valve AS350 dating from 1951; there was a similar 400cc model designated 51-A4.**

Military motorcycles in Belgium

During the first three or four decades of motorcycling, more than 100 factories had been established in Belgium but by the time the Belgian Army started mechanization in the 1930s, it seems that only a handful of these manufacturers remained in business. The three that were chosen to supply military motorcycles were all based in the Liège town of Herstal, some 65km/40 miles east of Brussels. The Sarolea company had established a workshop in the town in 1898, and was almost certainly the first Belgian motorcycle manufacturer. FN followed in 1901, becoming known for its use of shaft drive from 1903. Gillet-Herstal had started producing motorcycles in 1919, and was presumably so-named to differentiate it from the French René Gillet concern, which had been established in business some 20 years earlier.

Small numbers of basically civilian FN motorcycles were used by the Belgian Army before and during World War I, and a number of the company's 2.75hp machines were used by the Australian Army. It was not until the 1930s that the country started seriously mechanizing its army and, from 1935/36

onwards, Gillet-Herstal, Sarolea and FN machines were purchased for the Belgian Army, with numbers of the latter also supplied to the Soviet and Swiss armies.

There was nothing remarkable about the majority of Belgian motorcycles but in the mid-1930s, in response to a requirement for a heavy motorcycle capable of operating in all types of ground conditions, all three Belgian manufacturers started to produce specialized military sidecar outfits with sidecar-wheel drive, high ground clearance and reverse gear.

Dating from 1937, the FN M12-SM was the first of these to be taken into service. It was a big, heavy-duty machine powered by a 1,000cc horizontally opposed side-valve engine driving the rear wheel and the sidecar wheel through a four-speed forward and reverse gearbox together with a two-speed transfer case. The same year, Sarolea produced the 600cc single-cylinder S6, following this in 1939 with the horizontally opposed H1000 *Militaire*, the latter equipped with a three-speed forward and reverse gearbox and two-speed transfer case. Gillet-Herstal produced their 750 in 1938, powered by a vertical twin engine and also featuring sidecar-wheel drive and a four-speed forward and reverse gearbox, although this time lacking the low-ratio gears of the transfer case. A motor tricycle was also produced, based on the FN M12-SM, between 1939 and 1940.

These unique Belgian machines, which pre-date the big Zündapp and BMW 3x2 sidecar outfits, were both captured and copied by the *Wehrmacht*, and were also supplied to many other countries including Argentina, Chile, China and the Middle East.

Although motorcycle production in Belgium was certainly seriously curtailed during the war years, all three companies resumed manufacturing motorcycles in the post-war period. Sarolea had formed a co-operative with a number of other Belgian manufacturers, including Gillet-Herstal, and generally

ABOVE AND BELOW: **Dating from 1947, the single-cylinder FN M13 was typical of medium motorcycles of the period. Although it was fitted with front suspension, the rear end remained unsprung. A selection of engines was available, including 250cc, 350cc and 450cc units.**

concentrated on two-strokes, while FN attempted to regain their market share with a range of 250cc to 500cc models. Both Sarolea and FN stopped making motorcycles in 1957, while Gillet-Herstal managed to survive into the early 1960s.

The Belgian Army used British and American machines in the immediate post-war years including Indian, Harley-Davidson, Ariel, Matchless, and Norton. All three of the domestic manufacturers also supplied small numbers of 350, 400 and 450cc side-valve motorcycles to the Belgian Army during the 1950s. A number of Harley-Davidson FL Electra-Glides were also purchased by the *Rijkwascht* in 1967 for military police duties, possibly the last use of a full-size Harley-Davidson by a European army.

During 1959, FN produced about 500 examples of their three-wheeled AS24 air-portable tricycle that was built under licence from Straussler and could be used as an ambulance, cargo or personnel carrier, fire-fighter or missile launcher.

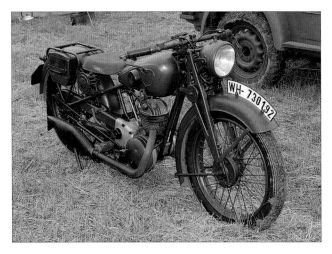

Military motorcycles in Germany

The German Imperial Army was quick to recognize the military potential of the motorcycle. The first such machines were trialled in 1899 and a number were taken into German military service as early as 1904, By 1918, the Germans had procured more than 5,400 motorcycles. Equally, of the main protagonists of World War II, Germany was always the most enthusiastic user of motorcycles – and, for that matter, horses – both of which were used in great numbers by all arms of the service during the early years of the conflict. Alongside the rather more mundane roles such as despatch riding, motorcycles were also employed by the elite and highly mobile combat troops known as *Kradschützen* which formed such an effective part of the lightning Blitzkrieg tactic.

At the end of the 1930s, the *Wehrmacht* had literally dozens of different, mostly civilian style, machines in service and it is said that there was a total of one million motorcycles in military service by 1937. Stockholding of parts was clearly something of a nightmare and, by 1940, the *Wehrmacht* had standardized

ABOVE: **Germany used thousands of motorcycles during World War II and not all were of the heavy variety. On the left is a 198cc NSU 201, on the right, a DKW NZ-350, with a capacity of 346cc.** BELOW: **The 340cc single-cylinder BMW R-35, dating from 1937, was widely used as a training machine.**

on motorcycles in three categories – light, medium and heavy – from a smaller number of manufacturers.

Light motorcycles, with engines under 350cc, were typically produced by BMW, DKW, NSU and TWN (Triumph). The most numerous of such machines was the NSU 251OS(L) of which some 35,000 were produced between 1934 and 1944. Basically a lightly modified commercial motorcycle, it was powered by an overhead valve engine of 241cc, had a top speed of 100kph/62mph, and a range of around 325km/200 miles. The rigid rear forks and parallelogram front suspension were typical of the period.

In the "medium" category, motorcycles were powered by an engine of between 350cc and 500cc and were typically produced by DKW, TWN and Victoria. Motorcycles in the "heavy" category were generally powered by a big 600 to 750cc flat-twin engine; Zündapp even had an 800cc model. These machines were invariably used in conjunction with a standardized military sidecar, often with a driven wheel. Such machines, produced by BMW, NSU and Zündapp, were used on all fronts as well as in airborne operations, and the BMW R-75 is representative of the type; produced between 1941 and 1944, it was powered by a 746cc horizontally opposed overhead-valve engine driving a rear axle which was shared by the motorcycle and sidecar, and which incorporated a lockable differential. A machine-gun was frequently mounted on the sidecar, which could also carry additional supplies of fuel and ammunition.

In addition, motorcycles produced by the Belgian FN and French Gnome & Rhône companies were also impressed into service, and there were also thousands of requisitioned civilian machines and other captured enemy motorcycles in service.

And, of course, Germany remained unique in employing a half-tracked motorcycle – the SdKfz 2, better known as the NSU HK-101 *Kettenkraftrad* – usually shortened to simply *Kettenkrad*. Offering excellent cross-country performance, it was powered by the 1,488cc engine of the contemporary Opel Olympia motorcar, and could accommodate a crew of three and tow a gun or light trailer.

But a combination of Allied bombing and the increasing demand for all kinds of military equipment meant that Germany struggled to produce sufficient motorcycles for the *Wehrmacht*'s needs. Between 1934 and 1939, the German armed forces took delivery of almost 70,000 motorcycles and, for the years 1940 to 1943, the number rose to 277,000. However, as Germany's factories strained to satisfy the war effort, many motorcycle manufacturers found themselves producing other war materials. By 1943, more than 80 per cent of the production facilities at

ABOVE: **Massed ranks of German motorcycle combinations taking the salute as they drive slowly past the *Führer*.**

the Ardie, Steyr, TWN, Victoria and DKW factories were devoted to producing tank components, stationary engines, arms and ammunition, rather than motorcycles.

Some German motorcycle production had resumed by the late 1940s and, while BMW might be a notable exception, many of the manufacturers never regained their pre-war markets.

ABOVE: **The band of the *Nationalsozialistisches Kraftfahrkorps*, NSKK (National Socialist Motor Corps – an organization of the Nazi Party), in 1937.**
RIGHT: **Lightweight motorcycles, with single-cylinder two-stroke engines of around 100cc, were widely used to provide mobility in the German Army. Typical machines were supplied by Ardie, Phänomen, DKW and TWN (Triumph).**

Military motorcycles in Great Britain

Britain was among the first users of military motorcycles, with motorcycle-mounted despatch riders used for the first time during manoeuvres in 1910. During World War I, the most numerous British Army motorcycles were lightly militarized civilian machines supplied by Triumph and Douglas which had been standardized for military service. Dozens of other, often unsuitable, types were also used, many being impressed civilian machines.

During the 1930s, the War Office attempted to standardize on a 500cc V-twin military motorcycle but, despite trialling dozens of UK and sometimes foreign machines, appeared unable to find anything which was suitable. By the outbreak of World War II, the typical British Army motorcycle was a low-cost single-cylinder machine that could be built in large numbers. Even so, production was not increased at a sufficient rate and in September 1939, some 30 per cent of the British Army's 21,000 motorcycles were impressed civilian types. Then, when the British Expeditionary Force abandoned thousands of its newest motorcycles in France and Belgium following the evacuations from Dunkirk, there was an immediate, and critical shortage of suitable machines. There was a period when anything that could move was purchased for military service, including hundreds of not terribly suitable civilian machines that happened to be in the showrooms or awaiting delivery.

With the immediate crises resolved, it would be fair to say that the typical British military motorcycle of World War II was a thoroughly conventional design, generally derived from a pre-war civilian machine. Most were powered by a 350cc or

TOP RIGHT: **Motorcycle outriders leading a transport convoy through the ruins of a town in Normandy.**
ABOVE RIGHT: **British despatch riders taking a break after the D-Day landings.**
RIGHT: **Introduced in 1939 and remaining in production until 1945, the 500cc side-valve BSA M20 was probably the longest-serving motorcycle in the British Army.**

ABOVE: **Sidecars were not widely used by the British services. This BSA M20 Swallow sidecar combination is marked as belonging to the RAF.** RIGHT: **The Royal Navy also used the M20; the civilian number plate suggests a very early machine.**

500cc single-cylinder side-valve engine driving the rear wheel through a four-speed gearbox and exposed chain; some manufacturers, for example Triumph, managed to graduate from side valves to overhead valves. With perhaps the notable exception of the Matchless G3L which had telescopic forks, front suspension was provided by coil-sprung parallelogram girder forks, while the rear end remained unsprung.

Sidecars were not widely used although the factory-produced Norton 633 Big Four should be mentioned as the only British combination outfit to be fitted with a driven sidecar wheel. At the other end of the scale, the tiny Excelsior Welbike "para-scooter", powered by a 98cc two-stroke engine which drove the rear wheel directly, was designed to be air-dropped in a standard container.

During this period, technical development generally took a back seat to the exigencies of production, often in the face of materials shortages and, occasionally, almost overwhelming *Luftwaffe* action, and a total of 425,000 military motorcycles poured out of Britain's motorcycle factories in the years 1940 to 1945. With the Jeep taking care of many roles for which the motorcycle would have been considered during the 1930s, this was more than enough for the needs of the British and the Commonwealth armies, with more than a few exported to the Soviet Union. Motorcycles were used by the Army, the RAF and the Royal Navy throughout World War II, as well as by the Home Guard and Civil Defence services.

The British manufacturers were quick to get civilian production underway again after the war, albeit with little more than warmed-over versions of pre-war models. The British Army retained the best, and least used, motorcycles from the war years, with the BSA M20 and the Matchless G3L notably remaining in service into the 1950s, but a number of Triumph TRW twins were bought at the end of the 1940s. When new machines were purchased in the 1960s, they were little more than lightly militarized versions of the then current BSA A65 and B40, Matchless G3LS, and the Triumph 500. In the late 1970s, the BSA-assembled Bombardier Can-Am 250 replaced the British

motorcycles and this, in turn, gave way to the Armstrong/Harley-Davidson MT350 and MT500, while powerful Norton police motorcycles were replaced by the Honda Pan-European.

Despite a few World War II experiments with machine-gun equipped sidecars, the British Army did not generally use motorcycles for a combat role, preferring to employ them for despatch riders, convoy escort, traffic control, and military police duties – and, of course, in the Royal Signals "White Helmets" display team that first saw the light of day in 1927.

ABOVE: **The side-valve Triumph 2SW was supplied to the War Office between 1938 and 1941, with more than 10,000 examples built.**

Military motorcycles in the Commonwealth

During World War I, Canadian and Australian forces were equipped with a similar range of machines as the British Army, notably the Douglas 2.75hp, BSA Model H, and Triumph Model H. It was much the same story for World War II, and although the industries of Canada, Australia, New Zealand, India and South Africa all constructed military vehicles during World War II, none of these nations produced military motorcycles. With but a single exception, there were no domestic motorcycle manufacturers in the Commonwealth and the armies generally operated motorcycles which had been manufactured in either Britain or the USA.

That exception was Australia, where there was a single domestic motorcycle, the lightweight Villiers-powered Waratah produced by Williams Brothers of Sydney who were in business from 1914 to 1948, but none appear to have been supplied to the Australian services. In Canada, Bombardier did not start producing motorcycles until 1973 and Royal Enfield did not establish their factory in India until 1955. Hence, all Commonwealth military motorcycles of World War II came from overseas.

The Canadian Army Vehicle Data Book, issued by Canadian Military Headquarters in March 1944, lists just three motorcycles: two from Britain – the Matchless G3L and the Norton 16H, both of which were classed as "light", and the US-built Harley-Davidson WLC, which was described as "heavy". However, the Canadians almost certainly also used Indian 340 and 640 machines and Harley-Davidson WLAs.

The Harley-Davidson WLC was developed especially for the Canadian Department of National Defense, and was introduced in 1941. It is the closest thing there is to a Canadian military motorcycle and was produced in what were described as "domestic" and "export" models, both incorporating a number of detailed changes when compared to the standard US Army WLA. These changes included British-style right-hand clutch-

ABOVE LEFT: **Canadian forces made use of the British BSA M20.** ABOVE: **South African Army Commandos mounted on Harley-Davidsons.** BELOW: **The machine nearest the camera is a Matchless G3 with a decidedly flat rear tyre.**

LEFT: **The ubiquitous BSA M20 was as popular with Commonwealth units as it was with British. These new machines, costing £49.50 each, were part of a contract for 4,000 dating from 1940.**
BELOW: **South African women riders on civilian machines; the motorcycle nearest the camera is a Royal Enfield, probably a Model C from which the WD/C was derived.**

ABOVE: **A Canadian despatch rider on a Norton 16H consults his rotating map while on exercise in England in 1943.**

and-throttle configuration, with the ignition-timing lever also on the right, and different lighting arrangements, which tended to reflect British military practice. There was also a different instrument nacelle, slightly smaller mudguards, and an ammunition/spare parts box carried on the front mudguard; the WLC did not carry the rifle scabbard or ammunition box of the US Army machines. A number of WLCs were fitted with a Goulding single-seat sidecar, in which form it may have been described as Model WLS.

Although the WLA remained in volume production to 1945, and even beyond, the WLC was discontinued in 1944 after 5,356 examples had been built.

As regards machines of British origin, BSA had been supplying motorcycles to both India and South Africa during 1938/39 and, of course, many of these machines remained in service during the war. After 1940, the armies of all of the Commonwealth countries were reinforced with equipment from Britain, including for example Matchless G3L, BSA M20, and Norton 16H motorcycles. Harley-Davidson, and Indian machines were also supplied under the Lend-Lease arrangements, in both solo and sidecar combination form as appropriate. It is also worth noting that in 1942/43 South Africa uniquely received 1,597 examples of the Harley-Davidson Model US sidecar outfit, fitted with a left-hand LLE sidecar, and supplied through the British Supply Council.

Many of these wartime machines remained in service well into the 1950s, the BSA M20 and Matchless G3L proving to have particular longevity. Australia, Canada, India and Pakistan, and South Africa all continued to buy British military motorcycles, the Triumph TRW and BSA B40 being particularly popular.

Military motorcycles in the USA

In 1900, Columbia was the first company to offer a proper motorcycle for sale in the United States. By the following year, there were more than a dozen competitors, including the Indian machine designed by George M. Hendee and Oscar Hedstrom; Harley-Davidson was established in 1904. During the early years of the industry, the US motorcycles differed from their European counterparts in using sturdier frames and well-sprung saddles as a response to the generally poor roads, and in being fitted with better lighting and braking equipment. By the end of the 20th century, the USA had been home to some 325 manufacturers of motorcycles. Hendee had initially laid claim to being the largest motorcycle manufacturer in the world, with sales growing from just 143 in 1902 to 20,000 in 1912, but the title soon passed to Harley-Davidson.

Harley-Davidson was probably the first US motorcycle manufacturer to supply machines to the military, having supplied the Japanese Imperial Army back in 1912. The US Army started buying motorcycles from Hendee (Indian) in 1913, with Harley-Davidsons following in 1916. During World War I, Indian, Harley-Davidson, Excelsior and Cleveland motorcycles were all supplied to the US Expeditionary Force as well as to the Western Allies. The machines were generally used by scouts and despatch riders but, as in Europe, there were also experiments with using sidecars as a stretcher carrier or machine-gun mount.

However, the appearance of cheap motorcars had a profound effect on the growth of the US motorcycle industry, with many pioneering companies forced into early bankruptcy. Cyclone, Thor, Pope, Yale, Iver Johnson and Peerless all closed before

ABOVE: **The iconic Harley-Davidson WLA was the most common US military motorcycle of World War II. A Dodge WC52 weapons carrier provides the backdrop.**
LEFT: **Derived from Harley-Davidson's civilian Model WL, something like 78,000 WLAs were produced between March 1940 and May 1945.**

ABOVE: **A US soldier of the 315th Engineer Battalion, 90th Infantry Division carries everything he needs for his daily routine on his Harley WLA**

the end of World War I, with Indian, Cleveland, Harley-Davidson and Excelsior – who had absorbed Henderson – being the only significant companies to survive into the 1920s. Cleveland failed in 1929 and when Henderson and Excelsior closed in 1931 only Harley-Davidson and Indian survived – the Hendee company having finally changed its name in 1923.

During World War II, the two surviving volume producers supplied the majority of the motorcycles used by the US Army, as well as supplying machines to Britain, the British Commonwealth, China and the Soviet Union. The military products of both companies were derived from pre-war civilian models although both also developed sidecar combination machines with a driven wheel in the style of the big German BMW and Zündapp motorcycles. By the time the machines were deemed ready for production, events had overcome them and the need had passed, with no series production being commissioned. Small

numbers of specialized motorcycles were also supplied by Cushman and Simplex, with tiny motorized package delivery vehicles coming from Salsbury and Strimple.

In the early days of World War II, motorcycles were widely held by US armoured and infantry combat units and were used for scouting and reconnaissance duties as well being considered a form of mechanized cavalry. The appearance of the Jeep put paid to this and after 1942, the role of the military motorcycle was downgraded and the machines were generally reserved for military police, traffic and convoy control, and despatch riding.

Both Indian and Harley-Davidson resumed civilian production in 1945 but Indian finally closed the doors in 1953, leaving Harley-Davidson as the only volume domestic motorcycle manufacturer. The company generally eschewed the lightweight end of the market and concentrated on the traditional heavy American motorcycle.

Sales continued to the US and other armies during the 1950s and 1960s but the numbers were not significant and it was not until 1987 that Harley-Davidson became, albeit briefly, a significant player in the military market again when the company purchased the rights to the British Armstrong MT350 and MT500. Hoping to secure a big US Army contract, they continued to manufacture the Rotax-engined MT, using parts from all over the world, and to supply the British and Canadian armies who had been buying from Armstrong. A number of MT500s were also used by USAF "combat control teams" but the big US order never materialized, the US Army going on to buy the Kawasaki KL-250D8. Total production of all MT models, by Armstrong and Harley-Davidson during a near 20-year production run was 4,470 units.

The US Army has been one of the prime developers in the RMCS/HDT diesel motorcycle project and continues to operate motorcycles although these days they are far more likely to be of Japanese manufacture.

BELOW LEFT: **The 1,213cc Harley-Davidson Model U was produced between 1937 and 1948, with more than 33,000 examples built, with several thousand of these supplied to the US Government for both sidecar and solo use.** BELOW: **The Cushman Package Kar.**

ABOVE: **The Bianchi 500M was unusual for the time in having plunger-type rear suspension.** LEFT: **Introduced in 1939, some 7,000 examples of the Moto-Guzzi 500cc *Alce* were produced during World War II.**

Military motorcycles in Italy

The Italian Army started mechanization by purchasing a single Fiat motorcar in 1903; motorcycles followed, in small numbers, from 1914 with essentially civilian machines coming from manufacturers such as Bianchi, Frera and Gilera. Of these, Bianchi, which had been established in 1897, was almost certainly the first motorcycle manufacturer in Italy, with Frera established in 1906 and Gilera in 1909.

During World War I, the belt-drive 500cc Bianchi Type A was probably the most numerous motorcycle in use with the Italian Army, but the 570cc and 795cc Frera machines were also widely employed, in both solo and combination form. By 1918, the Italian Army had almost 6,500 motorcycles in service, all of them being lightly militarized commercial models. Few purchases were made in the post-war years and many of the older machines remained in service into the early 1920s. Following the coming to power of Benito Mussolini in 1922, efforts were made to reorganize the Italian motorcycle industry and the army started buying motorcycles again from the early 1930s. The Moto-Guzzi *Militare* 32 motor tricycle was adopted by the army for a range of roles from 1932, including artillery tractor, cargo and personnel carrier, and as a gun platform.

The Benelli company, which had been established in 1917 to supply engines to other manufacturers, started producing motorcycles in 1921 and from the mid-1930s the company

became one of the big three suppliers to the Italian Army, alongside Moto-Guzzi and Gilera. For a number of years during the late 1930s, the Italian Army attempted to develop armoured motorcycles which could be used by snipers. One of these, based on the Moto-Guzzi GT17 could be fitted with armoured leg shields and a screen through which the rider was expected to aim and fire a light machine-gun but like all such efforts elsewhere, it was eventually abandoned as being top heavy and impractical.

Bianchi, Moto-Guzzi, Gilera and Sertum all produced specialized military motorcycles during World War II, with motor tricycles also coming from the first three named companies as well as Benelli. Volugrafo, a company which appears only to have operated during the war years, but which is notable for being the manufacturer of the first modern motor scooter, produced a very small air-portable machine for military use, which was derived from its scooter.

In the years immediately following World War II, the Italian motorcycle industry was quick to re-establish itself, with the Moto-Guzzi *Superalce* and the Gilera *Saturno* both launched in 1946. Both of these models, as well as the Gilera 175GT (1956) were widely used by the Italian Army. Benelli began production a little later, having had its factory destroyed. The company's first post-war machine was not launched until 1949 by which time it appears to have been too late to procure further military contracts.

The 1959 Moto-Guzzi *Mulo Meccanico* should also be mentioned as an all-terrain successor to the motor tricycles of the 1930s. With its 750cc V-twin engine, torque-dividing differential and 3x3 driveline, together with operator controls to reduce the rear tracks on the move, and the ability to be fitted with tracks on the rear wheels, it was far more capable than

LEFT: **First produced in 1942, the Moto-Guzzi 500U *Unificato* is a typical Italian *Motocarro* of the period.**

its predecessors and 200 units were supplied to the Alpine Regiment for use on mountain tracks and passes. In a similar vein, MV Augusta also built the German Faun *Kraka* under licence although, as a four-wheeled vehicle with a conventional steering wheel, this machine is outside the scope of this book.

During the 1960s, Moto-Guzzi made a name for itself as a producer of high-quality powerful motorcycles which might be considered as an alternative to the big BMWs and its 500–950cc machines were widely used in Italy and elsewhere, the V7 and the *Nuovo Falcone*, both dating from 1967, being particular favourites for convoy escort and military police duties. These machines were followed by the 850-T3 and the semi-automatic V1000 *Convert*, dating from 1973 and 1975, respectively.

Unique among European motorcycle industries, Italy seems to have survived the Japanese "invasion" with Benelli, Gilera and Moto-Guzzi all intact, and has even managed to find export orders for its military machines.

TOP AND ABOVE: **Moto-Guzzi retained the horizontal single-cylinder engine (installed along the axis of the machine) together with the exposed flywheel into the post-war years. This is the 500cc *Falcone*, introduced in 1966.** LEFT: **British riders on captured Italian machines, probably Gileras.**

Military motorcycles in the USSR

During World War I, the Russian Imperial Army used motorcycles supplied by, for example, Clyno, Sunbeam and Rudge in Britain, as well as others. Some efforts were made in the mid-1920s to design a heavy military motorcycle in the Soviet Union but these came to nothing and the earliest domestic machine in Soviet military service was probably the IZH-7 (L300) of 1933, a 293cc solo motorcycle produced by the Izhevsk Steel Plant (ISH). Other models followed from the same plant including the prototypes for the purpose-designed military motorcycle combination which subsequently entered production as the PMZ NATI A-750.

The PMZ NATI A-750 featured a mix of Indian and BMW design features and went into production in 1935, until it was eventually replaced by the M-72 in 1939. Between 1936 and 1943, the Tagnarog plant also produced the TIM-AM600 (sometimes identified as TIZ-AM600).

ABOVE RIGHT: **During World War II, the Soviet Union used large numbers of US and British motorcycles to supplement their own production.**
RIGHT: **The Red Army has always been an enthusiastic user of the military motorcycle, with more than 1.5 million machines taken into service over a 90-year period.** BELOW: **The Soviet M-72 was based heavily on the pre-war BMW R-71.**

The best-known Soviet military motorcycle is almost certainly the M-72, which was first produced in 1942, and was used in both solo and sidecar configuration. Based heavily on a pre-war BMW, probably the R-71 since this had been produced under licence in the Soviet Union in 1938, it was powered by a 750cc horizontally opposed side-valve engine and featured shaft drive to the rear wheel via a four-speed gearbox. The original Soviet plan was that the machine would be produced at factories in Moscow, Leningrad (now Saint Petersburg), and Kharkov. The imminent threat of German bombing and subsequent invasion led to the removal of the Moscow facilities to Irbit (the factory being known as IMZ, or Irbit Moto Zavod), and the Leningrad and Kharkov facilities to Gorkiy Moto Zavod (GMZ). During World War II, a total of 9,799 M-72 motorcycles were built and delivered to the Red Army.

In 1949, the M-72 production line was moved again, this time from Gorkiy, (now called Nizhny Novgorod) to the Kiev Motor Zavod (KMZ) in Ukraine, which had been established in 1946. By 1950, 30,000 machines had been produced.

LEFT: **The spirit of the M-72 lives on through various machines – this is the Dniepr M-12 of 1977, which retains the horizontally opposed side-valve engine.** BELOW: **The Mayday parades have always been used as a means of demonstrating the military might of the Soviet Union; these machine-gun equipped infantrymen are riding TIM (TIZ) AM600 solo machines.**

In various forms, and under names which have included Cossack, Ural and, from 1907, Dniepr, the M-72 has remained in almost continuous production. The original M-72 was produced until around 1956; subsequent variants were designated M-72K, M-72H and finally M-72M, with production finally ending in 1960. A civilian model was produced from 1954 by IMZ under the designation K-750. The Chinese motorcycle manufacturer, Chang Jiang, eventually bought the production line for the Ural M-72 to build its CJ-750 motorcycle.

The purely military MV-750, introduced in 1964, featured a power-sharing differential which allowed the rider to choose to feed equal power to the sidecar and motorcycle wheels or 67 per cent of the power to the rear wheel of the motorcycle, and 33 per cent to the sidecar.

The civilian K-750 provided the basis for the Dniepr MT-12 model of 1977, a 750cc heavy motorcycle for sidecar use, still retaining side valves, and fitted with a four-speed forward and reverse gearbox. Later models, such as the MT-9 and MT-10, used an overhead valve engine.

More than 1.5 million motorcycles have been constructed for use by the Red Army to date, and motorcycle production continues at the Kiev KMZ plant today, with the MT-11 and MT-16. Of course, the former Soviet Socialist Republic of Ukraine has been an independent state since 1990.

The Dniepr 750 machine was used for presidential escort work during the Soviet period and continues to be favoured by President Vladimir Putin. Soviet airborne forces continue to deploy lightweight motorcycles, using them at checkpoints and to control traffic and check dispersed communications installations. Current Soviet thinking has also seen motorcycle combinations armed with heavy machine-guns, and trials have also been conducted mounting anti-tank guided weapons on motorcycle sidecar chassis.

Military motorcycles in Japan

Although it should be pointed out that the Japanese Army has never been a great user of military motorcycles, no-one could argue that the Japanese motorcycle industry does not dominate the world. But it was not always thus and it would seem that the country did not actually start building motorcycles until 1932.

However, the first military use of motorcycles in Japan had begun in 1912 when Harley-Davidson had supplied a number of machines "without spares" to the Japanese Imperial Army for evaluation – almost certainly 492cc single-cylinder

Model X-8-A civilian machines. Japan's involvement in World War I brought this arrangement to an end and there were no further exports to the Japanese Army after 1917. But, like it or not, Harley-Davidson was inextricably linked with the emergence of the Japanese motorcycle industry; a fact which it certainly would have regretted had the implications been clear.

In 1922, the Murato Iron Works produced a copy of a contemporary Harley-Davidson. It was not taken up for production but, finding more success in producing motorcycle components, the Murato Iron Works evolved into Meguro Seisakusho. In the same year, Harley-Davidson's Export Manager, Alfred Rich Child, signed contracts to supply the Model J to Japan and, a year later, Child was nominated manager of the first Harley-Davidson dealer in Japan. In July of that year, he negotiated the purchase of 350 "big twins".

Sales to Japan remained important to Harley-Davidson in the following decade, with the 1,200cc VL V-twin finding particular favour with the Japanese Imperial Army. Civilian sales were also booming and, in 1932, Child signed a contract to supply blueprints, dies and machine tools to Sankyo Seiyako, a pharmaceutical company, who would produce Harley-Davidson motorcycles under the name Rikuo. It was intended that local content would gradually increase over a four or five year period. Some sources suggest that the machines were constructed by Meguro at their Shinagawa factory in Tokyo but, certainly, by 1935, the Rikuo was of 100 per cent Japanese origin.

After 1936 when the arrangement expired, Sankyo continued selling Harley-Davidson derived motorcycles, supplying to the Japanese Army from 1937 under the name Rikuo Type 97 – the "type number" indicating the year of development, 1937 (Year 2597 in the Japanese system). By the end of World War II, some 18,000 of these machines had been supplied for both solo and sidecar use, in the latter case, fitted with a three-speed and reverse gearbox. At this time, there were some 15 motorcycle manufacturers in Japan, but it would appear that only the Rikuo Type 97 was used by the Japanese Army.

In 1937, the Japanese Army had also trialled a four-wheel drive multi-terrain machine that was powered by a 1,200cc V-twin Harley-Davidson engine – or more likely, a Sankyo copy of a Harley-Davidson engine. It was approved for production but was never actually built in quantity, the five prototypes being all that existed.

Alongside the Rikuo Type 97, the Japanese Army and Navy were both enthusiastic users of motorized tricycles – known as *Sanrinsha*. These machines had first appeared

LEFT: **These Allied soldiers appear pleased with a captured Japanese motorcycle, almost certainly the Sankyo (Meguro) Rikuo Type 97 which was based on the Harley-Davidson.**

ABOVE AND RIGHT: **Produced from 1932, the Sankyo Rikuo Type 97 was the only motorcycle used by the Japanese Imperial Army during World War II; it was also available to civilian customers.** BELOW: **Abandoned Sankyo Type 97 at Balikapapan.**

in Japan in about 1930 for commercial use, and numbers of what was called the *Sanrinsha Type 1* (2601 or 1941) were supplied by Iwasaki and Kurogane.

After the end of World War II, Japan was banned from building passenger cars until 1949 but there was no such ban on motorcycles and Rikuo continued to build their Harley-Davidson copies into the late 1950s. However, it was one Soichiro Honda who changed everything when he purchased 500 military surplus two-stroke stationary engines and started fitting these into bicycle frames to produce a low-cost moped. In September 1948 he set up the Honda

Motor Company and the world of motorcycling was never going to be the same again.

Suzuki was established in 1952, with Yamaha following in 1955. Kawasaki started making motorcycles in 1960 after taking over the Meguro company who were producing a 500cc machine based on the BSA A7. By 1962, Kawasaki Motor Sales had been formed, the forerunner to the Kawasaki Motorcycle Company. Although these four companies have subsequently dominated the world's motorcycle markets, they came too late to have any significant effect on the military motorcycle scene, either in Japan or elsewhere.

Military motorcycles in neutral Europe

The total number of motorcycles constructed by the Allies during World War II was in the order of 541,000 – 425,000 were built in Britain, more than 106,000 in the USA, and almost 10,000 in the Soviet Union. For the other side, more than 277,000 machines were produced in Germany and Austria between 1939 and 1945, 18,000 in Japan, and thousands more in Italy. But of course this wasn't the whole story and military motorcycles were also produced and used by Ireland, Sweden and Switzerland, all of whom remained neutral during this period. Other countries, including for example Spain and Portugal, also remained neutral, but neither nation mobilized.

Ireland

Despite a proud rebel tradition and the boast of having been fighting the British for 800 years, the Irish Republic (Eire) is not a naturally militaristic nation. And, despite a single domestic motorcycle manufacturer – the Villiers-engined Fagan motorcycle having been manufactured in Dublin between 1935 and 1937 – neither does Ireland have an industrial tradition. Fagan had to close down by the time World War II, which Ireland always describes as "the emergency", broke out.

In 1939, the Irish Army comprised 7,500 men and, although Britain supplied some materiel and equipment, neither Britain nor the USA was prepared to supply more unless Ireland abandoned its policy of neutrality. De Valera kept Ireland neutral but the Irish

ABOVE: **The Irish Republic remained neutral for the duration of what was described there as "the emergency" but received military vehicles and other materiel from Britain. These BSA M20 motorcycles were supplied in 1940.**

Army eventually grew to 250,000 men and, although they were never particularly well supplied, among the equipment available there were 470 BSA M20 motorcycles that had come from Britain in 1940. By 1954, 372 of these were still in service, and many remained on strength into the 1960s.

Other motorcycles that have seen service with the Irish Defence Force (IDF) subsequently include the Kawasaki GT550, Honda 650 Deauville and Yamaha XS500. The IDF currently uses Suzuki DRZ400 machines, but the government has shown an interest in the RMCS/HDT diesel motorcycle.

Sweden

In 1939, Sweden was one of Europe's longest-standing neutral nations, having not been at war since 1814. However, while it must have helped that Germany was importing Swedish iron ore, the government recognized that a declaration of neutrality was no guarantee of safety, and the country had been re-arming since 1936. In 1937, the Swedish Army comprised 403,000 men, rising to 600,000 by 1945.

DKW military motorcycles had been procured from Germany but the government recognized that it would be better to employ

LEFT: **The Swedish M/42 was a rugged 500cc solo motorcycle built by both Husqvarna and Monark-Albin and was produced with both overhead and side valve engines.**
BELOW LEFT: **Dating from 1943, the Swedish NV M1000 was a heavy multi-terrain machine powered by an engine which was effectively two M/42 cylinders on a common crankcase.** BELOW AND BOTTOM: **The Swiss Universal A1000 was a V-twin machine intended for both solo and sidecar use.**

two new military-type motorcycles that were suitable for solo and sidecar use. Manufactured by both Universal and Condor in almost identical form, the machines were designated A680 and A1000, the former powered by a 676cc side-valve V-twin engine, the latter with a 990cc unit, and both were fitted with a four-speed Burman gearbox.

Both machines remained in service into the 1950s but were superseded by the Condor A580 and A750 from 1958, the latter also being manufactured by Universal.

domestic machines. Husqvarna had been the largest producer of motorcycles in Sweden during the 1920s and 1930s but by 1939 was committed to producing guns and armaments. In an attempt to solve the problem, the government approached Husqvarna to design a specialized military motorcycle which could be built by several companies. The result was the M/42, a 500cc, three-speed machine manufactured by Husqvarna, Monark and NV, with more than 3,000 built by 1945; two versions were produced, one with a side-valve engine and rigid rear end, the other with an overhead-valve engine and plunger suspension at the rear. The M/42 remained in service into the 1960s.

Switzerland

Despite being land-locked between Germany and Italy on two sides, and German-occupied France on the other, Switzerland was another European country with a long tradition of neutrality. Discretion generally proving the better part of valour, the Swiss Army, which was not mechanized to any significant degree, was mobilized on September 2, 1939, against the possibility of German invasion.

During the 1930s, the Swiss Army had used civilian motorcycles supplied by the Condor, Motosacoche (MAG), and Universal. While many of these remained in service during World War II, in 1943 the Universal company also designed

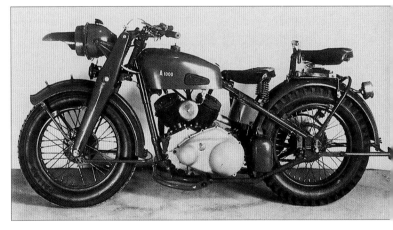

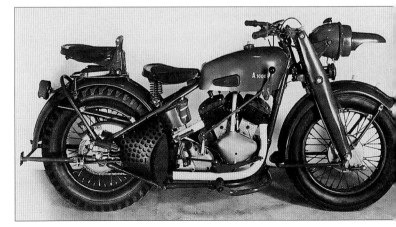

War surplus

When the war in Europe ended in May 1945, hundreds of defence contracts were terminated and the Allies found themselves with huge surplus stocks of every kind of imaginable item, including vehicles and motorcycles. Motorcycles that had further life in them – generally late models with low mileage – were retained, but thousands were put up for sale in the USA, Britain and across Europe as being surplus to requirements. Others were gifted to the governments of the newly liberated European nations.

In fact, the US government had actually started to dispose of large numbers of surplus motorcycles in the spring and summer of 1944. Among these were 15,000 Harley-Davidson WLAs, offered at a government-controlled retail price of $450; many were low-mileage machines which had never left the USA, some were even still crated. A quantity of shaft-drive XAs followed at $500 each. However, while this might not have been all of the surplus motorcycles that were available, US manufacturers were not faced with the situation of having to compete against their own products. It is said that there was an unwritten agreement between the US manufacturers and their government that, in order to protect the domestic market, surplus machines would not be returned to the USA from overseas.

The war had created considerable demand for motorcycles and, without having huge numbers of ex-services machines to depress the market, Harley-Davidson set about reactivating its network of franchised dealers and launching new civilian machines – albeit they were based on the militarized machines which they had already been selling to Uncle Sam.

ABOVE: **For the duration of the war, the major combatants continued to produce motorcycles in their thousands – Britain alone produced more than 1,400 machines every week between 1939 and 1945.** BELOW: **As soon as the fighting in Europe was over, enormous dumps were established where surplus equipment was collected prior to disposal.**

In Britain, the story was different. All of the Lend-Lease US-built machines, which had come from Indian and Harley-Davidson, were disposed of, and many of these found their way into the hands of UK dealers such as F. H. Warr, Marble Arch Motors and Pride & Clarke, where more than a few were converted to a more luxurious civilian specification. Unissued British motorcycles were generally returned to the manufacturers

LEFT: **Following the retreat of the British Expeditionary Force from France in May 1940, all available civilian motorcycles were purchased and stockpiled for military service.** BELOW: **Motorcycles were stored in massive depots prior to issue or, in later years, disposal.**

as being surplus to the Army's needs and were reworked back to civilian form and offered for sale to the public through the normal dealer channels. Other, usually more heavily used machines were offered direct to the public through the Ministry of Supply auctions, often at rock bottom prices. Since civilian machines were both expensive and in short supply, there was no shortage of eager buyers. Spares were equally plentiful and the ex-military motorcycle provided cheap transportation at a time when the only alternative was to use the bus or tram, or buy a pedal cycle.

Although the large number of surplus machines offered for sale must have depressed the British motorcycle industry, surprisingly it was these machines which allowed the British manufacturers to gain a foothold in the USA. Norton started it all off with civilian-finished versions of the 500cc 16H, but Ariel, Royal Enfield, BSA and Triumph soon followed, all of them offering what were essentially ex-WD 500cc motorcycles with a civilian finish. Royal Enfield even managed to find a market in the USA for the WD/RE "Flying Flea". The British machines were comparatively light and powerful and stood up well against the heavy domestic V-twins of Harley-Davidson and Indian. Almost 10,000 examples were imported into the USA in 1946.

As regards disposals to European governments, the French situation sums this up well. In the late 1940s and early 1950s, alongside small numbers of essentially pre-war domestic machines, the French Army operated a mixed bag of British and American motorcycles. Cushman airborne scooters and Harley-Davidson WLAs and WLCs were used along with machines such as the BSA M20 and B-30WD, the Norton 633 Big Four, and the Royal-Enfield WD/CO. Other European armies had similar mixed inventories.

Germany, of course, was obliged to stop building military motorcycles as soon as the fighting stopped but nevertheless, many ex-*Wehrmacht* motorcycles found their way on to the civilian market.

World War II almost certainly contributed to the demise of the British motorcycle industry. The combination of shattered and worn out production facilities, continuing austerity conditions at home, and the ready availability of surplus military motorcycles meant that it was more than a decade before the industry showed any real signs of recovering from the war.

LEFT: **Despite an innovative torsion-bar suspension at the rear, combined with the company's Radiadraulic bottom-link front forks, early post-war Douglas motorcycles sold badly. The 350cc Dragonfly featured a frame designed by Ernie Earles but it fared little better. By 1951, Douglas had been reduced to assembling Vespa scooters under licence from Italy. The company closed in 1964.**

The immediate post-war years

At the the end of World War II there was huge demand for cheap, utilitarian transport. Unlike the USA, the motorcar had yet to percolate through every level of European society and those domestic motorcycle manufacturers that were in a position to restart production found themselves with a ready market. It did not appear to matter that what was on offer was little more than a mixture of pre-war machines and wartime military models wearing a new coat of paint.

In Britain, despite the best efforts of the Luftwaffe, the motorcycle factories had produced 425,000 machines during the conflict and, although there was a ban on civilian sales, most of the larger manufacturers had survived. Civilian production was restarted almost immediately after the war ended, but it seemed that those companies that had failed to secure substantial military contracts generally made little or no impression on the civilian market in the immediate post-war years. For example, although the Brough Superior had been the chosen mount of T.E. Lawrence, the company

supplied no military motorcycles during World War II and, unable to resume production in 1945 because of a lack of suitable engines, had effectively closed in 1940, along with Rudge and Levis. Vincent struggled on until 1956, Sunbeam to 1957, with Scott and Excelsior barely surviving into the 1960s.

For others, the 1950s and 1960s were a time of plenty, with British 'bikes exported to military and civilian users across the globe. British motorcycle manufacturers quickly resumed their position as world leaders, but, sadly, it proved a false dawn and the success of those early years was insufficient to ensure long-term survival.

The demise of the once great BSA company, which had been responsible for producing one quarter of the British

ABOVE: **The British-built version of the DKW1 RT-125 was the BSA 125cc Bantam, a motorcycle used by the "Telegram Boys" of the GPO (General Post Office).**
LEFT: **The Matchless G80 "jampot" was firmly in the British tradition but could not save the company, which closed in 1969.**

LEFT: **Panther's iconic "sloper" design entered production in 1932, and the Panther-patented twin headlamps denotes this as the Model 100 De-Luxe. The Model 100 was put back into production after the war, using Dowty telescopic forks, but lasted only until 1963. The company closed in 1967.**

motorcycles of World War II, neatly sums up the fate of the post war British motorcycle industry. The company launched the DKW-derived Bantam in 1946 and, by 1948, was back in full civilian production. By 1951, BSA had bought Triumph, Ariel and Sunbeam, becoming the largest producer of motorcycles in the world. Expansion continued throughout the 1950s and into the 1960s. But, BSA had underestimated the impact of the Japanese machines, and, by the end of the decade, sales were dwindling. In 1973, in a rescue operation, the government merged Triumph with Norton-Villiers to create Norton-Villiers-Triumph. But, it was too late, and, by 1975 the receivers were called in.

In Germany, the big motorcycle companies lay in ruins, often literally, as a result of the war. The Allied Control Commission which was responsible for ensuring the Germans could not restart the production of military vehicles and equipment, forbade DKW, Zündapp, BMW and others from producing motorcycles, until the growing Soviet menace led to the restrictions being lifted. Zündapp had restarted production in 1947 with a 200cc two-stroke – a far cry from the company's massive wartime machines – following this with the Bella scooter in 1953. BMW launched its all-new 250cc R-24 in 1948. Based on the pre-war R-38, it was the only post-war BMW to lack rear suspension.

DKW saw its plants split between the Soviet and American zones. The company put an updated version of the lightweight RT-125 back into production in 1946, but had to watch the model also being produced in Britain, the USA, Japan, the Soviet Union and East Germany. NSU restarted production with pre-war models such as the Quick and the 251-OSL; they also managed to produce a number of Kettenkrad half-tracks for agricultural use. In 1949, DKW's first post-war model was launched and, in the same year, the company signed a licence to produce the Lambretta scooter.

France and Belgium never managed to resume the volume production of motorcycles. Only Peugeot survived, with companies such as Gnome & Rhône, FN, Gillet-Herstal, Monet-Goyon, Terrot and René Gellet scarcely struggling on into the late 1950s or early 1960s.

In Italy, the booming motorcycle industry initially concentrated on converting ex-military machines for civilian use, thus providing breathing space to develop new models. Well-established manufacturers such as Gilera, Benelli, and Moto-Guzzi all survived the war, the latter distinguished by being the oldest European manufacturer in continuous production of motorcycles, but the post-war years also saw some new companies established. For example, MV Augusta was set up in 1945, at first producing a 100cc two-stroke, but subsequently finding success with high-performance models. Laverda started producing motorcycles in 1949, again with a lightweight two-stroke, and scooters began to make an impact, with Piaggio, Vespa and Lambretta all starting production in 1946.

Curiously, Japan was not perceived as a threat during these immediate post-war years. Despite the country's industry being in ruins, Honda started motorcycle manufacture in 1948, launching its hugely successful Cub model in 1958. Suzuki joined the market in 1952, and Yamaha in 1955. These three companies were ultimately responsible for the death of the once-great British motorcycle industry.

Isolated from the European turmoil, Harley-Davidson survived a charge of restrictive practice in 1952 when it sought a tariff of 40% on imported motorcycles. It became the only US volume motorcycle builder when Indian collapsed in 1953, but, finding itself struggling against British, and then Japanese, imports, Harley-Davidson changed hands in 1969, almost going bankrupt in the process.

The Japanese "invasion"

At the end of World War II, Soichiro Honda purchased 500 military surplus two-stroke stationary engines and started fitting these in bicycle frames to make a simple low-cost moped. In September 1948 he established the Honda Motor Company and within 10 years had launched the Honda C50, a small 50cc motorcycle with a step-through frame, plastic leg-shields, and a fully enclosed engine and transmission. With its high-revving four-stroke engine, it was unlike other small machines of the period, and Honda set about breaking into a market sector totally dominated by the two-stroke models of other manufacturers.

But not only was the C50 unlike other similar machines of the period, it was also completely unlike the traditional British motorcycle and manufacturers such as BSA, Triumph and Norton, who were little interested in the bottom end of the market, failed to see the C50 as a threat. While it may not have been obvious at the time, the C50 was the start of the Japanese motorcycle "invasion". Having established a dealer network for their small commuter machine, Honda started to attack other market sectors and soon it was not just the bottom end of the market that the Honda wanted, it was the whole market.

The C50 went on to become the best-selling motorcycle of all time, providing cheap reliable transportation to millions across the globe. The machine is still in production today and has

RIGHT: **Suzuki's Power Free moped of 1952 featured a 36cc two-stroke engine and allowed the rider to choose between full power, pedal power or pedal assistance.**
MIDDLE RIGHT: **Yamaha's first motorcycle, the YA-1, was launched in 1954, with just 125 examples built during the first year.**
BELOW RIGHT: **Having established themselves with lightweight reliable machines that were little more than mopeds, Japanese manufacturers quickly learned how to produce ever-more powerful and sophisticated products.**

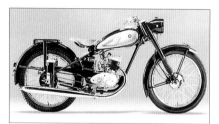

TOP: **The Honda C50, or Cub, is the world's most numerous motorcycle, with in excess of 100 million built over more than 60 decades.** ABOVE: **In 1947, Honda started to market the A-Type, the company's first motorcycle.**
LEFT: **Honda's Cub F-Type dates from 1952.**

achieved worldwide sales of more than 100 million units. And where Honda led, Yamaha, Suzuki, and Kawasaki followed.

Within little more than a decade, the Japanese "invasion" had wiped out most of the European motorcycle industry and even managed to bring the mighty Harley-Davidson to its knees.

During the 1950s and 1960s, Britain had been a world leader in producing motorcycles, but by the early 1970s, BSA, Ariel, Matchless, Norton, AJS and Royal Enfield had closed down. Norton managed to re-open as a builder of powerful machines, and it was a similar story at Triumph where production ceased in 1983 and restarted at a considerably reduced volume in 1985. But as volume producers they were finished. In France, only Peugeot survived and, of the German giants, DKW closed in 1981 and Zündapp followed in 1985. Only BMW managed to hold on to its traditional luxury market.

Over in the USA, Harley-Davidson became the only domestic motorcycle manufacturer of any note when Indian effectively closed in 1953; but the company had been weakened by British imports in the late 1950s and early 1960s, and was purchased by the American Machine & Foundry Company in 1969. The company lobbied successfully for tariffs to be imposed on imported Japanese motorcycles, but there had been considerable damage done. In 1981, Harley-Davidson passed back into private hands as the result of a management buyout, but it took four years to reverse the company's fortunes and bankruptcy was an ever-present threat.

This turmoil in the world motorcycle market coincided with the European and American armies losing interest in operating motorcycles in significant numbers. So, while it is true that the sales of domestic military machines dropped during this period, there was no commensurate increase in the purchase of Japanese machinery and it could appear that the Japanese "invasion" had little effect on military motorcycle usage. This is not the case, and when military motorcycles started to reappear in the late 1980s, even the US military were purchasing

RIGHT AND BELOW:
With virtually no domestic motorcycle industry remaining in Britain, the 250cc Kawasaki KL-250 and KLR-250D8 trail bike has found favour with the British Army. The machine has also been used by US forces and has seen service in Iraq and Afghanistan.

Kawasakis and Suzukis and the big Honda Pan European police motorcycle has proved popular with the British Army for convoy escort and military police duties.

Aside from small numbers of Armstrong/Harley-Davidson machines purchased by Canada and the UK, and small Peugeot trail bikes operated by the nationalistic French, the days of the European military motorcycle are gone.

In the end there is little doubt that the big four Japanese manufacturers have changed the face of military motorcycling, as surely as they changed the civilian market.

Diesel motorcycles

ABOVE: **The RMCS/Hayes M1030 is based on the Kawasaki KLR-650 and is produced in versions for the USA and Europe.** BELOW LEFT AND BELOW: **Details of the M1030.**

During World War II, both sides used a mixture of diesel and petrol engines in both logistical and combat vehicles. Clearly, this was far from an ideal situation since fuel transport and storage facilities needed to be duplicated. Worse still, the volatility and combustibility of petrol also presented unnecessary hazards. It should be no surprise then that NATO has been struggling to standardize on a single fuel for more than two decades and, these days, even the smaller vehicles, such as Land Rovers, are now diesel-engined. The only non-diesel machine has always been the motorcycle.

While most people would baulk at the idea of a diesel-powered motorcycle, surprisingly, the machine has more than a 100-year history and diesel motorcycles have something of a cult following in civvy street. The Indian company, Royal Enfield, produced and marketed a diesel version of their Bullet model, described as the Taurus, until the 1990s. But sadly, the slow-revving nature of many early diesel engines hardly lends itself to the sort of performance most motorcyclists expect, and the fuel consumption is less of an issue than it is for car drivers. Thus, the market has remained small and specialized.

However, perhaps unwittingly, the diesel-engined Bullet provided a starting point for the development of a specialized diesel-engined military motorcycle when, in 1992, Dr Stuart McGuigan and John Crocker of the British Royal Military College of Science (RMCS) produced a diesel-engined motorcycle demonstrator which they showed to the British Army. Their aim was to produce an engine with realistic power output and performance characteristics, that would allow it to replace conventional petrol motorcycle engines.

The prototype proved to be both reliable and usable, and the RMCS claimed it would lead to the world's first production diesel-powered military motorcycle. Unfortunately, the College

LEFT: **Astride a US Marine Corps M1010-M1, a member of the US 15th Marine Expeditionary Unit (MEU) waits his turn for a helicopter flight into Kuwait.**
BELOW: **The engine of the RMCS/Hayes M1030 was originally based on the bottom end of an Indian-built Royal Enfield Bullet. The production engine is manufactured by Hayes Diversified Technologies in California, USA.**

team experienced difficulty in finding a diesel-engine manufacturer who was prepared to work with them to refine the prototype. In the end, it was American money, appearing as a result of interest from the US Marines, which secured the future of the project, and the M1030-M1, as it was dubbed, became a joint collaboration between RMCS and Hayes Diversified Technologies (HDT) of Hesperia, California. US military interest also brought the British Ministry of Defence (MoD) to the table, and the development project ended up being sponsored by the MoD and the US Marine Corps (USMC).

The production machine was powered by a liquid-cooled wet sump indirect-injection diesel engine displacing 548cc, and incorporated the chassis, transmission and some engine components of the Kawasaki KLR-650. The custom-built engine will happily run on seven types of fuel, including diesel, aviation kerosene (AVTUR or JP8), and even rapeseed (canola) oil, and fuel consumption is said to be in the order of 50km per litre/140mpg, giving a range of 650km/400 miles. This performance compares well to a conventional 250cc machine, with a 0-100kph/0-62mph figure of just over 10 seconds, and a top speed of 130-135kph/80-90mph. The torque characteristics of the diesel engine also reduce the need for gear changing which improves the rider's control across country.

A pre-production version was demonstrated to the press in May 2001, and the machine went into production in March 2006. The US Marine Corps ordered a total of 440 examples, but received only 214, whilst an unspecified number of the slightly-modified M1030-M1E were supplied to the British Army as well as to several European NATO countries, including France. In Summer 2010, HDT presented an upgraded version of the machine at the Eurosatory Defence Equipment Exhibition, powered by a 670cc engine, and designated M1030-M2.

HDT has now withdrawn from the military motorcycles market, but the success of this machine led to the development of a diesel-powered military quad bike by Roush Technologies, using a Lombardini two-cylinder four-stroke diesel engine installed in a modified Arctic Sno Cat. Development began in 2004, with production in 2006.

ATVs and quad bikes

It is doubtful that anyone would consider that the history of All-Terrain Vehicles (ATVs) started with an 1897 Royal Enfield product, but that is certainly the case. In 1897, R.W. Smith, one of the financiers who had bailed out the original Royal Enfield company, built a quadricycle in which the engine was placed under the saddle, between the rear wheels. The machine went into production in 1899.

During World War II, the Standard Motor Company and Jaguar Cars both produced four-wheeled ultra-lightweight "buggies" that borrowed equally from motorcycle and motorcar technologies; an amphibious trailer was also produced that could be used for river crossing. The end of the war brought an end to this line of development, but, by the 1960s, civilian ATVs

were being produced in Europe and America. In the USA, for example, a number of manufacturers offered small amphibious off-road vehicles that could travel equally across swamps, streams, roads and cross-country tracks. In the UK, the Crayford Argocat and Cargocat appeared in 1980, and there was even a special military version.

Honda produced what could be considered the first modern ATV in 1970. It was a three-wheeled machine, featuring balloon tyres in place of conventional suspension, and borrowing heavily from Honda's motorcycle technology. The rider sat astride the machine, rather than inside, and it was controlled in the same way as a motorcycle, with the extra wheel providing stability at slow speeds. By the early 1980s, proper swing-arm coil-spring suspension had been introduced, and lower-profile tyres were fitted. In 1982, Honda introduced the ATC200E Big Red which, by including carrying racks, was effectively the first utility three-wheeled ATV.

Over the next few years both Yamaha and Kawasaki joined the market with high-performance two-stroke machines designed to break Honda's monopoly, and ATVs began to acquire a sporting image. Suzuki joined the fray in 1982/83, producing its first ATV, the LT125 QuadRunner; it was the QuadRunner's four wheels that spawned the name "quad bike". In 1985, Suzuki followed this up with the first high-performance four-wheeled ATV, the LT250R QuadRacer, but a year later, Honda produced the first all-wheel drive ATV, the TRX350 FourTrax 4x4. Its success was such that other manufacturers followed suit, and the 4x4 drive-line eventually became

TOP, ABOVE AND ABOVE RIGHT: **Widely used by the British and US forces in Iraq and Afghanistan, quad bikes are fast, powerful and easily manoeuvred, and can even be used with a small trailer to enhance the load-carrying capacity.**

standard. The three-wheeled machines were gradually discontinued due to safety concerns.

ATVs have proved popular with farmers, hunters, and construction workers, as well as with the sports fan, but it was probably the advent of all-wheel drive which encouraged military interest, almost to the point where ATVs have replaced military motorcycles.

Utility ATVs, which can reach speeds in excess of 125kph/77mph, have become a popular mount for airborne and special forces operations, where conventional vehicles such as the HMMWV and Land Rover are too large. They are exceptionally useful in close terrain, where tracks may be narrow and road surfaces poor, and, at the same time, ATVs offer massive versatility. In Afghanistan for example, ATVs were typically used for running replenishment operations, transferring stores to and from helicopter landing sites, evacuating casualties, and even as a firing platform. Larger ATVs are able to carry supplies on built-in racks, and there are 6x6 and 6x4 variants with a cargo-carrying rear load bed. Some are able to tow a small trailer.

The first ATVs supplied to the British Army came from Yamaha, but Honda, Kawasaki, and Suzuki have all supplied military ATVs, with a total of 1000 vehicles having been acquired by the British up to 2015. But the Japanese manufacturers do not have the market all to themselves. In 2004, for example, Essex-based Roush Specialist Vehicle Engineering, in association with Arctic Cat, developed a diesel-powered military quad bike, with some 450 units supplied under a British Army "urgent operational requirement" (UOR).

The US company General Dynamics demonstrated its "super light tactical vehicle, diesel", an ATV with four-wheel steering and automatic transmission, at the Eurosatory Exhibition in

2014, and Polaris Industries has supplied its automatic-transmission MV850 quad bike to the US Army since 2011, with examples also going to the defence forces of Germany, Latvia and Turkmenistan. Finally, the three-cylinder diesel-powered Defenture WRd-1 has been supplied to both the US and Netherlands Armies, the latter signing a contract for 250 examples in 2020.

Subsequent developments have seen ATVs begin to more closely resemble conventional four-wheeled vehicles.

LEFT AND BELOW: **Early quad bikes used balloon-type tyres for suspension and lacked all-wheel drive. Suzuki introduced their successful LT125 4x4 in 1982. Honda followed suit in 1986. The success of these machines means that all-wheel drive and independent suspension have now become standard features.**

Directory of Military Motorcycles

The armies of the world have used literally hundreds of different motorcycles over the last 100 years. While many have been essentially civilian in origin, there have been sufficient unique machines and military specials to provide interesting history.

Over those 100 years, many, many companies have disappeared. Great British names such as BSA, Triumph, Ariel, Velocette, AJS, and Norton have either ceased producing completely or been relegated to producing a few custom built machines where once they would have produced thousands a month. All across Europe, the motorcycle industries of France, Belgium, Sweden, Poland and Czechoslovakia have all but ended.

Today, the motorcycle world is dominated by the big four Japanese companies – Honda, Yamaha, Suzuki and Kawasaki. Outside Japan, only the USA, Germany and Italy appear able to support a sizeable domestic industry. In the USA, Harley-Davidson has continued to produce its own distinctive machines, after the demise of Indian, Excelsior and many other fledgling companies. In Italy the companies Benelli, Moto-Guzzi and Gilera survive. The mighty BMW company continues to produce its famous machines in Germany.

In the pages that follow you will find the products of a once global industry, an industry that had room for national characteristics and innovation – an industry that was full of names that have now been lost in time.

LEFT: **With a powerful engine and selectable sidecar-wheel drive, the German combination outfits of World War II probably represent the pinnacle of heavy military motorcycle design. The designs were copied by Chinese and Russian companies during the post-war years, and these machines are favoured by enthusiasts searching for a low-cost 'German' motorcycle.**

Laurin & Klement Slavia CCCC

Established in December 1895, the Austrian company Laurin & Klement (L&K) was one of the earliest producers of high-quality motorcycles, their first model dating from 1898. Never orthodox, the company produced both V-twin and, in the case of the CCCC, four-cylinder machines, some of which were water-cooled. Early L&K machines had the engine above the front wheel.

The CCCC was assembled on a stretched heavy-duty tubular-steel cycle frame, with auxiliary pedals and chain. The engine was a 570cc four-cylinder in-line unit, consisting of four separately cast cylinders mounted on a common crankcase. The magneto was installed under the engine, protected by a distinctive loop in the frame, and the narrow fuel tank was carried ahead of the seat tube. The length of the frame necessitated extended handlebars. There were no gears and the drive to the rear wheel was by means of a flat belt running on a large

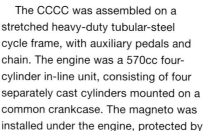

LEFT: **The distinctive frame on the CCCC.**

diameter pulley. The CCCC II, of 1905, employed a redesigned, shorter frame, and side-valve engine.

Alongside service with the Austro-Hungarian forces, the CCCC was widely exported, even as far as Japan.

Motorcycle production came to an end in 1909 but Laurin & Klement also produced a range of passenger cars. Skoda took control of the company in 1907 in 1925.

Laurin & Klement Slavia CCCC

Type: Motorcycle, heavy, solo
Manufacturer: Laurin & Klement Motorräder; Mladá Boleslav, Bohemia (later Czechoslavakia)
Production: 1904 to 1909
Engine: Laurin & Klement; four cylinders, in-line; 570cc; overhead inlet valves, side exhaust; air cooled; power output, 5bhp at 1500rpm
Transmission: Single gear ratio, with auxiliary pedals
Suspension: None
Brakes: Contracting belt, rear only
Dimensions: Not available
Performance: Maximum speed – 75kph/46mph

Puch R-1

Engineer Johann Puch opened a factory at Graz in Austria in 1899, constructing bicycles. Rapid expansion over the next decade or so saw the company producing lorries, motorcars, railway locomotives, tricycles and motorcycles. The first motorcycle appeared in 1903 and, in 1914, the Austrian Army purchased the company's R-1 and R-2 models for despatch and liaison duties. The two models were similar in design but the

R-1 was equipped with a 254cc single-cylinder engine, while a more powerful 300cc engine was fitted to the R-2.

Both were standard lightweight production machines, lightly modified for military service. The tubular frame was of typical bicycle pattern, with heavy-duty front forks. The single-cylinder engine was arranged to drive the rear wheel via a flat leather belt. Neither machine was fitted with a clutch, although there were auxiliary pedals to help start and to pull away. The R-1 had just a single gear ratio, while

LEFT: **The belt-driven Puch R-1.**

the R-2 offered two speeds. Military modifications were minor but most were provided with full acetylene lighting equipment and a small leather saddlebag.

In 1934, Puch merged with Steyr and Austro-Daimler to form Steyr-Daimler-Puch. The motorcycle manufacturing division of the Puch company was taken over by Piaggio in 1987.

Puch R-1

Type: Motorcycle, light, solo
Manufacturer: Johann Puch Erste Steirmärkische Fahrradfabrik, then Johann Puch AG; Graz
Production: 1914 to 1916
Engine: Puch; single cylinder; 254cc; side valves; air cooled; power output, 2bhp
Transmission: Single gear ratio, with auxiliary pedals
Suspension: None
Brakes: Contracting belt, rear only
Dimensions: Wheelbase – 1,300mm/51in Other dimensions not available Weight – 52kg/114lb
Performance: Maximum speed – 50kph/31mph

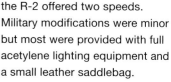

Puch P800

During the inter-war years Puch grew to become the largest supplier of motorcycles in Austria, merging with Steyr and Austro-Daimler to form Steyr-Daimler-Puch in 1934. Following the annexation of Austria by the Nazis, the company concentrated on producing small two-strokes, but this had not always been the case and the Puch P800 is a good example of the company's capabilities. A splendid,

powerful and unconventional machine, it was powered by a flat-four engine which gave it a top speed approaching 130kph/80mph. Although it had been developed for the civilian market, it was nonetheless pressed into service with the Austrian Army and later adopted by the *Wehrmacht*.

The machine was suitable for both solo and sidecar use which was not uncommon for a machine of this type, but it was the engine of the P800 that was its most interesting feature. A horizontally opposed side-valve unit with coil ignition, it could best be described as a "near flat-four", meaning that the cylinders were set at a very slight V. The engine was placed transversely across a hybrid tubular and forged-steel frame which was both low and compact, resulting in a handsome and purposeful machine. The front forks were fabricated from pressed-steel sections and suspended by means of a friction-damped coil spring; at the rear, the forks were unsprung.

Drive was taken to the rear wheel through a four-speed hand-change

ABOVE: **Powered by a flat-four engine, the P800 had a top speed of almost 125kph/70mph.** BELOW. **It was a handsome bike with a modern appearance that was somewhat ahead of its time.**

gearbox and open chain, and the clutch was placed in the rear hub rather than between the engine and transmission.

Military modifications included a rear luggage rack or pillion seat.

Just 550 examples were constructed before production ceased.

Puch P800

Type: Motorcycle, heavy, solo; and with sidecar
Manufacturer: Steyr-Daimler-Puch; Graz
Production: 1936 to 1938
Engine: Puch; four cylinder, horizontally opposed; 792cc; side valves; air cooled; power output, 20bhp at 4,000rpm
Transmission: 4F; hand gear-change
Suspension: Pressed-steel parallelogram front forks with friction-damped coil spring; rigid rear end
Brakes: Drums, front and rear
Dimensions: Length – 2,180mm/86in
  Width – 830mm/33in
  Height – 1,050mm/41in
  Wheelbase – 1,427mm/56in
  Weight (solo) – 195kg/430lb
Performance: Maximum speed – 125kph/78mph

ABOVE AND LEFT: **The Puch 175 MCH was a militarized version of a lightweight civilian two-stroke machine, and was typical of military motorcycles in the post-war years.**

Puch 175 MCH

Typical of the small two-stroke motorcycles favoured by many services during the immediate post-war years, the Puch 175 MCH was a militarized lightweight civilian machine. It was powered by a single-cylinder

split-piston engine and, despite a modest level of performance, was used by the Austrian Army for solo despatch duties, as well as being suitable for the occasional off-road excursion. Deliveries were made during 1958 and 1959.

The 175 MCH was constructed on a hybrid pressed steel/tubular duplex cradle frame with a single down-tube; the saddle was fitted very close to the fuel tank and an unusual padded groin protector was attached to the rear of the latter. The front forks were of the hydraulically-damped telescopic pattern, with a shortish

LEFT: **A Puch R-1 on cross-country trials.** BELOW: **The VDO speedometer.**

110mm/4.5in of travel; the rear suspension consisted of a trailing arm suspended on a hydraulically-damped coil spring.

Like all Puch two-strokes of the period, the 175 MCH used the company's unique double-piston – a feature that had been patented in 1923. Also known as a "twingle", the engine used two pistons, one controlling the inlet ports, the other controls the exhaust ports; the pistons ran in parallel cylinder bores but shared a single combustion chamber, spark plug and cylinder head. Using a coil ignition system, the 172cc engine produced 10bhp which gave a top speed just under 80kph/48mph. Drive to the rear wheel was via a unit-constructed four-speed foot-change gearbox and open chain.

Puch 175 MCH

Type: Motorcycle, light, solo
Manufacturer: Steyr-Daimler-Puch; Graz
Production: 1958 to 1959
Engine: Puch; single cylinder split piston; 172cc; two-stroke; air cooled; power output, 10bhp at 5,800rpm
Transmission: 4F; foot gear-change
Suspension: Hydraulically-damped telescopic front forks; load-adjustable hydraulically-damped coil-sprung trailing arm at rear
Brakes: Drums, front and rear
Dimensions: Length – 2,030mm/80in
    Width – 750mm/30in
    Height – 1,100mm/41in
    Wheelbase – 1,320mm/52in
    Weight – 135kg/298lb
Performance: Maximum speed – 80kph/48mph

Puch 250 MCH

Introduced in 1969 as a replacement for the earlier double-piston two-stroke Puch 250 SG, the 250 MCH was a standard lightweight civilian motorcycle that had been modified for service with the Austrian Army. It was light, fast for its size, and capable and, while the 250 MCH was not an off-road machine in the modern sense, it was nevertheless intended for multi-terrain use.

The construction was typical of lightweight machines of the period, using a tubular duplex cradle frame with a single down-tube, fitted with a modern-shaped squared-off tank and a double saddle. The front forks were of the hydraulically-damped telescopic type, with a total travel of almost 170mm/7in which would have helped the off-road use, and at the rear there was a hydraulically-damped load-adjustable coil-sprung trailing arm

with 80mm/3.25in of travel. As with the earlier 250 SG, the engine was a coil-ignition 248cc two-stroke with Puch's trademark double-piston arrangement, producing 14bhp. The 250 MCH was one of the last motorcycles to use Puch's "split single" engine, the company generally preferring conventional two-strokes during the 1960s. The transmission consisted of a unit-constructed four-speed foot-change gearbox with final drive by open chain.

Military modifications included braced handlebars, a large air filter, rear luggage rack, and pannier bags. There was a curiously long side-stand attached to a pivot just below the saddle rim.

Although the company Puch remains in business, it was taken over by Piaggio in 1991 when all motorcycle production ceased; today, the company builds motor scooters.

LEFT AND RIGHT: **One of the last motorcycles to use the Puch double-piston two-stroke design, the 250 MCH was a civilian machine, lightly modified for military use. Although essentially a road machine, the suspension was also designed to permit limited off-road usage.** BELOW: **The Puch badge.**

Puch 250 MCH

Type: Motorcycle, light, solo
Manufacturer: Steyr-Daimler-Puch; Graz
Production: 1969
Engine: Puch; single cylinder split piston; 248cc; two-stroke; air cooled; power output, 14bhp at 5,800rpm
Transmission: 4F; foot gear-change
Suspension: Hydraulically-damped telescopic front forks; load-adjustable coil-sprung trailing arm at rear
Brakes: Drums, front and rear
Dimensions: Length – 2,060mm/81in
Width – 850mm/33in
Height – 1,100mm/41in
Wheelbase – 1,350mm/53in
Weight – 155kg/341lb
Performance: Maximum speed – 100kph/62mph

FN Model 285 2.75hp

FN Model 285 2.75hp

Type: Motorcycle, light, solo
Manufacturer: Fabrique Nationale des Armes de Guerre; Herstal
Production: 1912 to 1920
Engine: FN; single cylinder; 285cc; overhead inlet valve, side exhaust; air cooled; power output, 2.75bhp
Transmission: 2 Forward; hand gear-change
Suspension: Hydraulically-damped girder parallelogram front forks; solid rear end
Brakes: Drum, rear only
Dimensions: Length – 1,860mm/73in
Width – 711mm/28in
Height – Not available
Wheelbase – 1,465mm/58in
Weight – 55kg/120lb
Performance: Maximum speed – 56kph/35mph

The Belgian company FN (Fabrique Nationale des Armes de Guerre) started producing bicycles in 1895 but by 1904, designer Paul Kelecom had produced the world's first four-cylinder motorcycle, equipped with a powerful five-bearing 362cc engine. The machine was quickly adopted by the Belgian and other European armies and by 1915 the engine had grown to 747cc, setting something of a pattern for large-capacity FN military motorcycles. However, in the early years the company also produced a number of smaller machines and the 285cc 2.75hp civilian model of 1912 – known as the Model 285 from 1915 – was typical of these.

The frame was a tubular-steel duplex cradle design, with hydraulically-damped girder parallelogram forks at the front, and a rigid rear end. The engine was a single-cylinder unit with an overhead inlet valve and side exhaust. It was fitted low in the frame, which necessitated a skid plate, and was connected to the rear wheel via a two-speed transmission and open shaft, with the gearbox at the rear hub. A chain and auxiliary pedals were provided for starting, and to provide assistance across difficult terrain. Military equipment included a rear carrying rack, leather panniers and full acetylene lighting.

The Model 285 was widely used by the Belgian Army and the Western Allies during World War I and may also have been used, and even produced for, the occupying German forces during the conflict. The machine remained in production until 1920 when it was replaced by the 285T.

ABOVE: **Dating from 1912, the FN Model 285 was widely used by the Belgian Army.**
BELOW: **Typical of very early motorcycles, the Model 285 is recognizably derived from a pedal cycle, even retaining the pedals and chain.** RIGHT: **With two cycle pedals and a carbine, the FN logo nicely summed up what the company was about.**

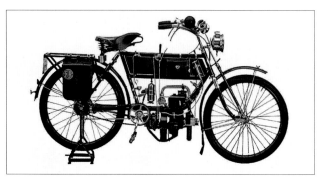

FN M86 *Militaire*

The Belgian Army was busy motorizing its armed forces during the 1930s and it was here, rather than in Germany, that the concept of the heavy military motorcycle with a driven sidecar was developed. However, that did not happen until 1937 and the FN M86 of 1934 was a straightforward modified civilian machine, which, although it was suitable for both solo, and sidecar use, lacked the driven wheel of machines such as the M12. Nevertheless, with a 497cc single-cylinder engine and no-nonsense presentation, it was typical of the high-quality Belgian heavy motorcycle and was also exported to a number of South American nations. For its day, the M86 was a fast machine and, in solo form, was capable of 130kph/80mph.

The frame was a conventional duplex design constructed from brazed steel tubes. At the front end the wheel was carried in coil-sprung girder parallelogram forks, while the rear end remained unsprung. Power came from an FN single-cylinder overhead-valve engine with coil ignition, coupled to the rear wheel via a unit-constructed four-speed foot-change gearbox and open chain. Military modifications included a pillion seat or rear carrying rack.

Various sidecars were used, the standard unit was a single-seat personnel carrier, with spare wheel and machine-gun mount, but there was also some development work with an armoured sidecar mounting a 9mm Bergmann MP 28.II machine-gun that was supplied to Argentina in 1934.

The M86 remained in production until the German occupation in 1940 and may also have been put back into production temporarily in 1946.

ABOVE: **The FN M86 was a modified single-cylinder motorcycle pressed into service with the Belgian Army in the 1930s. The coil-sprung girder front forks and unsprung rear end were typical of the period.** LEFT: **The engine was a 497cc overhead-valve unit producing 22bhp, sufficient to give the machine a top speed of 130kph/80mph.**

FN M86 *Militaire*

Type: Motorcycle, medium, solo; and with sidecar
Manufacturer: Fabrique Nationale des Armes de Guerre; Herstal
Production: 1934 to 1940
Engine: FN; single cylinder; 497cc; overhead valves; air cooled; power output, 22bhp at 4,800rpm
Transmission: 4F; foot gear-change
Suspension: Coil-sprung friction-damped girder parallelogram front forks; unsprung rear
Brakes: Drums, front and rear
Dimensions: Length – 2,150mm/85in
    Width – 711mm/28in
    Height – 1,041mm/41in
    Wheelbase – 1,380mm/54in
    Weight – 175kg/385lb
Performance: Maximum speed – 130kph/80mph

FN M12 SM (12a SM)

With a driven sidecar wheel, the Belgian FN M12 was a multi-terrain military motorcycle, very much in the mould of the larger German BMW and Zündapp machines but, of course, it pre-dated these machines by two to three years so should probably be considered as something of a pioneer. The powerful 992cc engine, four-speed forward and reverse gearbox with two-speed transfer case, and high ground clearance ensured a superb off-road performance, while the sprung front and rear forks also guaranteed a smooth riding experience on the road. Top speed was in the order of 90kph/56mph. As well as entering service with the Belgian Army, the machines were supplied to Greece, Iran and a number of countries in South America; many of the Belgian machines were commandeered by the *Wehrmacht* after the country's occupation.

Although the company had originally been founded to produce guns and ammunition, and had joined with a number of other Belgian gun manufacturers in 1889 to fulfil a large contract for the Belgian Army, FN started to construct bicycles in 1898, followed by motorcycles in 1903. Famous for their use of shaft-drive, the company's motorcycles found sporting success over the next two decades and FN went on to become Belgium's largest manufacturer of motorcycles. Shaft drive was abandoned on civilian machines as being too expensive in 1924.

ABOVE: **The M12 SM was fitted with a driven-wheel sidecar and low-ratio gears which gave an excellent cross-country ride.**

Dating from 1937, and designed to replace the essentially civilian FN M86 *Militaire* which had been supplied to the Belgian Army in 1936, the M12 SM was a purpose-built military motorcycle powered by a horizontally opposed side-valve twin mounted transversely in the frame, and unit constructed with the gearbox. The exhaust was run at a high level between the motorcycle and the sidecar, and air to the carburettor was supplied via a sand filter. The final drive was by means of a transverse exposed shaft. The frame was a conventional tubular duplex design with a bolt-on rear sub-frame. A wrap-around tubular sump guard was provided to protect the crankcase during off-road work, combined with crash bars to protect the protruding cylinders.

Coil-spring suspension was provided for the parallelogram front forks but the rear end was unsprung. A sprung pillion seat was also fitted to the machine to allow a crew of three to be carried. It was unusually positioned some way back over the rear mudguard and was provided with unusual knee grips.

The sidecar was a single-seat military design with a pintle mount for an FN or Browning machine-gun on the nose, and a small luggage rack at the rear; sidecars without gun mount were frequently fitted with

a windscreen. All three wheels were identical and were usually shod with heavy-treaded off-road tyres; a spare was carried on the rear of the sidecar.

An outstanding machine for its day, just 1,090 examples of the M12 were constructed between 1937 and 1939 and, of these, only 300 went to the Belgian Army. The FN 12a SM-T3

motor tricycle of 1939 was constructed using many of the components of the M12; some 331 examples were delivered before production came to an end in May 1940.

Although motorcycle production ended in 1963, the company remains a defence contractor and, these days, is part of the Herstal Group.

ABOVE: **The sidecar was a standard military design also used by Gillet-Herstal and Sarolea.**
LEFT: **In 1939, the M12 was also used as the basis for a military motorized tricycle.**

FN M12 SM (12a SM)

Type: Motorcycle, heavy, solo, with sidecar, 3x2
Manufacturer: Fabrique Nationale des Armes de Guerre; Herstal
Production: 1937 to 1939
Engine: FN; two cylinder horizontally opposed; 992cc; side valves; air cooled; power output, 22bhp at 4,000rpm
Transmission: 4F1Rx2; hand gear-change
Suspension: Girder parallelogram front forks with single friction-damped coil spring; solid rear end
Brakes: Drums, front and rear
Dimensions: Not available
  Wheelbase – 1,499mm/59in
  Weight – 240kg/528lb
Performance: Maximum speed – 90kph/56mph

FN M13

The FN M13 – sometimes described as the XIII M – was the military version of a standard civilian motorcycle, launched in 1947, and was used by the Belgian Army. Although at a glance, the M13 was a conventional medium motorcycle of the period, the front fork and suspension design remained decidedly distinctive.

The machine was constructed around a typical tubular-steel frame, but could be readily identified by the curious front suspension and what appear to be crash bars around the front mudguard. The original 1947 model used a patented Swiss design of balancing front forks, employing a cantilevered leading-arm suspended on a pair of

almost horizontal coil springs; the springs were subsequently changed to vertical rubber "loops" in 1949. Conventional hydraulically-damped telescopic front forks were adopted in 1951. On early models, the rear forks were rubber-bushed but remained unsprung; from 1954, a new frame was adopted which also used rubber to provide suspension at the rear; full hydraulic suspension was adopted in 1955. The Belgian Army appears only to have used the rubber-sprung version produced from 1949 to 1951.

As regards power unit, there was a choice of either a single-cylinder side-valve unit with magneto spark and an unusual 444cc capacity, as specified by the Belgian Army, or a 350cc side-valve engine. Overhead-valve engines were also offered with capacities of 250cc, 350cc and 450cc. In all cases, final drive from the unit-constructed four-speed foot-change gearbox was by open chain.

Small modifications were made to equip the machine for its service life, including the use of a lower compression ratio to reduce the top speed. A small pillion pad was fitted, together with a rear luggage rack and side pannier bags of leather. A total of almost 11,000 M13s were built of which perhaps 1,050 were of the military variant. FN produced its last motorcycle in 1963.

ABOVE: **With telescopic front forks and rigid rear end, the M13 was typical of European motorcycles produced immediately after the end of World War II.**
LEFT: **Although designed as a solo machine for despatch use, a small pillion pad was provided.**

FN M13

Type: Motorcycle, medium, solo
Manufacturer: Fabrique Nationale des Armes de Guerre; Herstal
Production: 1947 to 1952
Engine: FN; single cylinder; 444cc; side valves; air cooled; power output, 11.5bhp at 4,500rpm
Transmission: 4F; foot gear-change
Suspension: Cantilever balancing front forks with coil spring or rubber suspension; later telescopic front forks with rubber suspension; unsprung rear, although late models used a swing frame with either rubber or hydraulic suspension
Brakes: Drums, front and rear
Dimensions: Length – 2,220mm/87in
  Width – 830mm/33in
  Height – 1,030mm/41in
  Wheelbase – 1,220mm/48in
  Weight – 160kg/352lb
Performance: Maximum speed – 102kph/63mph

ABOVE AND BELOW: **A small trailer was also produced for use with the AS24, providing a useful 250kg/560lb load-carrying capacity.**

FN AS24

The FN AS24 was an air-portable four-seater lightweight folding vehicle produced under licence from Straussler for the Belgian Army and for export. Although it was steered by a conventional wheel, and driven by a conventional motorcar-style rear axle, it is something of a hybrid motorcycle-cum-utility vehicle and can be considered a forerunner of today's lightweight quad bikes and ATVs. A number of variants were produced including personnel carriers and fire-fighters, and there was also a

matching trailer. A total of 460 were produced between 1959 and 1962, most of them ending up with the Belgian Paracommandos.

Constructed on a composite folding frame consisting of tubular steel and box sections, the machine was powered by a 244cc vertical two-stroke twin mounted directly above the rear axle. Extended full-width crash bars were fitted to protect the seating area. There was a four-speed gearbox with hand gear-change and final drive was by a short open chain

to the rear wheel. Wide-section (12x22) Lypsoid tyres were fitted to the three wheels, and these provided the only form of suspension.

The most numerous variant was a four-seat personnel carrier that was equipped with a lightweight tubular-framed bench seat with canvas or vinyl covering; the machine could also be used as a 250kg/560lb load carrier.

When folded for transport, the length was reduced to 1,040mm/41in and it took just 60 seconds to make the vehicle ready for use after parachute dropping.

A single example was evaluated by the US Army in May 1963, but there were no serial purchases.

ABOVE: **Typical of the work of Nicholas Straussler, the Lypsoid tyres provided suspension and excellent traction. This AS24 is being tested by the US Army.**
LEFT: **Almost 500 AS24s were produced for the Belgian Paracommandos but, with a width of just 1,640mm/65ln, it must have made for a pretty tight fit with four soldiers seated abreast. The engine was placed over the rear axle, driving the rear wheels through a short chain.**

FN AS24

Type: Motor tricycle, light, air portable, 3x2
Manufacturer: Fabrique Nationale des Armes de Guerre; Herstal
Production: 1959 to 1962
Engine: FN; two cylinder; 244cc; two stroke; air cooled; power output, 15bhp at 5,300rpm
Transmission: 4F; hand gear-change
Suspension: By Lypsoid tyres only
Brakes: Drums, rear only
Dimensions: Length – 1,836mm/72in
    Width – 1,640mm/65in
    Height – 900mm/35in
    Wheelbase – 1,270mm/50in
    Weight – 220kg/484lb
Performance: Maximum speed – 56kph/35mph

Gillet 750

ABOVE: **The Gillet 750 was a high-quality V-twin powered motorcycle built for the Belgian military and intended for sidecar and solo use.**

Making its first appearance in 1938, the Gillet 750 was another of those very competent Belgian military multi-terrain heavy motorcycle outfits which featured a driven sidecar wheel, and which must have inspired the likes of the big BMW and Zündapp machines. The 750, which superficially resembled the FN M12, was a militarized version of a civilian sidecar outfit which had originally been produced for the Belgian *Gendarmerie* – both the military and police machines were widely used by the *Wehrmacht* after the German occupation in May 1940. Like FN, Gillet was also based in the Belgian town of Herstal.

Gillet produced its first motorcycle in 1919, and had enjoyed some competition success with a rotary two-stroke engine design in the mid-1920s, and this had led to similar engines being produced in a range of capacities. It was nevertheless unusual for a two-stroke to be fitted to such

a large and heavy machine. However, with 22bhp available from its 728cc capacity, the top speed of the machine was in excess of 80kph/50mph and the cross-country performance was excellent.

The two cylinders were arranged one behind the other in-line, and the engine was mounted in a duplex cradle in a conventional tubular frame. Both sump shield and crash bars were also provided and, as with the FN M12, the exhaust was run at a high level between the motorcycle and the sidecar. Drive to the rear wheel was conveyed through a unit-constructed four-speed and reverse gearbox, using gears for the primary transmission and an open chain for the final drive; the machine lacked the high/low ratio facility which made the FN so versatile. There was selectable shaft drive to the sidecar wheel, and the military version was fitted with over-sized cross-country tyres on the three identical wheels.

At the front end there was friction-damped coil-spring suspension for the girder parallelogram forks, and the rear end was unsprung. Performance on sand and gravel was said to be excellent, but the weight counted against the machine in wet mud.

A pillion seat was fitted to the rear mudguard, and the sidecar was a special military-pattern single-seater with a front pintle mount for an FN or Browning machine-gun, and a small luggage rack at the rear; a spare wheel was also carried, mounted upright on the rear panel. The sidecar could also be adapted to act as a stretcher carrier, and a different, and slightly smaller, sidecar was fitted to the police version.

The Gillet 750 was also tested by the British War Office in a head-to-head against the new Norton Model 633 Big Four in May 1939, the trials taking place at Farnborough. Aside

ABOVE: **In its original civilian form, the Gillet 750 was used by the Belgian** *Gendarmerie*. **The machine was fitted with coil-spring front suspension and had a solid rear end.**

from the presence of a reverse gear and the bonus of sidecar brakes, the Gillet was not felt to offer any particular performance advantage over the British machine and was eventually returned to the manufacturer.

Production of the 750 almost certainly ceased in 1940, although some say that a number were also produced under German control. The engine design continued to be available in civilian machines after the war, but Gillet turned to motor scooters and eventually stopped motorcycle production altogether in 1956, although the company survived another three years.

ABOVE: **The driven-wheel sidecar was a typical standardized military unit of the period. The engine was an in-line twin, producing 22bhp from 728cc.**

Gillet 750

Type: Motorcycle, heavy, solo, with sidecar, 3x2

Manufacturer: Gillet-Herstal; Herstal

Production: 1938 to 1940

Engine: Gillet; in-line two cylinder; 728cc; two-stroke; air cooled; power output, 22bhp at 4,000rpm

Transmission: 4F1R; foot gear-change

Suspension: Girder parallelogram front forks with a single friction-damped coil spring; solid rear end

Brakes: Drums, front and rear, including sidecar wheel

Dimensions: Not available
Weight – 300kg/660lb

Performance: Maximum speed – 85kph/53mph

Sarolea Type H-1000

Established in 1898, Sarolea was one of the first manufacturers of motorcycles in Belgium. In 1939, the company launched the H-1000, a

powerful multi-terrain sidecar combination developed for the Belgian Army. With its horizontally opposed two-cylinder engine, high/low ratio transmission, and shaft-drive sidecar, the machine followed the design principles already established by FN and Gillet.

The H-1000 was constructed around a heavy-duty pressed-steel duplex frame, that incorporated crash protection for the sidecar, crash bars and a heavy sump shield. Power came from a 978cc side-valve engine with coil ignition, driving the rear wheels through a three-speed gearbox, the latter also incorporating planetary reduction gears to improve off-road performance. Both the gear-change and selection of the low-ratio gears was effected by a single lever. Final drive was by Carden shaft. Front forks were typical

LEFT: **A Sarolea H-1000 with the standard single-seat sidecar.**

Sarolea H-1000

Type: Motorcycle, heavy, with sidecar, 3x2
Manufacturer: Sarolea; Herstal
Production: 1939
Engine: Sarolea; two cylinder, horizontally opposed; 978cc; side valves; air cooled; power output, 20bhp at 3,000rpm
Transmission: 3F1Rx2; hand gear-change
Suspension: Friction-damped girder parallelogram coil-sprung front forks; unsprung rear
Brakes: Drums, all three wheels
Dimensions: Not available
Weight – 524kg/1,155lb
Performance: Maximum speed – 85kph/53mph

of the period, consisting of parallelogram girders, using a single friction-damped coil spring; there was no rear suspension. The pillion seat was fitted with knee pads.

Standard sidecars included a single-seat design, together with variants adapted for the radio and machine-gun, the same range of sidecars was used by FN and Gillet. The H-1000 was also used by the *Wehrmacht*.

Sarolea 51A4

The Sarolea 51A4 was a standard production machine, modified for service with the Belgian Army. Typical of its period, it was a single-seater medium-weight multi-terrain motorcycle with both front and rear suspension. Military modifications were confined to fitting pannier racks and a small pillion post.

Constructed around a single-loop tubular frame, the 51A4 was powered

by a 400cc side-valve engine driving through a separate four-speed gearbox and exposed chain. Ignition was by battery and coil. Both front and rear forks were of the coil-sprung telescopic design, hydraulically-damped at the front. The engine was protected by tubular crash bars, and the mudguards were shaped with deep side skirts; a handle was fitted to the front mudguard

LEFT: **Sarolea produced motorcycles in the Belgian town of Herstal from 1898 to 1957, this modified civilian machine of 1951 was one of the company's last military motorcycles. The plunger rear end was typical of the transition from rigid rear ends to "full" suspension.**

Sarolea 51A4

Type: Motorcycle, medium, solo
Manufacturer: Sarolea; Herstal
Production: 1951
Engine: Sarolea; single cylinder; 400cc; side valves; air cooled; power output, 12bhp at 4,200rpm
Transmission: 4F; foot gear-change
Suspension: Hydraulically-damped coil-sprung telescopic front forks; coil-sprung plunger type suspension at rear
Brakes: Drums, front and rear
Dimensions: Length – 2,120mm/83in
Width – 700mm/28in
Height – 1,400mm/44in
Wheelbase – 1,400mm/55in
Weight – 132kg/290lb
Performance: Maximum speed – 100kph/60mph

to help manhandle the machine through mud and difficult terrain.

A similar 350cc model (AS 350) was also produced at the same time. The name Sarolea was applied to Italian Moto Rumi scooters during the 1950s but the company ceased involvement in motorcycle manufacture in 1957.

Chang Jiang CJ-750M1

The Chang Jiang CJ-750M1 is a 746cc heavy motorcycle combination much favoured by the Chinese People's Liberation Army (PLA). Although it is frequently stated as being a copy of the pre-war BMW R-71, it would be more accurate to describe it as being based heavily on the Soviet-built Dniepr M-72 which was largely copied from the BMW. The Chang Jiang – it derives its name from the longest river in China – was introduced in November 1957, at first solely for military use, and remains in

production today, with export sales handled through Dong Tian Enterprise.

Powered by a 746cc horizontally opposed twin-cylinder side-valve engine that would be familiar to any BMW enthusiast, the CJ-750M1 is constructed around a tubular-steel cycle type frame with telescopic front forks and coil-spring plunger-type suspension at the rear; as with the BMW, power is transferred to the rear wheel by carden shaft and the sidecar wheel is undriven. The original engine and transmission

Chang Jiang CJ-750M1, CJ-750M1M	
Type: Motorcycle, heavy, with sidecar	
Manufacturer: Jiang Xi Hong Du Hang Kong Gong Ye Ji Tuan; Nan Chang	
Production: 1957 to 2008	
Engine: Chang Jiang; two cylinder horizontally opposed; 746cc; side valves; air cooled; power output, 22–24bhp at 4,500rpm	
Transmission: 4F, 4F1R (reverse on M1M only); foot gear-change	
Suspension: Hydraulically-damped telescopic coil-sprung front forks; un-damped coil-sprung plunger suspension at rear	
Brakes: Drums, all three wheels	
Dimensions: Length – 2,400mm/94in Width – 1,580mm/62in Height – 1,000mm/39in Wheelbase – 1,400mm/55in Weight – 161kg/355lb	
Performance: Maximum speed – 90kph/56mph	

ABOVE: **Despite its somewhat dated technology it is widely used by the Chinese People's Liberation Army and remains in production today.** LEFT: **With a horizontally opposed side-valve engine and shaft drive, the Chinese Chang Jiang CJ-750M1 was essentially a copy of the Russian copy of the pre-war BMW R-71.**

were identical to that used in the Soviet M-72 but the Chinese introduced a new engine in September 1966, fitting an improved transmission at the same time.

The single-seat sidecar is a typical civilian-style product, carrying a single spare wheel and there is also a hinged pillion seat together with a small luggage carrier.

Early machines were produced by Guo Ying Gan Jiang Ji Xie Chang, frequently using Soviet-made frames, wheels and sheet metal. It was not until 1961 that the Chinese factory was able to produce the complete machine and apparently, even some complete Soviet M-72s were badged as CJ-750s, some with the engine changed to a Chinese-made unit. The factory name was changed several times during the 1960s and 1970s and today is known as Jiang Xi Hong Du Hang Kong Gong Ye Ji Tuan. Virtually the same machine was also produced by other Chinese State factories under other names.

Detail changes have been made to the machine throughout its production life and the improved CJ-750M1M was introduced in about 1980. Notable changes include the use of a 12V electrical system in place of the original 6V allowing the use of electric start, and the addition of reverse gear.

LEFT AND BELOW:

The Rotax-engined Bombardier Can-Am – the name often being reversed for some reason – was a specialized military motorcycle derived from the company's civilian TNT model. It became something of a standard NATO machine of its type in the 1970s.

Bombardier Can-Am

The Bombardier company, the world's largest producer of snowmobiles, began production of a range of Rotax-powered civilian trials and off-road motorcycles in 1973 at their factory at Valcourt, in the Eastern Townships of Canada's Quebec Province. The first such military machine, known as the Can-Am, appeared in 1978, and was based on the company's TNT ("track n trail") motorcycle of the mid-1970s, with modifications intended to better suit the machine to military service. It was initially intended to be made available with a choice of four engines from 125cc to 370cc although, in the event, only the 247cc machine actually went into production.

Not surprisingly, the Can-Am shares many parts with the TNT, as well as with the company's early MX motorcycles and, like these machines, is equipped with a single-cylinder Austrian Rotax engine of rotary-valve two-stroke design, in this instance with a displacement of 247cc, fitted with Bosch CDI 12V electronic ignition. Typical of many off-road machines of the period, the frame was a double-loop tubular cradle design offering a high ground clearance; a reservoir for the engine lubricating oil was contained in the tapered top tube. Power was transmitted to the rear wheel through an

oil-bath clutch and exposed roller chain, via a five-speed constant-mesh gearbox. The front suspension was of the Teledraulic type, with travel of up to 250mm/10in, and there was a load-adjustable, helically-sprung damped trailing arm at the rear. Most examples were fitted with a rear carrying rack and panniers for the despatch rider and reconnaissance role.

In 1978, the Royal Canadian Army purchased a total of 72 of these motorcycles to replace a fleet of ageing Triumph T100s, many of which had scarcely been used but which were proving expensive to store and maintain. The Belgian and British armies, and the US Marines, placed orders over the following three years, and the Can-Am was also trialled by the US Army, although in the latter case there were no series purchases. However, the machine did go on to become something of a standard NATO lightweight motorcycle.

The motorcycles intended for the British and Belgian armies, some 872 in total, and were assembled under licence by BSA at Coventry, and were the last military motorcycles to come out of the BSA factory. These machines included a percentage of domestic components, for example, the wheels and tyres, fuel tank, panniers, etc. With a maximum road speed of 90kph/56mph, the Can-Am was not fast, but it was able to offer excellent off-road performance. It was popular with users although it did gain a reputation for being somewhat fragile in military service.

ABOVE: **The Bombardier Can-Am was supplied to Britain, the USA, Canada and Belgium. Unusually for the time, the frame was used as a reservoir for the engine lubricating oil.**

Bombardier Can-Am military 250

Type: Motorcycle, light, solo
Manufacturer: Bombardier; Valcourt; with some machines assembled in the UK
Production: 1978 to 1987
Engine: Bombardier-Rotax; single cylinder; 247cc; rotary valve two-stroke; air cooled; power output, 26bhp at 7,500rpm
Transmission: 5F; foot gear-change
Suspension: Teledraulic telescopic front forks with hydraulic damping; helical-sprung trailing rear forks
Brakes: Drums front and rear
Dimensions: Length – 2,130mm/84in
    Width – 860mm/45in
    Height – 991mm/39in
    Wheelbase – 1,397mm/55in
    Weight – 130kg/286lb
Performance: Maximum speed – 90kph/56mph

ČZ 175

The first ČZ motorcycle was a 98cc twin cylinder machine produced in 1932. The ČZ company – the name is derived from Čveskà Zbrojovka (Czech arms factory) – soon became a leading domestic producer of civilian motorcycles as well as armaments. A good-looking single-cylinder 172cc machine was launched in 1934 and was immediately adopted by the Czechoslovak Army. It remained in production until 1939, by which time the army had 1,238 motorcycles of all types in service; the machine was also widely used by the occupying German forces. Further machines being produced under Nazi control.

Although modest in design and aspirations, the ČZ 175 was well-constructed and reliable. It was constructed around a compact pressed-steel external frame in the manner of pre-war BMWs, and mounted a twin-port two-stroke engine with Bosch coil ignition. Final drive was by open chain from an integral three-speed gearbox.

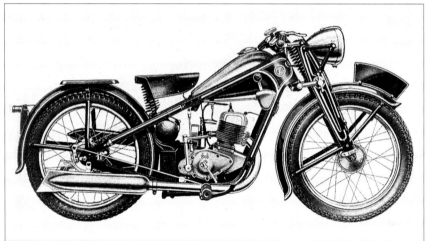

TOP: **The ČZ 175 had a twin-port two-stroke petrol engine.** ABOVE: **The distinctive-shaped pressed-steel frame in the pre-war BMW manner.**

The front forks were also of pressed-steel parallelogram construction, incorporating a single friction-damped coil-spring, while the rear forks were without suspension.

There was also a similar 250cc machine produced from 1936.

After the end of World War II, ČZ fell under state control and was linked with Jawa, the two companies sharing design and technology, as well as manufacturing expertise.

ČZ 175

Type: Motorcycle, light, solo
Manufacturer: Čveskà Zbrojovka; Strakonice
Production: 1934 to 1939
Engine: ČZ; single cylinder; 172cc; two stroke; air cooled; power output, 5.5bhp at 3,800rpm
Transmission: 3F; hand gear-change
Suspension: Friction-damped parallelogram coil-sprung front forks; unsprung rear
Brakes: Drums, front and rear
Dimensions: Length – 2,000mm/79in
　　Width – 770mm/30in
　　Height – 915mm/36in
　　Wheelbase – 1,300mm/51in
　　Weight – 97kg/213lb
Performance: Maximum speed – 80kph/50mph

Jawa Model 554-05

Frantiek Janecek began manufacturing German Wanderer motorcycles in Czechoslovakia under licence in 1927. In 1929 he produced a shaft-drive model of his own design, featuring a pressed steel frame and powered by a 498cc engine. He branded it with the name Jawa, derived from the first two letters of the words "Janecek" and "Wanderer". The *Wehrmacht* commandeered the factory in 1938 but Jawa apparently managed to conceal sufficient parts to restart motorcycle production in 1945, and even managed to carry on design work under the noses of the Germans.

The company's 350cc twin appeared in 1963, a development of the first post-war Jawa. As well as becoming the standard

RIGHT: **The standard civilian Jawa Model 554, adapted for military multi-terrain use as either solo or with a sidecar.**

Czech Army motorcycle, was also exported to Sweden and Finland. It was sold in more than 120 countries around the world under various trade names.

The Jawa 350 was a standard production model which was adapted for military multi-terrain use, either solo or with a sidecar; in Sweden it was also adapted by Fleron for use on skis. With

a lightweight hybrid pressed-steel/tubular frame, a twin-cylinder two-stroke engine, four-speed gearbox with both hand- and foot-change, and a semi-automatic centrifugal clutch, it was not quite in the mainstream of 1960s motorcycle design, but was nevertheless capable of a road speed of 120kph/75mph. Front suspension was by telescopic hydraulic forks offering 250mm/10in of travel, while the rear end consisted of a hydraulically-damped trailing arm. The final drive chain was fully enclosed. There was a similar 250cc model also available which shared many of the components and design features of the 350. The company was merged with ČZ and nationalized in 1945.

LEFT: **In service with the Swedish Army. Note the ski-type outriggers developed by Fleron to improve handling on icy surfaces.**

Jawa Model 554-05

Type: Motorcycle, medium, solo; and with sidecar
Manufacturer: Zbrojovka F Janecek; Prague
Production: 1963 to 1978
Engine: Jawa; two cylinder; 344cc; two stroke; air cooled; power output, 18bhp at 4,750rpm
Transmission: 4F; foot and hand gear-change
Suspension: Telescopic coil-spring front forks with hydraulic damping; coil-spring suspended swing-arm forks at rear with hydraulic damping
Brakes: Drums front and rear
Dimensions: Length – 1,980mm/78in
Width – 670mm/26in
Height – 1,025mm/40in
Wheelbase – 1,318mm/52in
Weight – 160kg/352lb
Performance: Maximum speed – 120kph/75mph

BD 500, Praga 500

The Praga BD was designed by Jaroslav Frantisek Koch, a gifted Czech designer who had produced his first machine in 1919 for the AVIA Aircraft company. Sadly, this never got beyond the prototype stage but when AVIA was taken over by Skoda in 1927, Koch moved to Brietfeld & Daněk and the military BD 500 appeared the same year. With its low compact styling, double overhead camshaft and hand-built quality, the BD 500 was a very advanced design for the period and quickly acquired a deserved reputation for reliability.

The BD 500 was powered by a 499cc overhead twin-cam engine, installed in a modern twin-cradle tubular frame; the transmission consisted of a unit constructed three-speed gearbox, with exposed chain final drive, and gear change was by a lever mounted on the crankcase. At the front, there were parallelogram tubular girder forks, with a single-coil spring and friction damping, while the rear end was unsprung. A tubular luggage rack was fitted at the rear.

A well-designed and expensive machine which was procured only in small numbers, the BD 500 was intended for despatch rider duties and, although it was no off-road machine, the engine was

LEFT: **The Praga-BD was also used by the** *Wehrmacht* **after the annexation of Czechoslovakia.**

BD 500, Praga 500	
Type: Motorcycle, medium, solo; and with sidecar	
Manufacturer: Breitfeld & Daněk (BD), and then Praga (Ceskomoravské Továrny na Stroje); Prague	
Production: 1927 to 1935	
Engine: BD/Praga; single cylinder; 499cc; overhead valves; air cooled; power output, 15bhp at 4,000rpm	
Transmission: 3F; hand gear-change	
Suspension: Parallelogram girder front forks with friction-damped single coil spring; solid rear end	
Brakes: Drum, front and rear	
Dimensions: Not available	
Wheelbase – 1,448mm/57in	
Weight – 170kg/374lb	
Performance: Maximum speed – 110kph/68mph	

sufficiently powerful to allow a top speed of 110kph/68mph. More than a few were used with a sidecar.

A very similar civilian model, known as the BD 500 OHC was launched in 1928 and, from 1929, when Brietfeld & Daněk merged with Praga, the machines were identified as the Praga-BD 500 and 500 OHC, and then simply as the Praga.

Fisker & Nielsen Nimbus 750 Model C

The Danish Fisker & Nielsen company produced its first motorcycle soon after the turn of the 20th century and, following a five-year period of inactivity, went on to become the largest supplier of motorcycles to the Danish police force and armed services. The four-cylinder 746cc Model C went into production in 1934 and, with only minor modifications, remained available until 1958.

The engine, which was mounted in a pressed-steel duplex cradle frame, featured four cylinders in-line, cast as a single block rather in the style of a motor-car engine. Power was transmitted to the rear wheels through a three-speed gearbox, via an exposed shaft; special sidecar gearing was available to order. The front forks were suspended on coil springs, and the rear end was solid.

Something like 12,750 examples were constructed during the model's 24-year production run and it was widely used by the Danish Army in both solo and combination form.

Fisker & Nielsen Nimbus 750	
Type: Motorcycle, heavy, solo; and with sidecar	
Manufacturer: Fisker & Nielsen; Copenhagen	
Production: 1934 to 1958	
Engine: Nimbus; four cylinders, in-line; 746cc; overhead valves; air cooled; power output, 18 to 22bhp at 3,500rpm	
Transmission: 3F; foot gear-change; shaft drive	
Suspension: Girder parallelogram front forks with a single coil spring; solid rear end	
Brakes: Front and rear	
Dimensions (solo): Length – 2,160mm/85in	
Width – 780mm/31in	
Height – 1,050mm/41in	
Wheelbase – 1,410mm/56in	
Weight – 185kg/408lb	
Performance: Maximum speed – 120kph/75mph	

LEFT: **A Nimbus 750 in service with the Swedish Army.**

Winha K-340

Produced by snow scooter manufacturers, Polar Metal Plast in Finland, and designed by Jussi Tiitola and Jussi Tapio, the Winha K-340 was an unconventional two-stroke multi-terrain machine. The standard gearbox was replaced by a stepless automatic primary belt drive rather in the fashion of the original DAF motorcars, which had been especially developed to make the motorcycle suitable for use in snow and other difficult conditions.

Although early examples of the K-340 were powered by a single-cylinder Sachs Snowmobile engine, this was eventually replaced by a Canadian twin-cylinder Kohler unit. The automatic transmission used a pair of expanding and contracting pulleys to give a stepless gearing which could adjust itself to the particular combination of ground and engine speed. Final drive was by open chain.

The frame was a tubular-steel duplex cradle design, with Ceriani hydraulically-

damped telescopic front forks, and a Girling or Marzocchi coil-spring swing-arm system at the rear.

Other features included braced handlebars, pillion seat, rear luggage

Winha K-340

Type: Motorcycle, medium, solo
Manufacturer: Polar Metal Plast; Rovaniemi
Production: 1974 to 1978
Engine: Sachs SA-340-R; single cylinder; 336cc; two stroke; air cooled; power output, 33bhp at 6,500rpm. Later fitted with a Kohler 340-2AX; two cylinder; 338cc; two stroke; air cooled; power output, 30bhp at 7,000rpm
Transmission: Stepless automatic
Suspension: Hydraulically-damped telescopic front forks with hydraulic damping; coil-spring suspended trailing arm forks at rear
Brakes: Drum, front and rear
Dimensions: Length – 2,235mm/88in
    Width – 787mm/31in
    Height – 1,270mm/50in
    Wheelbase – 1,540mm/61in
    Weight – 114kg/250lb
Performance: Maximum speed – 120kph/75mph

LEFT: **The K-340 was used by the Finnish Army and border guards.**

rack, a power take-off, high-level exhaust, and ski fittings. Another unusual provision was that heated air from the engine was directed towards the rider.

ACMA/Vespa TAP

Built under licence from the Italian Vespa company, the French ACMA 150 TAP (*Troupes, Aero Portées*) scooter was based on the company's 150GL model and was intended for use by paratroops. The original Vespa had been first produced in Italy by the Piaggio company in 1946 and was inspired by the American Cushman scooter which had been used by the US Army in World War II.

Like all Vespas, the 150 TAP was built on a unique spar-frame design, on this occasion using Vespa's "large frame", with the engine mounted to one side of the rear wheel, obviating the need for a chain or shaft. A front weather-shield provided wind and rain protection and, at least for civilians, the flat floor and step-through design gave the machine more universal rider appeal; the front mudguard was cutaway when compared to the civilian version.

The engine was a 147cc single-cylinder two-stroke, in unit construction with a three-speed gearbox.

The machine was also used as a mount – perhaps even a firing platform

LEFT: **The ACMA/Vespa TAP mounting the US-built 75mm M20 recoilless rifle.**

ACMA/Vespa TAP

Type: Motorscooter, two wheel, airborne; and with 75mm recoilless rifle
Manufacturer: Piaggio Ateliers de Construction de Motocycles et Accessoires (ACMA); Fourchambault
Production: 1956 to 1958
Engine: Vespa; single cylinder; 147cc; two-stroke; air cooled; power output, 6.2bhp
Transmission: 4F; hand gear-change
Suspension: Parallelogram front forks with coil spring. Engine, transmission and wheel mounted on trailing arm and horizontal coil spring and telescopic damper at rear
Brakes: Drum, front and rear
Dimensions: Length – 1,727mm/68in
    Width – 787mm/31in
    Height – 1,041mm/41in
    Wheelbase – 1,168mm/46in
    Weight – 114kg/250lb
Performance: Maximum speed – 80kph/50mph

– for the US-built 75mm M20 recoilless rifle. ACMA produced Vespas from 1951 to 1962 at a factory in Fourchambault, near Dijon.

Gnome et Rhône 750XA *Armée*

The Paris-based Gnome et Rhône company had made their name producing aircraft engines during World War I and started building motorcycles designed by Granville Bradshaw under licence from the English ABC company in 1919. The first "home-grown" machines appeared in 1923. The 750XA *Armée*, dating from 1935, was one of a number of heavy sidecar outfits purchased by the French Army in the years leading up to World War II. Although it should be considered to be a specialized military machine, it was based on the company's Type X *Grand Luxe* civilian model and, in military service, replaced the earlier V2 model. As well as entering service with the Belgian Army, the machines were supplied to Greece, Iran and a number of countries in South America; many of the Belgian machines were commandeered by the *Wehrmacht* after the country's occupation.

The 750XA was a big, heavy motorcycle, reliable and capable, and very much in the German style. However, despite the high-level exhaust and high ground clearance,

ABOVE: **With a big horizontally-opposed twin-cylinder engine and pressed-steel perimeter frame, the 750XA was similar in design to BMWs of the 1930s.**

it was not really suited to off-road work but, nevertheless, was more than capable of 80kph/50mph on the road.

As with all of the larger Gnome et Rhône machines, power was provided by transverse-mounted flat-twin engine, in this case an overhead-valve 749cc unit driving the rear wheel through a unit-constructed four-speed gearbox; final drive was by exposed shaft, while a hand lever on the right-hand side of the fuel tank controlled the gearchange. The company made much of the fact that the frame was of the pressed-steel perimeter type, extolling the modern form of construction and claiming that the historic and anachronistic links with the pedal cycle frame had finally been broken. At the front there were pressed-steel parallelogram forks with suspension by means of a friction-damped coil spring and, typically, there was no suspension at the rear.

ABOVE: The 750XA was a well-built and reliable machine. BELOW: The 750XA fitted with a civilian-type sidecar.

The standard military sidecar was designed for a single passenger, but could also be adapted to mount a machine-gun, or for use as an ammunition or wireless carrier, or as a stretcher bearer. Leg-guards and panniers were a standard fitment.

In civilian markets, the bigger Gnome et Rhône motorcycles would have been considered a competitor to the BMW and Zündapp machines so it should be no surprise that captured Gnome et Rhône motorcycles were widely used by the Wehrmacht after the fall of France in 1940. Some machines may have also been specially constructed for the Germans after 1940. After the war, the company resumed motorcycle production, producing small two-stroke machines, until closure in 1959.

ABOVE: Widely used by the French Army in both solo and sidecar form from 1935, the 750XA was derived from the company's V-twin Type X *Grand Luxe* civilian machine.

Gnome et Rhône 750XA *Armée*

Type: Motorcycle, heavy, solo; and with sidecar
Manufacturer: Gnome et Rhône; Paris
Production: 1935 to 1940
Engine: Gnome et Rhône; two cylinder, horizontally opposed; 749cc; overhead valves; air cooled; power output, 18bhp at 4,000rpm
Transmission: 4F; hand gear-change
Suspension: Pressed-steel parallelogram front forks with a single friction-damped coil spring; solid rear end
Brakes: Drum, front and rear
Dimensions (with sidecar):
  Length – 2,200mm/87in
  Width – 1,680mm/66in
  Height – 1,130mm/44in
  Wheelbase – 1,450mm/57in
  Weight – 320kg/704lb
Performance: Maximum speed – 80kph/50mph

Gnome et Rhône AX2

Appearing in 1936, the AX2 heavy sidecar outfit was a logical development of Gnome et Rhône's earlier V2 military model, albeit the side-valve engine was increased in capacity from 500cc to 800cc. Unlike the 750XA, which it was intended to replace, the AX2 featured selectable drive to the sidecar wheel and was provided with a reverse gear. Again, it was developed strictly for military use, and was intended for multi-terrain use in the reconnaissance and sidecar despatch roles, where the driven sidecar wheel provided a notable increase in off-road performance when compared to the earlier machines.

The AX2 was a fast and capable motorcycle with a speed better than 80kph/50mph on the road, although the speed was governed to this figure. The AX2 had a range of 130km/80 miles across country.

As with previous Gnome et Rhône machines, power was provided by transverse-mounted flat-twin engine, in this case an 804cc side-valve unit driving the rear wheel through a unit-constructed four-speed gearbox which incorporated reverse gear. Final drive was by exposed Carden shaft, and there was cross-shaft drive to the sidecar wheel which could be engaged or disengaged by the rider using an interlocked hand and foot control. A separate hand throttle was provided for off-road use.

ABOVE: **Splendidly restored example of the Gnome et Rhône AX2, a heavy military sidecar combination powered by a horizontally opposed flat-twin engine.** BELOW: **The Bernardet military sidecar allowed the mounting of a machine-gun on the front.**

At the front were pressed-steel parallelogram forks with suspension by means of a friction-damped coil spring and, typically, there was no suspension at the rear.

The standard boat-shaped Bernardet military sidecar was designed for a single passenger; a spare wheel was carried on the rear. Leg-guards and panniers, a rear carrying rack and pillion seat were provided as a standard fitment.

ABOVE: **With its lightly stressed 800cc side-valve engine, shaft drive and four-speed gearbox with reverse, the AX2 was a well-made and reliable machine capable of 85kph/53mph on the road. The external pressed-steel frame was combined with pressed-steel front forks.**

BELOW: **The use of a cross shaft to allow selection of sidecar-wheel drive improved off-road performance.**

This was an expensive and well-built machine very much in the German style and well suited to a hard military life. As with the earlier 750XA, the AX2 would have been seen as a direct competitor to the larger BMW and Zündapp machines and, again, captured examples were pressed into service with the *Wehrmacht*. After the fall of France in 1940, there are some reports that the AX2 continued to be constructed in the Dijon factories of the French Terrot company which, at the time, was France's largest manufacturer of motorcycles.

Not all of the AX2s were destroyed in German service, and a small number remained in use with the French Army in the immediate post-war years and into the early 1950s.

ABOVE: **A spare wheel was generally carried on the rear of the side-car.** BELOW: **The AX2 was popular with the *Wehrmacht* after the fall of France in 1940 and a handful survived the war years, re-entering French military service in 1945.**

Gnome et Rhône AX2

Type: Motorcycle, heavy, with sidecar, 3x2
Manufacturer: Gnome et Rhône; Paris
Production: 1936 to 1945
Engine: Gnome et Rhône; two cylinder, horizontally opposed; 804cc; side valves; air cooled; power output, 18.5bhp at 3,500rpm
Transmission: 4F1R; hand gear-change
Suspension: Pressed-steel parallelogram front forks with a single friction-damped coil spring; solid rear end
Brakes: Drum, front and rear
Dimensions (with sidecar):
Length – 2,700mm/106in
Width – 1,650mm/65in
Height – 1,000mm/39in
Wheelbase – 1,485mm/58in
Weight – 316kg/696lb
Performance: Maximum speed – 85kph/53mph

Monet-Goyon L5A, L5A1

First produced in 1917, the MAG-engined French Monet-Goyon motorcycle enjoyed considerable racing success during the 1930s. The L5A – and the slightly modified L5A1 – was a standard production machine widely used in solo and sidecar form by the French Army and the *Gendarmerie*.

ABOVE LEFT AND LEFT: **Although the L5 was not a powerful machine it was nevertheless used in both solo and combination form, and a number were commandeered by the *Wehrmacht* after the fall of France in 1940.**

Easily identified by its distinctive drooping fuel tank, the machine was superseded by the purpose-made Gnome et Rhône AX2 sidecar outfits just prior to World War II.

The frame of the L5A1 was of composite construction, consisting of a tubular upper structure with a single down-tube, combined with flat plates to support the engine. The engine was a 486cc single-cylinder unit driving the rear wheel through a four-speed gearbox and open chain. A single coil spring provided suspension for the friction-damped girder parallelogram front forks, while the rear was unsprung.

Military equipment was confined to a rear luggage rack and small leather pannier bags. The sidecar was a single-seater of typically civilian design, also with a small luggage rack at the rear, sometimes carrying a spare wheel.

ABOVE: **Looking a little the worse for wear but, nonetheless, proudly exhibiting the evidence of a long and arduous career. Note the distinctive shape of the L5A's fuel tank with its pronounced droop.**

A number of these machines remained in service in 1940 when France fell to the Germans in the Blitzkreig and were still available during the immediate post-war years. Monet-Goyon ceased motorcycle production in 1957.

Monet-Goyon L5A, L5A1

Type: Motorcycle, medium, solo; and with sidecar
Manufacturer: Monet-Goyon; Macon
Production: 1935 to 1936
Engine: MAG; single cylinder; 486cc; side valves; air cooled; power output, 12bhp at 4,000rpm
Transmission: 4F; hand gear-change
Suspension: Friction-damped coil-sprung parallelogram girder forks at front; unsprung rear
Brakes: Drums, front and rear
Dimensions (with sidecar):
Length – 2,250mm/89in
Width – 1,760mm/70in
Height – 1,020mm/40in
Wheelbase – 1,150mm/45in
Weight – 300kg/661lb
Performance: Maximum speed – 60kph/38mph

Motobécane Mobylette

Established in 1923, the French company Motobécane was originally a producer of both motorcycles and bicycles and for a long time was France's largest motorcycle manufacturer. In 1949, the company introduced its Mobylette, essentially a bicycle to which had been fitted a small two-stroke engine.

The first of these machines, which soon became known as mopeds, was the AV3, but the most popular was the 50 Series. However, all Mobylettes share what is essentially the same engine, with differences confined to the ignition system (6V or 12V), and the drive-line. During the life of the machine, two types of drive system were adopted. The Variator uses an expanding pulley to vary the gear ratio as engine speed increases; a low ratio allows the motorcycle to move off from idle speeds while the highest ratio is provided when the engine is running at speed. Other machines were fitted with a standard clutch and single, fixed gear ratio.

The frame was a simple step-through design, with the 49cc motor mounted low down, just ahead of the bottom bracket.

Late models, from the AV31, were provided with telescopic front forks but there was never any suspension at the rear. Pedals were provided to assist with starting – and indeed, might sometimes have been required to help the little machine up hills. Speed on the road was restricted to less than 40kph/25mph and off-road operation would have been diifficult at speeds above walking pace.

The French Army employed such machines widely, not only from Motobécane but also from other manufacturers such as VAP and Peugeot. The typical role was base messenger duties, but the machines may also have been issued to airborne troops where the light weight would have been an asset.

A total of 14 million Mobylettes were produced over almost half a century, and the machine was soon beset by competitors, the best known of which in the UK was probably the German NSU Quickly, but in France would have been the Vélo Solex. The Motobécane company went into receivership in 1981 but was rescued by Yamaha and renamed MBK.

TOP AND ABOVE: **The Motobécane Mobylette currently remains in production in India.**

Motobécane Mobylette

Type: Motor bicycle, two wheel
Manufacturer: Motobécane, MBK; Saint Quentin
Production: 1949 to 2002
Engine: Motobécane; single cylinder; 49cc; two-stroke; air cooled; power output, 1.33bhp
Transmission: 4F; hand gear-change
Suspension: Telescopic front forks on later models; solid rear end
Brakes: Cycle type rim brakes or drums, front and rear
Dimensions: Length – 1,750mm/69in
  Width – 600mm/24in
  Height – 1,000mm/39in
  Wheelbase – 1,000mm/39in
  Weight – 45kg/95lb
Performance: Maximum speed – 40kph/25mph

Peugeot P-135A

Peugeot was one of the pioneers of the French motor industry and started manufacturing motor tricycles in 1898, using De Dion engines. The company's first motorcycle appearing in 1901. The motorcar and cycle and motorcycle divisions of the company separated in 1926, and the P-135, which made its first appearance in 1936, was Peugeot's most successful pre-war production motorcycle. From 1939, the modified

P-135A was adopted by the French Army for liaison and despatch duties; the "A" suffix (*Armée*) indicating that the machine was intended for use by the army.

A compact, lightweight machine of surprisingly modern appearance, the P-135A was constructed around a standard tubular-steel cycle type frame with a single down-tube, and was powered by a single-cylinder twin-port engine of 346cc, driving through

a three-speed gearbox and exposed chain. Front suspension consisted of a single friction-damped coil spring on the girder parallelogram front forks, while the rear end was unsprung.

Military equipment was confined to a rear luggage rack or pillion seat, together with simple tubular pannier racks.

The machine was put back into production after the war, and Peugeot motorcycles continue to be manufactured today. Indeed, Cycles Peugeot claims to be the only surviving French motorcycle manufacturer from 300 such companies.

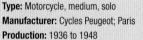

Peugeot P-135A

Type: Motorcycle, medium, solo
Manufacturer: Cycles Peugeot; Paris
Production: 1936 to 1948
Engine: Peugeot; single cylinder; 346cc; overhead valves; air cooled; power output, not available
Transmission: 3F; hand gear-change
Suspension: Friction-damped coil-sprung parallelogram girder forks at front; unsprung rear
Brakes: Drums, front and rear
Dimensions: Length – 2,150mm/85in
  Width – 700mm/28in
  Height – 1,000mm/39in
  Wheelbase – 1,400mm/55in
  Weight (solo) – 150kg/330lb
Performance: Maximum speed – 90kph/56mph

ABOVE AND RIGHT: **After the end of World War II, Peugeot was the largest motorcycle manufacturer in France. Production of the P-135A resumed and it remained available in civilian guise until 1948 by which time the large single-cylinder engine, girder front forks, and rigid rear end were looking a little dated.**

Peugeot SX8T *Armée*

The SX8 – also designated SX8T *Armée* – was a military version of a standard civilian lightweight two-stroke multi-terrain motorcycle. Some 75 machines were procured for trials by the French Army during 1977, with production commencing the following year. In service, the SX8T was intended to replace the older Honda CB 250 but the power output was found to be insufficient and off-road performance was disappointing so the machines were confined to driving school and convoy escort duties. Rather than replacing the Honda, in practice the two machines served alongside one another until they were both replaced in the 1980s.

The machine was constructed around a tubular-steel duplex-cradle frame and featured telescopic hydraulically-damped front forks with 130mm/5.5in of travel; at the rear was a coil-sprung load-adjustable trailing arm. The engine was a Peugeot two-stroke unit of just 80cc, driving through a five-speed gearbox and exposed chain. Military modifications included the use of a high-level exhaust, crash bars, and braced handlebars.

There was a dual seat, and military equipment was confined to a small rear luggage rack and vestigial pannier racks.

The machine remained in production until 1985; two years later the cycle and motorcycle aspects of Cycles Peugeot were separated, the latter being renamed Peugeot Motorcycles, with a 25 per cent stake held by Honda.

LEFT: **The similar, but more powerful, Peugeot X200 was trialled as a possible replacement for the SX8T, alongside an Italian Caglva machine. Budgetary constraints caused the project to be cancelled and the SX8T remained in service into the mid-1980s.**

Peugeot SX8T *Armée*

Type: Motorcycle, light, solo
Manufacturer: Cycles Peugeot; Valentigney
Production: 1978 to 1985
Engine: Peugeot; single cylinder; 80cc; two-stroke; air cooled; power output, 8bhp at 6,500rpm
Transmission: 5F; foot gear-change
Suspension: Hydraulically-damped telescopic forks at front; load-adjustable coil-sprung trailing arm at rear
Brakes: Drums, front and rear
Dimensions: Length – 2,000mm/79in
   Width – 800mm/31in
   Height – 1,092mm/43in
   Wheelbase – 1290mm/50in
   Weight – 77kg/169lb
Performance: Maximum speed – 80kph/50mph

René Gillet G1

René Gillet started producing high-quality motorcycles in 1898 and the company's heavy solo and sidecar outfits, which first appeared in 1928, were favourites with the French Army and police forces. The G1 became one of the French Army's standard road-going solo and sidecar combination machines of the late 1930s. Although military production ceased in 1940 when France fell to the Germans, the machine was put back into production after the war and remained available, with some design modifications, until the early 1950s.

The G1 was a typical heavy motorcycle of the period, and was constructed around a tubular-steel cycle type frame with a single down-tube. The front forks were of the leading-link type, and were suspended on a single friction-damped coil spring; the rear forks were unsprung. Power was provided by a 748cc side-valve V-twin, initially coupled to a three-speed gearbox, although this was subsequently superseded by a four-speed unit; final drive was by open chain. The distinctive front mudguards incorporated deep side skirts.

Standard military equipment included a rear luggage rack in place of the pillion seat, leather panniers and a heavy sump guard. Sidecars included a standard single-seat civilian-style unit, as well as machine-gun mount, radio, and stretcher carriers. A spare wheel was carried on the rear of the sidecar.

René Gillet ceased manufacture of motorcycles in 1957.

ABOVE: **The V-twin G1 was the standard French military motorcycle of the 1930s, both in solo and sidecar form.** RIGHT: **In its original form, the machine used a three-speed transmission with hand gear-change, but this was later superseded by a four-speed unit, still retaining the tank-mounted control.**

René Gillet G1

Type: Motorcycle, heavy, solo; and with sidecar
Manufacturer: René Gillet; Paris
Production: 1937 to 1940
Engine: René Gillet; two cylinders in V formation; 748cc; side valves; air cooled; power output, 14.6bhp at 4,000rpm
Transmission: 3F and then 4F; hand gear-change
Suspension: Friction-damped coil-sprung leading-link girder forks at front; unsprung rear
Brakes: Drums, front and rear
Dimensions (with sidecar): Length – 2,260mm/89in
　　Width – 1,640mm/65in
　　Height – 1,000mm/39in
　　Wheelbase – 1,500mm/59in
　　Weight (solo) – 254kg/560lb
Performance: Maximum speed – 65kph/40mph

Terrot RD-A

At one time, Terrot of Dijon was the largest motorcycle manufacturer in France and almost unique among French motorcycle builders also established a factory overseas – a division in Czechoslovakia built the company's 350cc model between 1933 and 1935. Although not a major supplier, the company did sell motorcycles to the French Army throughout the years leading up to World War II. Typical of these was the RD-A, a medium-duty military machine used in both solo and sidecar combination form and based on the civilian RD.

The RD-A was a 498cc single-cylinder overhead-valve machine and, although the engine was provided with magneto ignition. There was also a battery and generator for lighting. Power was transmitted to the rear wheel through a separate hand-change four-speed gearbox, with final drive by open chain. The engine was installed in a conventional tubular-steel frame with a single down-tube. Coil-sprung girder parallelogram forks were fitted at the front, and there was a rigid rear end.

The factory's Dijon location put it out of reach of the occupying Germans, but production was halted in 1944. Other Terrot machines used by the French Army at this time included the RGM-A, HD-A and VATT. Production resumed after the war and, in 1950 and 1951, the French Army took delivery of some 500cc RGST and 350cc HCT models. Terrot motorcycle production was halted in the early 1960s.

ABOVE: **The 498cc RD-A was a military motorcycle based on the company's civilian RD.** LEFT: **Terrot opened a factory in Czechoslovakia in 1933 and the company's products were sold across Europe.**

Terrot RD-A

Type: Motorcycle, medium, solo; and with sidecar
Manufacturer: Terrot; Dijon
Production: 1937 to 1944
Engine: Terrot RSSR; single cylinder; 498cc; overhead valves; air cooled; power output, 14bhp at 4,000rpm
Transmission: 4F; foot gear-change
Suspension: Friction-damped coil-sprung girder parallelogram front forks; unsprung rear
Brakes: Drums, front and rear
Dimensions (with sidecar):
  Length – 2,330mm/93in
  Width – 1,740mm/69in
  Height – 1,040mm/41in
  Wheelbase – 1,420mm/56in
  Weight – 284kg/625lb
Performance: Maximum speed – 85kph/52mph

Ardie VF125

Type: Motorcycle, light, solo
Manufacturer: Ardie Werke; Nürnberg
Production: 1939 to 1945
Engine: Ardie or Sachs; single cylinder; 123cc;
two stroke; air cooled; power output,
5bhp at 4,500rpm
Transmission: 3F; hand gear-change
Suspension: Friction-damped coil-sprung
parallelogram front forks; unsprung rear
Brakes: Drums, front and rear
Dimensions: Length – 1,920mm/76in
Width – 700mm/27in
Height – 1,000mm/39in
Wheelbase – 1,250mm/49in
Weight – 67kg/150lb
Performance: Maximum speed – 75kph/47mph

Ardie VF125

Not all German motorcycles of World War II were huge off-road sidecar outfits and the Ardie VF125 is a case in point. The Ardie works had been founded by former Premier designer Arno Dietrich, and had started making motorcycles in 1919. The machines enjoyed a degree of racing success, the company at first using their own engines but then adopting

ABOVE: **While the lightweight Ardie might be typical of many German machines of the period, the trailer is a novel touch.** BELOW: **The two-stroke Sachs engine, in this case with a capacity of 123cc, was widely used in lightweight German motorcycles.**

power units from JAP, alongside design features which included lightweight frames of Duralumin. Ardie resumed manufacture of their own engines in 1936, favouring small capacity two-strokes as well as similar power units supplied by Sachs. A range of lightweight 100, 125 and 200cc machines were produced from about 1937 and by the following year, the range included 12 models. The *Wehrmacht* started buying the little VF125 soon after it was launched in 1939. Some 9,000 of these simple lightweight two-stroke civilian machines were constructed before the end of the

war, the majority of which were pressed into military service. The *Wehrmacht* also used the company's slightly larger 200cc RBZ200 model.

Constructed around a simple cycle frame with a single down-tube, and featuring pressed-steel parallelogram front forks with a friction-damped single coil spring, the Ardie VF125 was powered by a kick-start 123cc single-cylinder two-stroke engine, driving through a three-speed hand-change gearbox. Ignition was by Bosch magneto and the machine was generally equipped with a rear carrying rack and twin leather panniers.

By 1942, the VF125 was the only machine being produced, although the engine was also used in a stationary generator. The Ardie factory was heavily bombed by the Allies but production resumed after the war with the company in the ownership of Dürkopp at Bielefeld. Ardie stopped motorcycle production in 1958.

BELOW: **From 1942, the VF125 was the only military motorcycle built by Ardie.**

Auto-Union DKW RT-125

DKW was founded in 1919 by the Danish-born engineer, J.S. Rasmussen and the company's first product was a clip-on engine designed for motorizing a standard bicycle. Various small two-stroke machines, designed by Hugo Ruppe, followed and within a very few years, the company was operating the world's largest motorcycle factory. In the 1930s, DKW became part of the Auto-Union conglomerate and the company enjoyed considerable racing success during the decade. The little two-stroke RT-125 was typical of the company's commercial output during this period and was widely used by the *Wehrmacht*.

Very early machines were powered by a 98cc two-stroke engine with magneto spark, but the large majority used a 123cc single-cylinder two-stroke, driving through a three-speed foot-change gearbox and open chain. The frame was a standard tubular cycle design with a single down-tube.

At the front end, there were pressed-steel parallelogram forks, at first suspended on rubber, but for most of the production run using a single coil spring. There was no suspension at the rear.

Although basically a civilian machine, military equipment included a rear luggage rack, and leather side panniers.

The RT-125 was possibly the only German motorcycle to remain in production throughout the war.

A near copy of the machine was produced in Britain during the war as the Royal Enfield WD/RE and, as part of war reparations in 1945, the design of the RT-125 was given, royalty-free, to both BSA in the UK, who put it into production as the Bantam in 1948, and to Harley-Davidson in the US, their version being described as the Model S. The design was also unofficially adopted by MZ in East Germany and Yamaha. DKW themselves put the design back into production in 1949.

ABOVE RIGHT, RIGHT AND BELOW: **The lightweight DKW RT-125 was an extremely capable machine, and was the only German motorcycle to remain in production throughout World War II. The type was copied by Royal Enfield as the WD/RE. The design was passed to BSA and Harley-Davidson as part of German reparations.**

Auto-Union DKW RT-125

Type: Motorcycle, light, solo
Manufacturer: Auto-Union, Werke DKW; Zschopau
Production: 1939 to 1945
Engine: DKW; single cylinder; 123cc; two-stroke; air cooled; power output, 4.3bhp at 4,000rpm
Transmission: 3F; foot gear-change
Suspension: Coil-sprung pressed-steel parallelogram front forks; unsprung rear
Brakes: Drums, front and rear
Dimensions: Length – 1,940mm/76in
  Width – 650mm/26in
  Height – 900mm/35in
  Wheelbase – 1,230mm/48in
  Weight – 91kg/200lb
Performance: Maximum speed – 50kph/30mph

Auto-Union DKW RT-175-VS

After the end of World War II, the DKW company was split in two as part of German war reparations. The original Zschopau factory fell into the Soviet-occupied East German zone and

became IFA and then MZ, while DKW set up a new factory at Ingolstadt, with production commencing in 1949. Production of the RT-125 continued with some small modifications after the move to Ingolstadt but it was not used by the military. In 1954, DKW introduced the more powerful RT-175-VS, a standard civilian machine based on the frame of the company's RT-250 and the engine of the RT-200. This machine was adopted by the *Bundeswehr* for general liaison and despatch duties.

The engine was a 174cc single-cylinder two-stroke unit with a power output of 9.5bhp, driving the rear wheel through a four-speed gearbox, with final drive by enclosed chain. The frame was a hybrid pressed-steel/tubular design

ABOVE AND LEFT: **After the war, DKW established a new factory at Ingolstadt and motorcycle production was restarted in 1949 with the pre-war RT-125. Typical of the company's lightweight two-stroke designs the single-cylinder RT-175-VS was introduced in 1954 and was widely used by the *Bundeswehr*.**

with a single down-tube, and the rear mudguard included a cowling which enclosed the seat tube. Leading-link telescopic pattern forks were used at the front, with hydraulic damping, while the rear end consisted of a trailing arm suspended on a single coil spring.

Although basically still a production civilian machine, military equipment included a rear luggage rack, crash bars and leather side panniers.

DKW motorcycle production came to an end in 1981.

DKW RT-175-VS

Type: Motorcycle, light, solo
Manufacturer: Auto-Union; Ingolstadt
Production: 1954 to 1958
Engine: DKW; single cylinder; 174cc; two-stroke; air cooled; power output, 9.5bhp at 5,000rpm
Transmission: 4F; foot gear-change
Suspension: Telescopic hydraulically-damped leading-link front forks; trailing arm at rear with coil spring
Brakes: Drums, front and rear
Dimensions: Length – 1,975mm/78in
    Width – 650mm/26in
    Height – 926mm/36in
    Wheelbase – 1,278mm/50in
    Weight – 135kg/298lb
Performance: Maximum speed – 95kph/59mph

ABOVE AND LEFT: **With its external pressed-steel frame, "boxer" engine, shaft drive and telescopic forks, the R-12 has all of the iconic features of the pre-war BMW.**

BMW R-12

Among the most numerous of the German military motorcycles of World War II was the BMW R-12, a big, 750cc, essentially civilian, machine which was widely used by the *Kradschützen* battalions of the *Wehrmacht*'s during the early stages of the conflict.

Although it could trace its lineage directly back to the R-62 of 1928, the unorthodox pressed-steel rigid perimeter frame of the R-12 was clearly derived from the similarly equipped R-11 and R-16 models of 1929. Originally introduced to resolve problems with cracked welds in earlier machines, BMW's then-unique perimeter frame was a major step away from the bicycle ancestry of the motorcycle and was the forerunner of today's perimeter-framed

machines. However, the R-12 was also fitted with telescopic front forks with hydraulic shock absorbers – the first production motorcycle to be so equipped – in an effort to improve handling, and it further differed from its predecessors in having a four-speed gearbox and interchangeable wheels.

Early problems with the riveted joints of the frame led to the adoption of electric arc welding in 1936, and the R-12 went on to become BMW's most numerous motorcycle until the introduction of the R-75/5 of the early 1970s.

Despite weighing more than 182kg/400lb, the powerful 746cc flat-twin engine, with shaft drive to the four-speed gearbox, ensured that the R-12 was a fast and reliable machine and, despite the rigid rear end, the telescopic front forks gave a comfortable ride on the road. However, the close-fitted mudguards, the result of

its civilian ancestry frequently caused difficulties in mud and snow, and it was easily defeated by winter conditions on the Eastern Front.

The R-12 was used solo, as well as with the typical German military sidecar but, unlike the R-75 which followed, the sidecar wheel was not driven. This reduced off-road performance.

Some 36,000 machines had been manufactured by the time production ended in May 1941, with more than 10,000 completed in the first 12 months alone; something like 10,000 R-12s were delivered directly to the *Wehrmacht*, but hapless civilians found that their machines were also impressed into service.

Although it remained in production, in 1938, the R-12 was effectively superseded by the R-71 and the smaller R-61.

LEFT: **Until the early 1970s, the R-12 was BMW's most numerous motorcycle, with 36,000 examples produced between 1935 and 1941. Although essentially a civilian machine, it was used by the *Wehrmacht* in both solo and sidecar form and provided the model for Soviet and Chinese copies.**

BMW R-12	

Type: Motorcycle, heavy, solo; and with sidecar
Manufacturer: BMW Werke; München
Production: 1935 to 1941
Engine: BMW; two cylinder, horizontally opposed; 746cc; side valves; air cooled; power output, 18bhp at 3,500rpm
Transmission: 4F; hand gear-change
Suspension: Telescopic hydraulically-damped front forks; solid rear end
Brakes: Drum, front and rear
Dimensions (solo): Length – 2,100mm/83in
 Width – 900mm/35in
 Height – 950mm/37in
 Wheelbase – 1,400mm/55in
 Weight – 190kg/418lb
Performance: Maximum speed – 100kph/62mph

BMW R-4

By the time the R-4 appeared in 1932, the BMW company had been making quality motorcycles for almost a decade. Originally established as an aeroplane manufacturer – hence the spinning propeller logo – BMW was forced to abandon the manufacture of aircraft under the Treaty of Versailles and turned to producing motorcycle engines for companies such as Victoria, SMW and Bison. In 1923, BMW's Chief Designer, Max Fritz, designed the now classic horizontally opposed "boxer" twin (which remained the mainstay of the company until 1984), mounting it in the R-32, the company's first motorcycle. Not all of the company's products were thus powered, and the R-4 was a low-priced single-cylinder machine, one of a number of lightweight motorcycles intended to help the company ride out the depression.

Although the R-4 was intended to complement the BMW's R-2 "people's" machine, a 200cc commuter model, BMW soon found that it was supplying the *Reichswehr*. After Hitler came to power, the R-4 also became the standard training machine of the *Wehrmacht*.

Powered by a 398cc single-cylinder four-stroke engine driving through a three-speed gearbox and exposed Carden shaft, the R-4 was relatively light and easy

to handle; top speed was in the order of 105kph/65mph and even if off-road performance was minimal, it was a useful machine for despatch riders and general reconnaissance work. Sidecar gears could also be specified.

The R-4 was constructed around the pressed-steel external frame – the so-called "star" frame – which was originally developed to handle the stresses produced by the company's larger machines. The front forks were similarly of pressed-steel construction, consisting of a friction-damped leaf-sprung trailing-link design.

The machines supplied to the military were little different to their civilian counterparts, and military modifications were restricted to a sump shield, rear luggage carrier, and twin pannier bags.

The launch price of the Series 1, produced during 1932, was 1,250RM. This was superseded by the Series 2 in 1933; the Series 3 in 1934, Series 4 in 1935; when the final model, the Series 5, was produced during 1936 and 1937 the price had fallen to 1,150RM. By the time production of the R-4 came to an

ABOVE: **The R-4 was widely used by the *Wehrmacht* in both solo and sidecar form, particularly as a training machine.**

end, the company had abandoned both the pressed-steel frame and the cantilever spring front forks on most models, the R-4 being one of the last to retain these features.

Although the R-4 stands in the shadow of such icons as the R-12 and the R-75, total production nevertheless, amounted to more than 15,000.

BELOW: **The curved pressed-steel front forks give the R-4 a curiously old-fashioned appearance which belies its technology.**

BMW R-4

Type: Motorcycle, medium, solo; and with sidecar
Manufacturer: BMW Werke; München
Production: 1932 to 1937
Engine: BMW; single cylinder; 398cc; overhead valves; air cooled; power output, 12bhp at 3,500rpm
Transmission: Three-speed; hand gear-change
Suspension: Friction-damped cantilever leaf spring on front forks; unsprung rear
Brakes: Drums, front and rear
Dimensions: Length – 1,950mm/77in
Width – 850mm/33in
Height – 950mm/37in
Wheelbase – 1,320mm/53in
Weight – 130kg/286lb
Performance: Maximum speed – 105kph/65mph

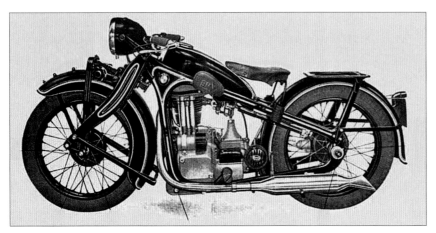

BMW R-61 and R-66

BMW R-61 & R-66

Type: Motorcycle, heavy, solo; and with sidecar

Manufacturer: BMW Werke; München

Production: 1938 to 1941

Engine: BMW; two cylinder, horizontally opposed; 597cc; side valves (R-61) or overhead valves (R-66); air cooled; power output, 18bhp or 30bhp, respectively

Transmission: 4F; hand gear-change

Suspension: Coil-sprung hydraulically-damped telescopic front forks; coil-sprung plunger suspension at rear

Brakes: Drums, front and rear

Dimensions: Length – 2,130mm/84in
Width – 810mm/32in
Height – 1,000mm/39in
Wheelbase – 1,400mm/55in
Weight (solo) – 187kg/412lb

Performance: Maximum speed – 120–145kph/ 70–90mph

By 1938, BMW had constructed 100,000 motorcycles and, during that year, launched the side-valve engined R-61 and the similar, overhead valve R-66 on the civilian market, the latter described as the "most powerful twin yet offered to the public". Although neither was designed specifically for military use, both were procured in small numbers by the *Wehrmacht* and employed for solo despatch duties and were even occasionally fitted with a civilian sidecar.

Both machines were firmly in the mainstream BMW mould and, although the company had abandoned the distinctive pressed-steel frame in 1935, the R-61 and R-66 were both powered by versions of the company's iconic flat-twin engine, and were fitted with the up-to-date telescopic front forks as well as being the first to employ plunger rear suspension.

The faster of the two was the R-66 with its overhead-valve engine – top speed was almost 145kph/90mph – but there is no doubt that these were both fast and capable motorcycles.

Like the R-61, the R-66 was constructed around a conventional tubular-steel duplex triangular-shaped frame, with hydraulically-damped coil-sprung telescopic front forks and a plunger-type rear end employing undamped coil springs. The engine was a coil-sparked twin-carburettor version of Max Fritz's classical flat-twin; in overhead valve form, as fitted to the R-66, it produced 30bhp from 597cc, while the side-valve version could only manage 18bhp. As had already become the BMW tradition – and a tradition which would persist for 60 years – final drive was by means of an exposed

carden shaft transmitting drive to a crown wheel and pinion set in the rear hub. The front and rear wheels were interchangeable. A hand gear-change lever was positioned directly below the saddle, coupled directly to the four-speed gearbox.

Although hardly a lightweight, the machines avoided the heavy appearance of the later big BMWs, and both could be considered handsome and purposeful-looking motorcycles with modern lines which belie their age. Needless to say, both also enjoyed the rugged reliability for which the company's products had become famous.

Military modifications included the use of a rear luggage rack or pillion seat, and twin leather pannier bags.

The R-61 is notable for being the last BMW to employ a side-valve engine, and both models remained in production until 1941 when they were discontinued in favour of larger machines like the R-75 and Zündapp KS750 which were designed especially for the armed forces. Total production of the R-61 amounted to 3,747 units, while the comparable figure for the R-66 was 1,669.

In 1940, a captured, or otherwise procured, BMW flat-twin was trialled at the Mechanical Warfare Experimental Establishment (MWEE) at Farnborough; this may well have been an R-66.

ABOVE: **Dating from 1938 and remaining in production until 1941, both the R-61 and the R-66 were used by the *Wehrmacht*.**

LEFT: **The R-61 and R-66 differed mainly in the location of the valves – side valves for the former (as here) and overhead valves for the latter.**

BMW R-75

Introduced in 1941, the big BMW R-75 was originally designed for use by the German *Afrika Korps* and other *Wehrmacht* outfits, and was intended to embody all the lessons learned by the elite *Kradschützen* motorcycle troops. Unlike the pre-war BMWs in *Wehrmacht* service at that date, the R-75 was designed as a military motorcycle from the outset; it was even equipped with a pintle hitch to allow a trailer or light gun to be towed. Indeed, with its powerful flat-twin engine, combined with features such as a driven sidecar wheel, lockable differential, hydraulic brakes, and multi-terrain capability, many might consider it the pinnacle of German military motorcycle design. Along with the similar Zündapp KS750, these big motorcycle combinations were able to fulfil many of the roles for which the US-built Jeep had been designed.

BMW had abandoned their pressed-steel frames by the time the R-75 entered production and the machine was constructed around a heavy-duty duplex tubular-steel frame, with telescopic coil-sprung front forks and a rigid rear end. The engine was an overhead-valve version of Max Fritz's iconic horizontally opposed twin, producing 26bhp from a capacity of 746cc. Following BMW tradition, final drive from the gearbox was by exposed propeller shaft and the hand-change gearbox itself offered the rider a total of six speeds – three standard road speeds, plus three low ratio speeds for off-road use – plus high and low reverse gears; by 1942/43 BMW had added a fourth road speed to the gearbox.

ABOVE: **Designed for the arduous conditions of the Western Desert, the BMW R-75 featured overhead valves, telescopic front forks, shaft drive, and selectable sidecar-wheel drive. It was even equipped for towing.** BELOW: **The rubber gaiter covers on the front forks were developed to exclude the sand and dust of the desert.**

Drive to the sidecar wheel was achieved by means of a cross-shaft, and the differential was lockable. Brakes were provided on all three wheels, those on the driving wheels having hydraulic operation.

Early machines had metal covers for the sliding components of the front forks, but it was found that the grit of the North African desert had a deleterious effect and rubber gaiters were subsequently fitted. A tank-mounted air filter was fitted from 1942. From 1943, the exhaust system was modified to allow heated air to be ducted to the rider's otherwise exposed hands and feet and into the sidecar, almost certainly a welcome modification to those exposed to the harsh Russian winter.

The 286/1 sidecar was a standard military design with a cut-away right-hand side, similar to that used with the Zündapp KS750. A spare wheel was carried on the rear and there was provision for mounting a machine-gun at the front. A rear rack was fitted to the motorcycle, together with a hinged pillion seat, and leather or metal panniers.

In order to allow components to be easily exchanged between the BMW R-75 and the KS750, items such as wheels, differentials, brake parts and sidecar drive were standardized. It was suggested that eventually the two companies might develop a Zündapp-BMW hybrid, with each company producing 20,000 machines a year, and it was agreed that production of the R-75 would cease once the factory had manufactured 20,200 units, a target which never was achieved.

Although it probably called for more maintenance than it was likely to get in the field, particularly on the Eastern Front where conditions were frequently appalling, the complex R-75 was a well-designed and powerful machine that could tackle almost anything that was asked of it. By the time production ceased in 1944, around 18,000 examples had been turned out of BMW's München, and later Eisenach factories. Some 750 examples were also supplied to Spain directly from the *Wehrmacht* in 1943.

ABOVE: **Although not fast, the R-75 was a powerful and well-designed machine which could tackle most types of terrain with ease.** LEFT: **The R-75 was among the first BMWs to use an overhead-valve engine.**

BMW R-75

Type: Motorcycle, heavy, with sidecar
Manufacturer: BMW Werke; München
Production: 1941 to 1944
Engine: BMW; two cylinder, horizontally opposed; 746cc; overhead valves; air cooled; power output, 26bhp at 4,000rpm
Transmission: 3F1R, then 4F1R; hand/foot gear-change
Suspension: Friction-damped coil-sprung telescopic front forks; unsprung rear
Brakes: Drums, all three wheels; hydraulic operation on driven wheels
Dimensions: Length – 2,400mm/94in
Width – 1,730mm/68in
Height – 1,000mm/39in
Wheelbase – 1,444mm/57in
Weight – 400kg/880lb
Performance: Maximum speed – 92kph/57mph

BMW R-80/7

ABOVE: **Dating from 1977, BMW's R-80/7 was typical of the company's high-quality post-war output.** BELOW LEFT: **Chosen by Germany, Austria, France, Belgium and the Netherlands, the R-80/7 was used for the convoy escort and military police roles.**

BMW had resumed motorcycle manufacture in 1949 with the single-cylinder R-24 but the company did not abandon the flat-twin engine for which it had become so well known and the first post-war "boxer" was the R-51/2, launched the following year. The new machines helped BMW to recapture its markets and to consolidate its position as a producer of high-quality, reliable machines

and, by 1954 all new BMWs featured telescopic forks and plunger rear ends. New ranges were launched in 1955 and 1969 but, by the 1970s the company found it was fighting the "japanese invasion". More powerful machines were developed, and the 798cc R-80/7 – the "/7" code indicating that it was launched in 1977 – was typical of the company's larger motorcycles produced during the closing decades of the 20th century

With its shaft drive, and iconic transverse-twin, the R-80/7 was a fitting tribute to Max Fritz's original design work and although it was a standard civilian machine, it was also available in modified form for police and military customers. As well as being used by the *Bundeswehr* in Germany, examples were exported to countries such as France, Austria, the Netherlands and Belgium, where typical roles included convoy escort and military police work.

The R-80/7 was constructed around a heavy-duty tubular-steel duplex cradle design, mounting hydraulically-damped telescopic front forks, offering 200mm/8in of travel, and with a long hydraulically-damped load-adjustable trailing arm at the rear which allowed a deflection of 125mm/5in. Power came from a typical BMW overhead-valve transverse-twin, with a wet sump and solid-state electronic ignition, available in 50bhp and 55bhp versions. In both cases, the transmission was a five-speed foot-change gearbox, driving

LEFT: **Although essentially a road-going machine, a lightweight Enduro variant known as the R-80G/S – *Gelände/Strasse* – was also built. This was BMW's first off-road machine and was produced from 1980 to 1986 and, in R-65G/S form, was used in small numbers by the military.**

the rear wheel through a shaft running in an oil bath in the right-hand leg of the rear trailing arm.

This was essentially a road machine and military modifications were confined to fitting a rear carrying rack for a radio, plastic panniers, front and rear crash bars, a windscreen, and lighting if required.

Total production over the lifespan of the machine, including civilian models, amounted to 18,500 units.

Of course, BMW remains among the world's leading motorcycle manufacturers. Although, the traditional boxer twins have, at least partly given way to flat-fours and even two-stroke singles and off-road machines, the company continues to supply military motorcycles to the world's armies. In the civilian world, BMW's reputation for producing the highest-quality riders' machines remains intact.

LEFT: **A version of the R-80G/S was used on the Paris–Dakar Rally in 1981.**

BMW R-80/7

Type: Motorcycle, heavy, solo
Manufacturer: BMW Werke; München
Production: 1977 to 1984
Engine: BMW; two cylinder, horizontally opposed; 798cc; overhead valves; air cooled; power output, 50 to 55bhp at 7,000rpm
Transmission: 5F, foot gear-change
Suspension: Hydraulically-damped telescopic front forks; load-adjustable hydraulically-damped trailing arm at rear
Brakes: Disc, front; drum, rear
Dimensions: Length – 2,180mm/86in, from 1978 – 2,210mm/87in
Width – 746mm/29in
Height – 1,080mm/43in
Wheelbase – 1,465mm/58in
Weight – 215kg/473lb
Performance: Maximum speed – 180kph/112mph

Heinkel Tourist 103A-2

Heinkel was better known for manufacturing aircraft during World War II but in 1954 changed to producing motor scooters under the model name Tourist. Early machines were powered by a 149cc overhead valve unit and included advanced features such as electric start, four-speed gearbox and 12V electrics. The range was eventually extended to include 125cc and 174cc machines. The US forces in West Germany purchased large quantities of the 174cc 103A-2, fitting it with a box-like sidecar for messenger and package delivery duties.

Constructed around a simple step-through tubular-steel frame, the power unit and four-speed gearbox were mounted immediately ahead of the rear wheel. A short enclosed chain was used to drive the rear wheel. The engine was fully enclosed, with the engine compartment cover also used to provide a spare-wheel mount and driver/pillion seat. At the front, both the forks and the 254mm/10in wheel were concealed by the deep streamlined fairing. The front and rear forks were suspended by means of hydraulically-damped coil-sprung telescopic units.

LEFT: **Large numbers of the 103A-2 with the 174cc engine were purchased for US forces in West Germany.**

While the use of a four-stroke engine in a scooter might seem unusual, it is said that the engine was actually designed and produced during World War II for bomb train tractors and that Heinkel simply found a civilian use. Nevertheless, it was a powerful unit which gave the scooter an excellent turn of speed and a reputation for reliability.

Heinkel Tourist 103A-2

Type: Motor scooter, two wheeled, with sidecar
Manufacturer: Ernst Heinkel Aktiengesellschaft; Warnemünde
Production: 1960 to 1965
Engine: Heinkel; single cylinder; 174cc; overhead valves; air cooled; power output, 9.5bhp at 5,750rpm
Transmission: 4F; hand gear-change
Suspension: Hydraulically-damped coil-sprung telescopic leg at front, trailing arm at rear
Brakes: Drums, front and rear
Dimensions: Length – 2,180mm/86in
Width – 746mm/29in
Height – 1,080mm/43in
Wheelbase – 1,465mm/58in
Weight – 215kg/473lb
Performance: Maximum speed – 92kph/57mph

Maico M250/B

Although not known as a supplier of military motorcycles prior to World War II, Maico had actually started building motorcycles in 1935, specializing in lightweight two-stroke machines which, presumably, were not to the liking of the *Wehrmacht*. The M250/B multi-terrain machine was introduced in 1959, remaining in production for ten years, by which time some 10,000 examples had been completed. It was supplied both to the West German Army (*Bundeswehr*) and to the border police (*Bundesgrenzschütz*) between 1961 and 1966, and was also exported.

The M250/B – the "B" indicating *Bundeswehr* – was a standard civilian machine, lightly modified for military use and was constructed around a tubular-steel frame, with hydraulically-damped telescopic front forks and a coil-sprung trailing rear end. The engine was a single-cylinder two-stroke unit driving the rear wheel through a four-speed gearbox; final drive was by enclosed chain.

Military modifications included a sump shield, braced handlebars, large rear toolbox, rear-carrying rack, mid-level exhaust, and twin pannier bags.

LEFT: **Maico did not produce motorcycles for the *Wehrmacht* in World War II. The company's first military machine appeared in 1959.**

Maico M250/B

Type: Motorcycle, light, solo
Manufacturer: Maico Fahrzeugfabrik; Pfaffingen
Production: 1959 to 1969
Engine: Maico; single cylinder; 247cc; two stroke; air cooled; power output, 14.5bhp at 5,250rpm
Transmission: 4F; foot gear-change
Suspension: Hydraulically-damped telescopic front forks; trailing rear forks with coil spring
Brakes: Drums, front and rear
Dimensions: Length – 2,200mm/79in
Width – 800mm/32in
Height – 1,075mm/42in
Wheelbase – 1,300mm/52in
Weight – 155kg/341lb
Performance: Maximum speed – 96kph/60mph

NSU 3hp

Better known as NSU, the German Neckarsulmer Fahrzeugwerke company started producing motorcycles in 1901. Early machines were nothing more than pedal cycles into which NSU had fitted a Swiss Zedel engine, but the company started manufacturing its own engines in 1903 and, two years later, also developed a simple clutch device and two-speed epicyclic gearbox that fitted into the engine drive belt pulley. NSU also seems to have come up with the idea of the V-twin engine in 1903. Using this type of power unit, the standard civilian 3hp machine of 1913 was widely used by the German Imperial Army throughout World War I, and was one of a range of seven

BELOW: **This early NSU 3hp lacks the coil-spring rear suspension which was fitted from 1915 on.**

NSU motorcycles with nominal power outputs ranging from 2hp to 7hp.

Although it employed a cycle-type triangular frame of tubular steel, the NSU 3hp model was not really typical of early motorcycle designs. Firstly, the engine was a relatively powerful V-twin unit of 396cc, driving the rear wheels through a single-speed gearbox and exposed V belt. But more importantly, NSU was among the pioneers of rear suspension and the 3hp, like all NSU motorcycles produced after 1915, was equipped with a coil-sprung rear sub-frame. The front forks were of the leading-link design, suspended on a single friction-damped coil spring. Military modifications were confined to a rear carrying rack.

NSU was quick to resume motorcycle manufacture after 1918 and

considerable sales success followed. By 1922 NSU had been forced to embrace mass production techniques to cope with demand, and was employing 3,000 people.

NSU 3hp		

Type: Motorcycle, medium, solo
Manufacturer: Neckarsulmer Fahrzeugwerke; Neckarsulm
Production: 1913 to 1918
Engine: NSU; two cylinders in V formation, 396cc; overhead inlet valves, side exhaust; air cooled; power output, 10.5bhp
Transmission: Single speed
Suspension: Coil-sprung friction-damped leading-link front forks; coil-sprung sub-frame at rear
Brakes: Block acting on belt rim at rear only
Dimensions: Not available
Weight – 75kg/165lb
Performance: Maximum speed – 80kph/50mph

NSU 7.5hp

NSU had pioneered V-twin engines back in 1903 using atmospheric inlet valves, and by 1914 was offering well-built 3hp and 5hp machines fitted with V-twins which, by now, were using an inlet-over-exhaust valve configuration. The 7.5hp V-twin was launched in 1915 and was the first NSU machine to incorporate such advanced features as kick-start, chain drive, leading-link sprung front forks and coil-spring rear suspension. Enthusiastically embraced by the Imperial German Army from the start, the 7.5hp was even kitted out with a machine-gun sidecar.

The 7.5hp was a standard production machine constructed around a cycle-type triangular frame of tubular steel, in which was installed a V-twin engine, with magneto ignition. The engine was capable of producing 12bhp from its almost 995cc capacity and this was an extraordinarily fast motorcycle for the time; in solo form, it was capable of 100kph/62mph. The transmission consisted of a hand-change three-speed gearbox, and final drive was by exposed chain. Like all NSUs of the period, the 7.5hp was fitted with leading-link coil-sprung front forks and a coil-sprung rear sub-frame.

Military modifications were confined to fitting a rear carrying rack but the machine was also used in combination form, both with single-seat personnel sidecars and a platform sidecar on which was mounted a tripod and machine-gun.

Most motorcycles employed by German troops during World War I came from NSU.

LEFT: **NSU's 7.5hp V-twin was widely used by German troops during World War I, in both solo and sidecar form. In the latter case it was often employed as a mount for a machine-gun. Unusually for the period, there was coil-spring suspension on both the front and rear forks and the machine also possessed a rare turn of speed, with a top speed of 100kph/62mph perfectly possible in solo form.**

NSU 7.5hp

Type: Motorcycle, medium, solo; and with sidecar
Manufacturer: Neckarsulmer Fahrzeugwerke; Neckarsulm
Production: 1915 to 1918
Engine: NSU; two cylinders in V formation, 995cc; overhead inlet valves, side exhaust; air cooled; power output, 12bhp
Transmission: 3F, hand gear-change
Suspension: Coil-sprung friction-damped leading-link front forks; coil-sprung sub-frame at rear
Brakes: Drum, rear only
Dimensions: Not available
Weight – 62kg/286lb
Performance: Maximum speed – 100kph/62mph

NSU 251 OS(L)

Having pioneered the mass production of motorcycles during the 1920s, NSU concentrated on smaller machines during the following decade under the English designer, Walter Moore, who had previously worked for Norton. Typical of these was the 251 OS(L), a standard lightweight civilian machine with a high-performance four-stroke engine of which some 35,000 examples were supplied to the *Reichswehr* and the *Wehrmacht* from 1933 on.

The triangular frame was constructed from tubular steel and designed to allow the crankcase to form the lower structural member. At the front, there were friction-damped girder parallelogram coil-sprung forks, while the rear end was unsprung. NSU's 241cc overhead-valve engine was a powerful unit for its size, producing more than 10bhp, which was sufficient to give the machine a top speed of just over 100kph/62mph. The transmission consisted of a four-speed foot-change gearbox with final drive by enclosed chain.

Military modifications were confined to the use of a rear carrying rack or pillion seat, and leather panniers. The exhaust

ABOVE AND BELOW LEFT: **The 251 OS(L) was a civilian lightweight solo machine widely used by the *Wehrmacht*. An interesting construction feature was the use of the crankcase as a load-bearing part of the frame. The overhead-valve engine gave a top speed of 100kph/62mph.**

system was generally carried at a high level to allow use in mud and snow.

Production ended in 1944, but NSU resumed the manufacture of civilian motorcycles after the war, using pressed-steel frames from 1947. Lambretta scooters were produced under licence from 1949, and the company became well known for the NSU Quickly moped. All motorcycle production ceased in 1965.

NSU 252 OS(L)

Type: Motorcycle, light, solo
Manufacturer: Neckarsulmer Fahrzeugwerke; Neckarsulm
Production: 1933 to 1944
Engine: NSU; single cylinder, 241cc; overhead valves; air cooled; power output, 10.5bhp
Transmission: 4F; foot gear-change
Suspension: Coil-sprung friction-damped girder parallelogram front forks; solid rear end
Brakes: Drums, front and rear
Dimensions: Length – 2,040mm/80in
    Width – 780mm/31in
    Height – 950mm/37in
    Wheelbase – 1,320mm/52in
    Weight – 144kg/317lb
Performance: Maximum speed – 100kph/62mph

139

NSU HK-101 SdKfz 2 *Kettenkraftrad*

In 1938, the *Luftwaffe* (German Air Force) sponsored the development of what was effectively a half-tracked motorcycle. Designed by WaPrüf6 and NSU, and known as the *kleines Kettenkraftrad* (or, more usually, just *Kettenkrad*), the vehicle was initially intended to be used as a small, but powerful, artillery prime mover for the paratroop (*Fallschirmjäger*) units. It was more than capable of towing a 7.5cm *Gebrigskanone* 15/28 gun, 2cm FlaK.30 or PaK.38 anti-aircraft gun, or 3.7cm PaK.36 anti-tank gun, all of which were suitable for air-dropping but which required a small tractor for deployment on the ground. Late in the war, *Kettenkrads* were also used as aircraft tugs. The vehicle was capable of 73kph/45mph on the road and possessed formidable off-road capabilities, being able to climb almost anywhere that a man could walk; it could even carry men through the Russian winter mud.

Derived from the wheel-cum-track *Motorkarette*, which had been designed for the Austrian Army following a patent lodged by the engineer Heinrich Ernst Kniepkamp, the *Kettenkrad* (designated *SonderKraftfahrzeug 2* [special purpose vehicle 2] SdKfz 2) consisted, essentially, of the front end of a motorcycle, attached to a small, box-like steel hull supported on a tank-type track system; less than 10 per cent of the vehicle's weight was carried by the front wheel, the remainder was supported by the tracks.

NSU was not able to produce a suitable power unit so the vehicle was powered by a centrally mounted Opel 1,478cc

ABOVE: **The smallest of the standardized German half-track vehicles, the Opel-powered NSU *Kettenkrad* was originally intended for use as a light artillery tractor. A number of small trailers were also designed for use with the machine.** LEFT: **The box-like hull provided a saddle for the driver, together with rear-facing seats for two men. The engine was placed centrally, under the driver's saddle.**

four-cylinder petrol engine, which was taken from the company's Olympia motor car. The engine was connected to a three-speed gearbox and two-speed transfer case (3F1Rx2), positioned under the driver's saddle, via a standard motor-car style clutch.

The driver sat on a saddle in the normal motorcycle position, behind the front wheel, and steered via handlebars; a transverse rear-facing seat for two was provided behind the engine compartment. The sides of the body formed the fuel tanks, giving a capacity of 42 litres/9.25 gallons.

The front wheel provided the initial steering input, but a differential braking system was automatically brought into action once the handlebars were turned beyond a certain angle which provided the skid-steering characteristics of a standard track-layer. The motorcycle-style front forks were originally adapted from those used on the 600cc NSU motorcycle but, when this proved to be a weak point, in 1942, they were replaced by a wholly new pattern incorporating a hydraulic damper as well as the original coil springs. Where early prototypes had 483mm/19in motorcycle-style spoked wheels

at the front, on production models, a steel disc wheel was adopted which was presumably stronger and easier to manufacture. The brakes were mechanically operated.

Production started in 1939 at NSU's Neckarsulm factory, with the first vehicles delivered during 1940/41; additional machines were produced by Stoewer from 1943. A total of 8345 vehicles had been constructed by the end of the war. Variants included:

SdKfz 2   Motorcycle, ½ ton, half-track, tractor;
            HK-100, HK-101
SdKfz 2   Motorcycle, ½ ton, half-track, crane; HK-101
SdKfz 2/1 Motorcycle, ½ ton, half-track,
            field telephone cable layer; HK-101
SdKfz 2/2 Motorcycle, ½ ton, half-track,
            heavy field telephone cable layer; HK-101

A number of trailers were also designed for use with the vehicle, including a small, amphibious, unit.

The vehicle remained in production for civilian users until 1948, where it was marketed as a light agricultural tractor, with perhaps 500–550 more examples constructed.

LEFT: The light weight of the machine, combined with the use of tracks for propulsion, gave the *Kettenkrad* excellent off-road performance. After the war, the machine remained in production as an agricultural tractor.

NSU HK-101

Type: ½ ton, half-track, tractor; SdKfz2
Manufacturer: NSU; Neckarsulm
Production: 1939 to 1945
Engine: Opel; four cylinder; 1,478cc; overhead valves; water cooled; power output, 36bhp at 3,400rpm
Transmission: 3F1Rx2; foot gear-change
Suspension: Coil spring with hydraulic damper (late production only) at front; torsion bars at rear
Brakes: Mechanical at rear via controlled differential
Dimensions: Length – 3,000mm/118in
Width – 1,000mm/39in
Height – 1,200m/47in
Length of track in contact with ground – 820mm/32in
Weight – 1,280kg/2816lb
Performance: Maximum speed – 73kph/45mph

Triumph 3hp

The British Triumph company was the brainchild of two Germans – Siegfried Bettman and Maurice Schulte established the company to construct bicycles in 1887, before experimenting with the production of motorcycles around the turn of the century. In 1903, the year that the first Triumph motorcycle was put on sale, a German factory was established in Nürnberg and, until 1929, the products of the two factories were almost identical.

LEFT: **Designed by Charles Hathway, the 363cc single-cylinder engine was the first to be constructed by Triumph, replacing JAP and Fafnir units in the company's motorcycles.**

In 1904, the German factory began selling motorcycles to the German Army, and a year later introduced the 3hp solo machine that was the first product to be fitted with a Triumph-built engine.

The engine of the 3hp Triumph was a 363cc vertical single-cylinder unit with side valves and magneto ignition. It had been designed by Charles Hathaway who had been employed to carry out this specific task, previous Triumph machines having used JAP and Fafnir engines. Hathaway also designed the curious cantilever forks which Triumph used for many years. The engine was installed in a conventional cycle type tubular-steel frame, with the magneto mounted ahead of the down-tube. For the first year there was no front suspension but from 1906, Hathaway's cantilever forks, with a horizontal coil spring, were fitted at the front, combined with unsprung forks at the rear. There was a choice of direct drive or a three-speed hub-mounted gearbox, and final drive was by exposed

V belt on a separate rim. Auxiliary pedals were provided for starting.

It was essentially a civilian machine but nevertheless, many hundreds provided excellent military service, often equipped with leather panniers and a rear carrying rack.

In 1907, it was superseded by a 4hp machine with a 550cc engine. Triumph sold the German subsidiary to Adler in 1929 and it continued in business as Triumph-Adler. German-built Triumph motorcycles were used by the *Wehrmacht* during World War II.

Truimph 3hp

Type: Motorcycle, medium, solo
Manufacturer: Triumph Werke; Nürnberg
Production: 1905 to 1907
Engine: Triumph; single cylinder, 363cc; side valves; air cooled; power output, 3.5bhp at 1,500rpm
Transmission: Direct drive or 2F; hand gear-change
Suspension: Coil-sprung friction-damped cantilever front forks (1906 to 1907); solid rear end
Brakes: Caliper at front, block acting on pulley wheel at rear
Dimensions: Not available
Performance: Maximum speed – 73kph/45mph

Victoria KR-VI

The Victoria company was founded in 1886 as a manufacturer of bicycles, but by 1899 had started to produce motorcycles by fitting Zedel and Fafnir engines into its own frames. In 1920, the company started using engines designed by BMW's Max Fritz in what was described as the KR-I and by the mid-1920s, was producing 150,000 machines a year. By 1927, the KR-I had evolved into the KR-VI, a standard civilian machine using a new Fritz-designed power unit. The KR-VI was supplied to the *Reichswehr* in large numbers for both solo and sidecar work.

Built around a conventional tubular-steel frame, the KR-VI was fitted with the standard parallelogram friction-damped, coil-sprung girder forks of the period, combined with a rigid rear end. Power was provided by a 596cc flat-twin engine driving through a three-speed gearbox and open chain.

There were twin panniers at the rear, a high-level exhaust system and either a pillion seat or a rear carrying rack.

The KR-VI was also used as the basis of an experimental track-driven machine.

LEFT: **The Victoria KR-V was very American in appearance.**

Victoria KR-VI		
Type: Motorcycle, heavy, solo; and with sidecar		
Manufacturer: Victoria Werke; Nürnberg		
Production: 1927 to 1932		
Engine: Victoria; flat-twin; 596cc; overhead valves; air cooled; power output, 16bhp at 3,800rpm		
Transmission: 3F; hand gear-change		
Suspension: Friction-damped coil-sprung girder parallelogram front forks; unsprung rear		
Brakes: Drums, front and rear		
Dimensions: Length – 2,315mm/91in		
Width – 850mm/33in		
Height – 1,020mm/40in		
Wheelbase – 1,500mm/59in		
Weight – 170kg/374lb		
Performance: Maximum speed – 95kph/60mph		

ABOVE: **The compact 596cc engine. Note the gear change lever.**

Victoria KR-9

The Victoria KR-VI was replaced by the completely redesigned KR-6 in 1933 and this was joined by the KR-9, which featured an entirely new engine design, in 1936. Unusual for its completely enclosed engine and transmission, which contrived to give the compact machine a very modern aspect, the KR-9 was supplied to both the *Reichswehr* and the *Wehrmacht* in small numbers for both solo and sidecar work. A handful saw service into World War II.

The frame of the KR-9 was of hybrid tubular and pressed-steel construction. The engine enclosure panels also incorporated leg shields and running boards. The engine was a 596cc side-valve flat-twin, mounted along the centre line of the frame. The rear wheel was driven through a four-speed gearbox and enclosed chain. The parallelogram front forks were also of pressed-steel construction, featuring a friction-damped coil; the rear end was unsprung.

LEFT: **The Victoria KR-9 featured a fully enclosed engine and drive chain.**

Victoria KR-9		
Type: Motorcycle, heavy, solo; and with sidecar		
Manufacturer: Victoria Werke; Nürnberg		
Production: 1936 to 1937		
Engine: Victoria; flat-twin; 596cc; overhead inlet valves, side exhaust; air cooled; power output, 16bhp at 3,800rpm		
Transmission: 4F; hand gear-change		
Suspension: Friction-damped coil-sprung pressed-steel parallelogram front forks; unsprung rear		
Brakes: Drums, front and rear		
Dimensions: Length – 2,130mm/84in		
Width – 860mm/34in		
Height – 920mm/36in		
Wheelbase – 1,380mm/54in		
Weight – Not available		
Performance: Maximum speed – 100kph/62mph		

Victoria KR-35-WH

Victoria KR-35-WH

Type: Motorcycle, medium, solo; and with sidecar
Manufacturer: Victoria Werke; Nürnberg
Production: 1938 to 1945
Engine: Colombus; single cylinder; 342cc; overhead valves; air cooled; power output, 14bhp at 4,000rpm
Transmission: 4F; foot gear-change
Suspension: Friction-damped coil-sprung girder parallelogram front forks; unsprung rear
Brakes: Drums, front and rear
Dimensions (solo): Length – 2,160mm/85in
Width – 780mm/31in
Height – 1,000mm/39in
Wheelbase – 1,400mm/55in
Weight – 155kg/342lb
Performance: Maximum speed – 100kph/62mph

Appearing in 1938, initially as the civilian KR-35-SN and SS *Pionier* models, the Victoria KR-35-WH was a 350cc sports lightweight machine produced in a modified form to satisfy the *Wehrmacht* "medium" motorcycle category. Military modifications included a high-level exhaust system, fuel-tank mounted toolbox, a high-set

ABOVE: **A Victoria KR-35-WH displayed at the National Military History Center, Auburn, Indiana, USA.**

pillion seat and leather panniers or rear carrying rack.

The frame was a conventional tubular-steel design, with a single down-tube, and there were girder parallelogram friction-damped, coil-

sprung forks, combined with a rigid rear end. Power was provided by a Colombus 342cc single-cylinder engine, driving through a four-speed gearbox and open chain.

Although the KR-35-WH remained in production almost until the end of the war, in May 1945 the Victoria plant was almost completely destroyed.

Wanderer 3hp

The first Wanderer motorcycle was built in 1902, and by the time the model 3hp appeared in 1908, the company had already acquired a reputation for the quality of its products.

Wanderer motorcycles were generally of advanced design, boasting features such as unit construction engines and front and rear suspension. The 408cc engine of the 3hp machine was an unusual V-twin design, mounted in

the frame so that the rear cylinder was upright, the other being inclined forward at 45 degrees, but with horizontal cooling fins. Final drive was by flat belt, with no clutch, but there were auxiliary pedals to assist in starting.

The frame was a conventional tubular-steel single down-tube design, but with additional reinforcement beneath the engine. There were friction-damped trailing-link coil-sprung forks, combined with a double coil-sprung rear subframe.

A modified version remained in production

LEFT: **Wanderer supplied around half of the German Imperial Army's motorcycles in World War I.**

throughout World War I, and Wanderer supplied almost half of all machines used by the German forces during that conflict. By 1918, the company had completed more than 10,000 motorcycles. Production ceased in favour of motorcars in 1929, the motorcycle side of the business was sold to Jawa.

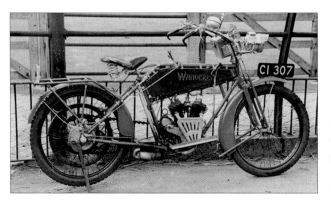

Wanderer 3hp

Type: Motorcycle, medium, solo
Manufacturer: Wanderer Werke, Winklhofer & Jäenicke; Schoneau, Chemnitz
Production: 1908 to 1913
Engine: Wanderer; two cylinders in V formation; 408cc; side valves; air cooled; power output, 3bhp at 2,000rpm
Transmission: Single gear, flat belt drive
Suspension: Friction-damped trailing-link coil-sprung forks, double coil-sprung rear subframe
Brakes: Drum, front; external contracting, rear
Dimensions: Not available
Weight – 67kg/148lb
Performance: Maximum speed – 100kph/62mph

Zündapp K800-W

Zündapp – the name was a contraction of Zünder & Apparatebau – was founded in 1917 as a munitions manufacturer, and started making motorcycles in Nürnberg in 1921. The first machines were little more than a copy of the British 211cc Levis two-stroke, powered by engines supplied from the UK. More Levis copies followed but, by 1926, the company had developed its own designs and, from the early 1930s started to specialize in heavy shaft-driven machines powered by a transverse horizontally opposed engine. Known as the "K Series", and designed

by Richard Küchen, the largest of the range was the K800-W, dating from 1934. Large numbers of K800-Ws – the "W" indicating that this was a military variant – soon entered into military service for both solo and sidecar work.

In common with all of the K Series, the K800-W was constructed around a heavy-duty pressed-steel external duplex frame, into which was mounted a horizontally opposed engine. In the K800-W, this was a huge 804cc four-cylinder side-valve unit with magneto ignition; power output was in the order of 20bhp and the heavy machine was capable of 110kph/68mph in solo form.

Final drive was via a hand-change integral four-speed gearbox, together with an exposed Carden shaft. Coil-sprung friction-damped pressed-steel parallelogram forks were used at the front, with an unsprung rear end. In military service, there was a hinged pillion seat, rear carrying rack, and leather panniers.

The formula was excellent, resulting in a series of reliable machines which were ideal for military and police service. Although production of the K800-W ended in 1938, the series continued through the war, with the overhead-valve KS600 also being reintroduced in 1951.

Zündapp K800-W

Type: Motorcycle, heavy, solo; and with sidecar
Manufacturer: Zündapp Werke; Nürnberg
Production: 1934 to 1938
Engine: Zündapp; four cylinder, horizontally opposed; 804cc; side valves; air cooled; power output, 20bhp at 4,000rpm
Transmission: 4F; hand gear-change
Suspension: Coil-sprung friction-damped pressed-steel parallelogram front forks; unsprung rear
Brakes: Drums, front and rear
Dimensions (solo): Length – 2,165mm/85in
Width – 815mm/32in
Height – 900mm/35in
Wheelbase – 1,405mm/55in
Weight – 215kg/474lb
Performance (solo): Maximum speed – 110kph/68mph

ABOVE: **Big, handsome and powerful, the Zündapp K800-W was a military version of a standard civilian machine and was supplied to the *Wehrmacht* between 1934 and 1938.**

LEFT: **Power was provided by a horizontally opposed side-valve engine driving the rear wheel through a four-speed gearbox and exposed drive shaft.**

Zündapp KS600-W

With the distinctive military sidecar, and 597cc horizontal twin engine, the big Zündapp KS600-W could be considered as the epitome of the German heavy motorcycle in World War II, and is believed by many to be the best such machine fielded by the *Wehrmacht* during the conflict. Introduced in 1937 to replace the same manufacturer's K500, the Zündapp featured heavily in the early German Blitzkrieg campaigns, remaining in production until it was replaced by the more powerful KS750 in 1941. Although it lacked the driven wheel to the sidecar typical of later German BMW and Zündapp heavy motorcycles, the relatively light weight of the machine, made it more than equal in performance to light all-wheel drive vehicles in many types of terrain even if, in common with much German equipment, it proved unequal to tackling the mud and snow of the Russian winter.

The KS600-W was a militarized version of the company's K600 civilian machine, which had been introduced in 1933, and featured the distinctive rigid pressed-steel perimeter frame typical of both the big Zündapp and BMW machines of the period. The flat footboards of the civilian model were replaced by foot pegs, and the machine was equipped with leather or steel panniers; a rear luggage rack was generally fitted. The machine was powered by a 597cc horizontally opposed twin-cylinder engine with overhead camshafts, producing 28bhp. The transmission to the rear wheel was via an exposed, universally jointed, Carden shaft (indicated by the "K", denoting *Kardanantrieb*, in the model designation); Zündapp had introduced this form of drive on the K600 in 1933. The driver had four speeds available, selected by either hand or foot control to suit the riding conditions, the hand control taking the form of a tank-mounted lever to the rider's right hand.

As usual, there was no suspension at the rear – the rider having to make do with the helically-sprung leather saddle – but the pressed-steel parallelogram front forks were both coil-sprung and friction damped.

LEFT AND BELOW:

The engine was a horizontally opposed 597cc twin-cylinder unit with overhead camshafts, capable of powering the heavy machine up to a top speed of 120kph/75mph in solo form.

Well built, clean-lined and purposeful in appearance, it was a fast, reliable and capable machine, offering a top speed of more than 120kph/75mph on the road in solo form, and was the ideal mode of transport for motorcycle-mounted *Kradschützen* troops. Some 18,000 examples were manufactured at Zündapp's Nürnberg factory between 1937 and 1941 and the machine was used by *Wehrmacht* and military police units, primarily with the Type 39 sidecar but occasionally in solo form. Early examples of the civilian KS600 model were also deployed by the German Army; this model was put back into production after the war, eventually to be replaced by the modified KS601 in 1951.

Zündapp KS600-W

Type: Motorcycle, heavy, solo; and with sidecar
Manufacturer: Zündapp Werke; Nürnberg
Production: 1937 to 1941
Engine: Zündapp; two cylinder, horizontally opposed; 597cc; overhead valves; air cooled; power output, 28bhp at 4,700rpm
Transmission: 4F; foot or hand gear-change
Suspension: Parallelogram front forks with single coil spring and friction damper; rigid rear end
Brakes: Front and rear
Dimensions (solo): Length – 2,150mm/85in
    Width – 820mm/32in
    Height – 900mm/35in
    Wheelbase – 1,390mm/55in
    Weight – 205kg/451lb
Performance: Maximum speed,
    solo – 120kph/75mph
    with sidecar – 100kph/62mph

ABOVE AND LEFT: **With the sidecar wheel driven, the Zündapp KS750 was a typically German heavy motorcycle – fast and powerful. It served with the _Wehrmacht_ from 1941 until the end of World War II.**

Zündapp KS750

Like the similar BMW R-75, the big Zündapp KS750 sidecar combination was the ultimate military motorcycle – a machine that could provide the German _Kradschützen_ motorcycle troops with a fast, highly mobile gun platform for attacking troops, a liaison and despatch machine that could deal with any terrain, and yet which was equally at home on the high-speed _Autobahns_. With its powerful engine, driven sidecar and towing capability, it was capable of travelling almost anywhere.

The KS750 was the largest motorcycle manufactured by Zündapp during World War II. Constructed around a pressed-steel external frame, it was powered by a horizontally opposed (although actually the pistons were at 170°) twin-cylinder overhead-valve engine of 750cc driving the two rear wheels through a four-speed gearbox, which also incorporated a crawler gear and reverse. Final drive was by exposed shaft, with a cross-shaft providing drive to the sidecar wheel; there was also a manual differential lock. Coil-sprung girder parallelogram forks were used at the front, whilst the rear end was unsprung. Brakes were provided on all three wheels, those on the driving wheels having hydraulic operation.

A rear rack was fitted, and there was also a hinged pillion seat and leather or metal panniers and, like the BMW R-75, the big Zündapp was used in conjunction with a military sidecar. A spare wheel was carried on the rear, and there was also provision for mounting a machine-gun at the front. A towing pintle could be fitted at the rear to allow the outfit to be coupled to a light gun or trailer.

Although it was slightly heavier, the Zündapp was probably the better of the two outfits, and when production came to an end in 1944, the Nürnberg factory had produced 18,635 examples.

Zündapp resumed civilian motorcycle manufacture in 1947 with a 200cc two-stroke. The KS600 was put back into production until it was replaced with an overhead-valve design in 1951. The company went into liquidation at the end of 1985 and was eventually sold to China.

LEFT: **The sidecar was a standard military pattern 286/1 and was often fitted with a machine gun on a pintle mount.**

Zündapp KS750	

Type: Motorcycle, heavy, with sidecar
Manufacturer: Zündapp Werke; Nürnberg
Production: 1941 to 1944
Engine: Zündapp; two cylinder, horizontally opposed (170°); 751cc; overhead valves; air cooled; power output, 26bhp at 4,000rpm
Transmission: 4F1R +1 low ratio; foot gear-change
Suspension: Coil-sprung girder parallelogram front forks; unsprung rear
Brakes: Drums, all three wheels; hydraulic operation on driven wheels
Dimensions: Length – 2,385mm/94in
    Width – 1,650mm/65in
    Height – 1,000mm/39in
    Wheelbase – 1,410mm/56in
    Weight – 420kg/925lb
Performance: Maximum speed – 92kph/57mph

EMW R-35

Originally badged as BMW, EMW cars and motorcycles were produced in the former BMW Dixi plant at Eisenach from 1945, in what became East Germany. At the time, BMW was forbidden from manufacturing motorcycles. When BMW production resumed in 1948, EMW was eventually forced to change its name as a result of a lawsuit from the West German company. EMW's only motorcycle was the R-35, a single-cylinder medium-weight machine based closely on the 1937 BMW of the same name, although it is said that frames and perhaps engines were also produced by EMW to provide the basis of the Soviet-built Ural machine. Despite being obsolete even before its

ABOVE: **The EMW R-35 was used by the East German Army. Some were available to civilians and even for export.**

release, the EMW R-35 was used by the East German military.

The R-35 was constructed on a pressed-steel frame with hydraulically-damped front forks and plunger-type suspension at the rear. The engine was a 340cc four-stroke unit driving the rear

EMW R-35

Type: Motorcycle, medium, solo
Manufacturer: VEB Eisenacher Motoren Werke; Eisenach
Production: 1946 to 1956
Engine: EMW; single cylinder; 340cc; overhead valves; air cooled; power output, 14bhp at 4,200rpm
Transmission: 4F; foot gear-change
Suspension: Telescopic hydraulically-damped front forks; plunger suspension at rear
Brakes: Drums, front and rear
Dimensions (solo): Length – 2,150mm/85in
　　Width – 725mm/29in
　　Height – 960mm/38in
　　Wheelbase – 1,400mm/55in
　　Weight – 170kg/375lb
Performance: Maximum speed – 95kph/60mph

wheel via a four-speed gearbox and exposed shaft. A pillion seat or luggage-carrying rack was generally fitted.

MZ ES250

The East German MZ company was a successor to the motorcycle arm of the state-owned IFA conglomerate, and inheritor of the motorcycle legacy – and the Zschopau factory – of DKW. The company's early products were developed from the DKW RT-125, a small two-stroke machine that, in the years immediately following the end of the war, had also been copied by both Harley-Davidson and BSA as part of war reparations. MZ was created in 1956, and the company's first product was the ES250, which was quickly adopted by the East German military. The company

enjoyed considerable racing success and had taken the lessons learned and applied these to the road machines.

Typical of all of MZ's products, the ES250 was a lightweight two-stroke machine of decidedly curious appearance, with a rubber-mounted engine driving via a four-speed gearbox and enclosed chain. The frame was of composite tubular and pressed-steel construction, featuring long-travel hydraulically-damped front and rear forks, the latter adjustable for load.

The first incarnation was the ES250/1; this was replaced by the improved and

MZ ES250/1, 250/2, 250/2A

Type: Motorcycle, light, solo; and with sidecar
Manufacturer: VEB Motorradwerk Zschopau (MZ); Zschopau
Production: 1956 to 1976
Engine: MZ; single cylinder; 243cc; two stroke; air cooled; power output, 17.5bhp at 5,300rpm
Transmission: 4F; foot gear-change
Suspension: Leading-link hydraulically-damped front forks; hydraulically-damped trailing arm at rear
Brakes: Drums, front and rear
Dimensions (solo): Length – 2,090mm/82in
　　Width – 862mm/34in
　　Height – 1,060mm/42in
　　Wheelbase – 1,325mm/52in
　　Weight – 156kg/343lb
Performance: Maximum speed – 120kph/75mph

restyled ES250/2 and ES/250/2A in 1967. In military guise, the machine was fitted with either a luggage rack or a separate pillion seat and a single pannier bag; a fully sprung sidecar was also available.

The ES250 was also supplied to other Eastern Bloc nations, notably to the Polish police force and remained in production well into the 1970s. MZ got into financial difficulties in 1991 with production eventually being transferred to Turkey and the company name was changed to MüZ (Motorrad über Zschopau).

LEFT: **Typical of Eastern Bloc products in the decades following the end of World War II. The East German-built MZ ES250 was a two-stroke machine, featuring rather extreme styling. Although originally intended for civilian usage, it was adopted by the military.**

Royal Enfield Bullet

The 350cc Royal Enfield Bullet was introduced in the UK in 1948 for off-road competition use, with a road model appearing the following year. The Bullet was the first UK motorcycle to use swing-arm rear suspension on a trials machine and, perhaps due to its handling, was quickly snapped up by the Indian Army and police

ABOVE: **Now into its sixth decade, the classic British lines of the Royal Enfield Bullet still have a timeless appeal.** BELOW LEFT: **A member of the Indian Army's motorcycle display team.**

authorities as the standard motorcycle for border patrol service, where it seemed to suit the difficult terrain on borders between India and its neighbours. From 1949, thousands were supplied to the Indian government through the Madras Motor Company.

In 1955, the Indian government declared that it would only continue to do business with Madras Motors if the Bullet was produced in India and a partnership deal was drawn up between the UK Royal Enfield Company and the Madras Motor Company which led to the opening of a factory devoted to building the Bullet in Chennai (formerly Madras). The earliest machines were actually sent out from the Redditch factory in knocked-down kit form to be assembled in India but, in 1957, tooling equipment was sold to Enfield India Limited thus allowing the manufacture of components. First the frames were produced and then the engines, and it was not long before the company was in a position to produce the Bullet, without any input from the UK.

At this point the design was effectively "frozen" and, despite the discontinuation of the Bullet in the UK during 1962/63 and the collapse of the "parent" Royal Enfield company in 1970, the Indian factory continues to produce what is effectively a 1955 "British" motorcycle.

The original 348cc machine was joined by a 499cc version in 1953, sharing many components and, similarly, the Indian manufactured Bullet is currently available in the same engine sizes. The model we are interested in here being described as the "military" or, in civilian form as the "Classic". Despite a claimed 100 improvements, the Bullet remains close to the original 1955 specification.

The engine is a free-revving overhead-valve single, constructed in the old-fashioned way with a separate engine and transmission case; elements of the design actually date back to the pre-war Model G. Final drive is by exposed roller chain via a four-speed gearbox. The spoked wheels are of traditional laced design and there are drum brakes at both front and rear. Eschewing modern electronics, the Bullet continues to have battery and coil ignition, and breaker points, albeit now rated at 12V rather than the original 6V. Until recently, there was no electric starter although the lighting equipment has been updated. The frame is a good substantial cruciform tubular design and the engine is solidly mounted. Despite its obviously dated origins, the Bullet is a handsome machine offering a safe and comfortable but "vintage" ride.

The Indian plant has supplied more than 100,000 machines to the Indian Army and a further 25,000 to the police. The Bullet was finally reintroduced to the UK in 1984, with marketing undertaken by Watsonian; the motorcycles were originally identified under the marque name "Enfield" for legal reasons. In 1993/94, the factory was taken over by Eicher Motors Limited during a merger with the Enfield India Company and the rights to the Royal Enfield name were acquired in 1995.

ABOVE: The Bullet remains in service with the Indian Army, with more than 100,000 examples purchased since 1948. LEFT: The machine has also served with the Indian Air Force.

Royal Enfield Bullet

Type: Motorcycle, medium, solo
Manufacturer: Enfield Cycle Co; Redditch
Production: 1949 (1955) to date
Engine: Royal Enfield; single cylinder; 346cc or 499cc; overhead valves; air cooled; power output, 18bhp at 5,650rpm
Transmission: 4F (5F optional on late model machines); foot gear-change
Suspension: Telescopic front forks with hydraulic damping; swing arm at rear with adjustable shock absorbers
Brakes: Drums, front and rear
Dimensions: Length – 2,120mm/84in
Width – 750mm/30in
Height – 1,080mm/43in
Wheelbase – 1,370mm/54in
Weight – 163 to 165kg/359 to 364lb
Performance: Maximum speed – 121kph/75mph

Bianchi 500M

The Bianchi company was founded in 1897 by Edoardo Bianchi initially to build bicycles, but within a decade or so the company had progressed from selling motorized pedal cycles to producing "proper" motorcycles. Never among the largest supplier of military machines to the Italian Army, nevertheless the company's standard civilian 500cc machine of 1936 was modified for military service and

remained in use throughout World War II and into the post-war era.

Typical of medium-weight machines of the period, the 500M was powered by a 498cc single-cylinder side-valve engine fitted into a standard cycle type tubular frame with a single down-tube. At the front, there were girder parallelogram forks with a friction-damped coil spring, and surprisingly, at a time when many contemporary machines still had a rigid

rear end, the 500M featured plunger-type rear suspension using an enclosed coil spring. The transmission consisted of a three-speed hand-change gearbox, with final drive to the rear wheel by open chain. A carrying rack was fitted at the rear, and side panniers and a pillion seat were frequently fitted.

The machine remained in production for some five years and gave sterling service as a despatch rider's mount and general-purpose liaison machine in North Africa during the early years of the war.

ABOVE: **The Bianchi 500M was introduced in 1936 and remained in production until 1941, serving with the Italian Army throughout World War II. Like most Bianchis of the period, it featured full suspension, using coil springs at the front and enclosed plunger units at the rear.**
LEFT: **The 500M was powered by a 498cc single-cylinder engine driving through a three-speed transmission.**

Bianchi 500M

Type: Motorcycle, medium, solo
Manufacturer: Edoardo Bianchi Moto Meccanica; Milano
Production: 1936 to 1941
Engine: Bianchi 500; single cylinder; 498cc; side valves; air cooled; power output, 9bhp at 4,000rpm
Transmission: 3F; hand gear-change
Suspension: Coil-sprung friction-damped girder parallelogram front forks; coil-sprung plunger suspension at rear
Brakes: Drums, front and rear
Dimensions: Length – 2,120mm/84in
  Width – 750mm/30in
  Height – 960mm/38in
  Wheelbase – 1,380mm/54in
  Weight – 170kg/375lb
Performance: Maximum speed – 75kph/46mph

Bianchi MT61

ating from 1961, the MT61 was a specialized military tactical motorcycle – "MT" (*Motociclo Tattico*) – produced by the Bianchi factory for despatch and liaison duties with the Italian Army. It was a handsome and compact machine, and included features such as long-travel front suspension, waterproofed exhaust and air inlet, and high ground clearance, and was clearly designed for maximum performance across all types of terrain.

The engine was a 318cc Bianchi single-cylinder overhead-valve unit with coil ignition, driving through a unit-constructed five-speed foot-change gearbox, with final drive by open chain.

BELOW: **The exhaust pipe was turned up to allow transit through water obstacles.**

The frame was an unusual tubular-steel duplex design with a single down-tube; the top-tube was upswept behind the seat to form a long horizontal extension to which the rear suspension units were attached. At the front, there were hydraulically-damped coil-sprung telescopic forks, while at the rear there was a trailing arm, also suspended on hydraulically-damped coil springs.

The carburettor was fitted with a waterproof air filter and the exhaust was turned upwards at the rear to allow deep-water fording. The high-clearance mudguard at the front suggest that Bianchi envisaged the MT61 being used seriously off-road. Also there were crash bars and leg shields to protect the rider. In typical Italian tradition, the pillion passenger

ABOVE LEFT, ABOVE AND BELOW: **Despite its modest-sized engine, the Bianchi MT61 was suitable for both solo and sidecar use, and almost 2,000 examples were supplied to the Italian Army.**

was presented with a grab handle. A small rear stowage compartment was provided, together with rear panniers. It was also used in conjunction with a standard military sidecar. Motorcycle production ended in 1967. The company continues to produce pedal cycles.

Bianchi MT61

Type: Motorcycle, medium, solo; and with sidecar
Manufacturer: Edoardo Bianchi Moto Meccanica; Milano
Production: 1961 to 1967
Engine: Bianchi; single cylinder; 318cc; overhead valves; air cooled; power output, 10.5bhp at 5,000rpm
Transmission: 5F; foot gear-change
Suspension: Hydraulically-damped coil-sprung telescopic front forks; hydraulically-damped suspension at rear
Brakes: Drums, front and rear
Dimensions: Length – 2,030mm/80in
　　　　　Width – 750mm/30in
　　　　　Height – 1,050mm/41in
　　　　　Wheelbase – 1,330mm/52in
　　　　　Weight – 170kg/375lb
Performance: Maximum speed – 88kph/55mph

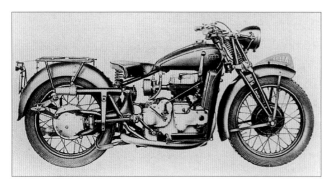

Gilera VL *Marte*

Although the business was founded in 1909, it was not until 1920 that Guiseppe Gilera started construction of motorcycles in Arcore. Early machines were powered by side-valve engines up to 500cc, with which the company achieved some racing success. The first military contracts were received in the 1930s when the company's *Marte* (Mars) model was modified for military service as the LTE. From 1941, the VL *Marte* was widely used by the Italian Army both as a solo despatch machine and, from the following year, as a purpose-designed military sidecar outfit, with a driven sidecar wheel. Broadly based on the 1936 LTE, the VL *Marte* differed mainly in having a unit-construction gearbox, sprung rear forks, and shaft drive.

The frame was a conventional tubular-steel cycle design with a single down-tube and, unusually for the period, was fully sprung. Girder parallelogram forks were fitted at the front using friction-damped coil springs, while at the rear there were friction-damped coil-sprung forks. Where the machine was used as a combination outfit, a similar form of suspension was used for the sidecar chassis; a folding stabilizing bar was fitted between the rear wheel of the motorcycle and the sidecar wheel which made the whole rear end act as a subframe. The sidecar was fitted on the right, using five attachment points.

Although Gilera had pioneered overhead valves in the *Saturno* (Saturn) of 1938, the Italian Army pressed for the reliability of side valves and the engine of the VL *Marte* was a 498cc single-cylinder side-valve unit, with magneto ignition. Power was transmitted through a four-speed gearbox and exposed Carden shaft. Sidecar drive could be disengaged when not required. The

standard single-seat sidecar had cut-away sides for ease of entry and was equipped with a machine-gun mount; a spare wheel was carried at the rear. Other military fittings included a rear luggage rack or pillion seat.

Total production may have amounted to 2,500 solo machines, and 8,500 sidecar outfits. The company continues to produce Piaggio scooters but production of full-size Gilera motorcycles ended in 1993.

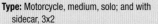

Gilera VL *Marte*

Type: Motorcycle, medium, solo; and with sidecar, 3x2

Manufacturer: Moto Gilera; Arcore

Production: 1941 to 1946

Engine: Gilera; single cylinder, 498cc; side valves; air cooled; power output, 14bhp at 4,800rpm

Transmission: 4F; foot or hand gear-change

Suspension: Girder parallelogram friction-damped coil-sprung front forks; friction-damped coil-sprung forks at rear, and for sidecar chassis (where fitted)

Brakes: Drums, front and rear, including sidecar wheel

Dimensions (with sidecar): Length – 2,300mm/91in
Width – 1,600mm/63in
Height – 1,020mm/40in
Wheelbase – 1,430mm/56in
Weight – 300kg/660lb

Performance: Maximum speed – 90kph/55mph

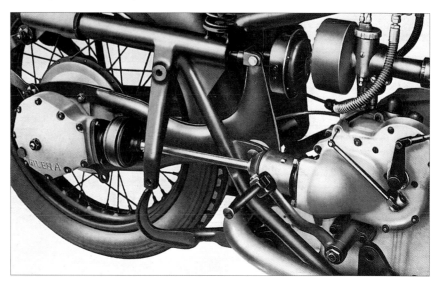

Moto-Guzzi GT17

Type: Motorcycle, medium, solo; and with sidecar
Manufacturer: Moto-Guzzi; Mandello del Lario
Production: 1932 to 1939
Engine: Moto-Guzzi; single cylinder; 499cc; overhead exhaust valve side inlet; air cooled; power output, 13.25bhp at 4,000rpm
Transmission: 3F; hand gear-change
Suspension: Coil-sprung friction-damped girder parallelogram front forks; coil-sprung, friction-damped trailing sub-frame at rear, adjustable for pre-load
Brakes: Drums, front and rear
Dimensions (solo): Length – 2,235mm/88in
  Width – 920mm/36in
  Height – 1,090mm/43in
  Wheelbase – 1520mm/60in
  Weight (solo) – 196kg/432lb
Performance: Maximum speed – 100kph/62mph

Moto-Guzzi GT17

Carlo Guzzi and Giorgio Parodi created the first Moto-Guzzi motorcycle in 1921, using a horizontal single-cylinder engine with a unit-constructed gearbox and exposed flywheel, installed in a low-slung frame. This theme continued until the 1960s. The first military orders came in 1928 for a modified GT model, which eventually provided the basis for the purpose-built military GT17 of 1932.

It was an unusual machine, not only for having rear suspension at a time when most motorcycles still had decidedly solid rear ends, but for the fact that the suspension could be adjusted for pre-load to suit either solo or pillion use.

The duplex frame was typical of Moto-Guzzi practice, consisting of a shallow triangle constructed from tubes and pressed-steel sections, the latter providing an engine mount and footboards for the rider. The girder parallelogram front forks were coil-sprung and friction-damped, and there was a trailing load adjustable sub-frame at the rear, with friction-damped coil springs.

A 499cc single-cylinder engine, with magneto-ignition, was mounted low down in the frame, with the horizontal cylinder facing to the front. The engine was coupled to a unit-constructed three-speed gearbox in which the gearbox ratios were closer-spaced than on the comparable civilian machine.

The machine was used in both solo and sidecar form by police, reconnaissance and despatch riders. Special military fittings included side panniers, a machine-gun mount, which also often included an armoured windshield, a rear luggage rack or hinged pillion saddle (*bi-posto*), the latter complete with its own handlebars. Special military sidecars were also available. More than 4,800 examples were completed between 1932 and 1939.

ABOVE LEFT: **Featuring Moto-Guzzi's trademark exposed flywheel, the GT17 was a modified version of a civilian machine used by the Italian Army in both solo and sidecar form.** LEFT: **The GT17 was unusual for the period in featuring a load-adjustable swinging subframe at the rear suspended on coil springs.**

Moto-Guzzi *Superalce*

Introduced in 1946, and also known by the name *Alce V*, the Moto-Guzzi *Superalce* (Super Moose) was a purpose-built 499cc military motorcycle which had been developed from the wartime *Alce* (Moose). While it remained very recognizable as a Moto-Guzzi, with its exposed flywheel, unusual rear suspension and single-cylinder horizontal engine, the major change was that the engine was now fitted with conventional overhead valves which gave a useful 5bhp increase in power. Like its predecessors, it was also suitable for both solo and combination use.

ABOVE AND LEFT: **Dating from 1946, the Moto-Guzzi *Superalce*, or *Alce V*, was a purpose-built military motorcycle derived from the wartime *Alce*. It retained the classic Moto-Guzzi layout but, for the first time, incorporated overhead valves. Some 3,500 examples were constructed over a 12-year period and it was never made available to civilians.**

ABOVE AND BELOW: **The engine was a 499cc single-cylinder horizontal type, installed low down in the hybrid tubular and pressed-steel frame; the exposed flywheel was a typical Moto-Guzzi feature. By the time it went out of production in 1957, this machine must have looked decidedly old fashioned.**

The duplex frame was a hybrid tubular/pressed steel design, with pressings for the engine mount and footboards, and for saddle support. Like its predecessors, it was fitted with friction-damped coil-sprung girder parallelogram front forks, which were now beginning to look a little archaic, together with the Moto-Guzzi coil-sprung trailing rear subframe.

A single cylinder 499cc engine was installed low down in the frame, with its horizontal cylinder facing forwards. The transmission was integral with the engine castings and offered four forward speeds with gear selection now by foot pedal. The final drive was still by open chain.

Standard military fittings included a pillion seat with folding handgrip, a rear luggage frame and side pannier bags. Special military sidecars were also available. The *Superalce* provided the standard Italian Army heavy motorcycle during the post-war years and remained in production until 1957.

Moto-Guzzi *Superalce*

Type: Motorcycle, heavy, solo; and with sidecar
Manufacturer: Moto-Guzzi; Mandello del Lario
Production: 1946 to 1957
Engine: Moto-Guzzi; single cylinder; 499cc; overhead valves; air cooled; power output, 18.5bhp at 4,300rpm
Transmission: 4F; foot gear-change
Suspension: Coil-sprung friction-damped girder parallelogram front forks; coil-sprung, friction-damped trailing sub-frame at rear
Brakes: Drums, front and rear
Dimensions (solo): Length – 2,220mm/87in
    Width – 790mm/31in
    Height – 1065mm/42in
    Wheelbase – 1,455mm/57in
    Weight (solo) – 195kg/429lb
Performance: Maximum speed – 110kph/68mph

Moto-Guzzi *Alce*

The Moto-Guzzi *Alce* (Moose) was a purpose-built 499cc military motorcycle suitable for both solo and sidecar combination use. It was introduced in 1939 to replace the GT17, and remained in production throughout the war years. In typical Moto-Guzzi style, it retained the rear suspension set-up, together with the exposed flywheel and large single-cylinder horizontal engine seen in its predecessor but within a wheelbase which was reduced by 50mm/ 2in, and with improved ground clearance. The tubular sections of the frame were also designed to provide a reservoir for the engine oil, a feature which become far more popular in post-war years.

Like the GT17, the duplex frame was a hybrid tubular/pressed-steel design, with the steel pressings forming the engine mount and footboards, as well as replacing the traditional tubular seat post. Again, following the pattern established with the GT17, this allowed for an unusual geometry to the sprung rear forks, which consisted of a sub-frame suspended on friction-damped coil springs, the latter positioned under the engine. At the front, there were girder parallelogram forks with a single friction-damped coil spring. Power was provided by essentially the

same 499cc single-cylinder engine as had been fitted to the GT17, with an overhead exhaust valve combined with side inlet, and magneto ignition. The engine was installed with the horizontal cylinder facing to the front, low down in the frame. The transmission was a unit-constructed four-speed unit with hand gear-change, and final drive was by open chain.

Special military sidecars were also available. The basic single-seat personnel sidecar was little different from civilian designs of the period. The body was carried on a tubular chassis with leaf-spring suspension, and the sidecar was fitted with a deep curved windscreen, and carried a spare wheel at the rear. Experiments were conducted into providing a sidecar with a driven wheel but there was no series production.

The *Alce* became the standard heavy motorcycle of the Italian Army and was used in both solo and sidecar form by military police units, and by reconnaissance and despatch riders; side-mounted skis could also be fitted for Alpine patrol units. Military fittings included side panniers, a machine-gun mount, rear luggage rack, and pillion saddle (*biposto*), the latter complete with its own folding handlebars.

ABOVE: **The Moto-Guzzi *Alce* (Moose) was produced between 1939 and 1945, with some 4,500 examples supplied to the Italian Army during that period. Replacing the earlier GT17, it retained most of the features of its predecessor including the unusual frame and suspension layout and the horizontal single-cylinder engine. The machine was suitable for both solo and sidecar use.**

More than 7,000 examples had been constructed by the time production ended in 1945; 6,390 were solo machines, 669 were fitted with a sidecar. In 1946, it was replaced by the improved *Superalce* (Super Moose).

Moto-Guzzi *Alce*

Type: Motorcycle, heavy, solo; and with sidecar
Manufacturer: Moto-Guzzi; Mandello del Lario
Production: 1939 to 1945
Engine: Moto-Guzzi; single cylinder; 499cc; overhead exhaust valve, side inlet; air cooled; power output, 13.25bhp at 4,000rpm
Transmission: 4F; hand gear-change
Suspension: Coil-sprung friction-damped girder parallelogram front forks; coil-sprung, friction-damped trailing sub-frame at rear
Brakes: Drums, front and rear
Dimensions: Length – 2,220mm/87in
  Width – 790mm/31in
  Height – 1,065mm/42in
  Wheelbase – 1,450mm/57in
  Weight – 196kg/432lb
Performance: Maximum speed – 95kph/60mph

Moto-Guzzi *Mulo Meccanico*

During the pre-war years and into World War II, the Italian Army had made widespread use of commercial motor tricycles, finding them useful in the narrow Alpine passes. Typically consisting of the front end of motorcycle attached to a two-wheeled rear sub-frame on which was mounted a cargo box. In 1959, Moto-Guzzi started the design work for a purpose-built military load-carrying tricycle which was described as the *Mulo Meccanico* (Mechanical Mule).

Although the rider was presented with a steering wheel, which turned the front wheel through a reduction gearbox, the *Mulo Meccanico* was clearly derived from motorcycle practice. The vehicle was built around a tubular-steel duplex frame and was powered by a 754cc V-twin fan-cooled engine installed transversely beneath the saddle. The front suspension consisted of coil springs, while the rear axle, on which the track was adjustable on the move between 1,300mm/51in and 850mm/33in, was carried on rubber-sprung trailing arms.

All three wheels were driven, through a six-speed plus reverse gearbox, and there was a torque-dividing locking differential at the centre which split the power between the front and rear wheels (80 per cent to the rear, 20 per cent to the front), as well as a locking differential on the cross shaft and bevels which took the power to the separate rear wheels. The front wheel was shaft driven through a bevel box at the steering head. Demountable tracks were available for the rear wheels, which were tensioned by drop-down idler wheels. There was a single seat up-front, mounted ahead of a superstructure which housed the battery, fuel tank, spare wheel, etc, as well as providing a rudimentary roll-over bar. At the rear, there was a small load platform with a capacity of 500kg/1100lb, which also included simple mudguards.

Some 500 examples were completed between 1961 and 1962.

ABOVE: The *Mulo Meccanico* is a hybrid vehicle which, although drawing mainly from motorcycle practice, also has some of the characteristics of the motorcar. All three wheels are driven, through locking differentials, and tracks could be fitted to improve traction at the rear. The distance between the rear wheels can be adjusted by the rider while on the move.

LEFT: With the rear tracks in place, the machine offers excellent climbing ability.

Moto-Guzzi *Mulo Meccanico*

Type: Motor tricycle, 3x3
Manufacturer: Moto-Guzzi; Mandello del Lario
Production: 1961 to 1963
Engine: Moto-Guzzi; twin cylinders in V formation; 754cc; overhead valves; air cooled; power output, 20bhp at 5,500rpm
Transmission: 6F1R; hand gear-change
Suspension: Coil-sprung friction-damped front forks; trailing arms at rear with rubber suspension
Brakes: Drums, front and rear
Dimensions: Length – 3,000mm/117in (maximum)
  Width – 1,570mm/62in
  Height – 1,420mm/56in
  Wheelbase – 2,030mm/80in
  Weight – 1,000kg/2,200lb
Performance: Maximum speed – 50kph/30mph

Moto-Guzzi 850-T3

In 1973, the Italian De Tomaso group purchased Moto-Guzzi, the Benelli motorcycle company and the Maserati car company. In the same year, Moto-Guzzi launched the 850-T3, a standard high-performance civilian touring machine that had been modified for military use. With its Lino Tonti-designed V-twin engine, the 850-T3 was capable of more than 195kph/120mph, and typical uses for these powerful road machines included convoy escort and military police work.

Built around a duplex cradle tubular frame, the machine was fitted with sealed hydraulically-damped telescopic front forks with suspension by coil spring; on late models, the front fork was a patented design, where the damping oil was contained in a sealed cartridge rather than in the fork tube itself. At the rear there was a load-adjustable trailing arm suspended on hydraulically-damped coil springs. The 850-T3 also employed a linked braking system where applying the back brake would also apply the left front pad.

Power was provided by a Moto-Guzzi 499cc 90 degree V4, installed across the frame, the engine featuring coil ignition and electric start. There was a foot-change five-speed transmission and enclosed final drive-shaft and, in 1975, the range was extended to include a model with automatic transmission.

Military equipment included a rear luggage rack which could accept a radio or pillion seat, windscreen, crash bars and leg shields, and metal or plastic panniers; sirens and police lights could also be specified.

The V1000 Convert, dating from 1975, shared many of the features of the 850-T3 and was also considered suitable for military and police service, although it was not procured for the Italian Army.

LEFT: **A Moto-Guzzi 850-T3 fully equipped for use by the Italian police forces.**

Moto-Guzzi 850-T3

Type: Motorcycle, medium, solo; and with sidecar
Manufacturer: Moto-Guzzi; Mandello del Lario
Production: 1973 to 2004
Engine: Moto-Guzzi; single cylinder; 499cc; overhead valves; air cooled; power output, 18.5bhp at 4,300rpm
Transmission: 5F; foot gear-change
Suspension: Hydraulically-damped telescopic front forks; hydraulically-damped coil-sprung trailing arm at rear
Brakes: Discs or drums, front and rear
Dimensions (solo): Length – 2,220mm/87in
  Width – 790mm/31in
  Height – 1,065mm/42in
  Wheelbase – 1,455mm/57in
  Weight – 195kg/429lb
Performance: Maximum speed – 195kph/120mph

Volugrafo Aeromoto

The Torino-based company Volugrafo was the first manufacturer of the modern motor scooter. Designed by Claudio Belmondo, the first Aeromotos were offered for sale on the civilian market in 1940, with a special military version intended for airborne use appearing two years later. Small, compact and light in weight, it was supposedly suitable for air-dropping in a special container alongside parachute troops, where it could provide immediate mobility after landing.

Rather like the American Cushman 53, the civilian Aeromoto resembled a child's scooter. The tubular-steel step-through duplex frame was of minimal construction, with a large triangulated brace at the front to carry the steering head, and with a continuation of the frame tubes forming the rear forks; two small platforms were provided for the rider's feet. There was no saddle, which forced the rider to stand. The 123cc two-stroke engine and two-speed gearbox were installed ahead of the rear wheel, with final drive by means of an exposed chain. There was no suspension fitted at front or rear.

The military version was even smaller and, with a rectangular duplex frame and tiny wheelbase, was more akin to a modern monkey bike. A rudimentary seat was provided on top of the fuel tank, and the engine was installed in a more "normal" position. The handlebars were designed to fold down to reduce the overall height. The front forks were of pressed-steel construction while the rear wheel was supported between the rear frame members. Twin wheels were fitted, front and rear, to help carry the load of a fully kitted airborne soldier. As with the civilian version, there was no suspension. A number were requisitioned by the *Wehrmacht*.

Sadly it was poorly designed and unstable and total production amounted to less than 2,000 units before Allied bombing put the factory out of commission. Civilian production may have resumed after the war but the company also went on to produce bubble cars using the unlikely name of "Bimbo".

TOP: **The military Aeromoto was derived from a small civilian motor scooter.** ABOVE AND LEFT: **Possibly the smallest military motorcycle produced, the folding Aeromoto was intended for airborne operations, with some 2,000 units produced between 1942 and 1944.**

Volugrafo Aeromoto

Type: Motor scooter, light, airborne
Manufacturer: Societa Volugrafo; Torino
Production: 1942 to 1944
Engine: Sachs; single cylinder; 123cc; two-stroke; air cooled; power output, 2bhp at 3,600rpm
Transmission: 2F; hand gear-change
Suspension: None
Brakes: Drums, front and rear
Dimensions: Length – 625mm/25in
    Width – 610mm/24in, reducing to 305mm/12in
    Height – 880mm/35in, reducing to 530mm/21in
    Wheelbase – 715mm/28in
    Weight – 53kg/114lb
Performance: Maximum speed – 50kph/30mph

Honda CB400T Hawk

LEFT: **A civilian specification CB400T Hawk. A modified version was available to the military.**

Honda may not have started making motorcycles until 1948 but, within two decades, the company was on its way to becoming the largest motorcycle manufacturer in the world. Imported Japanese machines all but wiped out the European, British and American domestic manufacturers during the 1960s and 1970s. The fact that this Japanese invasion had little effect on the military motorcycle scene, was simply because the Western armies had stopped buying motorcycles in large numbers. Nevertheless, the Honda CB400T, launched in 1978, was one of those machines that did manage to make its presence felt in uniform. It was a good all-round street machine with a reasonable turn of speed, and a modified version of the standard civilian model was purchased by both the armies of Denmark and South Africa.

The CB400T, sometimes known as the Hawk, was powered by a 395cc parallel-twin engine, with solid-state electronic ignition and electric start. Power to the rear wheel was by a five-speed – later six-speed – foot-change gearbox, with final drive by exposed chain. The engine was installed in a duplex cradle frame constructed from steel tubes, with hydraulically-damped telescopic forks fitted at the front, in combination with a load-adjustable coil-sprung trailing arm at the rear.

Honda ST1100 Pan European

Introduced in 1989 for the 1990 model year, the Honda ST1100 Pan European was a civilian touring machine designed to bridge the gap between the large Gold Wings and the smaller VFR models. It was fast and refined, and was adopted by the British Army for military police and convoy escort work, replacing the Norton Interpol 2.

The machine was powered by a 16-valve water-cooled V4 engine, with electronic ignition and electric start, producing 100bhp. Power was transmitted to the rear wheel through a five-speed foot-change transmission, with final drive by enclosed shaft fitted with integrated dampers. The front forks were air-assisted telescopic with Honda's Torque-Reactive Anti-dive Control (TRAC), and at the rear was a single-sided conventional swing-arm damper, adjustable for pre-load and bounce; the wheels were hollow-section three-spoke aluminium. From 1991, both automatic traction control and electronic ABS systems were fitted.

The engine was installed longitudinally, low down in a square-section external steel frame. Side guards were fitted and there was a full-width plastic fairing and windscreen. Side panniers were fitted at the rear.

LEFT: **One particular feature which made the ST1100 very suitable for military convoy work was the massive 28-litre/6-gallon fuel tank.**

**Honda ST1300P
Pan European**

Type: Motorcycle, heavy, solo
Manufacturer: Honda Motor Company;
 Shibuya Ku, Tokyo
Production: 2003 to date
Engine: Honda; four cylinders in V formation;
 1,216cc; overhead valves, four per cylinder;
 water cooled; power output, 117bhp
 at 7,500rpm
Transmission: 5F; foot gear-change; fitted
 with automatic traction control
Suspension: Air-assisted telescopic front forks;
 single-sided swing-arm damper at rear
Brakes: Discs, front and rear;
 with automatic ABS
Dimensions: Length – 2,282mm/90in
 Width – 935mm/37in
 Height – 1,332mm/52in
 Wheelbase – 1,491mm/59in
 Weight – 288kg/635lb
Performance: Maximum speed (restricted) –
 209kph/130mph

Honda ST1300P Pan European

The rate of technological change in Japanese motorcycle design is well demonstrated by the changes made to Honda's Pan European model when the ST1100 was replaced by the ST1300 in 2002 for the 2003 model year. A special single-seat military/police version was designated ST1300P. The capacity of the engine was increased from 1,084cc to 1,216cc with commensurate increases in acceleration and top-end speed. The frame was now constructed from lightweight aluminium, the front forks were increased in diameter from 41mm/1.61in to 45mm/1.81in, and the rear swing-arm was reduced in weight. The sum of these changes took nothing away from the original Pan European

concept but the result was a fast, refined touring bike with breathtaking performance that was almost certainly way over-specified for most of the military police and convoy escort duties for which the ST1300P would be procured.

The ST1300 was based on Honda's experimental X-Wing which had been powered by a V6 engine. The chassis of the X-Wing became the ST1300 but, like the ST1100 which it replaced, the new Pan European was powered by a lightweight 16-valve water-cooled fuel-injected V4 engine installed longitudinally in the frame. Power output was up to 117bhp from the enlarged 1,216cc capacity engine, which retained the electronic ignition system of the previous generation. In redesigning the engine, Honda's engineers managed to reduce the length by 60mm/2.4in and lower the centre of gravity by almost 20mm/0.8in, resulting in slight reductions in the wheel-base and overall height of the machine.

ABOVE: **The Honda ST1300 Pan European is typical of current big touring motorcycles.**
LEFT: **The ST1300P is a special model intended for military, police and emergency services. Unfortunately, it has exhibited a tendency to weave at speed which has led to a number of UK police forces discontinuing its use.**

Power was transmitted to the rear wheel through a five-speed foot-change transmission, with final drive by enclosed shaft fitted with integrated dampers; the drive-shaft was housed inside the rear swing-arm. The front forks were air-assisted telescopic, still with Honda's Torque-Reactive Anti-dive Control (TRAC), while the rear end consisted of a single-sided swing-arm damper, adjustable for pre-load and bounce; the wheels were hollow-section three-spoke aluminium. From the outset, Honda made maximum use of active ride control systems and the machine incorporated automatic traction control, and an electronic CBS-ABS system, the latter being optional for 2003.

The original steel frame was replaced by a lightweight aluminium unit, wrapped in new bodywork that included side guards, a full-width plastic fairing, and windscreen. Rear side panniers were also provided, together with twin blue lights on the ST1300P.

In 2006, a number of UK police forces announced that they were withdrawing the ST1300P from service because, at speed, the machine was found to exhibit a weaving tendency which had resulted in more than one accident.

Kawasaki KL-250D8

Originally founded as a shipyard back in 1878, Kawasaki started building motorcycles in 1949 and has grown to become one of the big four Japanese motorcycle

manufacturers, initially concentrating on two-strokes. The KL-250 was a civilian Enduro-style trail bike originally introduced in 1978. Following modification in the USA by Hayes Diversified Technologies to meet military requirements, the machine was adopted by the US Marines Corps as the KL-250D8, with 265 examples ordered in 1990/91.

Although it is constructed around a conventional duplex tubular-steel frame, unlike many such machines, the KL-250D8 is powered by a 246cc four-stroke water-cooled engine in combination with a six-speed

LEFT: **A US Army dispatch rider crossing the sand during Operation Desert Storm, the first Gulf War against the Iraqi invasion of Kuwait.**

transmission. Final drive is by open chain. There are long-travel telescopic front forks, together with a single-sided swing-arm at the rear.

Military versions were fitted with handlebar loops, a rear carrying rack and oversized rear tyres; there was also a 46-tooth rear sprocket giving improved fuel consumption.

Kawasaki KL-250D8

Type: Motorcycle, light, solo
Manufacturer: Kawasaki Heavy Industries; Ashaki
Production: 1991
Engine: Kawasaki; single cylinder; 246cc; overhead valves; water cooled; power output, 17bhp at 7,500rpm
Transmission: 6F; foot gear-change
Suspension: Air-assisted telescopic front forks; single-sided swing-arm damper at rear
Brakes: Discs, front and rear
Dimensions: Length – Not available
Performance: Maximum speed – 113kph/70mph

Kurogane *Sanrinsha* Type 1 or 2

With a big V-twin engine that was almost certainly derived from the Harley-Davidsons which had been imported into Japan in the 1930s, the Kurogane *Sanrinsha* was typical of standard commercial designs for load

BELOW: **A Kurogane *Sanrisha* captured in the Solomon Islands by Australian forces.**

carrying motor tricycles, thousands of which were pressed into service with the Japanese Imperial Army and the Special Naval Landing Force during World War II.

Known as *Sanrinsha*, the vehicle was a 3x2 cargo and personnel carrier modelled after the similar Italian Benelli and Moto-Guzzi machines. The front end resembled a conventional motorcycle, consisting of a pressed-steel frame carrying the front forks, engine, transmission and rider's seat, and attached to a box-like personnel, cargo or water carrier; on the cargo variant, the load-carrying box was provided with a bottom-hinged tailgate. Power from the 750cc V-twin engine was transmitted to a motorcar-type live rear axle by exposed carden shaft via a three-speed and reverse gearbox; unusually for a motorcycle of the period, ignition was by battery and coil. The front forks were of pressed-steel parallelogram design and the wheels were

pressed-steel disc pattern. A spare wheel was generally carried alongside the rider.

The manufacturer was originally known as the Nippon Nainenki Seiko Company, using the trade name Kurogane, but eventually changed its name to the Tokyo Kurogane Motor Company.

Kurogane *Sanrinsha* Type 1 or 2

Type: Motor tricycle, 3x2; Type 1 or 2
Manufacturer: Nippon Nainenki Seiko Co; Tokyo; Tokyo Kurogane Motor Co; Tokyo
Production: 1939 to 1945
Engine: Kurogane; two cylinders in V formation; 750cc; side valves; air cooled; power output, 23bhp
Transmission: 3F1R; hand gear-change
Suspension: Parallelogram front forks with friction-damped coil spring; live axle on semi-elliptical leaf springs at rear
Brakes: Drum, rear wheels only
Dimensions: Length – 2,730mm/107in
Width – 1,220mm/48in
Height – 1,220mm/48in
Wheelbase – 1,900mm/75in
Weight – 540kg/1,190lb
Performance: Maximum speed – 81kph/50mph

Sankyo *Shinagawa* Type 97

Sankyo *Shinagawa* Type 97

Type: Motorcycle, heavy, solo; and with sidecar, 3x2
Manufacturer: Sankyo, Shinagawa; Tokyo
Production: 1937 to 1945
Engine: Sankyo; two cylinders in V formation; 1,196cc; side valves; air cooled; power output, 24bhp at 4,000rpm
Transmission: 3F or 3F1R; hand gear-change
Suspension: Leading-link friction-damped coil-sprung front forks; solid rear end
Brakes: Drums, front and rear
Dimensions (solo): Length – 2,591mm/102in
Width – 915mm/36in
Height – 1,168mm/46in
Wheelbase – 1,600mm/63in
Weight – 280kg/617lb
Performance: Maximum speed – 97kph/60mph

Essentially a copy of the Harley-Davidson Model VL, the Sankyo *Shinagawa* 97 was launched on the Japanese civilian market in 1937 and was purchased by the Imperial Army for convoy escort and despatch work. With around 18,000 examples produced, it was the major Japanese military motorcycle of World War II. It is also described as the Rikuo Type 97 and

some suggest that it may have been built by the Japanese Meguro company.

Harley-Davidson had signed a deal with the Japanese Sankyo company in 1932 which allowed the company to build Harley-Davidsons under licence. When the licence expired in 1936, Sankyo continued to build the machine under the name Rikuo after World War II.

The machine was built around a tubular frame with a single down-tube, into which was installed a side-valve V-twin engine of 1,196cc that would have been recognizable to any Harley-

LEFT: **A Type 97 on display at the Technical Museum, Vladivostok, Russia.**

Davidson owner; a 750cc engine may also have been used. The rear wheel was driven via a three-speed hand-change gearbox – plus reverse when specified for sidecar use – and open chain. The leading-link, coil-sprung front forks were typical of Harley practice, and the rear end was unsprung. Military equipment usually comprised a rear luggage rack or pillion seat.

Yamaha DT-250MX

Yamaha DT-250MX

Type: Motorcycle, light, solo
Manufacturer: Yamaha Motor Co; Hamakita-Shi Shizuoka-Ken
Production: 1977 to 1980
Engine: Yamaha; single cylinder, 246cc; two stroke; air cooled; power output, 23bhp at 6,000rpm
Transmission: 5F; foot gear-change
Suspension: Hydraulically-damped telescopic front forks; trailing rear end with hydraulically-damped coil spring
Brakes: Drums, front and rear
Dimensions: Length – 2,145mm/84in
Width – 875mm/34in
Height – 1,140mm/45in
Wheelbase – 1,415mm/56in
Weight – 119kg/262lb
Performance: Maximum speed – 113kph/70mph

Although the Yamaha Fukin Works was established in 1887, the company did not start producing motorcycles until 1955, the first machine, the YA-1, being a copy of the pre-war DKW RT-125. But they learned fast and Yamaha was soon part of the Japanese motorcycle invasion that destroyed most of the UK motorcycle industry. Dating from 1978, the DT-250MX was a

standard civilian motocross machine that was modified for service with the Danish Army where it replaced older BSA and Nimbus machines during 1979.

The machine was assembled around a tubular-steel duplex frame, in which was installed a single-cylinder two-stroke engine of 246cc. The hydraulically-damped telescopic forks at the front provided predictably long travel to suit the multi-terrain role of the machine, while at the rear there was a trailing arm, suspended on a hydraulically-damped coil spring. A five-speed foot-change transmission drove the rear

LEFT: **A total of 450 Yamaha DT-250MXs were produced mainly for the Danish Army. However, in less than three years all had been replaced with the BMW-R65GS.**

wheel via an exposed chain. Military modifications included a 50 per cent increase in the size of the fuel tank, high-level exhaust, increased mudguard clearance and a rear radio rack.

CWS M-III

Largely designed by B. Fuksievich, the M-III motorcycle was produced by the Polish CWS State workshops in Warsaw. Design work for a heavy military motorcycle based on the Harley-Davidson pattern had started in 1928 and the first machine to be produced was the M55 S-0. Further development led to the M55 S-III of 1932, and then to the production M-III that appeared in 1933. A heavy, powerful machine, equally at home on and off the road, it was quickly adopted by the Polish Army and, although it was expensive, features such as the quality of build, and the ability to inject fuel directly into the cylinders for easy starting in low temperatures (down to –40°C), made it ideal for use in the harsh Polish winter.

The machine was designed primarily for use with a sidecar, and was constructed around a tubular-steel cycle-type frame with a single down-tube, and was powered by a 995cc V-twin side-valve engine with a power output of 18bhp; ignition was by magneto. The transmission set-up consisted of a three-speed gearbox with hand change, and exposed chain final drive. Leading-link friction-damped coil-sprung forks were employed at the front, and the rear end was solid.

Standard sidecars, always right-hand mounted, included personnel, ammunition and machine-gun variants, and experiments were in-hand with the M-121 variant, which had a driven sidecar wheel, when production ended. Military fittings included a gas mask case on the rear mudguard and a rear-mounted luggage carrier.

CWS was absorbed into PZInz (Panstwowych Zakladow Inzynierii) in 1934, but the motorcycles continued to be identified as CWS. A total of 3,400 M-IIIs had been completed by the time the German invasion of September 1939 brought production to a halt. A commercial version was marketed under the name Sokol 1000 M-III.

ABOVE AND RIGHT: **The Polish CWS M-III was a 995cc V-twin heavy motorcycle patterned on the contemporary Harley-Davidson. In military form, it was widely used by the Polish Army, with production continuing until 1939.**

CWS M-III

Type: Motorcycle, heavy, solo; and with sidecar
Manufacturer: Centraine Warsztaty Samochadowe; Warsaw
Production: 1933 to 1939
Engine: CWS; two cylinders in V formation; 995cc; side valves; air cooled; power output, 18bhp at 3,000rpm
Transmission: 3F; hand gear-change
Suspension: Leading link front forks with friction-damped coil springs; solid rear end
Brakes: Drums, all three wheels
Dimensions (with sidecar): Length – 2,450mm/96in
    Width – 1,740mm/69in
    Height – 1,135mm/45in
    Wheelbase – 1,465mm/58in
    Weight – solo, 230kg/507lb
    with sidecar, 375kg/825lb
Performance: Maximum speed – 100kph/62mph

IMZ Ural M-72

Based on the pre-war BMW R-71 – and often nicknamed Molotov – the IMZ Ural M-72 first appeared in 1941 and remained in production until the mid-1950s. Development started in about 1939 when the Soviets became nervous of Hitler's territorial aspirations and started to re-equip the Red Army. The Germans had been successful in the use of heavy motorcycle outfits and, keen to avoid the necessarily lengthy development time associated with a new machine, the Russians decided it would be simpler to "adopt" an existing design.

Through their neutral Scandinavian neighbours, Foreign Minister Molotov arranged to covertly acquire five BMW R-71 combinations and the Soviets set about copying it. The R-71 had been introduced in 1938 and was the last of the BMW flat-head twins, with a 746cc engine, four-speed gearbox and shaft drive to the rear wheel. The engine was installed in a conventional tubular steel frame with a duplex cradle support. Front suspension consisted of hydraulically-damped coil-sprung telescopic forks; at the rear, there was a coil-sprung plunger system.

The machine was used in both solo and sidecar form; in the former case, a pillion seat was often fitted together with a rear carrying rack and side panniers, while the sidecar carried a machine-gun mount and a spare wheel.

In late summer 1941, the German invasion of the Soviet Union led to various factories being moved away from the reach of the German bombers. The IMZ plant was moved into the Ural mountains, near the town of Irbit but production also took place at numerous other facilities including Leningrad, Kharkov, and Gorkyi.

ABOVE: **Between 1941 and 1945 a total of 9,799 were manufactured. The M-72 remained the workhorse of the Red Army well into the 1960s. Limited civilian sales started in 1946.**

IMZ Ural M-72

Type: Motorcycle, heavy, solo; and with sidecar
Manufacturer: Iskra Motor Zavod; Moscow and Irbit
Production: 1941 to 1956
Engine: IMZ; two cylinder, horizontally opposed; 746cc; side valves; air cooled; power output, 22bhp at 4,600rpm
Transmission: 4F; hand gear-change
Suspension: Hydraulically-damped telescopic front forks with coil springs; plunger suspension at rear using coil springs
Brakes: Drums, front and rear
Dimensions (solo): Length – 2,130mm/84in
    Width – 815mm/32in
    Height – 960mm/38in
    Wheelbase – 1,400mm/55in
    Weight – 205kg/451lb
Performance (solo): Maximum speed – 105kph/65mph

Izhevsk IZh-9

The Izhevsk Motorcycle Works in Ustinov had started manufacturing motorcycles in 1928, at first concentrating on heavy 1,200cc V-twin and 750cc models. The lighter IZh (or ISH) series appeared in 1938, with the IZh-9 dating from May 1940. This was a logical development of the earlier IZh-7 and IZh-8 series and was fitted with a 350cc two-stroke engine in place of the 293cc used in the previous machines.

The IZh-9 was a conventional medium-weight civilian motorcycle modified for military use. The machine consisted of a tubular-steel frame carrying the inclined, single-cylinder engine, with coil-sprung and friction-damped girder parallelogram front forks, and an unsprung rear end. Drive was transmitted to the rear wheel via a three-speed hand-change gearbox and exposed chain.

Production ceased in November 1941 although the more-powerful 350cc four-stroke IZh-12, which had been introduced at the same time, continued for a few more months.

IZh-9

Type: Motorcycle, medium, solo
Manufacturer: Izhevsk Motorcycle Works; Ustinov
Production: 1940 to 1941
Engine: IZh; single cylinder; 350cc; two stroke; air cooled; power output, 11bhp at 4,000rpm
Transmission: 3F; hand gear-change
Suspension: Coil-sprung friction-damped girder parallelogram forks at front; unsprung rear
Brakes: Drums, front and rear
Dimensions: Not available
Performance: Maximum speed – 125kph/77mph

LEFT: **The IZh-9 was a very conventional civilian motorcycle lightly modified for the military.**

KMZ Dniepr K-750M

Type: Motorcycle, heavy, with sidecar, 3x2
Manufacturer: Kiev Motor Zavod; Kiev
Production: 1963 to 1977
Engine: KMZ; two cylinders in V formation;
   746cc; side valves; air cooled; power output,
   26bhp at 4,900rpm
Transmission: 4F 1R; hand gear-change
Suspension: Hydraulically-damped leading-
   link telescopic front forks; coil-sprung
   plungers at rear
Brakes: Drums, front and rear
Dimensions (with sidecar): Length – 2,430mm/96in
   Width – 1,700m/67in
   Height – 1,100mm/43in
   Wheelbase – 1,510mm/59in
   Weight – 350kg/772lb
Performance: Maximum speed – 90kph/56mph

KMZ Dniepr K-750M

The first such machine to be built at the Kiev motorcycle factory, Ukraine, the Dniepr K-750M was a heavy military motorcycle combination outfit intended for the Soviet Army. In service, it replaced the earlier IMZ Ural M-72, which had started production in 1942 before being transferred to KMZ in 1951, but there were strong similarities between the two

ABOVE: **The Soviet Army Dniepr K-750M is considered a copy of the BMW.**

machines, both being clearly derived from pre-war BMW practice. Manufacture continued between 1963 and 1977.

The K-750M was powered by a 746cc horizontally opposed side-valve engine, with battery and coil ignition, installed in

a tubular duplex frame. Power was transmitted to the rear and sidecar wheels by means of a four-speed and reverse gearbox, with final drive by enclosed shaft. A cross-shaft was used to drive the sidecar wheel, and could be disengaged as required under hand control. The front forks were hydraulically-damped telescopic units, and the rear end was suspended on coil-sprung plungers.

PMZ A750

Designed by Pyotr Mozharov and manufactured by Podolskiy Motor Zavod between 1935 and 1939, the Soviet PMZ A750 was widely used by the Red Army and the civilian police authority. PMZ

PMZ A750

Type: Motorcycle, heavy, solo; and with sidecar
Manufacturer: Podolskiy Motor Zavod; Podolskiy
Production: 1935 to 1939
Engine: PMZ; two cylinders in V formation;
   747cc; side valves; air cooled; power output,
   15bhp at 3,600rpm
Transmission: 3F; hand gear-change
Suspension: Leading link front forks with
   friction-damped leaf springs; solid rear end
Brakes: Drums, front and rear
Dimensions: Wheelbase – 1,395mm/55in
   Other dimensions not available
   Weight – 220kg/485lb
Performance: Maximum speed – 100kph/62mph

had started producing bicycle engines in 1931 and had quickly progressed to motorcycles, using flat-twin engines in the style of BMW, and V-twins, which were similar to the standard Harley-Davidson products of the period. With its 747cc V-twin side-valve engine, the A750 fell into the latter and was procured in both solo and sidecar combination form.

Although the engine followed the Harley-Davidson pattern, it was installed in a decidedly BMW-style external pressed-steel duplex frame, with pressed-steel leading-link friction-damped leaf-sprung forks at the front,

ABOVE: **Some machines were fitted with a distinctive raised pillion seat, as shown in this photograph, and both single-seat and machine-gun sidecars were employed.**

and a solid rear end. The transmission set-up consisted of a three-speed gearbox with hand change, and exposed chain final drive.

PMZ ceased motorcycle manufacture at the end of World War II in 1945.

KMZ MB-650 M1

The MB-650 M1 was the military version of the civilian MT-16, and was manufactured at the Kiev Moto Zavod (KMZ) motorcycle factory in Ukraine from the mid-1980s until the factory closed in the late 1990s. With the horizontally opposed twin-cylinder engine and driven sidecar-wheel, it was possibly the finest incarnation of that type of Soviet heavy motorcycle, and its lineage could be traced directly back to the original Ural M-72 of 1942 which, in turn, had borrowed heavily from BMW practice. The machine was

also available without sidecar-wheel drive as the MT-11.

Constructed around a conventional tubular-steel duplex frame, the MB-650 M1 was powered by a 649cc two cylinder horizontally opposed overhead-valve engine, with alloy cylinder barrels and heads, and battery and coil ignition. The four speed and reverse gearbox transmitted power to the rear and sidecar wheels. The final drive was by means of an enclosed Carden shaft coupled to a cross-shaft to drive the sidecar wheel. This could

ABOVE: **Dniepr motorcycles were marketed in Britain between 1973 and 1979 by Satra.**

be disengaged as required by hand control. A locking differential lock was fitted to the rear axle.

The front forks were hydraulically-damped telescopic units and the rear end was suspended on decidedly old-fashioned coil-sprung plungers. The frame and suspension design offered exceptional ground clearance.

Outside of the USSR, KMZ motorcycles are also known as Dniepr. Between 1973 and 1979, were marketed by Satra, based in Byfleet in the United Kingdom, under the name Cossack.

The factory operated parallel production lines, one for military and police motorcycles, the other for the equivalent civilian machines. By the time the factory closed following the demise of the USSR, something approaching 1.5 million military motorcycles had been produced. The name continues to exist but the motorcycles are no longer produced in Kiev.

ABOVE AND LEFT: **Since World War II, Soviet heavy motorcycles have tended to be variations on the pre-war BMW theme. First produced in 1985, and powered by an overhead-valve horizontally opposed engine, the MB-650 M1 was a military version of the civilian MT-16, and was invariably used with a driven-wheel sidecar.**

KMZ MB-650 M1

Type: Motorcycle, heavy, with sidecar, 3x2
Manufacturer: Kiev Motor Zavod; Kiev
Production: 1985 to 1998
Engine: KMZ MT10.36; two cylinder, horizontally opposed; 649cc; overhead valves; air cooled; power output, 32bhp at 5,600rpm
Transmission: 4F 1R; hand gear-change
Suspension: Hydraulically-damped leading-link telescopic front forks; coil-sprung plungers at rear
Brakes: Drums, front and rear
Dimensions (with sidecar): Length – 2,430mm/96in
　　　Width – 1,700m/67in
　　　Height – 1,080mm/42in
　　　Wheelbase – 1,510mm/59in
　　　Weight (with sidecar) – 350kg/772lb
Performance: Maximum speed – 95kph/58mph

LEFT: **Although the prototype work was done by Hägglunds, technical difficulties meant that when the XM-74 eventually went into production it was with Husqvarna, the name being changed to MC-258-MT. Hägglunds's stepless belt-drive was replaced by a four-speed centrifugal automatic transmission and Husqvarna fitted their own 250cc engine in place of the single-cylinder Rotax.**

Hägglunds XM-74 (MC-258-MT)

In 1970, the Swedish military authorities prepared a specification for a military motorcycle with automatic transmission and approached Hägglunds, Husqvarna and Monark for prototypes. Although Hägglunds was an experienced defence contractor, the company had no previous experience with motorcycles. Their prototype, the XM-72 was nevertheless trialled during 1972 and selected for manufacture, against a bid from Husqvarna in 1974.

The frame was an unusual welded box-section design which incorporated both the fuel tank and the oil reservoir and which had the engine suspended below the box section. The front suspension was a single-sided telescopic leading arm, and the rear wheel was similarly mounted in a single-sided trailing arm; drum brakes were fitted front and rear. Power was initially provided by a 300cc Sachs single-cylinder two-stroke engine driving through a stepless belt-drive system similar to the DAF Variomatic system; final drive was by shaft housed in the rear fork arm.

Modifications made as a result of testing led to the XM-74 in which the Sachs engine was replaced by a single-cylinder 350cc Rotax unit and the leading arm front forks were replaced by a Ceriani telescopic unit. Further problems arose with the primary drive and in 1976 Hägglunds approached Husqvarna for design assistance, and this subsequently led to the whole project being transferred to Husqvarna for completion. Out went all of the innovative features introduced by Hägglunds. Designating the production machine MC-258-MT, Husqvarna simply modified the prototype that they had produced back in 1973, fitting their own 250cc single-cylinder electronic-ignition two-stroke engine, and introducing a four-speed unit-constructed centrifugal transmission. The frame was a conventional tubular-steel cycle design, with telescopic forks at the front, and a coil-sprung trailing arm at the rear.

Military equipment included a rear luggage rack, high-clearance mudguards, and braced handlebars; ski supports could also be fitted.

A total of 3,000 was supplied between 1980 and 1981, and a civilian version was also marketed. Hägglunds, now part of BAE Systems, continues to manufacture armoured vehicles but has not ventured back into motorcycle production.

Hägglunds XM-74/ Husqvarna MC-285-MT

Type: Motorcycle, medium, solo
Manufacturer: Hägglunds & Söner; Örnsköldsvik; then Husqvarna Motorcyklar; Odeshög
Production: 1973 to 1981
Engine: Husqvarna; single cylinder; 250cc; two stroke; air cooled; power output, 20bhp at 5,500rpm
Transmission: 4F; automatic
Suspension: Hydraulically-damped telescopic front forks; load-adjustable trailing arm at rear with coil-spring
Brakes: Drums, front and rear
Dimensions (production machine):
Length – 2,220mm/87in
Width – 860mm/34in
Height – 1,200mm/47in
Wheelbase – 1,480mm/58in
Weight – 130kg/286lbb
Performance: Maximum speed – 110kph/68mph

Husqvarna 145A

Located in the Swedish town of the same name, Husqvarna can trace its origins back to the 1600s, as a weapons manufacturer. During the 1800s, Husqvarna supplied the Swedish Army with Mauser bolt-action rifles, but, by the late 1800s the company had diversified into bicycle manufacture and the first motorcycle was produced in 1903, using a 1.5hp FN engine. In 1909, the FN power unit was replaced by Swiss-built Moto-Reve V-twin and this led to the company's first military order in 1916 for a lightly militarized variant of the standard civilian machine known as the Model 145A – the "A" indicating *Armé*. By the end of World War I, the Swedish Army had taken delivery of almost 500 examples.

The 145A was suitable for both solo and sidecar duty and, as befits a former cycle manufacturer, was constructed around a conventional tubular cycle-type frame with a single down-tube. The front forks were of the familiar friction-damped girder parallelogram pattern with twin coil-springs, and the rear end was solid. Power came from a Moto-Reve V-twin unit of 548cc, with magneto ignition, overhead inlet valves and side exhaust. On early civilian machines the engine drove the rear wheel directly via an open chain, but by the time the military orders were received, the machine was fitted with a three-speed hand-change gearbox.

BELOW: **A basic Husqvarna 145A with hand-change gearbox and chain drive.**

Husqvarna 145A	
Type: Motorcycle, heavy, solo; and with sidecar	
Manufacturer: Husqvarna Vapenfabriks; Husqvarna	
Production: 1909 to 1918	
Engine: Husqvarna; two cylinders in V formation, 548cc; overhead inlet valves, side exhaust; air cooled; power output, 4.25bh	
Transmission: 3F; hand gear-change	
Suspension: Girder parallelogram friction-damped coil-sprung front forks; solid rear end	
Brakes: Rear only, block acting on dummy rim	
Dimensions: Not available	
Weight (solo) – 118kg/260lb	
Performance: Maximum speed – 50mph/80kph	

Husqvarna 500A

From 1903, Husqvarna had been building motorcycles using proprietary engines but by 1920, the company started building their own V-twin engines designed by Folke Mannerstedt. One of the earliest machines to use these power units was the Husqvarna 500A, a heavy military motorcycle combination introduced in 1922 to replace the ageing military 145A which, by that time was six years old. The Swedish Army took delivery of 715 examples during 1922 and 1923 and, in a reverse of more normal practice, the machine was subsequently modified for civilian use and remained in production in this form until 1936 when Husqvarna stopped producing heavy motorcycles.

Built around a conventional tubular duplex frame, the 500A was powered by a 990cc V-twin side-valve engine. The rear wheel was driven via a separate three-speed hand-change gearbox and open chain; the gearbox included a foot-operated clutch. At the front, there were friction-damped girder parallelogram forks, using twin coil springs for suspension. The rear end was unsprung. Military equipment usually comprised a rear luggage rack or pillion seat and twin panniers. A spare wheel was carried on the sidecar.

The company was purchased by Cagiva in 1986, but continues to produce motorcycles to the present day.

LEFT: **The standard sidecar was a single-seat type of decidedly civilian appearance.**

Husqvarna 500A	
Type: Motorcycle, heavy, with sidecar	
Manufacturer: Husqvarna Vapenfabriks; Husqvarna	
Production: 1922 to 1923	
Engine: Husqvarna; two cylinders in V formation; 990cc; side valves; air cooled; power output, 8bhp at 3,500rpm	
Transmission: 3F; hand gear-change	
Suspension: Girder parallelogram friction-damped coil-sprung front forks; solid rear end	
Brakes: Drums, rear only	
Dimensions: Not available	
Weight (with sidecar) – 160kg/352lb	
Performance: Maximum speed – 100kph/62mph	

Monark Albin M/42

The Swedish Monark company originally produced two-stroke motorcycles under the name Essc but by the mid-1930s the name was changed with the introduction of four-stroke machines. Although Sweden remained neutral during World War II, the government was not immune to German militarization and as far back as 1935 had asked Husqvarna to design a multi-terrain military motorcycle, designated 112TV. In 1942, the design was put into production by Monark, as the M/42,

using a Monark frame and an Albin engine and transmission.

The frame was a hybrid pressed-steel and tubular design with coil-sprung girder parallelogram forks at the front, and coil-sprung plunger type suspension at the rear. Power came from a 495cc Albin single-cylinder engine driving through a three-speed foot-change gearbox. Final drive was by exposed chain. The machines were fitted with twin fuel tanks, the smaller generally being reserved for high-octane fuel to aid cold-starting.

Monark Albin M/42	
Type: Motorcycle, medium, solo	
Manufacturer: Cykelfabrieken Monark; Varberg	
Production: 1942 to 1943	
Engine: Albin; single cylinder; 495cc; overhead valves; air cooled; power output, 20bhp at 4,000rpm	
Transmission: 3F; foot gear-change	
Suspension: Friction-damped girder parallelogram coil-sprung front forks; coil-sprung plunger suspension at rear	
Brakes: Drums, front and rear	
Dimensions: Length – 2,120mm/83in	
Width – 740mm/29in	
Height – 940mm/37in	
Wheelbase – 1,410mm/56in	
Weight – 200kg/440lb	
Performance: Maximum speed – 110kph/68mph	

RIGHT: **The Monark Albin M/42 was a fully sprung single-cylinder 495cc motorcycle produced in Sweden during World War II and remaining in service in Sweden and Denmark into the 1960s.**

A rear carrying rack or pillion was fitted, together with leather pannier bags.

A similar machine was also produced, with a rigid frame and side-valve engine.

More than 3,000 M/42s were produced during 1942 and 1943, many remaining in service in Sweden and Denmark until the 1960s. Production of Monark motorcycles stopped in the mid-1970s.

Suecia 500 *Armé*

Suecia started production of motorcycles in 1928, initially using British-built Blackburn engines and Sturmey-Archer gearboxes but eventually replacing the Blackburn units with JAP or MAG engines. In 1937, the company launched a military motorcycle based on its civilian

500 Tourist model. Suitable for solo or sidecar use, the 500 *Armé* remained in production until 1940, by which time some 5,000 examples had been supplied to the Swedish Army. The 500 *Armé* was a well-built and reliable machine, and was rather British in overall design and manufacture. There was a tubular cycle-style frame with a single down-tube. Coil-sprung girder parallelogram forks were fitted at the front, together with a rigid rear end. The engine

was a 496cc Swiss-built MAG single-cylinder side-valve unit, driving the rear wheel through a separate four-speed Burman gearbox and exposed chain.

Either a rear carrying rack or pillion could be fitted, together with leather pannier bags. In combination form, the machine was supplied with a number of different commercial-built sidecars.

Suecia motorcycle production was terminated in 1940.

Suecia 500 *Armé*	
Type: Motorcycle, medium, solo; and with sidecar	
Manufacturer: Suecia Verken Motor; Orelljunga	
Production: 1937 to 1940	
Engine: MAG; single cylinder; 496cc; side valves; air cooled; power output, 11bhp at 3,600rpm	
Transmission: 4F; foot gear-change	
Suspension: Friction-damped girder parallelogram coil-sprung front forks; rigid rear end	
Brakes: Drums, front and rear	
Dimensions: Not available	
Wheelbase – 1,410mm/56in	
Weight – 165kg/363lb	
Performance: Maximum speed – 65kph/40mph	

RIGHT: **Although not widely known, the Swedish-built Suecia company produced motorcycles from 1928 until 1940. Based on a civilian machine, the MAG-engined 500 *Armé* was launched in 1937 and remained in production until 1940.**

Condor A250

LEFT: **Introduced in 1959 after an extended trial period, and remaining in production for a decade, the Swiss Condor A250 was a specialized military motorcycle, powered by a single-cylinder overhead valve engine, with a four-speed transmission and shaft drive.**

As heavy motorcycles fell from favour in the 1960s, most European armies sought to replace these machines with the new breed of faster lightweights. Remaining faithful to domestic suppliers, the Swiss Army

Condor A250

Type: Motorcycle, light, solo
Manufacturer: Condor; Courfaivre
Production: 1959 to 1968
Engine: Condor; single cylinder; 248cc; overhead valves; air cooled; power output, 13bhp at 6,000rpm
Transmission: 4F; foot gear-change
Suspension: Hydraulically-damped telescopic front forks; swinging-arm coil-sprung suspension at rear
Brakes: Drums, front and rear
Dimensions: Length – 2,050mm/81in
    Width – 690mm/27in
    Height – 1,050mm/41in
    Wheelbase – 1,350mm/53in
    Weight – 190kg/418lb
Performance: Maximum speed – 110kph/68mph

trialled more than 100 prototypes of the Condor A250 over an extended period before adopting it as the replacement for the A580.

Although only equipped with a 248cc single-cylinder engine, like its predecessors, the A250 was shaft-driven, via a four-speed unit-constructed gearbox, and was capable of almost 110kph/68mph on the road. The engine was mounted in a duplex cradle-type frame with hydraulically-damped

telescopic front forks; the rear end of the swing-arm type and was suspended on a single coil spring.

The machine was provided with crash bars, a pillion seat and leather panniers. A sub-machine-gun support bracket could also be fitted and there was provision for carrying two rifles.

Detail modifications were made in 1965 and 1968. A total of 573 examples were produced. It was replaced by the Condor A350 in 1973.

Condor A580, A580-1

The Condor A580 was a standardized shaft-driven heavy motorcycle produced exclusively for the Swiss Army from 1949. It was designed to supersede the company's previous A680 and A1000 machines.

Powerful and reliable, the A580 was equipped with a 577cc flat-twin engine in a duplex cradle-type frame which was capable of propelling the heavy machine

at speeds of up to 105kph/65mph on the road, while the two-speed transfer case also ensured that it could provide more than adequate off-road performance. The rear wheel was driven by a concealed Carden. Hydraulically-damped telescopic front forks were fitted. The rear end was unsprung until 1953 when the A580-1 variant appeared with plunger-type suspension.

Condor A580, A580-1

Type: Motorcycle, heavy, solo; sidecar variant designated A750
Manufacturer: Condor; Courfaivre
Production: 1949 to 1954
Engine: Condor; two cylinder, horizontally opposed; 577cc; side valves; air cooled; power output, 20bhp at 4,400rpm
Transmission: 4Fx2; foot gear-change
Suspension: Hydraulically-damped telescopic front forks; solid rear end (A580) or swinging-arm plunger-type suspension (A580-1)
Brakes: Drums, front and rear
Dimensions: Length – 2140mm/85in
    Width – 760mm/30in
    Height – 1,050mm/41in
    Wheelbase – 1,410mm/56in
    Weight – 210kg/462lb
Performance: Maximum speed – 105kph/65mph

RIGHT: **The Condor A580 was also a specialized military motorcycle, in production between 1949 and 1954, exclusively for the Swiss Army. Midway through the production run, the rigid rear end was updated with swinging-arm plunger-type suspension.**

The machine was fitted with a sump guard, crash bars and either a pillion seat or a rear carrying rack. A sidecar variant was also produced, designated A750.

A total of almost 4,500 examples were supplied to the Swiss Army between 1949 and 1954, and the machine remained in service until well into the 1970s.

Mercier Type 3

In 1936, the Mercier company – which was based either in France or Switzerland according to your source – produced a prototype for a curious hybrid tracked/wheeled motorcycle which was tested by the War Office in the UK during 1939.

The so-called Type 3 was constructed around a more-or-less conventional tubular frame, and was powered by a 349cc single-cylinder JAP engine placed between the handlebars, with the gearbox facing forwards. At the front, in the place where the wheel would normally be fitted, there was an aluminium-framed tracked bogie secured in tubular-steel forks with an idler wheel driven by a chain from the gearbox. A second train conveyed the power from the idler wheel to the rear, driven sprocket. The bogie used semi-elliptical multi-leaf springs to provide suspension and the rubber-faced track sections were about 150mm/6in wide. An exposed primary chain transferred power between the engine and gearbox. The rear wheel appears to have been both unsprung and undriven.

LEFT: **British test authorities considered the Mercier to be unsafe on wet roads. It was also said to be a poor hill climber.**

Mercier Type 3

Type: Motorcycle, medium, tracked, solo
Manufacturer: Mercier
Production: 1936
Engine: JAP; single cylinder, 349cc; overhead valves; air cooled; power output, not available
Transmission: Hand gear-change
Suspension: Front bogie suspended on semi-elliptical multi-leaf springs; unsprung rear
Brakes: Not known
Dimensions: Not available
  Weight – 160kg/352lb
Performance: Maximum speed – 65kph/40mph

Top speed was said to be in the order of 65kph/40mph which must have been a hair-raising experience.

It would not seem likely that this was a success but two years later the company prototyped a "motorcycle tank" which had a single rubber track running around an armoured body, with a stabilizing wheel fitted at either side. Neither went into series production.

Motosacoche 2C7

Motosacoche motorcycles were produced by Armand and Henri Dufaux in Genève. In 1899, the brothers had developed an engine which they supplied installed in a sub-frame that made it easy to fit into a standard bicycle frame. Marketed under the brand MAG (Motosacoche Acacias Genève), larger, more powerful engines soon followed and proved to be enormously successful. MAG engines were supplied to manufacturers across Europe and included Triumph, Ariel and Matchless in the UK. By 1914 the company had graduated to producing complete motorcycles, and the 497cc V-twin 2C7 model was purchased by the Swiss military.

Although the frame might be considered a conventional cycle-type design, the top-tube was curved upwards where it joined the steering head and the down-tube and seat-tube were shaped to accommodate a horizontal support for the engine. The engine was a V-twin four-stroke design coupled to the rear wheel through

Motosacoche 2C7

Type: Motorcycle, medium, solo
Manufacturer: H & A Dufaux SA; Genève
Production: 1914
Engine: MAG; two cylinders in V formation, 497cc; overhead inlet valves, side exhaust; air cooled; power output, 3.5bhp
Transmission: 2F, hand gear-change
Suspension: Friction-damped parallelogram front forks; unsprung rear
Brakes: Rear only, block acting on dummy rim
Dimensions: Not available
  Weight – Not available
Performance: Maximum speed – 50kph/30mph

a two-speed transmission and open chain; ignition was by magneto. There machine was fitted with girder parallelogram front forks, with a single friction-damped coil spring, and a rigid rear end.

An English subsidiary was established in 1908, but closed in 1928. The company had considerable racing success during the 1930s, but production in Switzerland ended in 1956.

LEFT: **The 2C7 had a very distinctively shaped frame.**

LEFT AND BELOW: **The AC Auto Carrier was launched in 1904 at a price of just £80 and was intended for local tradesmen making small deliveries. Three years later, in 1907, a passenger-carrying version was produced under the name Sociable. Both versions were powered by a single-cylinder engine of 648cc driving the rear wheel through a two-speed hub-mounted gearbox.**

AC Auto Carrier

It is hard to believe but AC, makers of the mighty Cobra sports car, actually started life producing a curious three-wheeled delivery vehicle known as the Auto Carrier. The company, which initially traded under the name Autocar & Accessories Limited, was an unlikely partnership between the engineer John Weller (who had already designed a motorcycle and a car) and John Portwine, the owner of a chain of butchers' shops in London. Launched in 1904, the Auto Carrier was intended for businesses who wished to replace a horse and cart, but who lacked the necessary capital to purchase a van.

In 1910, the August issue of *Motorcycling* reported that the 25th (County of London) Cyclists Battalion, London Regiment, TF – the "TF" standing for "Territorial Force" – had acquired four Auto Carriers; two were used to mount a forward-facing Maxim machine-gun, two provided support as ammunition carriers. This use of the Auto Carrier was one of the earliest examples of mechanization

in the British Army and it is said that the military authorities were impressed with the manoeuvrability of the machine. It would seem more likely that the War Office was impressed by the low price of £80.

Described as a motor tricycle, the Auto Carrier was not quite a motorcycle, but equally was not quite a cyclecar. It was constructed on a simple wooden frame, with tiller steering operating on the rear wheel, and was powered by a 648cc single-cylinder air-cooled engine located under the seat. Drive was transmitted by open chain to the single rear wheel, with a two-speed epicyclic gearbox in the rear hub. Suspension appears to have been limited to the pneumatic tyres.

A cargo box was normally fitted at the front and the vehicle was capable of carrying a load of 200–250kg/450–550lb; on the military versions the box was replaced by a flat bed which also provided seating for two additional crew members facing to the rear. The driver was placed centrally, just ahead of the rear wheel and

behind the load. In 1907/08, a passenger version of the Auto Carrier was launched under the name Sociable and in 1911 the company became Auto Carriers Limited and moved to Ferry Works, Thames Ditton, Surrey. Both models remained in production until 1914. The British Army had 12 Auto Carriers in service by 1918.

LEFT: **In 1910, the 25th County of London Cyclist Battallion acquired four Auto Carriers; two were used as a machine-gun mount, equipped with a Maxim machine gun, the other two acted as ammunition carriers. By 1918, there were 12 of these machines in British Army service.**

AC Auto Carrier	

Type: Motor tricycle, machine-gun and ammunition carrier, 3x1
Manufacturer: Autocar & Accessories Limited; West Norwood. Later, Auto Carriers; Thames Ditton
Production: 1904 to 1914
Engine: AC; single cylinder; 648cc; side valves; air cooled; power output, 5.6bhp
Transmission: 2F, hand gear-change
Suspension: None
Brakes: Rear only
Dimensions: Length – 2,440mm/96in
 Width – 1,220mm/48in
 Height – 1,066mm/42in
 Wheelbase – 1,525mm/60in
 Weight: Not available
Performance: Maximum allowable speed – 8kph/5mph

AJS M8

A.J. Stephens and his three brothers had been manufacturing motorcycles under the name AJS since 1909. They had some racing success, but eventually over-reached themselves financially and were forced to sell out to Matchless in 1931 and the products gradually started to move closer to those of the parent company, albeit the AJS brand was maintained.

The company was never a volume supplier to the War Office although they had supplied sample machines for evaluation from 1929.

Following the loss of every motorcycle in the British Expeditionary Force at Dunkirk in May 1940, the War Office was anxious to procure whatever was available. It seems that this included six assorted, strictly civilian machines from AJS – five of which were 500cc models (two Model 8SS, one M8, two M9s), the remaining machine, an M26, being equipped with a 350cc overhead-valve engine. Others were impressed civilian machines.

Costing the War Office £51.95, the M8 – or Model 8 – was a typical AJS product. It was similar in design and weight to the Matchless G3, but was powered by a 498cc single-cylinder overhead-valve engine, combined with a four-speed foot-change gearbox. Final drive was by open chain. The engine and gearbox were fitted into a conventional cycle type frame with a single down-tube. The front forks were of the girder parallelogram pattern, with suspension provided by a single friction-damped coil spring. The rear end was unsprung.

The machine was of civilian specification and, aside from being painted all-over olive drab, was almost certainly not modified at all.

ABOVE LEFT AND LEFT: **The Model 8 was powered by an overhead valve engine of 498cc, giving a top speed of 97kph/60mph. This racing model has a non-standard hand gear-change.**

ABOVE LEFT AND ABOVE: **Desperate for new motorcycles, the War Office purchased a single example of the AJS Model 8 – or M8 – in 1940. Although strictly civilian, it was certainly not stripped for racing like this preserved example.**

The AJS name continued after the war but Associated Motorcycles, owners of Norton, Francis Barnett, James, Matchless and AJS, went into receivership in 1969.

AJS Model 8 (M8)

Type: Motorcycle, medium, solo
Manufacturer: A J Stephens & Company; Plumstead, SE18
Production: 1940
Engine: AJS; single cylinder; 498cc; overhead valves; air cooled; power output, 14bhp at 4,500rpm
Transmission: 4F; foot gear-change
Suspension: Coil-sprung friction-damped girder parallelogram front forks; solid rear end
Brakes: Drums, front and rear
Dimensions: Not available
Weight – Not available
Performance: Maximum speed – 97kph/60mph

LEFT: **Possibly based on Ariel's 497cc civilian Red Hunter model, a small number of W/NH – or perhaps W/VH – were supplied to the War Office in 1940 as part of a contract for a selection of machines intended to help make good losses following the evacuation from Dunkirk.** BELOW: **The engine drive and clutch casing on the 497cc engine.**

Ariel W/VH or W/NH

Ariel motorcycles first appeared in 1902, powered by a 3.5bhp single-cylinder White & Poppe engine; in 1932, the company went into receivership and was purchased by Jack Sangster, the name changing to Ariel Motors (JS) Limited. The first military contracts came in 1935 when the War Office purchased a number of VA3 models. However, the company is probably best known for the W/NG which was supplied throughout World War II. The W/NH is something of a mystery. The Ministry of Supply contract records for the period show that a single 500cc model W/NH was supplied to the War Office under contract C7373 in 1940 amid a batch of 30 other 500cc machines of unspecified type.

The nomenclature "W/NH" would suggest that this was a War Office version of the NH – known as the "Red Hunter" in civilian form – but this was a 350cc machine and the contract record clearly states that the W/NH was 500cc. The Red Hunter was known as the VH which would suggest that the clerk in charge of recording the contract, or someone transcribing it at a later date confused the "V" with an "N". It would probably be safe to assume then that this was actually a W/VH machine – in other words, a militarized 497cc Red Hunter.

The Red Hunter had first appeared in 1933 and, with modifications remained available until the outbreak of the war. Although it was considered to be Ariel's competition machine, the shortage of equipment following the evacuation from Dunkirk was such that the War Office was glad of anything on which was readily available and apparently a small quantity of 497cc Red Hunters were available – perhaps 38 – so the War Office purchased them and issued them to the Army. It seems that they were not even all of the same specification; some had the single-port cylinder head (VH1), others had the twin port design – the latter being described as VH2.

As befits a sporting machine, the Red Hunter was designed with speed and tuning possibilities uppermost. For example, the crankcase was of exceptionally rigid design and there were features such as a dry sump, polished and lightened con rod, ground and polished ports, polished flywheel, and large diameter bearings. Combined with a four-speed gearbox this was able to guarantee that the machine could reach close to 129kph/80mph, almost certainly sufficient to scare the average despatch rider.

The frame was of conventional design, with friction-damped parallelogram girder front forks with

a single coil spring, and a solid rear end. Final drive was by exposed chain.

There were no more purchases after the initial few. Further Ariel military production was later concentrated on the far-more pedestrian Model W/NG.

Ariel Red Hunter W/VH (or W/NH)	

Type: Motorcycle, medium, solo
Manufacturer: Ariel Motors (JS); Birmingham
Production: 1933 to 1940
Engine: Ariel; single cylinder; 497cc; overhead valves; air cooled; power output, 26bhp at 5,600rpm
Transmission: 4F; foot gear-change
Suspension: Parallelogram girder front forks with friction-damped coil spring; solid rear end
Brakes: Drums, front and rear
Dimensions: Length – 2,083mm/82in
   Width – 762mm/30in
   Height – 1,016mm/40in
   Wheelbase – 1,397mm/55in
   Weight – 166kg/365lb
Performance: Maximum speed – 129kph/80mph

Ariel W/NG

The 348cc Model W/NG was Ariel's major contribution to the war effort, with some 40,000 examples completed between 1940 and the end of the war. While early examples were little changed from the machine's civilian counterpart, the Red Hunter NG, minor modifications and improvements were made throughout the production run. Despite its rather high weight compared to other similar machines, the W/NG was a reliable and lively performer, both on and off the road, and was a popular mount that served with all three British services.

The single prototype for what became the W/NG was supplied to the War Office on loan in mid-1940, and was demonstrated to both the British and a number of foreign military representatives; these demonstrations led to the French actually placing an order but, sadly, this could not be fulfilled following the German occupation. A number of faults came to light during the subsequent British trials during July 1940, and the War Office apparently rated the machine as "fair, for use only in an emergency". However, the evacuation from Dunkirk changed all that and, by August 1940, the Ministry of Supply had placed the first order for the W/NG, calling for some 2,700 machines at a price of around £55 each. Regular follow-up contracts continued throughout the war, the last being an order for the Royal Navy in April 1945.

Like its civilian predecessor, the W/NG was powered by an overhead-valve single-cylinder engine producing 12.8bhp from 348cc; this figure was down-rated from the 17bhp of the civilian equivalent. Drive to the rear wheel was via a four-speed gearbox and open chain.

In order to provide additional ground clearance for off-road work, the tubular steel frame was actually derived from Ariel's competition practice, rather than directly from the civilian NG. Nevertheless, it followed the conventions of the period, with a single down-tube,

ABOVE AND LEFT: **Based on the company's Red Hunter machine, the Model W/NG was produced by Ariel between 1940 and 1944 and supplied to Britain's Army and Royal Air Force.**

LEFT: **The W/NG was a conventional machine for the period, and was widely used by both the British Army and the Royal Navy, with many remaining in service into the 1950s.**

ABOVE: **The engine was a single-cylinder overhead-valve unit, producing almost 13bhp from 348cc. There was a four-speed gearbox, with final drive by open chain.**

and a solid rear end. The front forks were of the friction-damped parallelogram girder type with a single coil spring. The handlebars were originally rubber-mounted, but this method was discontinued since it was found that the attachment was not always secure. A rear carrying rack or a pillion post was fitted over the rear mudguard and there were dual toolboxes. Most examples produced after 1942 Included pannler frames, and late production models were fitted with the Vokes military universal air filter positioned on the top of the fuel tank.

In common with all British motorcycles of the period, the use of rubber items such as handgrips, footrests and so on was discontinued from 1942/43 due to severe shortages. Similarly, in an effort to conserve aluminum alloy, pressed steel or cast-iron primary chain case and timing covers were used. The steering damper was also removed.

The W/NG was the only motorcycle produced by Ariel between 1941 and 1945. After the war, many surplus machines were supplied to the liberated European nations, and some remained in use until the late 1950s.

ABOVE: **The Ariel Model NG was the company's major contribution to the British war effort. By 1945 some 40,000 machines had been manufactured.**

Ariel W/NG

Type: Motorcycle, medium, solo
Manufacturer: Ariel Motors (JS); Birmingham
Production: 1940 to 1944
Engine: Ariel; single cylinder; 348cc; overhead valves; air cooled; power output, 12.8bhp at 5,600rpm
Transmission: 4F; foot gear-change
Suspension: Parallelogram girder front forks with friction-damped coil spring; solid rear end
Brakes: Drums, front and rear
Dimensions: Length – 2,134mm/84in
Width – 762mm/30in
Height – 1,067mm/42in
Wheelbase – 1,397mm/55in
Weight – 171kg/376lb
Performance: Maximum speed – 109kph/68mph

Ariel W/VA

Typical of 500cc motorcycles of the period, the Ariel W/VA was a militarized version of the company's civilian VA model, launched in 1938, and procured in small numbers by the War Office during the difficult early years of World War II. Initial deliveries took place in September 1939, the machines supplied at a price of just over £47.50 each, with the last coming in October 1940, by which time just 184 had been procured, some possibly being diverted from French Army contracts which could not be completed. The first 97 machines were supplied to the Army, the others were issued to the Royal Air Force (RAF) and the Ministry of Agriculture.

The W/VA was a totally conventional machine, little altered from the civilian equivalent, and was assembled around a cycle-type tubular frame with a single down-tube; the front forks were of the parallelogram girder design, with a single coil spring and friction damper. No suspension was fitted at the rear. The engine was a 497cc single-cylinder side-valve unit with magneto ignition, driving the rear wheel through a separate Burman four-speed gearbox. Final drive was by open chain.

No pillion seat was fitted but there was a luggage carrier at the rear and some machines may have been used in conjunction with a sidecar. An experimental lightweight version of the

ABOVE AND BELOW LEFT: **The Ariel W/VA of 1939 was a military motorcycle based on the company's civilian VA model. The first examples were intended for the French Army but, when France fell in the Blitzkrieg of 1940, the machines were diverted for use by British forces.**

W/VA was also procured during 1939 and was trialled at Farnborough against a standard W/VA and a Norton 16H. There was no series production and, in 1940, the War Office settled on Ariel's W/NG as the company's major contribution to World War II.

Ariel did not become involved in supplying military motorcycles in the post-war years and ceased production in 1970.

Ariel W/VA

Type: Motorcycle, medium, solo; and with sidecar
Manufacturer: Ariel Motors (JS); Birmingham
Production: 1939 to 1940
Engine: Ariel; single cylinder; 497cc; side valves; air cooled; power output, 19bhp at 5,500rpm
Transmission: 4F; foot gear-change
Suspension: Coil-sprung friction-damped girder parallelogram front forks; solid rear end
Brakes: Drums, front and rear
Dimensions: Length – 2,134mm/84in
Width – 762mm/30in
Height – 1,067mm/42in
Wheelbase – 1,397mm/55in
Weight – 175kg/385lb
Performance: Maximum speed – 113kph/70mph

BSA Model H

Originally a manufacturer of guns – BSA stands for the Birmingham Small Arms Company – who began motorcycle production in 1910, having already been manufacturing cycles for five years. The British Army started to purchase BSA motorcycles in 1912 and, although they were outnumbered by the products of Douglas and Triumph, by 1918 there was a total of 1,088 BSA machines of various types in service. Most numerous of these was the Model H, a standard 557cc civilian model dating from 1914.

The Model H was powered by a 557cc vertical single-cylinder side-valve engine driving via a three-speed gearbox and concealed chain; power output was increased from 4hp to

4.25hp midway through the production run, in which form the machine was capable of a creditable 80kph/50mph. The frame was a heavy-duty version of that produced for the company's first motorcycle, the Model K, better suited to sidecar use. There were redesigned friction-damped coil-sprung cantilever front forks, together with a solid rear end. Typical of cycle practice of the period, the wheels had a diameter of 660mm/26in, with the brakes consisting of blocks acting on secondary rims, front and rear.

A square tank was carried below the top-tube of the frame and no pillion seat was fitted. Most examples were provided with full acetylene lighting and a rear luggage carrier.

ABOVE: The BSA Model H was a standard 557cc civilian machine, adopted by the British and other armies during World War I.

A number of these machines were also supplied to the South African Motor Cycle Corps during the early part of World War I.

BSA Model H

Type: Motorcycle, heavy, solo
Manufacturer: BSA; Birmingham
Production: 1914 to 1918
Engine: BSA; single cylinder; 557cc; side valves; air cooled; power output, 4 to 4.25bhp
Transmission: 3F; foot gear-change
Suspension: Coil-sprung friction-damped cantilever front forks; solid rear end
Brakes: Blocks and brake rims, front and rear
Dimensions: Not available
Weight – 118kg/260lb
Performance: Maximum speed – 80kph/50mph

BSA C10

In 1939, the War Office started purchasing a lightly militarized version of the BSA C10, a 249cc civilian motorcycle which had been introduced in 1938, and which it was deemed was suitable for training and domestic use. The first contract, in May 1939, called for 585 machines in what was described as "K" specification (K-C10), at a price of just £29.25 each. The second, in September of that year, covered a further 1,350 machines in "W" specification (W-C10). Deliveries took place during 1939 and 1940; a further four machines were also supplied to the Royal Navy in 1940.

BSA C10 (K-C10, W-C10)

Type: Motorcycle, light, solo
Manufacturer: BSA Cycles; Birmingham
Production: 1939 to 1940
Engine: BSA; single cylinder; 249cc; side valves; air cooled; power output, 8bhp at 4,500rpm
Transmission: 3F; foot gear-change
Suspension: Coil-sprung friction-damped girder parallelogram front forks; solid rear end
Brakes: Drums, front and rear
Dimensions: Wheelbase – 1,321mm/52in
Other dimensions not available
Weight – 114kg/250lb
Performance: Maximum speed – 97kph/60mph

Purchased as a replacement for the earlier BSA B20, the C10 was a relatively lightweight machine powered by a 249cc single-cylinder side-valve engine with magneto ignition, installed in a conventional cycle-type frame with a single down-tube. The rear wheel was driven via a three-speed foot-change gearbox and open chain. The front forks were of the girder parallelogram pattern, with suspension provided by a single friction-damped coil spring. No suspension was provided at the rear.

When tested by the Mechanical Warfare Engineering Establishment (MWEE), the C10 was considered to lack reliability but, nevertheless, it stayed in use with the Army, and presumably the Navy, until 1942 when whatever machines remained were passed to other government agencies.

The major difference between the civilian and military machines was in the use of wider wheel rims which allowed a standard WD tyre to be fitted and the use of a small luggage carrier on the rear mudguard.

The civilian C10 was put back into production after the war and survived until 1953.

LEFT: **The Royal Navy considered that the few BSA C10 motorcycles which they had acquired in 1940 were suitable for training and for women riders. Powered by a single-cylinder 249cc engine, the C10 was a militarized version of an earlier civilian machine.**

BSA B30-WD

Two prototypes for the military BSA B30-WD were supplied to the War Office in 1940 and were offered in direct competition to the Ariel W/NG. Based on the pre-war B29, it was essentially a standard production machine that had been lightly modified for military use. The B30 was found to perform well in the trials and an order was placed for 50 examples incorporating small modifications. These were delivered during 1941 and were issued to various units for service trials, including one example supplied to the USA and two to Canada. A follow-up order for 10,000 machines was cancelled

at the last minute in favour of the ubiquitous M20. Although the military B30 provided the basis for the company's post-war B31 off-road machine, it never went into series production.

A completely conventional but competent design, the B30 – which was also known as the WB30 – was a medium-weight motorcycle powered by BSA's 348cc single-cylinder overhead-valve engine, driving through a four-speed gearbox and exposed chain. The basis of the machine was a cycle-type frame of tubular construction, with friction-damped coil-sprung girder

ABOVE AND BELOW LEFT: **Total production of the B30-WD was only some 152 machines. Two prototypes, 50 machines for the Army and 50 for the Royal Navy.**

parallelogram forks at the front, and a rigid rear end. There was an occasional pillion post at the rear, while canvas pannier bags were carried on metal frames to suit the despatch role.

It was said to have been intended for multi-terrain use and, with a top speed of 120kph/75mph, it was fast on the road. However, at just 152mm/6in, the ground clearance was poor and the standard road-type front suspension cannot have made off-road riding easy or comfortable.

BSA B30-WD

Type: Motorcycle, medium, solo
Manufacturer: BSA; Birmingham
Production: 1940 to 1941
Engine: BSA; single cylinder; 348cc; overhead valve; air cooled; power output, 15bhp at 4,850rpm
Transmission: 4F; foot gear-change
Suspension: Parallelogram girder front forks with friction-damped coil springs; solid rear end
Brakes: Drums, front and rear
Dimensions: Length – 2,019mm/80in
   Width – 712mm/28in
   Height – 930mm/37in
   Wheelbase – 1,346mm/53in
   Weight – 154kg/339lb
Performance: Maximum speed – 120kph/75mph

BSA M20

The BSA M20 was first submitted to the War Office for consideration for possible military use in 1936, but was quickly rejected as being unreliable. The main complaint related to excessive wear in the cylinder bore – in fact the engine in this prototype machine wore to such a degree that a replacement piston and barrel had to be fitted after little more than 9,656km/6,000 miles. In 1937 three further machines were supplied in which BSA had attempted to address the problems. Two of these were put through a 16,093km/10,000 mile trial at the Mechanization Experimental Establishment (MEE) at Farnborough, while the third was issued for service trials.

Originally designed as part of the civilian M range, others of which were also supplied to the British Army, the M20 was a typical medium-weight single-cylinder machine of the period, a type favoured by the British Army. At the conclusion of the trials, the machine was reported to offer "fair" reliability and was accepted for military service. From this inauspicious start, the M20 went on to become the most numerous, and one of the longest-serving, motorcycles in the British Army, with almost 125,000 examples completed during the war years.

The M20 was powered by a 496cc low-compression side-valve single-cylinder air-cooled engine, with a cast-iron barrel and alloy crankcase. The rear wheel was driven via an exposed roller chain with the power transmitted through a non-adjustable Ferodo clutch – which was a source of trouble when contaminated by oil – and a four-speed foot-change gearbox. At the front, the forks were of the typical girder pattern, suspended by means of a single coil spring, initially with the addition a hand-adjusted damper knob. The damper knob adjustment was discontinued in October 1939 in favour of a

TOP: **The hybrid military/civilian M20 went into series production in 1939, with almost 125,000 manufactured during a nine-year production run.**
ABOVE: **Despite some initial problems, most users would have considered the side-valve M20 to be a reliable and very conventional machine and it was used by all three of the British services.**

nut adjustment, reinstated in 1941/42 as a result of experience gained in riding on poor road surfaces overseas. Both were finally deleted altogether in 1943. The rear end was unsprung.

Production started in earnest in early 1939 with a contract for 398 machines which were described as model K-M20 and were priced at £42.29 each. This was effectively a hybrid military/civilian machine which incorporated features such as a standard military lighting switch panel and 203mm/8in military-pattern headlight, but also included elements of the civilian M20 Standard and De-Luxe models.

More contracts followed, and a number of K-M20s were diverted to the British Army which had originally been intended for India and South Africa. The K-M20 was superseded by the W-M20 in October of that same year. The W-M20 featured new girder forks, simplified mudguards, and a new, smaller fuel tank. Despite being standardized in 1942, minor modifications continued throughout the life of the machine; for example, the headlight was superseded by a smaller 152mm/6in unit in 1941/42. All unnecessary rubber was removed from the machine in late 1942, when rubber was in short supply due to action in the Far East. Early examples were fitted with a long field stand which was subsequently deleted. In 1943, a new crankcase guard was designed, and the machine was fitted with a high-capacity Vokes air cleaner intended for use in dusty climates; the air cleaner was fitted to the top of the fuel tank, which in turn was also modified to accommodate it.

Typically, the machine was employed in the convoy escort and despatch rider/communications role and, by the time the war was over, the M20 was considered to be a reliable machine, and many remained in service well into the 1960s. However, despite some describing it as "the most reliable motorcycle ever made", the machine was not without its problems and throughout its service life there were difficulties with hot starting, burned valves, gasket failure and with oil contamination of the clutch. The latter not really being solved until the late 1950s. Another problem was that the engine was prone to catching fire as a result of backfiring.

The M20 was used by all three of the UK services and, particularly with the RAF, was often found in combination with an SS Swallow (Jaguar) built single-seat military sidecar

The last British military contract – for just three machines – was placed in 1947 by which time the price had risen to £79.70. Civilian production of the M20 continued until 1956, although its stablemate, the 600cc M21, continued in production until 1963.

ABOVE: **Very much in the style of the period, the M20 was fitted with girder parallelogram front forks and no rear suspension. The box on the fuel tank is the standard Vokes high-efficiency air cleaner.** BELOW: **The typical canvas pannier bags were invariably fitted on the rear luggage rack, together with an additional small luggage rack.**

BELOW AND BELOW RIGHT: **Suspension at the front was by a single coil spring and the engine was a single-cylinder side-valve producing 13bhp.**

BSA M20 (K-M20, W-M20)

Type: Motorcycle, medium, solo; and with sidecar
Manufacturer: BSA; Birmingham
Production: 1939 to 1947
Engine: BSA; single cylinder; 496cc; side valves; air cooled; power output, 13bhp at 4,200rpm
Transmission: 4F; foot gear-change
Suspension: Girder parallelogram front forks with a single coil spring; hand-operated damper on early and mid production models; solid rear end
Brakes: Drums, front and rear
Dimensions: Length – 2,134mm/84in
Width – 711mm/28in
Height – 991mm/39in
Wheelbase – 1,372mm/54in
Weight – 191kg/420lb
Performance: Maximum speed – 100kph/62mph

BSA B40-WD

Introduced for user trials in 1966 as a replacement for the wartime BSA B20 and Matchless G3L machines, many of which remained in service, the BSA B40-WD was a modified version of the company's standard B40 Star SS90 motorcycle dating from 1960. The B40 Star was effectively the frame of the 250cc C15 machine, into which had been fitted a larger, 343cc, engine. The B40-WD started to enter British service in 1967, with a total of 2,000 procured before production was halted. The B40 was also used by the Australian, Belgian, and Danish armies.

With telescopic front forks, 343cc overhead valve engine and four-speed transmission, the B40-WD was a distinct improvement on earlier production machines. Military modifications included a special engine filtration system, dust-proof carburettor and improved protection for the vulnerable areas of the drive chain

and front forks. In order to improve service life, the engine was down-rated by reducing the compression ratio.

The machine was standardized in the late 1960s and was used for convoy control, military police and despatch rider duties; motorcycles used for police escort duties were frequently fitted with a full fairing.

In those pre-Japanese "invasion" days, this could probably have been considered to be a modern motorcycle although it was not particularly fast on the road. It offered a surprisingly lively standard of cross-country performance, with many saying that the military version offered a better performance in this respect than the civilian machine.

Production of the civilian B40 ended in 1965, but the military version remained available until 1971 when the BSA company was effectively closed down.

ABOVE: **The BSA B40-WD was effectively a replacement for the wartime B30, albeit updated with an overhead-valve engine and full suspension. It was based on the civilian B40 Star.**

BSA B40-WD, Mk 1; FV2003

Type: Motorcycle, medium, solo; and with sidecar
Manufacturer: BSA; Birmingham
Production: 1966 to 1971
Engine: BSA; single cylinder; 343cc; overhead valves; air cooled; power output, 18bhp at 6,000rpm
Transmission: 4F; foot gear-change
Suspension: Telescopic coil-spring front forks with hydraulic damping; coil-spring suspended swing-arm forks at rear with hydraulic damping
Brakes: Drums, front and rear
Dimensions: Length – 2,108mm/83in
Width – 762mm/30in
Height – 1,080mm/43in
Wheelbase – 1,372mm/54in
Weight – 156kg/343lb
Performance: Maximum speed – 88kph/55mph

Clyno 5-6hp

Most of the combination outfits used by the British Army's Motor Machine Gun Corps during World War I were supplied by Clyno and were based on the company's standard civilian 5–6hp motorcycle of 1910. The special sidecar was designed and built by Vickers and carried a .303in tripod-mounted water-cooled Vickers machine-gun behind a armoured steel screen; there was also provision for spare ammunition, cooling water for the gun and sundry spares. The gun could also be demounted and used in a ground position.

The machine was powered by a Stevens V-twin side-valve engine producing a nominal 5–6hp from a capacity of 744cc, the rear wheel driving through a three-speed transmission and enclosed roller chain.

Clyno had also been one of the first companies to adopt interchangeable detachable wheels.

As is so often the case, the contracts for these military machines saved the Clyno company from bankruptcy and something like 1,800 of the outfits had been supplied by 1918. A further 1,500 were supplied to Russia but these were fitted with a JAP engine.

The same machine was also used in solo form, and with either a standard passenger sidecar or with a stretcher sidecar for use as a light ambulance. The latter intended for ferrying injured casualties from the front line to the clearing stations. The company more or less ceased motorcycle production after the end of the war to concentrate on motorcars.

ABOVE: **As well as being used as a mount for a machine gun, the Clyno 5–6hp was used in solo and standard sidecar form.**

Clyno 5–6hp

Type: Motorcycle, heavy, solo; and with machine-gun, passenger or stretcher sidecar
Manufacturer: Clyno; Wolverhampton
Production: 1910 to 1918
Engine: A.J. Stevens (or JAP); two cylinders in V formation; 744cc; side valves; air cooled; power output, 5 to 6hp (nominal)
Transmission: 3F; hand gear-change
Suspension: Girder parallelogram front forks with a single coil spring; friction damper; solid rear end; three-point suspension on sidecar
Brakes: Drum, rear only
Dimensions: Not available
Weight – 136kg/299lb
Performance: Maximum speed – 81kph/50mph

Douglas 2.75hp Model WD

Founded in 1882, Douglas Engineering started producing motorcycles in 1907 after acquiring the flat-twin engine design of W.J. Barter when Barters Light Motors went into liquidation. The company achieved considerable success in the Junior TT competition, and it was this that led to a contract to supply the British War Office. The Douglas Model WD appeared in 1914 and was used by the British and Belgian armies and by the Australian Expeditionary Force; by 1918, the British had some 14,000 of these motorcycles in service, a number exceeded only by the Triumph Model H.

Derived from the Model W, the WD was a standard civilian machine modified for military service and, although it was well-made and reliable, features such as V-belt drive and exposed flywheel would have been considered archaic by some even in 1914. However, the lightweight construction gave the machine a reasonable top speed of close to 80kph/50mph.

True to the company's origins and, unusually for the period, it was a horizontally opposed two-cylinder machine, with the engine arranged along the axis of the frame. Drive was by open

LEFT: **Production of the Model W ended in 1917, but was restarted a year later. The military version ended in 1921. The civilian model continued until 1926.**

Douglas 2.75hp	

Type: Motorcycle, medium, solo
Manufacturer: Douglas Engineering; Bristol
Production: 1914 to 1920
Engine: Douglas; horizontally opposed twin-cylinder; 348cc; side valve; air cooled; power output, 6.5bhp at 3,600rpm
Transmission: 2F, then 3F; hand gear-change
Suspension: Parallelogram front forks with friction-damped coil springs; solid rear end
Brakes: Caliper brakes at front; block acting on drive pulley at rear
Dimensions: Not available
   Weight – Not available
Performance: Maximum speed – 77kph/48mph

primary chain to a two-, and later three-speed gearbox, with belt drive to a pulley on the rear wheel; the transmission was mounted under the rear-most cylinder. The tubular frame was typical of cycle-derived designs, and incorporated a large mud shield behind the front wheel. The girder front forks incorporated friction-damped coil springs. Although the solid rear end was typical of the period; there were unsuccessful experiments with a swinging-arm rear fork arrangement. Acetylene lighting was provided together with leather pannier bags.

Douglas 4hp Models A, B

Although derived from the company's 3.5hp (500cc) civilian model, which also saw military service, the Douglas 4hp was a specialized military sidecar machine. Something like 5,000 examples were procured over a two-year period, with the machines being used by both the British Army and the Royal Naval Air Service.

The machine was constructed around a duplex frame, with a horizontally opposed two-cylinder engine engine installed longitudinally. This type of engine remained associated with the Douglas company almost until its demise and, unlike most such designs, the cylinders were arranged at something like 160 degree. Transmission was by chain, via a two- or three-speed gearbox. The front forks were of the girder type, with suspension provided by

LEFT: **The 3.5hp machine was discontinued in 1916. Civilian production of the 4hp machine continued until 1923.**

Douglas 4hp	

Type: Motorcycle, heavy, with sidecar
Manufacturer: Douglas Engineering; Bristol
Production: 1915 to 1918
Engine: Douglas; horizontally opposed twin-cylinder; 593cc; side valve; air cooled; power output, 6.5bhp at 3,600rpm
Transmission: 2F or 3F; hand gear-change
Suspension: Parallelogram front forks with friction-damped coil springs; solid rear end
Brakes: Caliper brakes at front; block acting on inside rim of drive pulley at rear
Dimensions: Not available
   Weight – Not available
Performance: Not available

a pair of friction-damped coil springs. The rear end was solid.

The single-seat sidecar was used to provide transport for officers in the field as well as occasionally providing carriage for the primitive radio sets of the period.

Douglas DV60

ABOVE: Douglas was a key supplier during World War I but made only the smallest contribution during the later conflict when the company produced two prototypes for a two-cylinder horizontally opposed flat-twin machine in the style of the big German motorcycles. The project was abandoned in 1945 with no series production.

Despite having been among the largest suppliers of motorcycles to the British War Office during World War I, the contribution of the Douglas Motors during World War II amounted to just two prototypes of a heavy 602cc horizontally opposed two cylinder machine – which never entered production. The DV60 was a decidedly un-British machine, much more in the style of the big German motorcycles. It was produced in response to a specification issued by the War Office for what was hoped would become a standardized heavy military motorcycle. Key features of the specification included a top speed of 100–115kph/62–71mph, a weight of less than 136kg/300lb and a totally enclosed transmission. Prototypes were bult by BSA, Douglas, Royal Enfield and Triumph.

Photographs of the DV60 show a large impressive machine built around a substantial duplex frame with twin top- and down-tubes, and with bracing tubes running underneath the tank to provide additional stiffness. The telescopic front forks were of the company's Radiadraulic pattern, employing hydraulic damping and, although the rear forks were unsprung, there was a fully sprung seat pillar offering 75mm/3in of movement. The engine was a 602cc side-valve transverse twin, with magneto ignition, driving through a three-speed gearbox and enclosed chain.

A substantial skid plate was fitted beneath the crankcase and there were also crash bars to protect the protruding cylinders. Twin panniers were fitted at the rear together with a hinged pillion seat and luggage rack. The fuel tank was fitted well forward in the frame and there were separate knee pads provided for the rider on a saddle extension.

Although the DV60 met the War Office specification in most respects, the total weight was well over the 136kg/300lb limit. Presumably if development had continued, this would have been reduced.

Two prototypes were completed during 1944/45 and were submitted to the Mechanical Warfare Experimental Establishment for trials. Nothing came of the project, it being was abandoned when the war ended.

When the British Army was looking for new motorcycle designs in the immediate post-war years, Douglas attempted to resurrect elements of the design in a new frame, but the War Office chose to purchase the Triumph TRW.

Douglas DV60

Type: Motorcycle, heavy, solo
Manufacturer: Douglas Motors; Bristol
Production: 1944 to 1945
Engine: Douglas; two cylinder, horizontally opposed; 602cc; side valves; air cooled; power output, Not available
Trancmiccion: 3F; foot gear-change
Suspension: Hydraulically-damped telescopic leading-link front forks; solid rear end
Brakes: Drums, front and rear
Dimensions: Not available
   Weight – 163kg/360lb
Performance: Maximum speed – 113kph/70mph

Excelsior Welbike

Known colloquially as the "parascooter", the Excelsior Welbike was one of the smallest military motorcycles produced and was certainly among the smallest military vehicles of World War II. It was designed with the intention of being air-dropped alongside parachute troops in order to provide mobility in the drop zone, and was packed into a special air-drop container, in a partly knocked-down condition.

The Welbike, which derived its name from the British city of Welwyn where it was designed, first appeared in 1942, and was developed under the direction of Lieutenant-Colonel J.R.V. Dolphin. Manufacturing was undertaken by the Excelsior Motor Company of Birmingham who, before the war, had been producing small motorcycles. The engine was a 98cc single-cylinder two-stroke unit produced by Villiers, mounted horizontally in the frame. The rear wheel was driven via a roller chain in the conventional manner but there was no gearbox, the rider having to make do with a single fixed ratio.

In order to fit the machine into the parachute container, the saddle was pushed down until it rested on the top of the seat tube. The handlebars were similarly folded back over the engine. It took little more than 10 seconds to make the machine ready for use after it had been removed from the container. It must be said that, without suspension or gears, and with just a rear brake, this machine was not suitable for travelling long distances but, nevertheless, it was capable of achieving 48kph/30mph on the flat.

The first production machines (1,183 examples) were designated Mk I while later machines were described as Mk II Series I and Mk II Series II, although the modifications were very modest. A total of some 3,923 units were produced under three separate contracts.

A similar, civilian, machine was produced after the war under the name Corgi.

ABOVE: **The Excelsior Welbike was developed especially for use by airborne troops and with its single-cylinder push-start engine and single gear ratio was of minimum specification. The handlebars were folded back across the tank and the seat was slid down into the seat tube to reduce the height to allow the tiny machine to be packed into an air-drop container.** LEFT: **Paratroopers unpack and assemble a Welbike that has been air-dropped in the container that also formed a transport trailer.**

Excelsior Welbike Mks I & II	

Type: Motorcycle, solo, folding, 98cc
Manufacturer: Excelsior Motor Co; Birmingham
Production: 1942 to 1945
Engine: Villiers Junior; single cylinder; 98cc; two-stroke; air cooled; power output, 2.7bhp at 3,750rpm
Transmission: Single fixed gear ratio
Suspension: None
Brakes: Drum, rear only
Dimensions: Length – 1,321mm/52in
    Width – 559mm/22in
    Height – 787mm/31in, reducing to 381mm/15in
    Wheelbase – 1,003mm/39.5in
    Weight – 31.8kg/70lb
Performance: Maximum speed – 48kph/30mph

LEFT: **This pre-production machine for what became the Hayes-RMCS M1030 was photographed at the Defence Equipment Research Agency (DERA) in May 2001. The engine, was developed by Hayes Diversified Technologies (HDT) to provide a power curve similar to a conventional petrol unit. The engine for the production machine is being produced by HDT. The frame and other components are derived from the Kawasaki KLR–650.**

while at the rear there is a swing arm with a Uni-Trak multi-link set-up. A skid plate is fitted to protect the engine and there are engine crash bars. The five-speed transmission is also taken from the Kawasaki, but the gear ratios are changed to suit the different characteristics of the diesel engine.

The prototype for the engine was based on the bottom end of the venerable Royal Enfield Bullet but later development machines used a custom-built liquid-cooled engine manufactured in the USA which will happily run on diesel fuel, aviation kerosene and even rapeseed oil. A single-cylinder indirect-injection type, the engine has double overhead cams with four valves, and uses some components of the base Kawasaki.

A heavy-duty rear equipment rack is fitted and a rigid plastic holster and side cases can also be fitted.

At a late stage in the development programme it was being said that the US Marines had ordered 500 machines, the MoD had ordered 1,500, and interest was also being shown by the governments of Germany, France, Belgium and Ireland. Production started in March 2006, with two models, the M1030M1 for the US Marines, and the M1030M1E for the UK and Europe.

Hayes–RMCS M1030M1

As far back as 1992, the British Royal Military College of Science (RMCS) had produced a diesel-engined motorcycle demonstrator. This work led to a collaboration between RMCS and Hayes Diversified Technologies (HDT) to develop what was claimed would be the world's first production diesel-powered motorcycle. Diesel fuel had already become the fuel of choice for NATO armies but, until this development work started, no diesel motorcycles were available. The development project was sponsored by the British Ministry of Defence (MoD) and the US Marine Corps (USMC).

The design of the motorcycle was carried out by Dr Stuart McGuigan and John Crocker of RMCS, with development and production being spearheaded by Fred Hayes of HDT. The project aimed to produce an engine with realistic power output and performance characteristics which would allow it to replace the conventional petrol engine.

The motorcycle itself is a development of the Kawasaki KL–R650, a standard dual-purpose military trail machine. The welded steel frame and suspension of the Kawasaki are unchanged; the front forks are hydraulically-damped telescopic units,

LEFT: **The original prototype, seen here, was produced by the Royal Military College of Science and used the bottom end of a Royal Enfield Bullet petrol engine.**

Hayes–RMCS M1030M1, M1030M1E

Type: Motorcycle, heavy, solo
Manufacturer: Hayes Diversified Technologies; Hesperia, California
Country: Joint United Kingdom/United States project
Production: 2006 to date
Engine: HDT; single cylinder; 584cc; overhead valves; diesel; liquid cooled; power output, 25bhp at 4,800rpm
Transmission: 5F; foot gear-change
Suspension: Hydraulically-damped telescopic front forks; swing arm at the rear suspended on a Uni-Trak multi-link system
Brakes: Discs, front and rear
Dimensions: Length – 2,160mm/85in
  Width – 915mm/36in
  Height – 1,345mm/53in
  Wheelbase – 1,448mm/57in
  Weight – 167kg/369lb
Performance: Maximum speed – 138kph/85mph

James K17

James K17

Type: Motorcycle, light, solo
Manufacturer: James Cycle Company; Birmingham
Production: 1939
Engine: Villiers 9D; single cylinder; 122cc; two stroke; air cooled; power output, 3.3bhp at 4,000rpm
Transmission: 3F; hand gear-change
Suspension: Pressed-steel parallelogram front forks with a single coil spring; solid rear end
Brakes: Drums, front and rear
Dimensions: Length – 1,854mm/73in
  Width – 889mm/35in
  Height – 851mm/34in
  Wheelbase – 1,219mm/48in
  Weight – 72kg/157lb
Performance: Maximum speed – 64kph/40mph

Just two examples of the civilian James K17 were supplied to the War Office for evaluation and trials in 1942/43. Since the model was out of production at that time and had been introduced in 1939 they must have been either old stock or assembled from parts. Although it was not purchased in quantity, the K17 could be considered as the

ABOVE: **More than 5,000 James ML (Military Lightweight) were purchased by the British War Office during World War II.**

pre-production or prototype version of the considerably more numerous, and similar, ML which remained in production from 1943 to 1945. A lightweight machine, it was envisaged that it might be suitable for use by airborne and assault units.

Like the ML which followed, the K17 was powered by a 122cc Villiers

9D single-cylinder engine – a type which had been introduced in 1939 – mounted in a simple cycle-type tubular frame, driving through a three-speed gearbox in unit construction with the engine. The front suspension consisted of a single coil spring in combination with pressed-steel parallelogram forks and the rear end was unsprung.

James J10 Comet

James J10 Comet

Type: Motorcycle, light, solo
Manufacturer: James Cycle Company; Birmingham; AMC; Woolwich
Production: 1948 to 1952
Engine: Villiers Mk 1F or Mk 4F (1952 models); single cylinder; 99cc; two stroke; air cooled; power output, 2.8bhp at 4,000rpm
Transmission: 2F; foot gear-change
Suspension: Tubular telescopic front forks with a single coil spring; solid rear end
Brakes: Drums, front and rear
Dimensions: Length – 2,007mm/79in
  Width – 648mm/26in
  Height – 851mm/34in
  Wheelbase – 1,171mm/47in
  Weight – 58kg/128lb
Performance: Maximum speed – 65kph/40mph

Although James had produced some larger machines during the pre-war years, wartime production consisted only of lightweight machines. The company's Birmingham factory was badly damaged during air raids in November 1940 and never really recovered. The tiny Comet was typical of post-war production. Powered by a 99cc Villiers engine in what was effectively a strenghtened cycle-type

frame, the Comet was little more than a moped capable of just 65kph/40mph on the road. A single, undamped coil spring was provided at the front, while the rear end was without suspension.

BELOW: **The James J10 Comet was a standard lightweight civilian motorcycle which was lightly modified for use by the RAF and the Air Ministry for despatch rider duties.**

Leather panniers and a rear luggage rack were provided and most examples were also fitted with leg shields and a small plastic windscreen.

The company was taken over by Associated Motorcycles (AMC) in 1951, and the J10 was superseded by the J11 with plunger rear suspension in 1953.

Matchless G8

Hundreds, possibly thousands of British Army motorcycles were abandoned in France following the evacuation from the Dunkirk beaches in May 1940 and, desperate to bring stocks back up to an acceptable level, the War Office procured large numbers of what were essentially civilian machines, almost regardless of suitability.

Among these were 15 examples of the pre-war Matchless G8, a 498cc single-cylinder machine which, slightly modified, was to remain a mainstay of the company's products for another 25 years.

The G8 had first been introduced in 1937 and, although it was a fast road motorcycle, intended for enthusiastic riding, it was not really suitable for

ABOVE AND BELOW LEFT: **The Matchless G8 was one of those civilian machines which was purchased by the British Army in a desperate attempt to make up for the motorcycles which had been abandoned in France following the evacuation from Dunkirk.**

military use and no further examples were purchased.

The machine went back into production in modified form in 1949 as the Clubman G80, remaining available until 1966. The designation became G80L when Teledraulic front forks were fitted.

Matchless G8

Type: Motorcycle, medium, solo
Manufacturer: Matchless Motor Cycles; Woolwich
Country: United Kingdom
Production: 1937 to 1940
Engine: Matchless; 498cc single cylinder; overhead valves; air cooled; power output, 23bhp at 5,400rpm
Transmission: 4F; foot gear-change
Suspension: Parallelogram girder front forks with damped coil spring suspension; solid rear end
Brakes: Drums, front and rear
Dimensions: Not available
    Wheelbase – 1,397mm/55in
    Weight – Not available
Performance: Maximum speed – 121kph/75mph

Matchless G3L

Matchless had provided the War Office with an example of their lightweight G3 in 1940 for trials. Known as the G3L, the production machine, which was scarcely recognizable when compared to the prototype, started to be delivered in the latter part of 1941. The changes which were made were intended to speed production and to suit the machine better for a service life.

It was a modern 347cc single-cylinder despatch riders' motorcycle of compact, perhaps too compact design; a feature which frequently brought problems in maintenance. The difficulties of access often making it less than popular with workshop staff. Nevertheless, with Teledraulic (telescopic hydraulic) front forks, a feature which had been introduced by Matchless in 1941 on

this model, combined with a powerful four-stroke power unit and four-speed gearbox, it was a fast and popular machine with riders. Although it was better suited to road duties, its popularity and reliability ensured that it remained in service into the 1950s.

As was usual, the machine was scarcely suitable for military service initially and development continued even after it had entered service. There were many minor changes during the model's production life, not always for the better. For example, at some stage a shortage of alloy meant that the timing cover was produced from cast iron. During 1942, several thousand machines were fitted with Miller electrical equipment rather than the more usual Lucas item. After 1942, the universal War Office pattern

ABOVE LEFT: **Almost unique among British military motorcycles of the period, the G3L was equipped with telescopic front forks which gave a fast, smooth ride, making the machine a popular mount for despatch riders.** ABOVE: **It is surprising what a difference the telescopic forks make to the overall appearance of the machine, giving it a modern look when compared with other motorcycles in service.**

Vokes air filter was fitted, positioned on the top of the fuel tank.

Production started in 1941, with more than 63,000 examples delivered for the War Office before the last contract was completed in 1945. The machine continued in production as the G3 Clubman after the war.

RIGHT: **The engine on the G3L was a 347cc overhead-valve unit, producing 16bhp; in combination with a four-speed gearbox, this was sufficient to propel the machine at speeds up to 109kph/68mph. More than 63,000 G3Ls were built between 1941 and 1945.**

Matchless G3L	

Type: Motorcycle, medium, solo
Manufacturer: Matchless Motor Cycles; Woolwich
Production: 1941 to 1945
Engine: Matchless; 347cc single cylinder; overhead valves; air cooled; power output, 16bhp at 3,500rpm
Transmission: 4F; foot gear-change
Suspension: Teledraulic (telescopic hydraulic) front forks; solid rear end
Brakes: Drums, front and rear
Dimensions: Length – 2,108mm/83in
    Width – 762mm/30in
    Height – 1,041mm/41in
    Wheelbase – 1,295mm/51in
    Weight – 149kg/328lb
Performance: Maximum speed – 109kph/68mph

Norton 16H, WD-16H

Norton was among the most significant suppliers of military motorcycles to the British Army and the company's earlier 16H model was the most numerous of the more-than 100,000 machines built by Norton during World War II. Effectively a lighter version of the company's Big Four, the 490cc 16H had originally been submitted to the War Office for trials back in 1932, and then again, in updated form in 1936. The latter model was among the most successful motorcycles tested at the Mechanical Engineering Establishment that year and series purchases began in 1936. Despite numerous detail improvements, the War Office stuck to the 1936 specification until production ceased in 1945.

The 16H was powered by a 499cc single-cylinder side-valve engine driving

through a four-speed gearbox – with a foot change replacing the hand change at the request of the War Office – and exposed roller chain. Top speed was 113kph/70mph. With a tubular steel cycle-type frame, girder parallelogram front forks and rigid rear end, the Norton was thoroughly conventional and totally reliable.

There were changes to the air-cleaner arrangements during the life of the machine, and a crankcase shield was fitted from 1938. Other changes included the fitting of a pillion seat and pannier racks during 1941/42. A new headlamp design appeared at around the same date.

Most of the 84,200 machines supplied were intended for solo use but a number were equipped with a single-seat sidecar, often supplied by The Swallow

ABOVE LEFT AND ABOVE: **Norton produced more than 100,000 motorcycles between 1939 and 1945 – some 80 per cent of which were the 16H, and the militarized WD-16H. With its 490cc single-cylinder side-valve engine, girder forks and rigid rear end, it was typical of British motorcycles of the period.**

Sidecar Company. The 16H was supplied to the British and Canadian armies, also the RAF, and was widely used for despatch rider, convoy control and reconnaissance duties.

A special lightweight version was also prepared for trials in 1936 but, with a weight reduction of less than 13kg/30lb, was found to offer no particular advantage. In 1938, the machine was also trialled with a driven sidecar wheel. Following the delivery of some 400 of these machines, the Big Four entered production.

Norton 16H, WD-16H

Type: Motorcycle, medium, solo; and with sidecar
Manufacturer: Norton Motors; Birmingham
Production: 1936 to 1945
Engine: Norton; 490cc single cylinder; side valves; air cooled; power output, 14bhp at 4,500rpm
Transmission: 4F; foot gear-change
Suspension: Parallelogram girder front forks with friction-damped coil spring; solid rear end
Brakes: Drums, front and rear
Dimensions (solo): Length – 1,880mm/74in
  Width – 762mm/30in
  Height – 991mm/39in
  Wheelbase – 1,372mm/54in
  Weight – 176kg/388lb
Performance: Maximum speed – 113kph/70mph

LEFT: **The 16H was employed by the British and Canadian armies and by the RAF, and was suitable for both solo and sidecar use. In the latter case, during the early years of the conflict, could sometimes be found mounting a machine-gun.**

Norton Model 633, WD–Big Four

Norton's 500cc 16H had been trialled with what the War Office referred to as Sidecar Wheel Drive (SWD) in May 1938, and the success of this machine led to the development of the sidecar-equipped Norton Big Four, the only British motorcycle of World War II to offer 3x2 drive. The Big Four had originally been

ABOVE AND BELOW: **The Norton Big Four had been launched as a civilian machine in 1936 before being trialled with sidecar-wheel drive by the British War Office in 1938. Military production started the same year but, sadly, the machine lacked sufficient power for the weight of the sidecar. The change of role for the military motorcycle and the appearance of the Jeep brought production to a premature end in 1942.**

launched on the civilian market in 1936, and had proven to be a reliable and successful machine. The military variant followed the pattern established by the 16H 3x2 development model, incorporating the Baughan live axle system, with improvements made to the drive-line, for example by incorporating universal joints. In this form, the machine appeared to offer a satisfactory cross-country performance and pre-production examples were issued for troop trials in 1938.

The "Model 633 number 1", better known as the military Big Four was put into production the same year. Sadly, the Norton was never as successful as the German, French and Belgian machines of this type. The 633cc single-cylinder side-valve engine was decidedly dated; although it had been updated for 1938, it had its origins in the 1920s. As a result the machine lacked sufficient pulling power off the road. In addition, with the sidecar drive engaged, the machine became difficult to steer on the road since there was no differential. Several attempts were made to improve the performance, but the appearance of the US-built Jeep, which offered effective four-wheel drive in a similar-sized package, brought this development to an end. Production ceased in 1942 after some 4,779 examples had been completed under nine separate contracts.

The frame of the machine was a standard cycle-type tubular design. On the civilian machines the frame was identical to that used with the 16H, but for the military Big Four the frame was enlarged and the rear forks were also modified to take larger diameter bearings. Front forks were of the girder parallelogram pattern, with friction-damped helical coil springs. The rear end was unsprung. The gearbox was a four-speed unit, with widely spaced ratios to suit cross-country work, and there was exposed chain drive to the rear wheel. The sidecar was driven by a simple cross shaft engaged by a hand control operated by the rider through a dog clutch.

The sidecar was a special military pattern not unlike that used on trials machines. Handles were fitted to the front and rear, behind the pillion seat, and on the front mudguard, to assist with manhandling the machine through heavy mud.

A stowage box for ammunition was provided behind the sidecar seat and the sidecar was also was equipped to mount a Bren gun on clips on the right-hand side. The sidecar body could also be removed and replaced by a flat platform designed to mount a mortar. All three wheels were interchangeable, and a spare wheel was carried on the back of the sidecar.

In 1947, the Norton Big Four was put back into production as a civilian solo machine; engine capacity was reduced to 596cc, achieved by shortening the stroke.

TOP AND ABOVE: **The standard military sidecar was a decidedly utilitarian unit which would have been equally at home on a civilian trials machine. The sidecar-wheel drive could be engaged by the rider via a hand control which operated a dog clutch on the cross shaft. When the drive was engaged, the machine was not easy to control.**

Norton Model 633, WD-Big Four

Type: Motorcycle, heavy, with sidecar, 3x2
Manufacturer: Norton Motors; Birmingham
Production: 1938 to 1942
Engine: Norton Big Four; single cylinder; 633cc, (post-war production, 596cc); side valves; air cooled; power output, 14.5bhp at 4,500rpm
Transmission: 4F; foot gear-change; shaft drive to sidecar wheel via dog clutch
Suspension: Parallelogram girder front forks with friction-damped coil spring; solid rear end
Brakes: Drums, front and rear
Dimensions (solo): Length – 2,182mm/86in
   Width – 1,702mm/67in
   Height – 1,168mm/46in
   Wheelbase – 1,372mm/54in
   Weight – 170kg/375lb
Performance: Maximum speed – 109kph/68mph

OEC (medium) Caterpillar Tractor 3x2

OEC motorcycles were produced between 1901 and 1954 by the Osborne Engineering Company. Early examples were powered by Minerva and MMC engines. From 1920 Blackburn engines were used and for a period the machines were identified as OEC-Blackburn. Although the RAF had purchased a number of OEC machines in the late 1920s, the company tended to concentrate on the specialized market and would not generally have been asked to supply to the military. However, in 1928, OEC completed a series of experimental 3x2 motorcycles in which the single rear wheel was replaced by two in-line.

The first of these was a medium weight single-cylinder machine which was trialled against a Triumph Model P which had been converted to this unusual configuration by the Royal Army Service Corps workshops. The OEC may have been purpose-built or it may have been a conversion of a standard motorcycle. Presumably in an effort to restrain the length, the down-tube was curved and the front wheel was pulled back into the curve. At the rear, a centre-pivoted walking beam carried a pair of small wheels driven by a secondary enclosed chain. A track could be fitted around these wheels, and the machine could also be readily converted back to the standard configuration. The front forks were of the sliding-pillar type with what was described as duplex steering.

LEFT: **The engine was a 490cc JAP V-twin side-valve, tilted back in the frame. The same machine has also been attributed to JAP as a manufacturer.**

OEC (medium) Caterpillar Tractor 3x2

Type: Motorcycle, medium, solo, 3x2
Manufacturer: Osborne Engineering Company; Gosport
Production: 1928
Engine: JAP; V-twin; 490cc; side valves; air cooled; power output, Not available
Transmission: 4F; hand gear-change
Suspension: Sliding pillar front forks; solid rear end
Brakes: Drums, front and rear
Dimensions: Not available
  Weight – 206kg/453lb
Performance: Not available

OEC (light) Caterpillar Tractor 3x2

The second of OEC's Caterpillar Tractor motorcycles was a 250cc machine, almost certainly using a Blackburn engine. Like the larger model, it was part of an experiment to try to improve the off-road performance of motorcycles by increasing the vehicle's tractive power. At the end of the trials, which were carried out in India and Egypt as well as at Aldershot, it was concluded that the improvements in cross-country performance were more than offset by rider fatigue and the complexity of the machine. The concept was abandoned.

The basic configuration of the lighter machine was similar to the first prototype – the frame was of similar unconventional design in order to minimize the wheelbase but various changes were made to reduce the weight. As before, the down-tube was shaped to allow the front wheel to run close-in, and there was a centre-pivoted walking beam chain case at the rear on which was mounted a pair of small wheels. Drive to the first of the rear wheels was by standard open chain from the gearbox. A caterpillar track could be fitted around these wheels, and, once again, the machine could also be readily converted to the standard configuration.

Sliding-pillar front forks type were fitted and the company favoured duplex steering, although this may have been removed during the trials and converted to the standard single pivot.

LEFT: **The OEC (light) is identifiable by the straight exhaust pipe from the 250cc Blackburn engine.**

OEC (light) Caterpillar Tractor 3x2

Type: Motorcycle, light, solo, 3x2
Manufacturer: Osborne Engineering Company; Gosport
Production: 1928
Engine: Blackburn; single cylinder; 250cc; side valves; air cooled; power output, Not available
Transmission: 4F; hand gear-change
Suspension: Sliding pillar front forks; solid rear end
Brakes: Drums, front and rear
Dimensions: Not available
  Weight – 141kg/310lb
Performance: Not available

Roush Arctic Cat

Roush Arctic Cat

Type: ATV quad bike, 4x4
Manufacturer: Roush Specialist Vehicle
Engineering/Arctic Cat; Brentwood
Production: 2006 to date
Engine: Lombardini; in-line two cylinders; 686cc;
overhead valves; diesel; water cooled; power
output, 18bhp at 4,300rpm
Transmission: Automatic CVT system; central
differential lock
Suspension: Hydraulically-damped coil-sprung
A arms at each wheel station
Brakes: Discs, front and rear
Dimensions: Length – 2,362mm/93in
Width – 1,220mm/48in
Height – 1,245mm/49in
Wheelbase – 1,473mm/58in
Weight – 357kg/785lb
Performance: Maximum speed – 80kph/50mph

In 2004, Roush Specialist Vehicle Engineering started the development work for a diesel-powered military quad bike in association with Arctic Cat, a manufacturer of ATVs for commercial and recreational applications. The machine combined high mobility in the roughest terrain, with portability and excellent riding characteristics, while also offering a high payload and towing capability. Manufacture of the vehicle began in 2006 at the Arctic Cat plant in Austria, and the machine is being marketed to both defence and commercial customers.

Based on the Arctic Cat Sport 4x4, the machine is built around a tubular-steel frame with load-adjustable coil-sprung double wishbone suspension, front and rear, with 250mm/10in of travel. Power comes from a 686cc Lombardini four-stroke twin-cylinder diesel engine, with optional turbocharger, driving all four wheels through an IBC automatic Constant Velocity Transmission (CVT) system and central differential lock.

The front wheels can be deselected when not required. To maintain stability and mobility in the event of tyre damage, the machine can be fitted with a run-flat system.

LEFT: **The diesel-powered Roush Arctic Cat was developed from the civilian sport model. The vehicle is air portable, highly mobile over the severest of terrain.**

Two seats are provided, and there are load-carrying racks fitted at front and rear, together with a cargo box, giving a total cargo capacity of 227kg/500lb.

Military fittings includes camouflage equipment, a self-contained shelter, gun racks and a man-pack radio. Roush also offers a range of options such as winches and communications equipment, combat lighting and auxiliary power supplies.

Royal Enfield Model D, WD/D

**Royal Enfield
Model D, WD/D**

Type: Motorcycle, light, solo
Manufacturer: Enfield Cycle Co; Redditch
Production: 1939 to 1941
Engine: Royal Enfield; single cylinder; 248cc;
air cooled; power output, 10bhp
Transmission: 4F; foot gear-change
Suspension: Girder parallelogram front forks
with friction-damped coil spring
Brakes: Drums, front and rear
Dimensions: Length – 2,159mm/85in
Width – 698mm/28in
Height – 1,016mm/40in
Wheelbase – 1,422mm/56in
Weight – 151kg/330lb
Performance: Maximum speed – 88kph/55mph

By 1938, Royal Enfield was offering no less than 20 different motorcycles to the public, among them was the 248cc Model D. The machine was among those pre-war civilian motorcyles pressed into service with the British Army following the outbreak of war in 1939. The first order came in 1939 when the War Office ordered 600 motorcycles intended for light despatch duties. Although these were essentially identical to the motorcycles available on the civilian market, those machines supplied under subsequent orders, for what was described as the Model WD/D, were modified in a number of small ways.

Very much a product of its time, the Model D was a large but relatively light motorcycle, fitted with a 248cc single-cylinder side-valve engine in a tubular cradle frame. Parallelogram girder-type forks with a friction-damped coil spring were fitted to the front. The rear end was unsprung. Transmission was by a four-speed gearbox and open chain. In original civilian form, the machine was a single seater, but later War Office contracts may have included a pillion pad.

BELOW: **During the war a total of some 2,100 examples were ordered, the WD/D was generally employed for training duties, particularly for ATS personnel.**

Royal Enfield Model WD/CO, WD/CO/B

TOP AND ABOVE: **Royal Enfield's overhead-valve WD/CO was introduced in 1942 and was derived from the company's civilian Model CO.**

ABOVE: **The WD/CO remained in production until the end of the war, by which time some 30,000 examples had been produced. It was widely used by all three British services.**

The Royal Enfield WD/C was introduced in 1940, and remained in production for two years, during which time, some 16,500 examples were supplied. The WD/C was a lightly militarized version of the company's pre-war Model C, a 346cc side-valve solo machine, much criticized in military service for its lack of power. This was addressed in early 1942 when the WD/C was superseded by the overhead valve WD/CO which, in turn, was derived from the civilian Model CO.

Although the two are often confused, presumably because the model designations are so similar, the machines share very few components, although the WD/CO was a direct replacement for the earlier machine. Despite sharing bore and stroke dimensions, and being fitted with the same type of Lucas magneto ignition, the overhead-valve engine, designed by E.O. (Ted) Pardoe, was considerably more efficient. With something like 50 per cent more horsepower than the earlier side-valve unit, the top speed was raised from 90kph/56mph to almost 110kph/68mph. An Albion four-speed foot-change gearbox was fitted, driving through an exposed chain. During late 1942, shortages led to the Albion gearbox being temporarily replaced by a Burman type. Machines which were so-equipped were designated WD/CO/B.

The frame was a conventional tubular-steel cycle-type in design with a single down-tube, although changes made during the production run meant that there were actually three distinct frame designs used; the last adopting a pressed-steel top tube for reasons of economy. The front forks were the familiar girder parallelogram type, using a friction-damped coil spring for suspension. All but the earliest production examples were equipped with side-mounted check springs on the forks.

Early models were equipped with a steering damper, but this was subsequently deleted. The first two frame designs differed in the area of the rear forks, but on all three, the rear end was unsprung.

These were essentially civilian motorcycles and the only concessions made to the military were by virtue of an all-over olive drab finish and the provision of a rear carrying rack or pillion seat and pannier racks. The Vokes tank-mounted air cleaner was fitted from late 1944 onwards. Total production of the two types of WD/CO amounted to almost 30,000 machines and the type was widely used by the British Army, Royal Navy and the RAF, as well as by Civil Defence units. Although it was a compact and well-designed machine, its use was mainly confined to convoy escort and similar work since the lack of ground clearance and exposed crankcase reduced suitability for cross-country usage.

Remaining machines were rapidly disposed of at the end of the war.

ABOVE RIGHT AND RIGHT: **The engine, designed by Ted Pardoe, was a 346cc overhead-valve unit producing 14bhp from its and was coupled to an Albion four-speed foot-change gearbox. Top speed was a creditable 110kph/68mph.** BELOW: **Front forks were of the conventional parallelogram girder design, with a friction-damped coil spring for suspension. The friction settings on both the steering and suspension could be adjusted by handwheel.**

Royal Enfield Model WD/CO, WD/CO/B

Type: Motorcycle, medium, solo
Manufacturer: Enfield Cycle Company; Redditch
Production: 1942 to 1945
Engine: Royal Enfield; single cylinder; 346cc; overhead valves; air cooled; power output, 14bhp at 4,800rpm
Transmission: 4F; foot gear-change
Suspension: Friction-damped coil-sprung girder parallelogram front forks; solid rear end
Brakes: Drums, front and rear
Dimensions: Length – 2,159mm/85in
Width – 698mm/28in
Height – 1,016mm/40in
Wheelbase – 1,422mm/56in
Weight – 154kg/340lb
Performance: Maximum speed – 109kph/68mph

Royal Enfield WD/RE "Flying Flea"

The lightweight Royal Enfield "Flying Flea" was procured as an expendable despatch rider's motorcycle which could be used by airborne troops. The design brief called for a machine which would be reliable and robust and could offer adequate performance on both roads and across country. It was essential that it be of lightweight construction since it would be carried in gliders or aircraft and, inevitably, would need to be manhandled across rough ground.

It was based on a civilian machine which Royal Enfield had launched, initially in the Netherlands, in 1939 and which, in turn, was said to be based on the German DKW RT-125. The examples which were initially supplied to the War Office for evaluation were little changed from the cilvilian offering. A 125cc single-cylinder two-stroke engine provided 2.6bhp, driving the rear wheel via a three-speed gearbox and roller chain. The front forks were suspended on rubber bands while the rear end was unsprung.

The War Office evaluation proved that the motorcycle was suitable for the intended role and, subject to a number of minor modifications it was approved for production. A twin-box silencer was fitted to reduce exhaust noise, and the War Office requested that the Amal carburettor be replaced with a Villiers type. Other changes involved modifying the frame to increase the saddle height, repositioning the toolbox. Folding kick-start, footrests and handlebars were fitted to reduce the envelope dimensions when packed in the protective cradle for air-dropping. The rear sprocket was reduced by one tooth (34 rather than 35) to lower the gear ratios.

Production started in 1942 and almost 8,000 examples had been constructed by the time the last military contract was completed in 1944.

ABOVE, ABOVE RIGHT AND LEFT: **The single-cylinder 125cc Royal Enfield WD/RE – better known as the "Flying Flea" – was based on a pre-war civilian machine which was said, in turn, to have been derived from DKW's RT-125. It was a lightweight motorcycle intended for use by airborne troops and considered to be expendable. A special protective cradle was developed which allowed the machine to be air-dropped. Some 8,000 examples were built over a three-year period.**

Royal Enfield WD/RE "Flying Flea"

Type: Motorcycle, light, solo
Manufacturer: Enfield Cycle Co; Redditch
Production: 1942 to 1944
Engine: Royal Enfield; single cylinder; 125cc; two stroke; air cooled; power output, 2.6bhp at 4,000rpm
Transmission: 3F; foot gear-change
Suspension: Girder parallelogram front forks with rubber band suspension; solid rear end
Brakes: Drums, front and rear
Dimensions: Length – 1,880mm/74in
 Width – 864mm/34in
 Height – 965mm/38in
 Wheelbase – 1,220mm/48in
 Weight – 62kg/137lb
Performance: Maximum speed – 65kph/40mph

Rudge-Whitworth 3.5hp Multi

Although best known for its bicycles, Rudge-Whitworth started making motorcycles in 1911, using a 499cc inlet-over-exhaust engine and achieved considerable racing success. In 1912, the company launched its civilian "Multi-gear" model, receiving an order for 400 of these from the Belgian Army in 1914, with a similar number also supplied to the Russian Imperial Army. None went to the British Army, although a small number were supplied to the Royal Navy for shore patrol work and to the Royal Naval Air Service (RNAS).

The machine employed a standard cycle-type tubular frame and was powered by a 499cc single-cylinder engine with magneto ignition, overhead inlet valves and side exhaust. Starting was by hand lever. Final drive was by belt and there was no gearbox in the accepted sense. The engine speed could be varied to the required road speed by means of hand-adjustable pulley on the rear wheel, adjustment drawing the flanges of the pulley together to change the diameter. The tension of the drive belt was handled automatically as the pulley diameter changed. A clutch was fitted on the engine output shaft.

At the front, friction-damped girder parallelogram forks, with a single coil spring were fitted. The rear remained unsprung.

The company supplied frames, wheels and front forks to the War Office for a standard British military motorcycle but this was not progressed. Production of the Multi stopped in 1916 to allow the company to concentrate on manufacturing aircraft wheels and ammunition. A few of these machines were supplied to the War Office between 1936 and 1939, but Rudge stopped making motorcycles in 1940.

LEFT: **The Rudge-Whitworth Multi was fitted with a unique manually controlled stepless transmission system which employed an adjustable pulley on the rear wheel, together with an automatic belt-tensioning device. The machine saw service with the Belgian and Russian armies and with the Royal Navy and RNAS.**

Rudge-Whitworth 3.5hp Multi

Type: Motorcycle, medium, solo
Manufacturer: Rudge-Whitworth; Coventry
Production: 1912 to 1916
Engine: Rudge-Whitworth; single cylinder; 499cc; overhead inlet valve, side exhaust; air cooled; power output, 3.5bhp
Transmission: Variable by hand adjustment of drive-belt pulley
Suspension: Coil-sprung friction-damped girder parallelogram front forks; solid rear end
Brakes: Caliper at front; block acting upon the drive pulley at the rear
Dimensions: Wheelbase – 1,397mm/55in
Other dimensions not available
Weight – 97kg/214lb
Performance: Maximum speed – 65kph/40mph

Scott 3.75hp

The Yorkshire engineer Alfred Scott built six prototypes of a two-cylinder motorcycle engine in 1908 and began production of motorcycles the following year, with early machines being produced on his behalf by the Jowett car company. The earliest examples of the motorcycle used air-cooled cylinder heads with water-cooled cylinders, but full water cooling was soon adopted. The 3.75hp model was launched in 1912 and became the basis for a machine-gun carrier outfit.

Known as the Scott/Vickers machine-gun carrier, the motorcycle was attached to a special armoured sidecar on which a 0.303in Vickers water-cooled machine-gun was tripod-mounted. In

this form, the machine was adopted by the Motor Machine Gun Service and was deployed in teams of three, one equipped with a gun, one with the tripod mount but no gun and one carrying spares and ammunition. The outfit was demonstrated to Winston Churchill and King George V in 1914. The company received contracts for 200 machine-gun carriers and 100 solo motorcycles, at least one of which was demonstrated with a machine-gun mounted on the handlebars. In use, it seems that the engine was insufficiently powerful for the weight of the machine.

The motorcycle used a step-through duplex tubular frame in which was mounted Scott's 499cc water-cooled two-cylinder engine, the radiator being carried ahead of the rider, immediately behind the leg shields. The fuel tank was mounted at the junction of the seat tube and the top tube. There was no gearbox, but two speeds were available via an innovative rocking-pedal foot-operated gear change that also doubled as a clutch; the final drive used a pair of open chains. Ignition was by magneto. At the front, there were undamped girder parallelogram forks, with a single coil spring, while the rear was unsprung.

LEFT: **A contemporary advertisement for the Scott 3.75hp machine-gun carrier.**

ABOVE: **The 3.75hp water-cooled Scott was one of the first British motorcycles to be adapted to carry a machine gun on a purpose-built sidecar. The machine lacked a conventional gearbox but two speeds were available via two chain wheels each of which could be selected by a foot pedal. The engine lacked sufficient power for the weight of the sidecar and gun.**

Although Alfred Scott left the company in 1918, the business which he had started prospered on the basis of producing high-quality water-cooled machines throughout the 1920s and 1930s. No motorcycles were supplied to the British Army during World War II and although production resumed after the war, there were further changes of ownership and production ended in the 1960s.

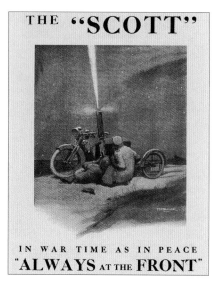

THE "SCOTT"

IN WAR TIME AS IN PEACE
"ALWAYS AT THE FRONT"

Scott 3.75hp

Type: Motorcycle, medium, solo; and with sidecar
Manufacturer: Scott Engineering; Bradford
Production: 1912 to 1914
Engine: Scott; two cylinder, 499cc; two stroke; water cooled; power output, 3.75bhp
Transmission: 2F by manual selection of chain sprocket
Suspension: Coil-sprung girder parallelogram front forks; solid rear end
Brakes: Caliper, front and rear
Dimensions: Wheelbase – 1,296mm/51in
Other dimensions not available
Weight – 100kg/220lb
Performance (solo): Maximum speed – 56kph/35mph

Sunbeam 3.5hp

Together with designer J.E. Greenwood and consultant Harry Stevens of AJS, John Marston started making motorcycles under the name Sunbeam in 1912, launching a 3.5hp model fitted with a 395cc engine in late 1913. Following the outbreak of hostilities in 1914, Marston modified the machine to make it suitable for military service. Changes included an improved magneto drive, a new more robust constant-mesh gearbox, and a strengthened clutch. Unfortunately, the high price of the machine deterred the War Office, and only 79 were in British service by the end of the war, although some were supplied to other Western Allies.

It was a well-built and interesting machine, powered by a 395cc single-cylinder side-valve engine installed in a cycle type diamond-pattern tubular frame, with drive by open chain to the rear wheel via a three-speed hand-change gearbox. At the front, there were Druid friction-damped coil-sprung parallelogram forks, while the rear end remained unsprung.

Acetylene lighting equipment was fitted and there was a rear luggage rack and small leather side panniers.

The 3.5hp model was also modified to form the FMM, a model specially designed for the French Army who specified belt drive; this necessitated an increase in engine power to 4hp achieved by increasing the capacity to 445cc.

After the war, the 3.5hp military model was offered to civilians alongside models from the 1916 range. Marston's death in 1918 led to the Sunbeam company being sold, eventually ending up with Nobel Industries (ICI), before passing to Associated Motor Cycles, and then to BSA during World War II.

ABOVE: **At the end of World War I, many Sunbeam 3.5hp machines were sold as surplus to civilians.**

Sunbeam 3.5hp

Type: Motorcycle, medium, solo
Manufacturer: John Marston; Wolverhampton
Production: 1912 to 1918
Engine: Sunbeam; single cylinder, 395cc; side valves; air cooled; power output, 3.5bhp
Transmission: 3F; hand gear-change
Suspension: Friction-damped coil-sprung girder parallelogram front forks; unsprung rear
Brakes: Caliper at front; drum at rear
Dimensions: Not available
Weight – Not available
Performance: Maximum speed – 64kph/40mph

Triumph Model H

Triumph motorcycles were the product of German immigrants, Siegfried Bettman and Maurice Schulte, at first constructed using Minerva and JAP engines. The company's first all-Triumph machines were launched in 1905 and racing success helped boost sales. The belt-drive Model H, launched in 1915, was the company's most successful machine to date, with more than 30,000

supplied to the British Army and the Western Allies between 1914 and 1918.

The Model H was a civilian machine, which made little concession to life in the Army, but, nevertheless, the reliability of the machine under difficult conditions earned it the nickname "Trusty" from the Allied troops. It was developed from the company's earlier 3.5hp model and it shared that model's tubular-steel cycle-type frame and exposed V-belt drive. The engine was a 550cc side-valve unit with magneto ignition and drove a separate Sturmey-Archer three-speed gearbox drive, connected by the V belt to a pulley on the wheel rim. The front forks were of

LEFT: **The Triumph Model H was to remain in production until 1920, and was then replaced by the Model SD.**

Triumph Model H

Type: Motorcycle, heavy, solo
Manufacturer: Triumph Motors; Coventry
Production: 1915 to 1920
Engine: Triumph; single cylinder, 550cc; side valves; air cooled; power output, 4bhp
Transmission: 3F; foot gear-change
Suspension: Coil-sprung friction-damped cantilever front forks; solid rear end
Brakes: Caliper at front, acting on wheel rim; block at rear, acting on drive pulley
Dimensions: Not available
Weight – 95kg/200lb
Performance: Maximum speed – 72kph/45mph

the coil-sprung cantilever type, and there was a rigid rear end. Brakes operated cycle-style by caliper on the front rim and by a block acting on the drive pulley at the rear.

The Model H was replaced by the Model SD "Spring Drive" in 1920 which used the same frame.

Triumph P-II

Triumph's Model P was a standard civilian machine, of utilitarian and decidedly pre-war design which the company hoped would help maintain sales in the face of recession. With a 1925 launch price of less than £43, it quickly became the best-selling 500cc motorcycle in Britain and by May 1925 the company was producing 1,000 machines a week. In improved P-II form, the machine was procured by

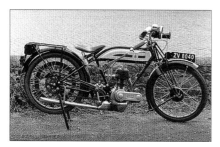

ABOVE: **The Model P also provided the basis for an experimental three-wheeled motorcycle produced by the Royal Army Service Corps.**

the British Army to replace the earlier Triumph Model H.

In its original form, the machine was powered by a 499cc single-cylinder side-valve engine driving via a chain and three-speed gearbox. The cycle-type frame featured an unsprung rear end, together with parallelogram girder front forks suspended on twin coil springs.

Clearly, the Model P was designed down to a price: the valves lacked guides, operating directly in the cylinder block; the front brake was little more than asbestos rope. The rear brake was a dummy rim upon which a brake block was activated. There were also problems with the clutch. The company's reputation began to suffer and after 20,000 examples of the early machine had been produced, in late 1925 it was replaced by the Model P-II which addressed some of these shortcomings. The military version differed little from the

Triumph Model P-II

Type: Motorcycle, medium, solo; and with sidecar
Manufacturer: Triumph Engineering; Coventry
Production: 1925 to 1927
Engine: Triumph; single cylinder; 499cc; side valves; air cooled; power output, 5bhp at 2,600rpm.
Transmission: 3F; hand gear-change
Suspension: Parallelogram girder front forks with friction-damped coil springs; solid rear end
Brakes: Drum at front, block and dummy rim at rear
Dimensions: Length – 2,160mm/85in
　Width – 700mm/28in
　Height – 950mm/37in
　Wheelbase – 1,410mm/56in
　Weight – 110kg/241lb
Performance: Maximum speed – 80kph/50mph

civilian machine, and although most were used in solo form, sidecars were also fitted. Drive to the rear was by chain, but a belt was also used to distribute the power between a pair of single-track twinned wheels. This machine was the forerunner of the OEC three-wheelers dating from 1928.

Triumph Silent Scout

Designed by Val Page, who had moved to Triumph from JAP, Triumph's Silent Scout range was introduced in 1932; the name was also associated with a 150cc two-stroke machine introduced in 1931. The Silent Scout range comprised three models, the Model A was powered by a 550cc side-valve engine, while the Models B and BS used a 493cc twin-port over-head valve engine, the Model BS being fitted with high-compression cylinder heads. Engine lubrication was by dry

sump and there was magneto ignition. The Model B was purchased in small numbers by the War Office for military service.

All of the Silent Scouts fitted Val Page's silent cams and followers and inclined "sloper" cylinder, the latter in the style established by BSA the previous year. The frame was a tubular design, using the crankcase as the lower structural member, and the machines fitted a new, rubber-bushed, saddle-type fuel tank straddling the

top-tube, the first time this feature had been employed on a Triumph motorcycle. Drive from the engine was passed through a separate four-speed hand-change gearbox and the final drive was by open chain. The front forks were of the coil-sprung girder parallelogram design combined with a rigid rear end.

Triumph Silent Scout

Type: Motorcycle, medium, solo
Manufacturer: Triumph Motors; Coventry
Production: 1932 to 1934
Engine: Triumph; single cylinder, 493cc; overhead valves; air cooled; power output, 5bhp
Transmission: 4F; hand gear-change
Suspension: Coil-sprung friction-damped girder parallelogram front forks; solid rear end
Brakes: Drums, front and rear
Dimensions: Not available
　Weight – 95kg/200lb
Performance: Maximum speed – 80kph/50mph

LEFT: **Despite the extended wheelbase, the Silent Scout was a modern-looking machine. The range was only in production for just two years and fewer than 2,000 were built.**

Triumph 3SW

In 1937, the War Office purchased a Triumph Model 3S for trials, before specifying various changes to make it suitable for military service. The resulting side-valve Model 3SW was built in large numbers during the early years of World War II, continuing to be produced even after the 1940 bombing of Triumph's Coventry factory. It was superseded by the 3HW.

The economy 3SE was used as a basis for the 3SW, and early examples cost the War Office less than £40 each. It was assembled around a cycle-type frame with a single down-tube and duplex engine cradle, and was powered by a 343cc single-cylinder side-valve dry-sump engine, with magneto ignition. There was a separately mounted four-speed foot-change gearbox, with wider ratios than the civilian equivalent; final drive was by

open chain. Friction-damped coil-sprung girder parallelogram forks were used at the front, while at the rear there was no suspension.

Few changes were made during the machine's production life and it saw service with all three UK services, the Royal Navy assigning it to the WRNS.

Triumph 3SW	
Type: Motorcycle, medium, solo	
Manufacturer: Triumph Motors; Warwick	
Production: 1938 to 1941	
Engine: Triumph; single cylinder, 343cc; side valves; air cooled; power output, 10bhp	
Transmission: 4F; foot gear-change	
Suspension: Parallelogram girder front forks with friction-damped coil springs; solid rear end	
Brakes: Drums, front and rear	
Dimensions: Length – 2,057mm/81in	
Width – 762mm/30in	
Height – 1,016mm/40in	
Wheelbase – 1,334mm/53in	
Weight – 161kg/355lb	
Performance: Maximum speed – 105kph/65mph	

ABOVE: **An enthusiast in Military Police uniform on a well-restored 35W.**

Some 13,500 examples were ordered before the contracts stopped in 1941.

Triumph Model 5TW

Designed by Bert Hopgood, the 5TW 499cc twin was the first Triumph motorcycle to be fitted with telescopic front forks. The first prototype was handed to the War Office in 1942 for comparative trials against the company's own 3TW model. Although it apparently performed well, there was insufficient development time available to continue the project and it was shelved until 1944 when there was

a resurgence of interest by the War Office. The 5TW never entered full-scale production, but did provide the basis for the post-war TRW machine.

The frame was a standard tubular-steel cycle type and the telescopic front forks gave the machine something of an extended look at the front end but, in order to compensate, the rear of the frame was shortened, with the rear wheel placed closer to the seat

Triumph 5TW	
Type: Motorcycle, medium, solo	
Manufacturer: Triumph Engineering; Meriden	
Production: 1942 to 1944	
Engine: Triumph; twin cylinder; 499cc; side valves; air cooled; power output, 18bhp at 5,000rpm	
Transmission: 4F; foot gear-change	
Suspension: Hydraulically-damped telescopic front forks; solid rear end	
Brakes: Drums, front and rear	
Dimensions: Length – 2,096mm/83in	
Width – 724mm/29in	
Height – 1,042mm/41in	
Wheelbase – 1,346mm/53in	
Weight – 170kg/375lb	
Performance: Maximum speed – 88kph/55mph	

LEFT: **Alongside the Matchless G3L, the side-valve Triumph 5TW was one of the few British military motorcycles of the period to be equipped with telescopic front forks. However, unlike the Ariel G3L, the Triumph never entered series production.**

tube. At the rear, there was no suspension, the rider having to rely on the sprung saddle.

Power was provided by a side-valve parallel twin, with siamesed exhausts through a four-speed gearbox. Drive was an enclosed chain. A small pillion seat was fitted and there were frames for canvas pannier bags. Just two examples were completed.

Triumph Model 3HW

Triumph was forced to abandon its Coventry factory in 1940, due to the night bombing raids carried out by the *Luftwaffe* during November of that year. The factory was all but destroyed, as was much of the centre of Coventry and many completed motorcycles. For a period, Triumph operated out of temporary premises in Warwick but, by early 1942, the new factory at Meriden was completed. In April 1942, the company started full-scale production of the new 3HW - "H" meaning "overhead valve" in Triumph model codes, and "W" meaning "War Office".

The 3HW was an overhead-valve engined machine, designed to replace the earlier side-valve 3SW and, aside from the new engine, it resembled the earlier 3SW and the larger 5SW, with which it also shared the frame and other components.

The frame was a standard tubular-steel cycle type with a single down-tube and a duplex engine cradle. The rear forks were unsprung, and there were friction-damped girder-type parallelogram forks at the front, using a single coil spring for suspension. The 343cc engine, now with overhead valves, was fitted with magneto ignition, and was based on that used in the civilian 3H Tiger 80, some

ABOVE: **The Triumph 3HW was the first motorcycle to be produced at the company's new Meriden factory following the destruction of the Coventry works.** LEFT: **Note, an ammeter was fitted in the headlamp housing as on civilian machines.**

143 examples of which had been supplied to the War Office in 1940 when almost any motorcycle that could move under its own power was considered acceptable. For the military 3HW, certain design aspects of the engine were simplified in order to speed assembly and, later in the production run, pressed-steel was used for components such as the chain case and oil pump cover to reduce the consumption of vital aluminium alloys. As was standard practice at the time, the machine was fitted with a four-speed foot-change gearbox, with final drive by means of an open chain.

A rear luggage carrier was fitted, together with standard pannier frames and, from 1943, provision was made for a pillion seat. The standard War Office-type Vokes tank-mounted air cleaner was fitted from early 1945.

A compact and very reliable machine, the 3HW was much favoured by the Royal Navy; a small number also went to the RAF. Military production continued until 1945 by which time something like 30,500 examples had been ordered, although it is likely that less than 28,000 were actually built. The level of parts held in stock by the factory allowed the 3HW to remain in production after the war when it was offered to civilians until around 1947.

The powerful engine made ex-military machines a popular basis for a grass-track racing motorcycle.

There had been trials with a lightweight welded-frame, overhead-valve variant designated 3TW in 1939, but this was abandoned in 1940 after approximately 100 pre-production models had been produced.

ABOVE LEFT: **The 343cc overhead-valve engine was of modern design, the power of which gave the 3HW a top speed of 113kph/70mph.**

ABOVE: **The machine retained the conventional rigid rear end and parallelogram girder front fork suspension of the earlier pre-war machines.**

Triumph 3HW

Type: Motorcycle, medium, solo
Manufacturer: Triumph Engineering; Meriden
Production: 1942 to 1945
Engine: Triumph; single cylinder; 343cc; overhead valves; air cooled; power output, 17bhp at 5,200rpm
Transmission: 4F; foot gear-change
Suspension: Parallelogram girder front forks with friction-damped coil springs; solid rear end
Brakes: Drums, front and rear
Dimensions: Length – 2,057mm/81in
Width – 762mm/30in
Height – 1,016mm/40in
Wheelbase – 1,334mm/53in
Weight – 164kg/360lb
Performance: Maximum speed – 113kph/70mph

Triumph TRW

The Triumph TRW was a specialized military motorcycle which can be considered a hybrid of the wartime 5TW and the company's post-war TR5 Trophy model. Standardized parts were used wherever possible in order to reduce costs. Although the side-valve configuration was virtually obsolete by the end of the war, nevertheless, the TRW was powered by a variant of the Bert Hopgood-designed 499cc side-valve twin which delivered a respectable performance. There were Mk 1 and Mk 2 versions differing mainly in the design of the cylinder head which was alloy on the Mk 1 and cast-iron on the Mk 2 – but, at least the telescopic front forks of the earlier machine were retained.

The frame was a rigid tubular-steel cycle type, fitted with hydraulically-damped telescopic front forks which gave a degree of off-road performance in conjunction with a 4.00x19 rear tyre. At the rear there was no suspension. The power unit was derived from that originally developed in 1942 for the 5TW. However things had moved on since then and it was now effectively a de-tuned version of the side-valve parallel twin from the TR5 Trophy, featuring aluminium barrels and aluminium cylinder heads and a car-type carburettor. The transmission was a standard four-speed gearbox driving through an open chain.

A small pillion seat was fitted and there were frames for canvas pannier bags.

In 1951, Triumph had been sold to BSA and, although the two marques retained their autonomy, there was some rationalization across the ranges. In 1953, the TRW Mk 2 was introduced. As well as being fitted with cast-iron cylinder heads, which many would have considered a retrograde step, the Mk 2

ABOVE AND LEFT: **Although derived from the war-time 5TW and the post-war Trophy model, the twin-cylinder Triumph Model TRW was a purpose-designed military motorcycle not available to civilians. As well as serving with all three of the British Services, it was also supplied to Canada.**

ABOVE: **A small carrier rack was fitted to the top of the fuel tank.**

also employed an alternator and coil ignition in place of the magneto of the original. The changes reduced the overall weight by some 9kg/20lb.

The TRW was supplied to both the British and Canadian armies. Also to the Royal Navy and the RAF. The TRW was also widely exported.

Triumph TRW	
Type: Motorcycle, medium, solo; FV2001	
Manufacturer: Triumph Engineering; Meriden	
Production: 1948 to 1962	
Engine: Triumph; twin cylinder; 499cc; side valves; air cooled; power output, 18bhp at 5,000rpm	
Transmission: 4F; foot gear-change	
Suspension: Hydraulically-damped telescopic front forks; solid rear end	
Brakes: Drums, front and rear	
Dimensions: Length – 2,134mm/84in	
Width – 711mm/28in	
Height – 1,067mm/42in	
Wheelbase – 1,346mm/53in	
Weight – 154 to 163kg/340 to 360lb	
Performance: Maximum speed – 121kph/75mph	

Triumph 3TA Special

The Triumph 3TA Special was a militarized version of the standard civilian 3TA – or "Twenty One" – and was developed for the Netherlands Army in 1963. Designed by Edward Turner and Jack Wickes, the machine had been launched on the civilian market in 1957 and was easily recognized by its over-sized "bathtub" rear mudguard – which was omitted from the military version. With the 349cc four-stroke

engine, the 3TA marked Triumph's return to a size of engine, which had been ignored since the war years.

It was a handsome motorcycle, constructed around a conventional tubular-steel frame with hydraulic telescopic suspension at the front, and Girling coil-spring units in conjunction with a trailing arm at the rear. The engine was a coil-ignition two-cylinder unit producing almost 20bhp, which was sufficient to give a top speed, in civilian form, of 135kph/84mph although this was deliberately restricted to 121kph/ 75mph for the military role. Power was transmitted through a four-speed

LEFT: **A total of 1,100 Triumph 3TA Specials were built for the Dutch military.**

Triumph 3TA Special

Type: Motorcycle, medium, solo
Manufacturer: Triumph Engineering; Meriden
Production: 1963
Engine: Triumph; twin cylinder; 349cc; overhead valves; air cooled; power output, 19bhp at 6,500rpm
Transmission: 4F; foot gear-change
Suspension: Hydraulically-damped telescopic front forks; trailing arm at rear suspended on coil springs
Brakes: Drums, front and rear
Dimensions: Length – 2,110mm/83in
    Width – 680mm/27in
    Height – 960mm/38in
    Wheelbase – 1,360mm/53in
    Weight – 152kg/340lb
Performance: Maximum speed – 121kph/75mph

foot-change gearbox in unit construction with the engine, driving the rear wheel through an exposed chain. The 3TA Special was equipped with either a rear luggage rack or pillion seat and pannier side crash bars.

Triumph Tiger Cub T20WD

The Triumph T20WD was a militarized version of the company's standard civilian Tiger Cub model, which had originally been launched in 1954 as a successor to the successful Terrier. With a 199cc overhead-valve engine, it was fast, good-looking and economical and quickly became a success, remaining in production in various forms until 1968. The British Army started buying the Tiger Cub in 1962, specifying a down-rated engine

BELOW: **The Triumph T20WD was the last military motorcycle to be produced by the company.**

and other simple modifications to make the machine more suitable for service use.

It was a compact and mainly conventional lightweight motorcycle, constructed around a tubular-steel cycle-type frame with a single down-tube. Power was provided by a 199cc single-cylinder four-stroke engine, with battery and coil ignition, driving through a four-speed unit-constructed gearbox and exposed chain. The front forks were of the hydraulically-damped telescopic type, with twin coil springs incorporated into the swing-frame rear end.

The Tiger Cub also proved popular with other armies, and in 1965, a modified version was also produced for the French Army using an adapted version of the 20S/H Sports Cub; this model was designated as T20MWD and was built at the BSA Small Heath, Birmingham, factory. The company remains in business as a motorcycle manufacturer.

Triumph Tiger Cub T20WD

Type: Motorcycle, light, solo
Manufacturer: Triumph Engineering; Meriden
Production: 1962 to 1968
Engine: Triumph; single cylinder; 199cc; overhead valves; air cooled; power output, 10bhp at 6,000rpm
Transmission: 4F; foot gear-change
Suspension: Hydraulically-damped coil-sprung telescopic forks at front; damped coil-sprung swing frame at rear
Brakes: Drums, front and rear
Dimensions: Length – 1,880mm/74in
    Width – 660mm/26in
    Height – 1,070mm/42in
    Wheelbase – 1,350mm/53in
    Weight – 111kg/244lb
Performance: Maximum speed – 113kph/70mph

Velocette MAF

Following some early forays into motorcycle design under other names, Percy and Eugene Goodman's Veloce company started building motorcycles using the name Velocette in 1913. Despite considerable success, it was not until 1939, when the War Office purchased two 500cc MAC models for evaluation that the company became involved with the military. But, disregarding some 1,200 militarized MAC machines originally intended for the

ABOVE AND BELOW: The Velocette MAF was a reliable and popular military motorcycle. It was a basic civilian motorcycle progressively developed by including a number of modifications and improvements. The man responsible was Philip Irving, the designer at Velocette.

French Army which were diverted to the UK in 1940, the company's most significant military motorcycle of World War II was the MAF.

The MAF was effectively a militarized version of the 349cc MAC. Under the watchful eye of Velocette's designer, Philip Irving, a standard civilian MAC machine was progressively

developed to incorporate a large number of refinements and improvements intended to better suit the machine to service use. For example, although the frame was of conventional tubular steel construction with a single down-tube and duplex engine cradle, it was redesigned and strengthened by the inclusion of a large forging beneath the engine that also served as a sump shield. Rubber bump stops were added to the front forks, which were of traditional coil-sprung girder design, to improve handling off-road. The rear brake plate was mounted via a torque arm. A lower chain guard was fitted and the exhaust system was re-routed. There were many other detail changes, all of which had the effect of both improving the machine but increasing unit price by some 35 per cent when compared to the standard MAC.

Nevertheless, this was a fine motorcycle, fast, reliable and well suited to despatch rider duties, providing it was ridden mainly on the road. The War Office placed a contract for 2,000 in July 1941, replacing a contract for the same number of MACs.

The engine was Velocette's 349cc single-cylinder unit, with a high camshaft operating the overhead valves via short pushrods. The engine produced almost 15bhp, which was certainly sufficient power to provide a top speed of 109kph/68mph. The gearbox was a four-speed unit, with the normal Velocette gear-change pattern reversed to match that of other British military motorcycles of the period. To improve slow-speed cross-country work, first gear was reduced to 18.7:1. Final drive was by exposed chain.

At the front end were the usual leading-link girder parallelogram forks, with a single friction-damped coil spring for suspension; although they were "borrowed" from the

ABOVE: **The standard military-pattern headlamp and speedometer fitting on the Velocette MAF.**

MAC, the length of the top links was extended to improve off-road handling and performance.

Unfortunately, Velocette lacked the production facilities of larger companies such as BSA and Triumph. In the event, the single contract for the MAF is all that the company received, the Ministry of Supply believing that the quantities produced were insignificant and that Velocette might be better suited to other war work. Although the original quantity ordered was 2,000, the contract was never actually completed, being cancelled in September 1942 after only 947 examples had been completed.

Civilian production resumed after the war with what were little more than pre-war models and the Velocette company went into liquidation in 1968.

LEFT: **Powered by an overhead-valve engine, the Velocette MAF was a (British) militarized version of the MAC, differing in many ways from the MAC (WD) which had been developed for France. Less than 1,000 examples were built during 1941 and 1942.**

Velocette MAF

Type: Motorcycle, medium, solo
Manufacturer: Veloce; Birmingham
Production: 1941 to 1942
Engine: Velocette; single cylinder; 349cc; overhead valves; air cooled; power output, 14.9bhp at 5,500rpm
Transmission: 4F; foot gear-change
Suspension: Coil-sprung friction-damped leading-link parallelogram front forks; unsprung rear
Brakes: Drums, front and rear
Dimensions: Length – 2,159mm/85in
Width – 711mm/28in
Height – 965mm/38in
Wheelbase – 1,321mm/52in
Weight – 154kg/340lb
Performance: Maximum speed – 109kph/68mph

Velocette MAC (WD)

Officially described as the MAC (WD), but frequently designated "MDD" after the frame serial number prefix, this was a militarized version of Velocette's civilian MAC model, which had originally been launched in 1933. It had been developed for the French Army who had ordered 1,200 examples after seeing the civilian MAC demonstrated in October 1939. It is said that the first 25 were lost at sea and that, of course, subsequent machines could not be delivered when France fell in 1940. Supplies were diverted to the British Army and a further 200 examples were ordered in late 1940.

The MAC (WD) was a conventional medium-weight multi-terrain motorcycle of the period, powered by a 350cc single-cylinder, overhead-valve engine, with magneto ignition. The engine was installed in a conventional cycle type frame with a single down-tube; unlike the civilian version, a steel undertray was fitted to protect the engine. A four-speed foot-change gearbox, installed separate from the engine, and fitted with a lower first gear to help slow-speed riding. A strengthened clutch was fitted to withstand the anticipated abuse from untrained riders. The final drive to the rear wheel was by open chain.

TOP: **The Velocette MAC (WD) was a militarized version of the company's civilian MAC model that had originally been developed for the French Army. When France fell in 1940, the order was diverted to Britain, with a further 200 ordered later in the year.** ABOVE: **Power was provided by a 350cc overhead-valve engine driving through a four-speed foot-change gearbox.**

Coil-sprung friction-damped girder parallelogram forks were fitted at the front, the rear end was unsprung.

With some modification, the civilian MAC remained in production until 1959, but Velocette closed in 1968.

Velocette MAC(WD), or MDD

Type: Motorcycle, medium, solo
Manufacturer: Veloce; Birmingham
Production: 1939 to 1940
Engine: Velocette; single cylinder; 350cc; overhead valves; air cooled; power output, 15bhp at 6,300rpm
Transmission: 4F; foot gear-change
Suspension: Coil-sprung friction-damped girder parallelogram front forks; solid rear end
Brakes: Drums, front and rear
Dimensions: Height – 864mm/34in
  Wheelbase – 1,346mm/53in
  Other dimensions not available
  Weight – 145kg/320lb
Performance: Maximum speed – 120kph/75mph

Autoped Ever Ready

Autoped Ever Ready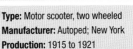

Type: Motor scooter, two wheeled
Manufacturer: Autoped; New York
Production: 1915 to 1921
Engine: Autoped; single cylinder; 155cc;
    side valves; air cooled; power output, 1.5bhp
Transmission: Direct drive
Suspension: None
Brakes: Drum, front only
Dimensions: Not available
    Weight – 44kg/96lb
Performance: Maximum speed – 16kph/10mph

The Autoped was trialled by the US Army for possible despatch duties in 1917. It was designed by Arthur Hugo Cecil Gibson, with patents issued to the

Autoped Company of New York in 1915, and was originally launched as the Marks Motorscooter. In truth, it was hardly more than a motorized skateboard, on which the rider was forced to remain standing; it does not appear to have entered service.

Looking just like a child's scooter of the period, the Ever Ready was powered by a 155cc engine located over the front wheel; the fuel tank sat alongside the engine. There were no gears and there was no separate "proper" clutch; the rider pushed forward on the handlebars to engage the drive, and then used the hand throttle control to accelerate; pulling part-way back on the bars disengaged the drive. The front brake

LEFT: **The Autoped Ever Ready was arguably the first example of a true motor scooter.**

was operated by pulling the bars all the way back. There was no rear brake.

No suspension was fitted but Autoped manufactured their own – red coloured – pneumatic tyres, which must have helped to cushion some of the road shocks.

Licensed copies were produced in Germany by Krupp, in Britain by Imperial Motor Industries (Douglas), and in Czechoslovakia by CAS.

Cushman 39 Package Kar

One of the weirdest motorcycles of the World War II period was surely the little Cushman 39 Package Kar of which some 600 examples were purchased by the US Army between 1943 and 1944. The machine was designed for industrial delivery work, but proved ideal for despatch duties around the typical military base.

Little more than a cargo box on wheels, the three-wheeled Package Kar comprised the back end of Cushman's production scooter, complete with its

engine, attached via a pivot to a simple ladder chassis at the front. A single seat was provided on the top of the engine compartment. At the front was a 0.21m³/7.5ft³ rectangular cargo box with a side-hinged top-opening lid; carrying capacity was 160kg/353lb. Headlamps attached to the corners of the box gave the vehicle a decidedly bug-eyed look.

Cushman was originally an engine manufacturer, eventually becoming part of the Johnson-Evinrude Group, and had entered the scooter business in 1936, seeing this as a way of increasing engine sales. Unsurprisingly, the Package Kar was powered by a 246cc Evinrude

engine, driving the rear wheel through a two-speed gearbox and a short chain. Aside from the over-sized tyres, suspension appears to have been non-existent, and the machine was steered via the central pivot.

Cushman 39 Package Kar

Type: Motor scooter, three-wheeled,
    package delivery
Manufacturer: Cushman Motor Works;
    Lincoln, Nebraska
Production: 1943 to 1944
Engine: Evinrude Husky 10M70; single cylinder;
    246cc; overhead valve; air cooled; power output,
    4bhp at 3,600rpm
Transmission: 2F; hand gear-change
Suspension: None
Brakes: Drum, rear only
Dimensions: Length – 2,324mm/92in
    Width – 1,143mm/45in
    Height – 1,194mm/47in
    Wheelbase – 1,575mm/62in
    Weight – 188kg/415lb
Performance: Maximum speed – 48kph/30mph

LEFT: **The Cushman 39 Package Kar remained in US military service until well into the 1950s.**

Cushman 53 Autoglide

Powered by a 246cc single-cylinder engine and fitted with lifting rings front and rear, the Cushman was intended to be used to provide immediate transportation to airborne troops – although travelling at the stated maximum speed of 64kph/40mph must have been scary. The scooter was assembled on a simple fabricated steel frame, with the engine located at the rear; crude mudguards and a footboard were provided to protect the rider. Drive to the rear wheel was via a two-speed gearbox and a short chain. The rider sat above the engine and steered the machine through conventional handlebars. Brakes were pedal-operated on the rear wheel only and the gearshift was a hand lever protruding from the front of the engine compartment. Suspension was achieved only through the use of over-sized tyres.

A total of 4,734 examples were completed over a two-year period and the machine was classified as "limited standard", remaining on the US Army's inventory into the 1950s. Photographs of the Autoglide in use are rare. In 1946, the basically similar Autoglide 53A was offered to civilians up until 1948. Cushman abandoned scooter production in 1965.

BELOW: **The Cushman airborne scooter dates from 1944 and was one of four types used by the US Army during World War II.**

Cushman Model 53 Autoglide	
Type: Motor scooter, airborne, two wheeled	
Manufacturer: Cushman Motor Works; Lincoln, Nebraska	
Production: 1944 to 1945	
Engine: Evinrude Husky 16M71; single cylinder; 246cc; overhead valves; air cooled; power output, 4.6bhp at 3,600rpm	
Transmission: 2F; hand gear-change	
Suspension: None	
Brakes: Drum, rear only	
Dimensions: Length – 1,956mm/77in Width – 584mm/23in Height – 965mm/38in Wheelbase – 1,448mm/57in Weight – 118kg/260lb	
Performance: Maximum speed – 64kph/40mph	

Crosley

Although better known for their microcars, the first of which had been built in 1939, Powel Crosley's company produced prototypes for a novel military motorcycle during 1940–41. Sadly, it never entered production, but one example has survived in the USA.

The machine was assembled around a hybrid pressed-steel and tubular frame, and was powered by a two-cylinder horizontally opposed engine, produced by Crosley from a Waukesha design. There may have been an electric starter, there was certainly a sizeable battery beneath the saddle. The rear wheel was driven through a three-speed gearbox, with final drive by exposed Carden shaft.

Although single-bladed forks have now become commonplace, the first Crosley prototype was equipped with a single rear fork on the left-hand side, and a standard telescopic double front fork; in the second version, the single rear fork was moved to the right; the third prototype used single-bladed forks at front and rear, the rear fork being on the right, and the front fork on the left.

Pressed-steel wheels were fitted. The rear mudguard was the fuel tank. During World War II, Crosley also produced prototypes for a 3x2 motor tricycle and a lightweight Jeep-type vehicle.

Crosley	
Type: Motorcycle, heavy, solo	
Manufacturer: Crosley Corporation; Cincinnati, Ohio	
Production: 1940 to 1941	
Engine: Waukesha-Crosley Model 150 Cub; two cylinder, horizontally opposed; 580cc; side valves; air cooled; power output, 12bhp	
Transmission: 3F; hand gear-change	
Suspension: Coil-sprung telescopic front forks; rigid rear end	
Brakes: Drums, front and rear	
Dimensions: Not available Weight – not available	
Performance: Not available	

LEFT: **Crosley only built prototypes of this innovative 580cc motorcycle.**

Excelsior 7–10hp

One of the "big three" American manufacturers, the Excelsior Motor Manufacturing & Supply Company started producing motorcycles in 1908. The smallest of the range was a 269cc two-stroke not unlike the British-built Triumph Baby, but there was also a 500cc single, and 750cc and 997cc V-twins. In 1911, the company was purchased by Ignaz Schwinn. In 1917, Schwinn also purchased the Henderson Motorcycle Company, moving all production to the Excelsior factory and initiating a period of vigorous expansion. By the end of 1918, the US Army had received 2,600

ABOVE: **An Excelsior 7–10hp in service with the US Cavalry during the campaign against Pancho Villa.**

examples of the Excelsior 997cc V-twin, a 7–10hp machine, using them for both solo and sidecar applications.

Many European motorcycles of the period still owed much to the pedal cycle in terms of both appearance and design, but the 7–10hp Excelsior was surprisingly modern in appearance, perhaps due in part to the tear-drop shaped fuel tank and upright frame geometry. It was also capable of a very creditable 121kph/75mph.

The tubular frame was of cycle type with a single downtube and parallel top-tubes. The engine was a powerful V-twin driving the rear wheel through a separate three-speed hand-change gearbox and exposed chain. At the front, the forks were of the trailing-link pattern, suspended on a friction-damped leaf spring. The rear end was solid. The 7–10hp was replaced by the Model H in 1919, but all Excelsior production ended in 1931.

Excelsior 7–10hp

Type: Motorcycle, heavy, solo; and with sidecar
Manufacturer: Excelsior Motor Manufacturing & Supply Company; Chicago, Illinois
Production: 1917 to 1918
Engine: Excelsior; two cylinders in V formation; 997cc; overhead inlet valves, side exhaust; air cooled; power output, 7 to 10bhp
Transmission: 3F; hand gear-change
Suspension: Leaf-sprung friction-damped trailing-link front forks; solid rear end
Brakes: Drums, front and rear
Dimensions: Wheelbase – 1475mm/58in
Other dimensions not available
Weight (solo) – 160kg/350lb
Performance: Maximum speed – 121kph/75mph

GM-Delco motor tricycle

Between 1938 and 1940, the US Army experimented with all-wheel drive three-wheelers which would have taken on the kinds of role for which the Jeep was so well suited. Prototypes were completed by four companies. Harley-Davidson supplied a field car based on their Model G motor tricycle, and Indian supplied a three-wheeler using the frame of their Model 340 followed by a further 16 examples using the Chief as a basis. The other two suppliers might

be considered wild cards. Crosley supplied a tricycle using the frame of an experimental lightweight motorcycle which they had built in 1940. GM-Delco, better known today for electronics products and aerospace work, prototyped a very durable shaft-drive tricycle powered by a two-cylinder horizontally opposed engine.

It was powered by a 745cc two-cylinder side-valve horizontally opposed engine, installed in the front end of a conventional duplex motorcycle frame, at the rear of which

LEFT: **Delco submitted their tricycle to the Infantry Board for testing in 1939. No data are available detailing testing or the machine's final fate.**

was a shortened motorcar drive axle. The transmission was a four-speed and reverse unit, with a hand gear-change. The front forks were hydraulically-damped telescopic units, while the rear end was either unsprung or fitted with simple leaf springs. All three wheels were of the pressed-steel disc type.

GM-Delco motor tricycle

Type: Motor tricycle, heavy, 3x2
Manufacturer: GM-Delco; Kokomo, Indiana
Production: 1939
Engine: Unknown make; two cylinder, horizontally opposed; 745cc; side valves; air cooled; power output, 22bhp at 4,500rpm
Transmission: 4F; hand gear-change
Suspension: Hydraulically-damped telescopic front forks; unsprung or leaf-sprung rear end
Brakes: Drums, all three wheels
Dimensions: Not available
Weight – Not available
Performance: Not available

Harley-Davidson Model X-8-A

ABOVE: The Harley-Davidson X-8-A was the first motorcycle supplied by the company for military use – albeit to Japan. BELOW LEFT: The X-8-A was powered by a 492cc single-cylinder engine and was driven by means of a flat belt running on a pulley on the rear wheel.

William S. Harley and Arthur Davidson founded what became the Harley-Davidson Motor Company in 1901 and within 20 years had become the world's largest manufacturer of motorcycles. Bearing in mind the catastrophic effects on the European and American motorcycle industries of the Japanese "invasion" of the 1960s and 1970s, a situation from which Harley-Davidson was not immune, it is ironic that the company supplied its first military motorcycle to Japan. In 1912 the company minutes record that several

examples of the civilian Model X-8-A were supplied to the Japanese Imperial Army for evaluation.

Like all H-D models of these early years, the X-8-A was assembled around what was essentially a tubular-steel cycle frame, although a downward angle was introduced into the top tube to allow a lower saddle height. There were steel-tube leading-link parallelogram front forks, with suspension by a single coil spring, together with a solid rear end. The engine was a 492cc single-cylinder

unit with overhead inlet valves and side exhaust, and magneto ignition.

These were early days for motorcycling and just one gear was available, with drive to the rear wheel effected by means of a flat leather belt running on a separate rim. A clutch was integrated into the rear wheel hub and cycle-type pedals were provided for starting. Production of the Model X-8-A ceased after just one year.

Harley-Davidson Model X-8-A

Type: Motorcycle, medium, solo
Manufacturer: Harley-Davidson Motor Company; Milwaukee
Production: 1912
Engine: Harley-Davidson; single cylinder; 492cc; overhead inlet valves, side exhaust; air cooled; power output, 4bhp at 3,000rpm
Transmission: Direct drive
Suspension: Parallelogram leading-link steel-tube front forks with friction-damped coil springs; solid rear end
Brakes: Expanding band, rear only
Dimensions: Wheelbase – 1,425mm/56in
Other dimensions not available
Weight – 142kg/312lb
Performance: Maximum speed – 65kph/40mph

LEFT: **The V-twin Harley-Davidson Model J was the company's standard military offering during World War I, remaining in production until 1929. It was used by the US, British, Russian and Dutch armies and was suitable for both solo and sidecar operation.** BELOW: **A military Model J, alongside is the ammunition carrier version of the sidecar.**

Harley-Davidson Model J

While not actually designed for the US Army, the Harley-Davidson Model J was the first of the company's motorcycles to enter US military service. Originally designated 11-J, the machine was announced to the public in the autumn of 1914; from 1916 the description was changed to include a prefix indicating the year of production, so the model description became 16-J, and then 17-J, 18-J, onward. The Model J went on to become one of the company's most successful early models.

The Model J was powered by the 999cc four-stroke V-twin engine which had been introduced on Model X-8-E in 1912; typical of period practice, the inlet valves were in the cylinder head, while the exhaust valves were in the cylinder casting. Drive to the rear wheel was via an adjustable multi-plate clutch and open chain. The new three-speed transmission made better use of the engine's torque and power output.

On March 16, 1916, the US government ordered 12 Model 16-J motorcycles, which were used in pursuit of Francisco "Pancho" Villa's troops into Mexico. Following this initial purchase, large numbers of the Model J were shipped overseas from 1916. By 1917, around half of all Model J production was going to the US military.

Special military sidecars were introduced for 1916, including the 16-GC machine-gun car, with a tripod-mounted machine-gun behind a folding armoured screen, together with a small seat for the gunner. Other military sidecars included the 16-AC ammunition car, and the 16-SC ambulance, in which the patient was carried at saddle height on a built-in stretcher. Standard (civilian) sidecars were also supplied to the military, including single-passenger sidecars for either right- or left-hand mounting, and a commercial box sidecar.

A dedicated sidecar version of the Model J, known as the JS appeared in 1919, featuring revised gearing as well as a lower compression ratio.

Production of the Models J and JS ended in 1929, after a total of 85,500 machines had been manufactured. During its 15-year life, the Model J was widely used by the US Army during and after World War I, as well as also seeing service with the Dutch, Russian and British armies.

Harley-Davidson Model J

Type: Motorcycle, heavy, solo; and with sidecar
Manufacturer: Harley-Davidson Motor Company; Milwaukee
Production: 1914 to 1929
Engine: Harley-Davidson 61; two cylinders in V formation; 999cc; overhead inlet valves, side exhaust; air cooled; power output, 11bhp at 3,000rpm
Transmission: 3F; hand gear-change
Suspension: Parallelogram leading-link steel-tube front forks with a single coil spring; solid rear end
Brakes: Drum, rear only until 1928, then Drums, front and rear
Dimensions (1916 model):
  Length – 2,336mm/92in
  Width – 762mm/30in
  Height – 762mm/30in
  Wheelbase – 1,524mm/60in
  Weight – 148kg/325lb
Performance: Maximum speed – 97kph/60mph

Harley-Davidson Model E

Launched in 1912, less than a decade after the company had been founded, the Harley-Davidson Model E was a utility V-twin model based on the popular Models J and F, but with single-speed transmission. During 1917 and 1918, very small numbers of these machines were procured by the US Army, probably for domestic use.

Like the Models J and F, the Model E was powered by a 999cc V-twin engine with overhead inlet valves and side exhaust. For 1912, drive to the rear wheel was by means of a flat leather belt, with a rear wheel clutch, and there was just the one gear ratio; from 1913 on the final drive was by open chain. Cycle type pedals were provided for starting until 1916. The frame was a conventional tubular-steel design, with a downward angle in the top tube to allow a lower saddle height. The steel-tube front forks were of the leading-link parallelogram type with a single coil spring, and a solid rear end.

Production of the Model E ceased in 1918 after 12,239 examples had been constructed but, in truth, the machine was very dated and sales had been slow since 1914.

LEFT: **The Model E shared the same 999cc inlet-over-exhaust V-twin engine as the Models J and F but the direct-drive transmission, using a flat leather belt, must have often made starting and hill-climbing difficult.**

Harley-Davidson Model E

Type: Motorcycle, heavy, solo;

Manufacturer: Harley-Davidson Motor Company; Milwaukee

Production: 1912 to 1918

Engine: Harley-Davidson; two cylinders in V formation; 999cc; overhead inlet valves, side exhaust; air cooled; power output, 11bhp at 3,000rpm

Transmission: Direct drive

Suspension: Parallelogram leading-link steel-tube front forks with friction-damped coil springs; solid rear end

Brakes: Expanding band, rear only

Dimensions: Wheelbase – 1,425mm/56in
Other dimensions not available
Weight – Not available

Performance: Maximum speed – 97kph/60mph

Harley-Davidson Models F, FS, FUS

The Harley-Davidson Model F, together with the sidecar FS, was a close relation of the Model J, introduced in 1915 and the first Harley to be supplied to the US Army in quantity. In truth, the only differences between the models lay in the fact that the Model F had magneto ignition and no electrical lighting equipment. Although in nothing like the quantities of Model J that were shipped overseas from 1916, both the F and the FS also saw limited military service. In addition, there was a special "government only" version of the Model F, produced in 1918 and 1919, designated Model FUS – effectively a Model F fitted with standard Presto-Lite electrical equipment.

The Model F was powered by the 999cc V-twin engine which had been introduced on the Model X-0-E in 1912; the inlet valves were in the cylinder head, while the exhaust valves were in the cylinder casting. Drive to the rear wheel was through a new three-speed transmission, which was now mounted immediately behind the engine, rather than in the rear hub, with final drive by open chain. For the first time, the cycle pedals

were omitted and there was a kick starter. The frame was a conventional tubular-steel design, with parallelogram leading-link steel-tube front forks with a single coil spring, and a solid rear end.

Special military sidecars were introduced for 1916, including the 16-GC, mounting a machine-gun behind a folding armoured screen; the 16-AC ammunition car, and the 16-SC ambulance, in which

the patient was carried at saddle height on a built-in stretcher.

Production of the Models F and FS ended in 1925. The total number produced was 15,616.

While never a pure military motorcycle, both the Models F and J were used by the US Army during and World War I, as well as seeing service with the Dutch, Russian and possibly the British armies.

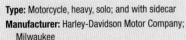

Harley-Davidson Models F, FS, FUS

Type: Motorcycle, heavy, solo; and with sidecar
Manufacturer: Harley-Davidson Motor Company; Milwaukee
Production: 1915 to 1919
Engine: Harley-Davidson; two cylinders in V formation; 999cc; overhead inlet valves, side exhaust; air cooled; power output, 11bhp at 3,000rpm
Transmission: 3F; hand gear-change
Suspension: Parallelogram leading-link steel-tube front forks with friction-damped coil springs; solid rear end
Brakes: Expanding band, rear only until 1928, then Drums, front and rear
Dimensions (solo):
Length – 2,337mm/92in
Width – 762mm/30in
Height – 762mm/30in
Wheelbase – 1,524mm/60in
Weight – 148kg/325lb
Performance: Maximum speed – 97kph/60mph

ABOVE: **Differing from the Model J only by virtue of its magneto ignition and acetylene lighting equipment, the Harley-Davidson Model F was also used by the US Army during World War I and was similarly suitable for both solo and sidecar work.**
RIGHT: **The special machine-gun sidecar, said to have been designed by William Harley himself, was introduced in 1916.**

Harley-Davidson Model V

Launched in 1930, Harley-Davidson's Model V was powered by a new V-twin engine although initial teething problems led to the first 1,326 examples being dismantled and reassembled with improved engines. The Model V range grew to become the most complex that the company had offered, although the 1930 offering was simple enough, comprising the Model V solo motorcycle; the VL, with higher compression heads; the VS with medium-compression heads and sidecar gearing; and the VC, a so-called "commercial" model with low-compression heads.

The machine was built around a conventional tubular-steel cycle-type frame into which was installed a 45-degree 1,213cc V-twin side-valve engine. Although still using total-loss

lubrication, the engine was initially offered with a choice of magneto or coil ignition. For 1935/36, certain models were fitted with a 1,311cc engine, although none of these larger-engined machines seem to have been supplied for military use. The gearbox was a three-speed hand-operated unit. Final drive to the rear wheel was by open chain. The front forks were of the parallelogram leading-link design with a single friction-damped coil spring, and the rear end was unsprung.

Out of the bewildering complexity of models that made up the Model V range over the years – in all there were more than 20 variants – the Models VL, VS and a low-compression sidecar model introduced in 1934 and designated VDS, certainly saw military use, mostly in the USA. The Chinese Imperial Army specified the Model

VL with a single-passenger sidecar, and a number of sidecar-equipped Model VS machines were supplied to Denmark in 1934 for trials against Danish-built Nimbus motorcycles. At least one of the Harley-Davidsons was fitted with a Landsverk armoured sidecar, designed to mount a machine-gun, designated Landsverk 210, but the weight made it hard to steer and there was no series production.

Total production of the Model V during its seven-year life was 43,042.

ABOVE, ABOVE RIGHT AND LEFT: **The Harley-Davidson Model V remained in production for seven years and although it was not intended for military use, a number were purchased for the US and Chinese armies and at least one was converted to an armoured reconnaissance vehicle by the Swedish Landsverk company. The engine was a 1,213cc V-twin; during 1935–36, the larger 1,311cc V-twin was also offered.**

Harley-Davidson Model V

Type: Motorcycle, heavy, solo; and with sidecar
Manufacturer: Harley-Davidson Motor Company; Milwaukee
Production: 1930 to 1936
Engine: Harley-Davidson; two cylinders in V formation; 1,213cc (or 1,311cc); side valves; air cooled; power output, 30bhp at 4,600rpm
Transmission: 3F; hand gear-change
Suspension: Parallelogram leading-link steel-tube front forks with a single coil spring; solid rear end
Brakes: Drums, front and rear
Dimensions (with sidecar):
Length – 2,235mm/88in
Width – 1,930mm/76in
Height – Not available
Wheelbase – 1,525mm/60in
Weight – 240kg/529lb
Performance: Maximum speed – 145kph/90mph

Harley-Davidson Model WL

Harley-Davidson's Model W replaced the ageing Model R in 1937. It was powered by an updated version of the iconic 737cc side-valve V-twin, and adopted the more modern external styling of the 1936 Model E. At launch, the range was made up of five models – Model W was a solo machine; WS was the sidecar equivalent; WL was a solo sports machine with high-compression heads; WLD had higher compression cylinder heads; and WLDR was described as a "competition special". There was also a Model WSR intended for export to Japan.

A typical heavy Harley-Davidson of the period, the machine was built around a steel-tube cycle-type frame into which was fitted the big 737cc V-twin engine. Power was transmitted to the rear wheel via a three- or four-speed gearbox and open chain. The frame was redesigned in 1941 to accept the new four-speed transmission. At the front, there were conventional parallelogram leading-link forks with twin coil springs and adjustable "ride control", while the rear end was unsprung.

Of the range, only the WL saw military service, the US Army taking delivery of small numbers in 1937, 1939 and 1945, and classifying it as "standard". These were more-or-less standard civilian machines, although one interesting variation involved the use of 4.00-18 section wheels and tyres on the 1945 models; these would have been normal in 1937, but their use on machines built in 1945 was presumably to provide commonality with the WLA. The WL also formed the basis of the military WLA and WLC.

The sidecar-equipped Model WLS was also trialled by the Danish Army in 1939, but was deemed unsuitable on account of its size and weight.

Civilian production had all but ceased in 1942, not being resumed until 1945 when the WL was reintroduced. Production of all W series models, excluding the military WLA and WLC, totalled 26,960 by the time the range was deleted in 1951.

Harley-Davidson Model WL

Type: Motorcycle, heavy, solo; and with sidecar
Manufacturer: Harley-Davidson Motor Company; Milwaukee
Production: 1932 to 1952
Engine: Harley-Davidson W45; two cylinders in V formation; 737cc; side valves; air cooled; power output, 23bhp at 4,600rpm
Transmission: 3F; hand gear-change
Suspension: Parallelogram leading-link front forks with twin friction-damped coil springs; solid rear end
Brakes: Drums, front and rear
Dimensions: Length – 2,235mm/88in
Width – 914mm/36in
Height – 1,041mm/41in
Wheelbase – 1,437mm/58in
Weight – 217kg/477lb
Performance: Maximum speed – 113kph/70mph

Harley-Davidson Models WLA, WLC

Although little more than a militarized pre-war Model WL, the Harley-Davidson Model WLA is the most numerous, and best known, of the company's military products. The WL had first appeared in 1937 and was supplied to the US Army in small numbers before a couple of modified machines, designated WLA, were submitted for military trials in 1939. Production of the new machine started in March 1940 and continued until 1945, with small numbers also produced after the war.

The Army had originally wanted a purpose-built 500cc machine for military police, convoy escort, despatch rider and reconnaissance duties and invited tenders for the contract from Harley-Davidson, Indian and GM-Delco. Harley-Davidson had nothing with a suitable engine and was not prepared to produce a "special", so a compromise was agreed upon whereby the company would provide the 737cc Model WL, modified to be more suitable for military service. Two prototypes of what would become the WLA were sent to Fort Knox, Kentucky, and Camp Holabird, Maryland.

In its specification, the Army had been insistent that the machines should not overheat when used for slow-speed work and the engine of the WL was down-rated accordingly. Harley-Davidson's engineers fitted aluminium cylinder heads and larger cooling fins. There were also improvements to the bearings, the lubrication system and the clutch. A hand-change three-speed gearbox was fitted, with lower ratio gears, making the machine better suited to convoy escort duties. Final drive was by open chain.

ABOVE: **Sometimes called the "Liberator" in honour of its World War II role, the 737cc V-twin Harley-Davidson WLA, and the related WLC, is probably the best-known military motorcycle of all time. It was based on the pre-war WL and production started in 1940 and continued into the early post-war years.**

The front forks of the prototypes were of the parallelogram girder design, with twin coil-springs and an adjustable steering damper. The rear end was typically "solid", relying on a softly sprung leather saddle. Additional military fittings included a lower chain guard, engine skid plate and side crash bars.

This was never intended to be an off-road bike and, although the wide-section open mudguards provided increased clearance to prevent a build-up of mud, ground clearance was little more than 100mm/4in, this tended to discourage off-roading. On the road, despite somewhat poor acceleration, the WLA was capable of about 110kph/68mph – but it was extremely reliable.

In slightly modified form, the WLA went into production in March 1940. The front forks were redesigned using the tubular style of the WL and were extended by 69mm/2.75in to increase ground clearance. Further small design changes were made over the years, but the machine remained essentially as it had been when introduced in 1940.

In 1941, the WLC appeared. Intended for the Canadian Army and produced in what were described as "domestic" and "export" models. The model featured a right-hand clutch-and-throttle configuration, with the ignition-timing lever also on the

ABOVE: **The WLC with sidecar, the design of which dated back to World War I.** RIGHT: **Not all WLAs were green; this white-painted machine is in service with the US Military Police.**

right. There were also a number of differences in the lighting, as well as a different instrument nacelle, slightly smaller mudguards, and an ammunition/spare parts box carried on the front mudguard. The WLC did not carry the rifle scabbard or ammunition box of the US Army machines.

It was essentially a solo machine, but small numbers of WLAs and WLCs were fitted with pillion seats. The WLC could also be found mounting a Goulding single-seat sidecar, in which form it may have been described as Model WLS.

All remaining production of the WLA was cancelled in August 1945. In all, about 78,000 examples were completed – 60,000 of these went to US forces, 30,000 reputedly went

to the USSR. The remainder were supplied to the various Allies, including Australia, India and China. A number were supplied to the RAF. The WLCs went to Canada.

After the war, many were rebuilt and supplied to various European armies, including France, Belgium and the Netherlands as part of the post-war Marshall Plan. And, for some curious reason, there was some very limited production of the WLA for the US Army, alongside the WL, during the period 1949 to 1952.

ABOVE: **The WLC was produced especially for the Canadian Army and incorporated detail changes to lighting and other equipment.**

Harley-Davidson Models WLA, WLC

Type: Motorcycle, heavy, solo
Manufacturer: Harley-Davidson Motor Company; Milwaukee
Production: 1940 to 1952
Engine: Harley-Davidson 45; two cylinders in V formation; 737cc; side valves; air cooled; power output, 23bhp at 4,600rpm
Transmission: 3F, hand gear-change
Suspension: Parallelogram leading-link steel-tube front forks with twin coil springs, friction damped; solid rear end. Steel parallelogram leading-link I-beam front forks on prototypes
Brakes: Drums, front and rear
Dimensions: Length – 2,235mm/88in
Width – 915mm/36in
Height – (with windshield) 1,499mm/59in (without windshield) 1,041mm/41in
Wheelbase – 1,473mm/58in
Weight – 234kg/515lb
Performance: Maximum speed – 105kph/65mph

Harley-Davidson Model U

The Harley-Davidson Model U was launched in 1937 as a replacement for the Model V. There was a choice of new engines, with capacities of either 1,213cc or 1,311cc and the range initially comprised six models, three with the smaller engine and three with the larger. Of the smaller-engined machines, the Model U was for solo use, the similar US was intended to be fitted with a sidecar, while the UL was fitted with high-compression heads. The UH, USH and ULH offered the same range of features, respectively, but with the larger engine.

Regardless of capacity, the engine was a side-valve 45-degree V-twin with magneto ignition and a dry sump, installed in a conventional tubular-steel duplex frame. Gear change was by a

hand lever fitted to the fuel tank and the gearbox had three speeds, with final drive to the rear wheel by open chain. The front forks were of the parallelogram leading-link design with friction-damped twin coil springs, and the rear end was unsprung.

The civilian Model UL was purchased by the US Army in 1938/39, with the standard single-passenger sidecar. Other military experiments during 1939/40 included a Model UL fitted with a special machine-gun sidecar, and a single Model UH fitted with an RCA radio set. The US Army also purchased a number of civilian Model U solo machines in 1939 before specifying a militarized version of the sidecar Model US, under the designation UA - the "A" suffix indicating "Army". Changes from the civilian specification included high-clearance mudguards,

blackout lighting and revised gearing; the sidecar was the standard civilian model. The Model US sidecar outfit, fitted with a left-hand sidecar, was also supplied to South African troops through the British Supply Council in 1943.

A total of around 2,100 examples of the Model U, in its various forms, were supplied for military use between 1938 and 1945. Full-scale civilian production resumed in 1945. Total production of all variants of the Model U during its 12-year life was 33,129.

ABOVE: **With the huge V-twin engine, the Harley-Davidson Model U was a massive machine. It surprisingly was capable of a top speed little better than 88kph/55mph.** LEFT: **The engine was a side-valve V-twin unit, with a capacity of either 1,213cc or 1,311cc, and with power output in the order of 33–35bhp.**

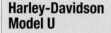

Harley-Davidson Model U	
Type: Motorcycle, heavy, solo; and with sidecar	
Manufacturer: Harley-Davidson Motor Company; Milwaukee	
Production: 1937 to 1949	
Engine: Harley-Davidson; two cylinders in V formation; 1,213cc or 1,311cc; side valves; air cooled; power output, 33 to 37bhp at 4,600rpm	
Transmission: 3F, hand gear-change	
Suspension: Parallelogram leading-link steel-tube front forks with twin friction-damped coil springs; solid rear end	
Brakes: Drums, front and rear	
Dimensions (with sidecar): Length – 2,438mm/96in	
Width – 1,753mm/69in	
Height (with windshield) – 1,092mm/43in	
Wheelbase – 1,525mm/60in	
Weight – 386kg/850lb	
Performance: Maximum speed – 88kph/55mph	

Harley-Davidson Model GA "Servi-Car"

First appearing in 1932, the three-wheeled Harley-Davidson Model G "Servi-Car" was the company's longest-running model, with a 42-year production life. It was originally aimed at service stations where it was used to collect and deliver motorcars for servicing or repair, but also found some favour with the US Army. The "Servi-Car" was essentially a motorcycle front end, with the frame extended at the rear to mount a live rear axle. A small compartment over the rear axle provided a locker for storing tools or other equipment; early examples were available with a bench seat over the storage box.

Throughout its production life, the "Servi-Car" was powered by the 737cc side-valve V-twin engine. Power from the engine was transmitted to the rear axle via a three-speed, forward and reverse transmission, with an open chain driving a sprocket in the differential housing. The latter also housed a central drum brake.

Originally, there were four variants – the basic Model G was supplied with a special tow bar; Model GA was identical, but no tow bar; GD had a larger-capacity

rear compartment and no tow bar, and GE also had the large-capacity compartment, plus an air tank for tyre inflation. In 1933, the range also included the GDT, with the large-capacity rear compartment and the tow bar. The GE was dropped in 1940, the GD and GDT disappeared in 1942. Between 1964 and 1973, all that remained was the standard "Servi-Car" without tow bar, now designated GE.

In 1941, the US Army purchased four GA "Servi-Cars", one of which was fitted with a General Electric mobile radio. Military modifications were confined to the use of blackout lighting, but the speed may have been restricted by the use of lower gear ratios.

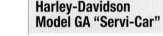
ABOVE: **Originally intended for service station work, the Model GA was trialled by the US Army with mobile radio equipment as well as being used post-war for convoy escort duties.**

Full-scale civilian production resumed in 1947 and the US Army purchased more "Servi-Cars" in 1950, for use by Military Police as convoy escort and messenger vehicles. The total number produced was approximately of 32,160.

BELOW: **In 1940 the "Servi-Car" was used as the basis for a three-seat 3x2 "field car", designated Model TA.**

Harley-Davidson Model GA "Servi-Car"

Type: Motor tricycle, 3x2
Manufacturer: Harley-Davidson Motor Company; Milwaukee
Production: 1932 to 1973
Engine: Harley-Davidson R45 or W45; two cylinders in V formation; 737cc; side valves; air cooled; power output, 22 to 23bhp at 4,600rpm
Transmission: 3F 1R, hand gear-change
Suspension: Parallelogram leading-link front forks with twin friction-damped coil springs; rear axle suspended on twin quarter-elliptical cantilevered multi-leaf springs; rear body suspended on coil springs
Brakes: Drums (discs, 1973 only), front and rear
Dimensions: Length – 2,718mm/107in
Width – 1,321mm/52in
Height – 1,321mm/52in
Wheelbase – 1,550mm/61in
Weight – 618kg/1360lb
Performance: Maximum speed – 105kph/65mph

Harley-Davidson Model XA

Dating from 1941, the XA is the closest thing there is to a purpose-made military Harley-Davidson and was said to have been inspired by the iconic BMW horizontal twins of the German Army. Although the XA was powered by a 739cc two-cylinder engine, with almost exactly the same capacity as Harley's legendary WLA, it could not have been more different, and shared very little with other models in the Harley range, either in components or design thinking.

The Model XA – the designation was supposed to have stood for "experimental, army" – was intended for use in the desert war which was at its height in 1941. It arose from a specification drawn up by the US War Department in 1941, describing a shaft-driven military motorcycle. Indian, GM-Delco and Harley-Davidson were all invited to compete for a production contract of 25,000 units.

Designed largely by John Nowak, the XA was said to have been based on a captured BMW R-12. Like the BMW, it featured a horizontally opposed side-valve engine, with a separate carburettor for each cylinder, while the balanced double-throw crankshaft meant that no flywheel was required. There was a distributor-less ignition system which sparked both plugs on every upstroke, and automatic spark advance. Again emulating the BMW, the engine was installed across

ABOVE: **Although, at a glance, it appears similar to the ubiquitous WLA, the horizontally opposed XA was like no Harley that had gone before.**

RIGHT: **The XA was the first Harley-Davidson manufactured to be trialled with telescopic front forks.**

Harley-Davidson Model XA

Type: Motorcycle, heavy, solo; and with sidecar

Manufacturer: Harley-Davidson Motor Company; Milwaukee

Production: 1941 to 1943

Engine: Harley-Davidson; two cylinder, horizontally opposed; 739cc; overhead valves; air cooled; power output, 23bhp at 4,600rpm

Transmission: 4F; foot and hand gear-change

Suspension: Parallelogram leading-link steel-tube front forks with friction-damped twin-coil spring; telescopic front forks on 1943 models; sprung telescopic rear suspension

Brakes: Drums, front and rear

Dimensions: Length – 2,286mm/90in
Width – 915mm/36in
Height – (with windshield) 1,525mm/60in (without windshield) 1,022mm/40in
Wheelbase – 1,499mm/59in
Weight – 241kg/525lb

Performance: Maximum speed – 97kph/60mph

the frame, which on the Harley-Davidson was a tubular duplex design, with the cylinders exposed to the natural air flow; heat shields were fitted to protect the rider's boots from the cylinder heads. There was a unit-constructed four-speed gearbox, similar to that used on the WLA.

The Germans had already discovered that the desert dust and grit quickly took a toll on a conventional roller-chain and realized that shaft drive was the only way to achieve reliability. Following their lead, the XA was also shaft-driven, with the final drive via an exposed universally jointed splined propeller shaft to a crown wheel and pinion set, driving the rear wheel through a flexible rubber coupling.

A lengthened, friction-damped version of the WLA front fork assembly was fitted, with telescopic coil-spring suspension units at the rear end. A handful of machines constructed in 1943 were fitted with an extended frame in which the engine sat a little further back, and these also used Harley-Davidson's first telescopic front forks. Most of the machines constructed used spoked wheels, but between 50 and 100 were delivered with solid disc wheels which it was believed would be more durable in tough conditions.

Other features intended to cope with desert conditions included increased ground clearance when compared to the WLA, and the use of a large skid plate under the engine, high-clearance mudguards, and an oil-bath air filter. Breaking with Harley-Davidson tradition, the clutch was hand-operated, with the gearshift foot-operated in the European style, although an auxiliary hand control was also provided. There was a rear rack, designed to carry a radio receiver, together with the usual saddlebags, ammunition box, rifle scabbard, and other stowage facilities. At least one XA was experimentally fitted with a driven-wheel sidecar (designated Model XAS), with drive to the sidecar wheel by means of a cross-shaft driven by the crown-wheel and pinion.

During military trials at Camp Holabird, Maryland, Fort Knox, Kentucky and Fort Carson, Colorado, problems were found with the lubrication of the engine and with the valve gear but, by the time the US government was ready to award the contract,

ABOVE: **The standard front fork was derived from that fitted to the WLA, but the rear end was also sprung, using telescopic plunger units.**

the war in Africa was essentially over. The Jeep was now used for most of the roles intended for the XA.

Harley-Davidson terminated the XA project in 1943 after completing between 1,000 and 1,011 examples.

MIDDLE AND ABOVE: **The engine of the XA was a 739cc horizontally opposed side-valve, supposedly based heavily on the pre-war BMW engine. Shaft drive was another feature copied from the big German motorcycles.**

LEFT AND BELOW LEFT:

The Harley-Davidson Model EL was the first to feature the company's new knucklehead engine and, although it was primarily aimed at a civilian market, it found some favour with the US Army and Navy for military police and shore patrol work, both in solo and sidecar form.

Harley-Davidson Model EL

Designed by William S. Harley and Lothar A. Doerner, Harley-Davidson's Model EL was launched in 1936 to replace the Model V. It was an all-new design, with a powerful new engine which quickly became known as the "knucklehead" for the shape of the valve covers, which resembled clenched knuckles. For the first two years, the range consisted of the Model E, a medium-compression solo machine, the sidecar ES, and the EL "Special Sport", a solo machine with high-compression heads.

The new engine was an overhead-valve design producing 40–45bhp from 999cc, and driving the rear wheel through four-speed gearbox and exposed roller-chain. The frame was a conventional steel tube duplex design, with parallelogram leading-link steel-tube front forks with a single friction-damped coil spring; the rear

end was solid. Teething troubles during the first year led to the frame being redesigned to prevent cracking. There were changes to the cylinder heads, oil tank and the kick-start gearing.

The base Model E was dropped in 1938, and in 1939 the US Army specified a militarized version of the sidecar Model ES, designated ELA, which was standardized the following year. Changes from the standard civilian machine included a utility finish, increased mudguard clearance, low-compression cylinder heads, lower gear ratios, standard military lighting fittings, possibly including blackout lighting, an oil-bath air cleaner, and the addition of various stowage fittings including a rear luggage rack. A small windscreen was fitted and there were also crash bars. The sidecar was a simple single-seater design.

Supplied in very small numbers, the ELA was typically used for convoy escort work, messenger duties, and naval shore and base patrols.

A similar model to the ELA was produced for the Canadian Army in 1941/42, described as the ELC, differing only in detail from the US Army counterpart. One example, fitted with a left-hand sidecar was delivered to the British War Office at the end of 1941 for evaluation, but was not adopted.

The Model ES was dropped in 1942 and the E was reintroduced, meaning that

the range now comprised the civilian Models EL and E, also the military ELA and ELC. The sidecar Model ES was reinstated for 1944, which probably indicates that the ELA was no longer in production. All military production of the Model E came to an end in 1945. Civilian production continued until 1948, with the new "panhead" engine being fitted for the final two years.

Total production of all Model E variants during the period 1936–48 was 28,958.

Harley-Davidson Models ES, ELA, ELC

Type: Motorcycle, heavy, solo; and with sidecar
Manufacturer: Harley-Davidson Motor Company; Milwaukee
Production: 1936 to 1948
Engine: Harley-Davidson 61; two cylinders in V formation; 999cc; overhead valves; air cooled; power output, 40 to 45bhp at 4,800rpm
Transmission: 4F; hand gear-change
Suspension: Parallelogram leading-link steel-tube front forks with single coil spring, friction damped; solid rear end
Brakes: Drums, front and rear (including sidecar)
Dimensions (with sidecar):
    Length – 2,438mm/96in
    Width – 1,753mm/69in
    Height – 1,092mm/43in
    Wheelbase – 1,525mm/60in
    Weight – 234kg/515lb
Performance: Maximum speed –
    solo 161kph/100mph
    with sidecar 88kph/55mph

Harley-Davidson Model FLH Electra-Glide

LEFT: **Launched as the Model FL Electra-Glide in 1965, but also offered as the higher-performance FLHB – later simplified as FLH – this was possibly the last full-size Harley-Davidson to be purchased for military work.** BELOW: **In 1967, the Belgian Military Police purchased a small number of FLHB Electra-Glides.**

Launched in 1965, the big Harley-Davidson FLB Electra-Glide had evolved from the Model FL of 1941, which, in 1949, had become the Hydra-Glide. The new model was possibly the last of the full-size Harley-Davidson to be used in military service. In 1967, the Belgian *Rijkswacht* (military police) purchased small

Harley-Davidson Model FLH Electra-Glide

Type: Motorcycle, heavy, solo
Manufacturer: Harley-Davidson Motor Company; Milwaukee
Production: 1965 to 1981
Engine: Harley-Davidson 74; two cylinders in V formation; 1,213cc; overhead valves; air cooled; power output, 54 to 62bhp at 5,400rpm. 1,311cc engine offered as an option (Model FLH-80) from 1978 to 1980, fitted as standard from 1981
Transmission: 4F (3F1R on sidecar outfits); foot- or hand-change according to model and year
Suspension: Hydraulically-damped telescopic front forks; trailing coil-spring rear end
Brakes: 1965 to 1971, Drums, front and rear; 1972, disc at front, drum at rear; 1973, discs, front and rear
Dimensions: Length – 2,362mm/93in
    Width – 889mm/35in
    Height – 1,460mm/58in
    Wheelbase – 1,550mm/61in
    Weight – 252kg/555lb
Performance: Maximum speed – 166kph/103mph

quantities of what was essentially a civilian Model FLHB Electra-Glide.

At launch, the Electra-Glide range comprised four models, the FLB and FLFB, the high-performance FLHB and FLFHB, all of them fitted with Harley-Davidson's 1,213cc "panhead" V-twin engine; a year later, this was replaced by the more-powerful "shovel-head" unit. There was a four-speed gearbox (or three-speed plus reverse for sidecar outfits) with exposed roller-chain drive to rear wheel. The frame was a conventional steel tube duplex design, with hydraulically-damped coil-spring suspension on the front forks, and a swinging arm with coil springs at the rear.

In 1970, the "B" was dropped from the model designation but, over the years, a considerable number of detail changes were made to the line-up. For example, by 1976, the range stood at just one model, the FLH-1200, although for 1977, this was joined by a so-called limited edition with different finish and accessories. For 1978, the range was back up to three, including the FLH-80 which was fitted with a larger 1,311cc engine. A year later, the line-up was five different models, some of which used the 1,213cc engine, others were fitted with the 1,311cc unit. From 1981,

the 1,213cc engine was finally deleted and production of the original Electra-Glide came to an end. By this time, total production amounted to 128,120 units, of which it must be said that just a few entered military service.

Although it was fast and comfortable, and very much at home on the highway, the Electra-Glide was a big, heavy motorcycle, very much in the Harley-Davidson tradition, and not at all suited to off-road work. Even at launch, the design was considerably different to the European trend for lower-profile, lighter, high-performance motorcycles.

Harley-Davidson MT350, MT500

ABOVE LEFT: **A standard MT350 fitted with a rack for pannier bags.** ABOVE: **A later MT350 equipped with moulded plastic document boxes.**

Originally badged Armstrong, the Harley-Davidson MT350 and MT500 machines were derived from a motorcycle developed in the early 1980s by the Italian SWM company to provide a street-legal model to sell alongside their competition machines. SWM ran into financial difficulties and the rights to the model were sold to

ABOVE: **Rights to the British-designed Rotax-powered Armstrong MT350 and MT500 were acquired by Harley-Davidson in 1987.**

Armstrong who also had the UK rights to produce the Canadian-designed Can-Am Bombardier which was in use with UK and other NATO forces. Harley-Davidson became involved in 1987, buying the rights to the model when Armstrong withdrew from the market.

Armstrong claimed that the company had spent two years developing the Italian machine into a reliable military motorcycle, beating-off competition for a British Ministry of Defence (MoD) contract from 16 competing manufacturers. In 1985 Armstrong announced that it had been asked to supply 2,300 MT500s to the MoD, as a replacement for the rather more fragile 250cc Can-Am Bombardier.

Powered by a Rotax four-valve single-cylinder engine of 485cc, key features of the MT500 included five-speed transmission, heavy-duty hydraulic suspension at front and rear, solid-state ignition system, sealed-for-life drive chain with O-ring seals, water- and dust-resistant brakes and aluminium wheel rims. Although the MT500 was generally equipped with a kick-starter, a number were fitted with electric-start and supplied to the Jordanian and Canadian armies. The Canadians confusingly designated theirs as the MT50. Alongside the MT500, Armstrong also offered a 348cc engine in what was substantially the same package, designated MT350.

In 1993, the MoD ordered a further 1,570 of these motorcycles from Harley-

Davidson, this time specifying the smaller-engined MT350, with the addition of electric start, changing the designation to MT350E. New disc brakes were fitted at the front and rear, and the old-fashioned panniers were changed in favour of one-piece moulded plastic "document boxes" with a waterproof hinged lid. In an attempt to conceal the thermal signature of the engine, the boxes were fitted to the frame down-tube to "obscure" the engine. A gun box was often fitted to the right-hand rear.

Total production of all MT models, by Armstrong and Harley-Davidson was 4,470 units.

Harley-Davidson MT350, MT500

Type: Motorcycle, medium, solo
Manufacturer: Armstrong Motorcycles; Bolton. Harley-Davidson Motor Co; Milwaukee
Production: 1985 to 1993
Engine: Rotax; single cylinder; 485cc (MT500, MT50), 348cc (MT350E); overhead valves; air cooled; power output, 33bhp at 6,200rpm, or 30bhp at 8,000rpm, respectively
Transmission: 5F; foot gear-change
Suspension: Telescopic front forks with hydraulic damping; trailing helical-spring rear end
Brakes: MT50, MT500, Drums, front and rear; MT350E, Discs, front and rear
Dimensions: Length – 2,210mm/87in
Width – 787mm/31in
Height – 1,168mm/46in
Wheelbase – 1,499mm/59in
Weight – 1,448mm/57in
Performance: Maximum speed – 145kph/90mph

Hendee Indian Powerplus

George M. Hendee started making Indian brand motorcycles in 1901, fitting a De Dion type engine which he had commissioned from Oscar Hedström into a cycle frame. In 1907, the company built a V-twin engine, using it to win races and break speed records. The company was the first to produce a motorcycle with electric start in 1914, even if this was also the subject of the industry's first recall in which it was replaced by a kick-start mechanism. George Hendee stepped down in 1915 and Hedström left in 1916, his place as Chief Designer being taken by Charlie Gustafson. A year later Gustafson's Powerplus machine was launched. With a 998cc V-twin engine, innovative rear suspension and three-speed gearbox it was an immediate success and thousands were pressed into service with the US Army during

World War I, both as solo machines and with a standard sidecar.

The Powerplus was constructed around a tubular steel cycle frame, with a single down-tube, into which Gustafson fitted his large V-twin engine, described in sales literature as the "most powerful and economical engine ever fitted to a motorcycle". A magneto/dynamo was used for ignition and the engine was lubricated by means of a dry sump. Power from the engine was passed through a helical gear train to a three-speed gearbox that was bolted directly to the engine in an early type of the unit-construction configuration. Final drive was by open chain. Girder-type parallelogram forks were fitted at the front, with suspension by a horizontal leaf spring. At the rear, there was a trailing arm similarly provided with leaf-spring suspension. A total of almost 40,000 Powerplus machines were

ordered by the US Army during the years 1917 and 1918 and Indian devoted virtually its entire production to the war effort. Something like 18,000 machines had been completed and delivered to the military by the end of 1918.

The company changed its name from the Hendee Manufacturing Company to the Indian Motocycle Company in 1923 – and the curious spelling is correct. In 1929, E. Paul and Francis du Pont purchased large blocks of Indian stock and were given seats on the board, eventually forcing Indian's management team out, thus taking control of the company.

Hendee Powerplus

Type: Motorcycle, heavy, solo; and with sidecar
Manufacturer: Hendee Manufacturing Company; Springfield, Massachusetts
Production: 1917 to 1919
Engine: Hendee; two cylinders in V formation; 998cc; side valves; air cooled; power output, 15 to 18bhp
Transmission: 3F; foot gear-change
Suspension: Leaf-sprung friction-damped trailing-link front forks; leaf-sprung trailing arm at rear
Brakes: Drum, rear only
Dimensions (with sidecar): Length – 2,337mm/92in
    Width – 1,575mm/62in
    Height – 1,016mm/40in
    Wheelbase – 1,524mm/60in
    Weight – 266kg/586lb
Performance: Maximum speed – 121kph/75mph

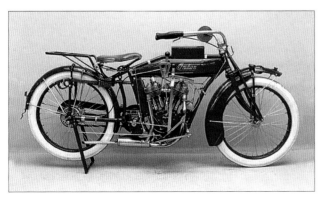

ABOVE: **Produced by the Hendee Manufacturing Company, more than 40,000 examples of the V-twin Indian Powerplus were acquired by the US Army in 1917 and 1918.**

LEFT: **The Powerplus was introduced in 1917 and remained in production until 1919.**

Indian Junior Scout

By 1923, Hendee Manufacturing had changed its name to Indian Motocycle Company, reflecting the brand name which had been used since the company's earliest days. The Powerplus had established the company as a major manufacturer but the post-war years were not always easy and it must have been a relief to stockholders and dealers alike when the successful 600cc Scout model was launched in 1920. Designed by Briggs Weaver, the name covered a variety of different machines over more than two decades and while the most famous was the Scout 101 of 1928, five years later the 493cc Scout Pony – later to be renamed the Junior Scout – also proved to be popular with the US Army.

Although a large machine by European standards, the Junior Scout was marketed as a lightweight or utility machine suitable for women riders, and was billed as the "lowest priced twin in America". It employed the conventional tubular-steel single down-tube frame of the company's Sport Scout but was powered by a dry-sump engine driving through a three-speed hand-change gearbox and exposed chain. The traditional leaf-sprung front forks were changed in favour of a girder parallelogram design using a single friction-damped coil spring. The trailing arm rear-end was replaced by a more economical rigid design. These changes lightened the

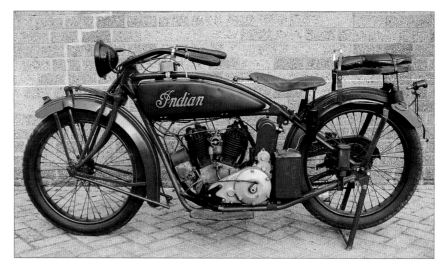

TOP AND ABOVE: **The Indian Junior Scout – or Scout Pony – remained in production for the best part of a decade and was used by the US Army throughout its life.** TOP RIGHT AND MIDDLE: **The V-twin engine, combined with a relatively light weight, gave the machine a reasonable level of performance.**

machine considerably and it resulted in a reasonable turn of speed that made it popular with sporting riders. Machines used by the military were frequently fitted with a pillion seat and side panniers.

Although the Junior Scout survived in production until 1942, it was eventually replaced in military service by the Model 741B which employed elements of the Junior Scout. It was not included in the line-up when Indian resumed civilian production in 1946.

Indian Junior Scout

Type: Motorcycle, heavy, solo;
Manufacturer: Indian Motocycle Company; Springfield, Massachusetts
Production: 1932 to 1942
Engine: Indian; two cylinders in V formation; 493cc; side valves; air cooled; power output, 15 to 18bhp at 4,000rpm
Transmission: 3F; hand gear-change
Suspension: Friction-damped coil-sprung parallelogram girder front forks; unsprung rear end
Brakes: Drums, front and rear
Dimensions: Length – 2,237mm/88in
Width – 851mm/34in
Height – 1,016mm/40in
Wheelbase – 1,442mm/57in
Weight – 163kg/359lb
Performance: Maximum speed – 88kph/55mph

Indian 741

Developed from Indian's 1939/40 model 640-A, and dating from 1941, the Indian 741 – sometimes described as the 741-A or 741-B – was effectively a militarized version of the Scout intended for supply to America's allies under the Lend-Lease Act. The majority of the machines built came to Britain and to the Commonwealth nations but, by British standards it was an unwieldy machine and, with unfamiliar clutch and gear-change

Indian 741

Type: Motorcycle, heavy, solo
Manufacturer: Indian Motocycle Company; Springfield, Massachusetts
Production: 1941 to 1943
Engine: Indian; two cylinders in V formation; 493cc; side valves; air cooled; power output, 15 to 18bhp at 4,000rpm
Transmission: 3F; hand gear-change
Suspension: Friction-damped coil-sprung parallelogram girder front forks; unsprung rear end
Brakes: Drums, front and rear
Dimensions: Length – 2,237mm/88in
Width – 826mm/33in
Height – 1,016mm/40in
Wheelbase – 1,442mm/57in
Weight – 209kg/460lb
Performance: Maximum speed – 88kph/55mph

controls was probably disliked by those who had to ride the machine. During the early years of World War II, the 741 was used by the British Army, but from about 1943, the machines were passed to various other official bodies, as well as being used by the RAF.

With a big 493cc V-twin engine, the 741 was a typical heavy US motorcycle that could not match the performance of British motorcycles of the time. The machine was totally conventional, with a tubular cycle-type frame having a single down-tube, coil-sprung girder parallelogram front forks, and rigid rear end. The transmission was a three-speed hand-change unit, with final drive by open chain.

Standard military equipment included a rear luggage rack, leather side panniers and front and rear crash bars.

A total of 35,044 were produced over three years. When production ended in 1943/44, large numbers

TOP: **The Indian 741 was a militarized Scout, and was developed for the armies of Britain and Canada.** ABOVE: **A close-up of the distinctive top of the fuel tank on the 741. Note the motorcycle's right-hand gear change lever.**

of machines which remained in the USA were disposed of to civilians as "surplus". Those machines which remained in the UK after the war ended were also rapidly disposed of.

Indian Chief 340B

The Indian Chief Model 340B – which indicates "model 3" of 1940, but which was also identified as the Model 74 – was a typical American civilian heavy sidecar outfit which had been lightly modified for military use, and was almost certainly derived from the Police Chief model. Some 5,000 had been ordered by the French Government in 1940, but France had fallen to the Germans before any machines were deliveried. Some were known to have been lost at sea due to U-boat action but others were diverted to the UK where they served with the British Army, the RAF and the Military Police, as well as with the "free" forces of, for example, Poland and Denmark, based in the UK.

Very much in the mould of the big Harley-Davidsons, the engine was Indian's 1,206cc V-twin side-valve unit, producing sufficient power to allow a top speed of around 88kph/55mph. The frame was a heavy-duty tubular affair with a single down-tube, and the final drive was via three-speed gearbox and

ABOVE: **The Indian Chief 340B – or Model 74 – was a lightly militarized machine, retaining the company's archaic leaf-spring front suspension. It had originally been intended for the French Army but was diverted to Britain after the fall of France in May 1940.**
RIGHT: **Powered by the 1,206cc V-twin engine, the machine was suitable for both sidecar and solo work, but was not popular with British riders due to size and weight and the unfamiliarity of the controls.**

RIGHT: **Like the Harley-Davidson WLA, war-surplus Indians were popular with US customizing enthusiasts in the 1950s and 1960s.**
BELOW: **Unlike the big Harley-Davidsons of World War II, the Indian Chief was fitted with coil springs at the rear.**

exposed chain; gear-change was by hand control on the fuel tank. Sadly, it seems that the brakes were not up to the task of stopping what was a large, powerful and heavy machine. Ground clearance was also poor. When these factors were combined with Indian's traditional leaf-sprung front forks together with the rather primitive undamped rear suspension, it meant that the machine was not really suitable for off-road use and, even on the road, needed to be in the hands of an experienced rider.

Taking note of all this, the fact that the War Office continued to order further supplies of the machine, placing six contracts covering some 750 machines over an 18–20 month period, is a measure of how desperate the British Army was for transport during the months following Dunkirk. To the average British motorcyclist the big Indian would have seemed a very strange machine indeed. However, it was a popular police motorcycle, and some 3,000 more were supplied to the US Army during the course of World War II.

The sidecar was a standard commercial single-seat unit, although some provision was made for mounting a machine-gun on the front. Early ex-French motorcycles were fitted with leg shields, a pillion seat and a spare wheel, the latter being carried on the rear of the sidecar. These fittings were omitted from later machines. The most obvious recognition point for "French'" against "UK" machines is that motorcycles ordered direct by the War Office were fitted with an oil-bath air filter and standard military light fittings.

However, the 340B was too big and heavy and was never ideal for UK conditions. And the fact that the machines had originally been intended for use in France meant that the sidecars were mounted on the "wrong" side; the Model 344B of 1944 had the sidecar moved to the rider's left-hand side.

Most of the early machines in the UK had been disposed of by 1943, but it is interesting to note that the Chief was Indian's only production machine between 1946 and 1947.

Indian Chief 340B

Type: Motorcycle, heavy, solo; and with sidecar
Manufacturer: Indian Motocycle Company; Springfield
Production: 1939 to 1942
Engine: Indian; two cylinders in V formation; 1,206cc; side valves; air cooled; power output, 30bhp at 4,000rpm
Transmission: 3F; hand gear-change
Suspension: Leaf-sprung trailing link front forks; plunger-type trailing rear forks with undamped coil springs; leaf-spring suspension to sidecar
Brakes: Drums, front and both rear wheels
Dimensions: Length – 2,464mm/97in
  Width – 1,829mm/72in
  Height – 1,118mm/44in
  Wheelbase – 1,575mm/62in
  Weight – 384kg/845lb
Performance: Maximum speed – 88kph/55mph

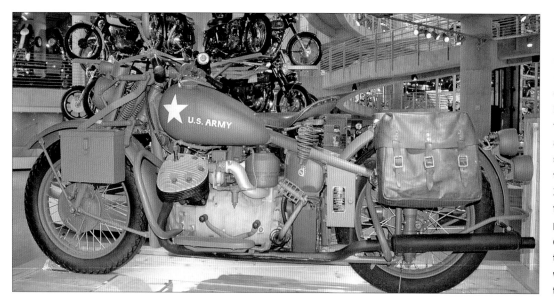

LEFT: **Developed for use in the punishing conditions of the North African desert, the Indian 841 was a product of the same programme as the Harley-Davidson XA. In a departure from normal Indian practice, the V-twin engine was set across the frame and there was shaft drive to the rear wheel.**

Indian 841

The Indian 841 was a purpose-designed military motorcycle developed for use in the North African desert. Like the Harley-Davidson Model XA which was produced as a result of the same design brief, it was said to have been inspired by the big German multi-terrain machines. It must be said that it shared little with those machines. In a departure from normal Indian practice, the V-twin engine was set across the frame, and shaft drive was a standard fitment, as well as suspension for both sets of forks. Although 1,056 examples were

completed, changing requirements in the field led to the termination of the project with most of the machines never leaving the factory.

The frame was a conventional tubular structure with a duplex engine cradle and front and rear suspension. The front forks were the familiar hydraulically-damped coil-sprung girder parallelogram units but, at the rear, Indian copied BMW and used a coil-sprung plunger design. The engine was a new transverse 90 degree V-twin, displacing 744cc and producing a governed 24bhp. Power was conveyed

to the rear wheel by a four-speed foot-change gearbox, with an exposed Carden shaft for the final drive.

The standard military equipment was fitted, including a rear luggage rack and leather side panniers. Front and rear crash bars were fitted.

Bearing in mind the size and weight of the machine, it is a surprise to find that it was easy to ride. Indian suggested that there might be a civilian model when the war ended. The unissued military 841s were sold as surplus but the planned civilian model was not produced.

ABOVE: **Although more than 1,000 examples of the Indian 841 were constructed, the majority apparently never left the factory. A planned civilian version of the motorcycle never appeared.**

Indian 841

Type: Motorcycle, heavy, solo
Manufacturer: Indian Motocycle Company; Springfield, Massachusetts
Production: 1942
Engine: Indian; two cylinders in transverse V formation; 744cc; side valves; air cooled; power output, 24bhp at 4,000rpm
Transmission: 4F; foot gear-change
Suspension: Friction-damped coil-sprung parallelogram girder front forks; coil-sprung plunger suspension at rear
Brakes: Drums, front and rear
Dimensions: Length – 2,305mm/91in
Width – 934mm/37in
Height – 1,016mm/40in
Wheelbase – 1,499mm/59in
Weight – 256kg/564lb
Performance: Maximum speed – 97kph/60mph

Indian 144 Aerocycle

Like Harley-Davidson, Indian is best known as a manufacturer of heavy motorcycles but as World War II unfolded, it became obvious that there was a need for lightweight machines suitable for use in airborne operations. The Indian 144 – designated by the US Ordnance Corps as "motorcycle, extra light, M1" – was manufactured in 1944 for just such a role, almost certainly replacing the Simplex Servi-Cycle. Weighing just 114kg/250lb, and capable

ABOVE AND RIGHT: **The Indian "motorcycle, extra light M1" weighed 114kg/250lb, making it ideal for airborne forces.**

of carrying a similar payload, it was powered by a 225cc single-cylinder engine and remained in service throughout World War II until it was replaced by the Indian 148 and 149 Arrow. A lightweight machine built on a simple cycle-style tubular frame with a single down-tube, the Aerocycle was fitted with coil-sprung front forks and a rigid rear end. There was magneto ignition and the single-cylinder engine and three-speed transmission was sufficient to propel the machine at a maximum of 72kph/45mph. Final drive was by open chain.

Additional military equipment included crash bars. Some machines were fitted with handles on the rear forks for manhandling the machine through difficult terrain. Also parachute lifting rings were fitted front and rear. The machine was classified as "standard" by the US Army and remained in military service into the early 1950s. It was replaced by the 148 in 1948 and the Model 149 Arrow in 1949, the latter having the distinction of being the last Indian to be built for the military.

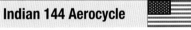

Indian 144 Aerocycle

Type: Motorcycle, light, solo
Manufacturer: Indian Motorcycle Company; Springfield
Production: 1944
Engine: Indian; single cylinder; 225cc; side valves; air cooled; power output, 6.3bhp at 4,800rpm
Transmission: 3F; foot gear-change
Suspension: Coil-sprung friction-damped cantilever front forks; solid rear end
Brakes: Drums, front and rear
Dimensions: Length – 1,977mm/78in
    Width – 711mm/28in
    Height – 940mm/37in
    Wheelbase – 1,270mm/50in
    Weight – 114kg/250lb
Performance: Maximum speed – 72kph/45mph

J A Strimple Keen Power Cycle

During World War II the US Army investigated a number of ultralight motorcycles and scooters which could be used around bases with a view to saving fuel. One such was the Keen Power Cycle produced by J A Strimple. Little more than a motorized skateboard, these small machines were in production between 1936 and perhaps 1948.

In standard guise, the Keen Power Cycle was made up of a simple step-through tubular and pressed-steel frame on which was mounted a steel box. The lid of the box provided seating for the rider and there was a storage compartment behind. The box concealed the engine and transmission. A trailer hitch could be specified but the US Army chose to equip

J A Strimple Keen Power Cycle

Type: Motorcycle, light, solo
Manufacturer: J A Strimple; Janesville, Wisconsin
Production: 1936 to 1948
Engine: Lauson; single cylinder; 145cc; two stroke; air cooled; power output, 2.2bhp
Transmission: Single gear
Suspension: None
Brakes: Rear only
Dimensions: Not available
   Weight – Not available
Performance: Maximum speed – 24kph/15mph

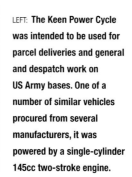

LEFT: **The Keen Power Cycle was intended to be used for parcel deliveries and general and despatch work on US Army bases. One of a number of similar vehicles procured from several manufacturers, it was powered by a single-cylinder 145cc two-stroke engine.**

the scooters they trialled in January 1944 with an open-topped sidecar which resembled a bathtub. There was no suspension other than that provided by the balloon tyres. Only the rear wheel was fitted with a brake.

It is possible that a limited number were acquired by the US Army following the trials.

Simplex GA-1 Servi-Cycle

Most American military motorcycles of World War II were heavy, traditional machines from Indian and Harley-Davidson, but the Simplex Servi-Cycle was completely the opposite. The machine was little more than a heavy bicycle, small and lightweight, it was intended for airborne troops.

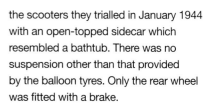

Simplex GA-1 Servi-Cycle

Type: Motor-driven bicycle
Manufacturer: Simplex Manufacturing; New Orleans
Country: USA
Production: 1942 to 1953
Engine: Simplex; single cylinder; 194cc; two stroke; air cooled; power output, 4bhp at 4,000rpm
Transmission: 2F; foot gear-change
Suspension: Coil-sprung leading-link parallelogram front forks; unsprung rear
Brakes: Drum, rear only
Dimensions: Length – 1,778mm/70in
   Width – 711mm/28in
   Height – 965mm/38in
   Wheelbase – 1,422mm/56in
   Weight – 75kg/165lb
Performance: Maximum speed – 48kph/30mph

However, since fewer than 700 examples were produced, it can hardly have been considered a huge success.

The machine was built around a triangulated tubular duplex frame which embraced the fuel tank at the top. At the lower end there was a mount for the engine. Drive to the rear wheel was transmitted through two of V-belts, one providing a high ratio, the other low. Final drive was by a third V-belt which used a variable tension control to provide a basic clutch. Unusually, the two-stroke 194cc engine was cast in light alloy, without a removable head, twin spark

plugs were fitted, presumably to solve the problem of plug-fouling.

The front forks were of the leading-link parallelogram design, with a single coil spring; there was no rear suspension, but the leather saddle was generously sprung. The spokes of the wheels were arranged in an unlaced radial pattern in the way that was common on American bicycles. Standard equipment included parachute rings, lights at front and rear, a rear pintle hook and a luggage carrier.

An improved version was supplied during the early 1950s, and the company continued to produce similar civilian machines into the 1960s.

RIGHT: **The Simplex Servi-Cycle was a lightweight machine intended for use by airborne troops. At just 75kg/165lb, it was light enough to be airdropped and could easily be manhandled. A towing pintle was provided to allow the machine to pull a small trailer.**

Military motorcycle data, from 1899

Make	Date	Model	Description	Engine: capacity	cyls*	Gears	Notes
Austria							
Laurin & Klement	1904	Slavia CCCC	Motorcycle, heavy, solo	570cc	4	1F	
Steyr-Daimler-Puch	1914	R-1	Motorcycle, medium, solo	254cc	1	1F	
	1914	R-2	Motorcycle, medium, solo	308cc	1	2F	
	1929	S204	Motorcycle, medium, solo	250cc	1	3F	
	1936	800	Motorcycle, heavy, solo; and with sidecar	792cc	V4	4F	
	1937	200	Motorcycle, light, solo	198cc	1	3F	split piston
	1938	350 GS	Motorcycle, medium, solo	347cc	1	4F	split piston
	1940	125T	Motorcycle, light, solo	125cc	1	3F	
	1940	250 S4	Motorcycle, light, solo	248cc	1	4F	split piston
	1956	250 SG	Motorcycle, light, solo	248cc	1	4F	split piston
	1958	175 MCH	Motorcycle, light, solo	172cc	1	4F	split piston
	1969	250 MCH	Motorcycle, light, solo	248cc	1	4F	split piston
Belgium							
FN	1904	4hp	Motorcycle, medium, solo	362–747cc	4	1F, 2F, 3F	according to user and year
	1906	3.5/4hp	Motorcycle, medium, solo	412cc	4	1F, 2F	
	1912	2.75hp	Motorcycle, light, solo	285cc	1	2F	
	1934	M86 *Militaire*	Motorcycle, medium, solo; and with sidecar	497cc	1	4F	
	1937	M12-SM	Motorcycle, heavy, with sidecar, 3x2	992cc	H2	4F1Rx2	
	1937	M86 *Militaire*	Motorcycle, medium, with armoured sidecar	497cc	1	4F	
	1939	Tricar 12A SM-T3, T8	Motor tricycle, personnel/load carrier, 3x2	992cc	H2	4F1R	
	1947	(M13) *Militaire*	Motorcycle, medium, solo	444cc	1	4F	also 250cc, 350cc engines
	1950	X III-M	Motorcycle, medium, solo	450cc	2	4F	
	1959	AS24	Motor tricycle, light, air portable, 3x2	244cc	2	4F	
Gillet-Herstal	1938	750	Motorcycle, heavy, with sidecar, 3x2	728cc	2	4F1R	
	1950	400 *Latéral*	Motorcycle, medium, solo	400cc	1	4F	
	1950	500 *Latéral*	Motorcycle, medium, solo	500cc	1	4F	
Sarolea	1936	AS 350	Motorcycle, medium, solo	349cc	1	4F	
	1937	S6	Motorcycle, heavy, solo; and with sidecar	589cc	1	4F	
	1939	H-1000 *Militaire*	Motorcycle, heavy, with sidecar, 3x2	978cc	H2	3F1Rx2	
	1951	51A4	Motorcycle, medium, solo	400cc	2	4F	
	1951	AS 350	Motorcycle, medium, solo	349cc	1	4F	
Canada							
Bombardier	1978	Can-Am	Motorcycle, light, solo	250cc	1	5F	also by Armstrong (UK)
China (People's Republic)							
Chang Jiang	1957	CJ-750M1, CJ-750M1M	Motorcycle, heavy, with sidecar	746cc	H2	4F1R	
Czechoslovakia							
Autfit Machek	1935	Ogar Model 4	Motorcycle, light, solo	250cc	2	4F	
CZ	1934	175	Motorcycle, light, solo	172cc	1	3F	
	1936	250	Motorcycle, light, solo	250cc	1	3F	
	1938	500	Motorcycle, medium, solo	500cc	2	3F	
Jawa	1934	350	Motorcycle, medium, solo	344cc	1	3F	
	1937	175	Motorcycle, light, solo	173cc	1	3F	
	1963	350 military	Motorcycle, medium, solo	344cc	2	4F	
	1978	350 military	Motorcycle, medium, solo, air portable	344cc	2	4F	
J Janatka	1924	Itar	Motorcycle, heavy, solo	700, 746cc	2	3F	
Praga	1926	BD 500	Motorcycle, medium, solo; and with sidecar	499cc	1	3F	
	1928	500	Motorcycle, medium, solo; and with sidecar	499cc	1	3F	
Walter	1922	Type A, B	Motorcycle, heavy, solo	750cc	V2	3F	
	1926	–	Motorcycle, medium, solo	500cc	1	3F	

KEY: H = cylinders horizontal or in horizontally opposed configuration; R = rotary; S = square configuration; V = Vee formation

Make	Date	Model	Description	Engine: capacity	cyls*	Gears	Notes
Denmark							
Fisker & Nielsen	1934	Nimbus 750 Model C	Motorcycle, heavy, solo; and with sidecar	746cc	4	4F	
	1934	Nimbus 750 Model C	Motorcycle, heavy, ammunition carrier	746cc	4	4F	
	1934	Nimbus 750 Model C	Motorcycle, heavy, ambulance	746cc	4	4F	
Smith	1937	SCO Type 3	Motorized bicycle, solo	48cc	1	3F	
Finland							
Winha	1977	340 Automatic	Motorcycle, medium, solo	338cc	1	Variomatic	
France							
ACMA	1956	TAP 150	Motor scooter, 2-wheel, airborne	150cc	1	3F	licence-built
Vespa	1956	TAP 150	Motor scooter, 2-wheel, airborne; 75mm recoilless rifle	150cc	1	3F	licence-built
Gnome et Rhône	1935	750 *Armée*	Motorcycle, heavy, with sidecar	750cc	H2	4F	
	1938	AX2	Motorcycle, heavy, with sidecar, 3x2	804cc	H2	4F1R	
	1938	D5A	Motorcycle, medium, solo	500cc	1	4F	
	1957	LX200	Motorcycle, light, solo	196cc	1	4F	
Koehler-Escoffier	1937	KL5A	Motorcycle, medium, with sidecar	500cc	1	4F	
Lehaitre	1938	–	Motorcycle, full-track	500cc	1	n/a	experimental
Merlin-Guerin-Debuit	1946	TT MGD	Motorcycle, light, solo	n/a	n/a	n/a	experimental
Monet-Goyon	1935	L5A, L5A1	Motorcycle, medium, solo; and with sidecar	486cc	1	4F	
Motobécane MBK	1940	B1V2	Motorcycle, light, solo	100cc	1	3F	
	1955	Mobylette S5C	Motorcycle, light, solo	48cc	1	1F	

RIGHT: **A Zündapp KS600-W painted with the tactical mark for a towed gun battery.**

Make	Date	Model	Description	Engine: capacity	cyls*	Gears	Notes
Peugeot	1914	2.5hp	Motorcycle, medium, solo	380cc	V2	1F	
	1934	P112	Motorcycle, medium, solo	350cc	1	4F	
	1936	P135A	Motorcycle, medium, solo	346cc	1	4F	
	1939	P53	Motorcycle, light, solo	100cc	1	3F	
	1956	176 TD4, 176 TC4	Motorcycle, light, solo	170cc	1	4F	
	1978	SX8, SX8T *Armée*	Motorcycle, light, solo	80cc	1	5F	
René Gillet	1916	–	Motorcycle, heavy, solo	748, 996cc	V2	2F	
	1926	G	Motorcycle, heavy, solo; and with sidecar	748cc	V2	3F	
	1937	G1	Motorcycle, heavy, with sidecar	748cc	V2	4F	
Simca-SEVITAME	1938	Type B *Armée*	Motorcycle, medium, solo	330cc	2	4F	
Terrot	1912	2hp	Motorcycle, medium, solo	317cc	1	1F	
	1934	VATT	Motorcycle, heavy, solo; and with sidecar	750cc	V2	4F	
	1935	HD-A	Motorcycle, medium, solo	346cc	1	4F	
	1937	RD-A	Motorcycle, medium, solo; and with sidecar	498cc	1	4F	
	1939	RGM-A	Motorcycle, medium, solo	498cc	1	4F	
	1950	RGST	Motorcycle, medium, solo	494cc	1	4F	
	1951	HCT	Motorcycle, medium, solo	346cc	1	4F	

Germany (including Federal Republic)

Make	Date	Model	Description	Engine: capacity	cyls*	Gears	Notes
Ardie	1939	RBZ200	Motorcycle, light, solo	197cc	1	3F	
	1939	VF125	Motorcycle, light, solo	123cc	1	3F	
Auto-Union DKW	1935	KM-200	Motorcycle, light, solo	198cc	2	3F	
	1936	SB-500	Motorcycle, medium, solo	489cc	2	3F	
	1937	NZ-250	Motorcycle, medium, solo	245cc	1	4F	
	1937	RT-3	Motorcycle, light, solo	98cc	1	3F	
	1938	KS-200	Motorcycle, medium, solo	198cc	1	3F	
	1938	NZ-350	Motorcycle, medium, solo	346cc	1	4F	
	1938	NZ-500	Motorcycle, medium, solo	489cc	2	4F	
	1938	RT-100	Motorcycle, light, solo	97cc	1	3F	
	1939	RT-125	Motorcycle, light, solo	123cc	1	3F	
	1030	RT 176	Motorcycle, solo	175cc	1	3F	
	1954	RT-175-VS	Motorcycle, light, solo	175cc	1	3F	
	1958	RT-200-VS	Motorcycle, light, solo	200cc	1	3F	
	1975	505P	Motorcycle, light, solo	49cc	1	1F	
BMW	1928	R-52	Motorcycle, medium, solo	500cc	1	3F	
	1928	R-62	Motorcycle, heavy, solo	745cc	H2	3F	
	1929	R-11	Motorcycle, heavy, solo; and with sidecar	745cc	H2	3F	
	1932	R-4	Motorcycle, medium, solo	398cc	1	3F	
	1935	R-12	Motorcycle, heavy, solo; and with sidecar	745cc	H2	4F	
	1936	R-5	Motorcycle, medium, solo	494cc	H2	4F	
	1937	R-35	Motorcycle, medium, solo	340cc	1	4F	
	1938	R-61	Motorcycle, heavy, solo	597cc	H2	4F	
	1938	R-66	Motorcycle, heavy, solo	597cc	H2	4F	
	1938	R-71	Motorcycle, heavy, solo	745cc	H2	4F	
	1941	R-75	Motorcycle, heavy, with sidecar, 3x2	746cc	H2	3F1Rx2	plus overdrive
	1950	R-25	Motorcycle, light, solo	247cc	1	4F	
	1951	R-51/3	Motorcycle, medium, solo	490cc	H2	4F	
	1955	R-25/3	Motorcycle, light, solo	247cc	1	4F	
	1955	R-26	Motorcycle, light, solo	247cc	1	4F	
	1955	R-50	Motorcycle, medium, solo	498cc	H2	4F	
	1960	R-27, R-27 TS	Motorcycle, light, solo	247cc	1	4F	
	1964	R-28 *Militar*	Motorcycle, light, solo	247cc	1	4F	pre-production only
	1969	R-60/5	Motorcycle, heavy, solo	599cc	H2	4F	
	1972	R-50/5	Motorcycle, medium, solo	498cc	H2	4F	
	1977	R-80/5	Motorcycle, heavy, solo	785cc	H2	5F	
	1977	R-80/7	Motorcycle, heavy, solo	785cc	H2	5F	
	1984	K100 RT	Motorcycle, heavy, solo	987cc	4	5F	
	1988	R-65 GS	Motorcycle, heavy, solo	650cc	H2	5F	
Bücker	1955	*Ilona* II	Motorcycle, medium, solo; and with sidecar	250cc	2	4F	
Cudell	1900	–	Motor tricycle, with gun carriage	n/a	n/a	n/a	
Goericke	1956	G100X	Motorcycle, light, solo	97cc	1	1F	
Heinkel	1960	Tourist 103A-2	Motor scooter, two wheeled, with sidecar	174cc	1	4F	
Hercules	1978	505P	Motorized bicycle, solo	47cc	1	1F	
	1981	K125BW	Motorcycle, light, solo	122cc	1	5F	
Horex-Columbus	1938	SB35	Motorcycle, medium, solo	342cc	1	n/a	
Maico	1959	M250/B	Motorcycle, light, solo	247cc	1	4F	
	1975	M250/M	Motorcycle, light, solo	247cc	1	5F	

Make	Date	Model	Description	Engine: capacity	cyls*	Gears	Notes
NSU (Neckarsulm)	1904	2.75hp	Motorcycle, medium, solo	375cc	1	1F	
	1911	3hp	Motorcycle, medium, solo	396cc	V2	3F	
	1912	1.5hp Pony	Motorcycle, light, solo	190cc	1	3F	
	1915	3.5hp	Motorcycle, medium, solo	499cc	V2	3F	
	1915	7.5hp	Motorcycle, heavy, with sidecar	995cc	V2	3F	
	1933	201 OS(L)	Motorcycle, light, solo	198cc	1	3F, 4F	
	1933	251 OS(L)	Motorcycle, light, solo	242cc	1	3F, 4F	
	1934	351 OS(L)	Motorcycle, medium, solo	346cc	1	4F	
	1935	601 OS(L)	Motorcycle, heavy, solo; and with sidecar	562cc	1	4F	
	1936	501 OS(L)	Motorcycle, medium, solo	500cc	1	4F	
	1939	125 ZDB	Motorcycle, light, solo	122cc	1	3Fx2	
	1940	Kettenkraftrad HK-101	Motorcycle, tractor, half-track; SdKfz 2	1,478cc	4	3Fx2	
Phänomen	1938	AHOI	Motorcycle, light, solo	124cc	1	3F	
TWN (Triumph)	1904	4.25hp	Motorcycle, medium, solo	489cc	1	1F	
	1905	3hp	Motorcycle, medium, solo	363cc	1	1F, 2F	
	1907	3hp	Motorcycle, medium, solo	453cc	1	1F	
	1908	3.5hp	Motorcycle, medium, solo	476cc	1	3F	
	1910	3.5hp	Motorcycle, medium, solo	499cc	1	1F, 3F	
	1914	Type A	Motorcycle, heavy, solo	550cc	2	4F	split piston
	1932	STM500	Motorcycle, medium, solo	500cc	1	3F	
	1935	Herren Mofa	Motorcycle, light, solo	98cc	1	3F	
	1937	S350	Motorcycle, medium, solo	346cc	1	4F	
	1938	B350	Motorcycle, medium, solo	346cc	1	4F	
	1938	BD250W	Motorcycle, light, solo	248cc	1	4F	
	1956	BDG200SL	Motorcycle, light, solo	250cc	1	4F	
Victoria	1923	KR-II	Motorcycle, heavy, solo	497cc	H2	3F	
	1927	KR-VI	Motorcycle, heavy, solo	596cc	H2	3F	
	1933	KR-6	Motorcycle, heavy, solo; and with sidecar	596cc	H2	4F	
	1936	KR-9	Motorcycle, medium, solo; and with sidecar	498cc	H2	4F	
	1938	KR-35-WH	Motorcycle, medium, solo	342cc	1	4F	
Wanderer	1908	3hp	Motorcycle, medium, solo	408cc	V2	1F	
	1920	4.5hp	Motorcycle, heavy, solo	616cc	V2	3F	
	1924	750	Motorcycle, heavy, solo	708cc	V2	3F	
Zündapp	1934	K500-W	Motorcycle, medium, solo	498cc	H2	4F	
	1934	K800-W	Motorcycle, heavy, solo; and with sidecar	804cc	H4	4F	
	1935	DBK-200 Derby	Motorcycle, light, solo	198cc	1	3F	
	1937	KS600-W	Motorcycle, heavy, solo; and with sidecar	597cc	H2	4F	
	1941	KS750	Motorcycle, heavy, with sidecar, 3x2	751cc	H2	4F	

Germany (Democratic Republic)

Make	Date	Model	Description	Engine: capacity	cyls*	Gears	Notes
EMW	1946	R-35	Motorcycle, medium, solo	340cc	1	4F	
MZ	1969	ES 250/1A, 2A	Motorcycle, light, solo; and with sidecar	243cc	1	4F	
	1975	TS 250/1	Motorcycle, light, solo	243cc	1	4F	

India

Make	Date	Model	Description	Engine: capacity	cyls*	Gears	Notes
Royal Enfield	1949	Bullet Military	Motorcycle, medium, solo	346, 499cc	1	4F, 5F	

Italy

Make	Date	Model	Description	Engine: capacity	cyls*	Gears	Notes
Benelli	1935	VLM-500	Motorcycle, medium, solo	493cc	1	4F	
	1939	250	Motorcycle, light, solo	250cc	1	2F	
	1942	Motocarro 500	Motor tricycle, load carrier/artillery tractor, 3x2	493cc	1	4F	
Bianchi	1914	Type A	Motorcycle, medium, solo	499cc	1	1F	
	1936	500M	Motorcycle, medium, solo	498cc	1	3F	
	1961	MT61	Motorcycle, medium, solo; and with sidecar	318cc	1	5F	
Cagiva	1985	350 T4A	Motorcycle, medium, solo	349cc	V2	5F	
	1994	W16	Motorcycle, heavy, solo	605cc	1	5F	
	1998	W8	Motorcycle, light, solo	125cc	1	6F	
Frera	1914	3.5hp	Motorcycle, heavy, solo	570cc	1	2F, 3F	
	1914	8hp	Motorcycle, heavy solo; and with sidecar	795cc	V2	2F, 3F	
	1929	250	Motorcycle, light, solo	250cc	1	n/a	
	1934	500	Motorcycle, medium, solo, heavy	500cc	1	3F	
Gilera	1936	LTE500	Motorcycle, medium, solo	498cc	1	4F	
	1940	600	Motorcycle, heavy, solo	600cc	1	4F	
	1942	Mercurio 500	Motor tricycle, load carrier, 3x2	499cc	1	4F	

Make	Date	Model	Description	Engine: capacity	cyls*	Gears	Notes
Gilera (continued)	1942	*Marte* VL	Motorcycle, medium, solo; and with sidecar, 3x2	499cc	1	4F	
	1942	*Gigante* VT	Motor tricycle, load carrier, 3x2	499, 600cc	1	4F	
	1946	*Saturno*	Motorcycle, medium, solo	500cc	1	4F	
	1956	175GT	Motorcycle, light, solo	175cc	1	4F	
Moto-Guzzi	1932	GT17	Motorcycle, medium, solo; and with sidecar	499cc	H1	3F	
	1932	*Militare* 32	Motor tricycle, load carrier, 3x2	499cc	H1	3F	
	1934	GTV	Motorcycle, medium, solo	488cc	H1	4F	
	1938	GT20	Motorcycle, medium, solo	499cc	H1	4F	
	1939	*Alce*	Motorcycle, medium, solo; and with sidecar	499cc	H1	4F	
	1940	*Aerone*	Motorcycle, light, solo	247cc	H1	4F	
	1941	*Alce*	Motorcycle, medium, with sidecar	499cc	H1	4F	
	1941	*Trialce*	Motor tricycle, load carrier/machine gun, 3x2	499cc	H1	4F	
	1942	500U *Unificato*	Motor tricycle, load carrier/self-propelled gun, 3x2	499cc	H1	4F	
	1942	*Trialce Smontabile*	Motor tricycle, load carrier, folding, 3x2	499cc	H1	4F	
	1946	*Superalce* (*Alce* V)	Motorcycle, medium, solo; and with sidecar	549cc	H1	4F	
	1959	*Mulo Meccanico*	Motor tricycle, load/personnel carrier, 3x3	754cc	V2	6F1R	
	1966	*Falcone*	Motorcycle, medium, solo	498cc	H1	4F	
	1967	V7	Motorcycle, heavy, solo	703cc	V2	4F	
	1968	*Stornello* 160	Motorcycle, light, solo	160cc	1	4F	
	1970	*Nuovo Falcone Militare*	Motorcycle, medium, solo	498cc	H1	4F	
	1971	*Ambasciatore* V7	Motorcycle, heavy, solo	703cc	V2	4F	
	1971	*Ambasciatore* V7 850GT	Motorcycle, heavy, solo	844cc	V2	5F	
	1973	850-T3	Motorcycle, heavy, solo	844cc	V2	5F	
	1975	V1000 *Convertito*	Motorcycle, heavy, solo	948cc	V2	5F	semi-automatic
	1977	V35	Motorcycle, medium, solo	346cc	V2	5F	
	1977	V50, V50-2	Motorcycle, medium, solo	490cc	V2	5F	
	1978	V1000 G5	Motorcycle, heavy, solo	948cc	V2	5F	
Moto-Morini	1952	175, M175	Motorcycle, light, solo	175cc	1	3F	
Sertum	1937	250 MCM	Motorcycle, light, solo	248cc	1	3F	
Volugrafo	1942	*Aeromoto*	Motor scooter, light, airborne	125cc	1	2F	

Japan

Make	Date	Model	Description	Engine: capacity	cyls*	Gears	Notes
Honda	1968	CB250	Motorcycle, light, solo	249cc	2	5F	
	1972	XL250	Motorcycle, light, solo	248cc	1	5F	
	1975	C90	Motorcycle, light, solo	90cc	1	3F	
	1978	CB400T Hawk	Motorcycle, medium, solo	395cc	2	5F, 6F	
	1986	R250 military	Motorcycle, light, solo	248cc	4	5F	
	1986	TRX-350	ATV quad bike, 4x4	329cc	2	5F	
	1989	Pan European ST1100	Motor cycle, heavy, solo	1,084cc	V4	5F	
	1998	Deauville 650	Motorcycle, heavy, solo	650cc	V2	5F	
	2002	Pan European ST1300P	Motor cycle, heavy, solo	1,260cc	V4	5F	
Iwasaki	1941	*Sanrinsha* Type 1	Motor tricycle, load/personnel carrier, 3x2	n/a	n/a	n/a	
Kawasaki	1973	650 Police Special	Motorcycle, heavy, solo	652cc	4	5F	
	1983	GT550	Motorcycle, heavy, solo	553cc	4	6F	
	1991	KL-250D8, KLR-250D8	Motorcycle, light, solo	249cc	1	6F	
Kurogane	1941	*Sanrinsha* Type 1	Motor tricycle, load/personnel carrier, 3x2	750cc	V2	3F1R	
	1941	*Sanrinsha* Type 1	Motor tricycle, water carrier, 3x2	750cc	V2	3F1R	
Sankyo (Meguro)	1937	Rikuo Type 97	Motorcycle, heavy, solo	750cc	V2	3F	
	1937	Rikuo Type 97	Motorcycle, heavy, solo; and with sidecar, 3x2	1,196cc	V2	3F1R	
Suzuki	1978	GS400	Motorcycle, medium, solo	398cc	2	6F	
	1989	Bandit GSF250	Motorcycle, light, solo	250cc	4	6F	
Yamaha	1972	XS-500	Motorcycle, medium, solo	499cc	2	5F	
	1978	DT-250MX	Motorcycle, light, solo	246cc	1	5F	
	1989	XT-125	Motorcycle, light, solo	125cc	1	5F	

Netherlands

Make	Date	Model	Description	Engine: capacity	cyls*	Gears	Notes
Eysink	1914	3.5hp	Motorcycle, medium, solo	408cc	1	3F	

Norway

Make	Date	Model	Description	Engine: capacity	cyls*	Gears	Notes
Tempo	1961	175 *Militar*	Motorcycle, light, solo	175cc	1	4F	

Make	Date	Model	Description	Engine: capacity	cyls*	Gears	Notes
Poland							
CWS	1928	M-55 S-0	Motorcycle, heavy, solo; and with sidecar	995cc	V2	3F	trials only
	1931	M55 S-III	Motorcycle, heavy, solo; and with sidecar	995cc	V2	3F	limited production
	1933	M-III	Motorcycle, heavy, solo; and with sidecar	995cc	V2	3F	
Junak	1960	M10	Motorcycle, medium, solo	350cc	1	4F	
MOJ	1938	130	Motorcycle, light, solo	128cc	1	3F	
Sokol	1936	600RT M211	Motorcycle, heavy, solo; and with sidecar	575cc	1	3F	
Soviet Union							
IMZ (Ural)	1942	M-72	Motorcycle, heavy, solo; and with sidecar	746cc	H2	4F	
	1954	M-72K (K-750)	Motorcycle, heavy, solo; and with sidecar	746cc	H2	4F	
	1956	M-72H, M72M	Motorcycle, heavy, solo; and with sidecar	746cc	H2	4F	
Izhevsk	1933	IZh-7 (L300)	Motorcycle, medium, solo	293cc	1	3F	
	1933	NATI-A750	Motorcycle, heavy, solo; and with sidecar	747cc	V2	3F	development only
	1938	IZh-8	Motorcycle, medium, solo	293cc	1	3F	
	1940	IZh-9	Motorcycle, medium, solo	350cc	1	3F	
	1940	IZh-12	Motorcycle, medium, solo	350cc	1	3F	
	1946	IZh-350	Motorcycle, medium, solo	350cc	1	3F	
KMZ (Cossack, Dniepr)	1963	K-750M	Motorcycle, heavy, solo; and with sidecar; 3x2	746cc	H2	4F1R	
	1964	MV-750	Motorcycle, heavy, solo; and with sidecar	746cc	H2	4F1R	
	1968	MT-9, MT-10 (K-650)	Motorcycle, heavy, solo; and with sidecar	649cc	H2	4F1R	
	1977	MT-12	Motorcycle, heavy, solo; and with sidecar	649cc	H2	4F1R	
	1985	MB-650 M1	Motorcycle, heavy, solo; and with sidecar, 3x2	649cc	H2	4F1R	
PMZ	1935	A-750 (NATI-A750)	Motorcycle, heavy, solo; and with sidecar	747cc	V2	3F	
TIM (TIZ)	1936	AM600	Motorcycle, heavy, solo; and with sidecar	595cc	1	4F	
Ukremto	1930	KhMZ-1M	Motorcycle, medium, solo	347cc	1	3F	
Spain							
Bultaco	1981	Commander	Motorcycle, light, solo	238cc	1	5F	
Sweden							
Hagglünds	1972	XM-72	Motorcycle, medium, solo	293cc	1	Variomatic	
	1974	XM-74 (MC-258-MT)	Motorcycle, medium, solo	347cc	1	Variomatic	trials only
Husqvarna	1916	145	Motorcycle, heavy, solo	548cc	V2	3F	
	1922	500A	Motorcycle, heavy, with sidecar	990cc	V2	3F	
	1942	M/42	Motorcycle, medium, solo	496cc	1	3F	
	1972	350A	Motorcycle, medium, solo	350cc	1	auto	
	1978	250A	Motorcycle, light, solo	245cc	1	4F auto	trials only
	1980	MC258-MT	Motorcycle, light, solo; also with skis	245cc	1	4F auto	
Monark, Monark-Albin	1942	M/42	Motorcycle, medium, solo	496cc	1	3F	
	1952	M500	Motorcycle, light, solo	250cc	1	4F	
	1954	M550	Motorcycle, light, solo	244cc	2	4F	
	1955	M560	Motorcycle, light, solo	250cc	1	4F	
	1965	MC356A	Motorcycle, medium, solo	344cc	2	4F	
	1972	M/72	Motorcycle, medium, solo	292cc	1	auto	trials only
	1980	MC258-MT	Motorcycle, light, solo; also with skis	245cc	1	4F auto	
NV	1942	M/42	Motorcycle, medium, solo	496cc	1	3F	
	1943	M1000	Motorcycle, heavy, with sidecar	990cc	V2	6F1R	
	1955	Model 38	Motorcycle, light, solo	246cc	1	4F	
Suecia	1937	500 *Armée*	Motorcycle, medium, solo; and with sidecar	496cc	1	4F	
Switzerland							
Condor	1908	1.25hp	Motorcycle, light, solo	n/a	1	2F	
	1922	A-641	Motorcycle, heavy, with sidecar	992cc	V2	3F	
	1930	A-752	Motorcycle, heavy, with sidecar	992cc	V2	3F	
	1943	A-680	Motorcycle, heavy, solo	676cc	V2	4F	
	1943	A-1000	Motorcycle, heavy, solo; and with sidecar	990cc	V2	4F	
	1948	A-580	Motorcycle, heavy, solo	577cc	H2	4F	
	1948	A-750	Motorcycle, heavy, solo; and with sidecar	749cc	V2	4F	
	1950	A580-1	Motorcycle, heavy, solo	577cc	H2	4F	

Make	Date	Model	Description	Engine: capacity	cyls*	Gears	Notes
Condor (continued)	1962	A-250	Motorcycle, light, solo	250cc	1	4F	
	1973	A-350	Motorcycle, medium, solo	340cc	1	5F	
Mercier	1936	Type 3	Motorcycle, medium, tracked, solo	350cc	1	n/a	
Motosacoche	1914	2hp	Motorcycle, medium, with sidecar	497cc	V2	2F	
(MAG)	1933	Type 512	Motorcycle, medium, solo; and with sidecar	497cc	V2	3F	
Universal	1940	A-500	Motorcycle, medium, solo	497cc	1	4F	
	1943	A-680	Motorcycle, heavy, solo; and with sidecar	676cc	V2	4F	
	1943	A-1000	Motorcycle, heavy, solo; and with sidecar	990cc	V2	4F	
	1950	A-580	Motorcycle, heavy, solo	578cc	H2	4F	

United Kingdom

Make	Date	Model	Description	Engine: capacity	cyls*	Gears	Notes
AC (Auto Carriers)	1904	Auto Carrier	Motor tricycle, machine gun, and ammunition, 3x1648cc		1	2F	
AJS (A J Stevens)	1917	Model D military	Motorcycle, heavy, machine gun carrier	748cc	V2	3F	
	1917	Model D military	Motorcycle, heavy, ammunition carrier	748cc	V2	3F	
	1917	Model D military	Motorcycle, heavy, light ambulance	748cc	V2	3F	
	1929	Model 6	Motorcycle, medium, solo	350cc	1	3F	trials only
	1940	Model 8	Motorcycle, medium, solo	498cc	1	4F	
	1940	Model 8SS	Motorcycle, medium, solo	498cc	1	4F	
	1940	Model 9	Motorcycle, medium, solo	498cc	1	4F	
	1940	Model 26	Motorcycle, medium, solo	347cc	1	4F	trials only
Ariel	1935	VA3	Motorcycle, heavy, solo	557cc	1	4F	trials only
	1936	4F	Motorcycle, heavy, solo	597cc	S4	4F	trials only
	1936	4G	Motorcycle, heavy, solo	997cc	S4	4F	trials only
	1940	MG	Motorcycle, medium, solo	349cc	1	4F	
	1940	NG De-Luxe	Motorcycle, medium, solo	347cc	1	4F	
	1940	NH Red Hunter	Motorcycle, medium, solo	347cc	1	4F	
	1940	VA	Motorcycle, medium, solo	497cc	1	4F	
	1940	VB De-Luxe	Motorcycle, heavy, solo	598cc	1	4F	
	1940	VG De-Luxe	Motorcycle, medium, solo	497cc	1	4F	
	1940	VH Red Hunter	Motorcycle, medium, solo	497cc	1	4F	
	1940	W/NG	Motorcycle, medium, solo	347cc	1	4F	

LEFT: **British soldiers from a machine-gun company with a Clyno combination mounting a .303in Vickers water-cooled machine-gun.**

Make	Date	Model	Description	Engine: capacity	cyls*	Gears	Notes
Ariel (continued)	1940	W/NH (or W/VH)	Motorcycle, medium, solo	497cc	1	4F	
	1939	W/VA	Motorcycle, medium, solo	497cc	1	4F	
	1940	W/VG	Motorcycle, medium, solo	497cc	1	4F	
Armstrong Bombardier (Canada)	1978	Can-Am	Motorcycle, light, solo	250cc	1	5F	also by
Aveling-Barford	1938	125	Motorcycle, light, solo	125cc	1	1F	trials only
BSA	1911	3.5hp	Motorcycle, medium, solo				
	1914	Model H	Motorcycle, heavy, solo	557cc	1	3F	
	1929	S29	Motorcycle, medium, solo	499cc	1	3F	trials only
	1933	500 (War Office) Twin	Motorcycle, medium, solo	498cc	2	3F	
	1933	A14	Motorcycle, medium, solo	498cc	2	3F	
	1934	WD 500 Twin	Motorcycle, medium, solo	498cc	V2	4F	trials only
	1935	W35-6	Motorcycle, medium, solo	499cc	1	4F	trials only
	1936	B23	Motorcycle, medium, solo	348cc	1	4F	trials only
	1936	B26	Motorcycle, medium, solo	348cc	1	4F	trials only
	1936	M20 (K-M20, W-M20)	Motorcycle, medium, solo; and with sidecar	496cc	1	4F	
	1937	B20 (H-B20, J-B20)	Motorcycle, light, solo	249cc	1	4F	
	1938	G14	Motorcycle, heavy, solo	986cc	V2	4F	
	1938	G14	Motorcycle, heavy, with machine-gun sidecar	986cc	V2	4F	
	1938	Gold Star M24 (J-M24, K-M24)	Motorcycle, medium, solo	496cc	1	4F	
	1938	W-B27	Motorcycle, medium, solo	348cc	1	4F	
	1939	C10 (K-C10, W-C10)	Motorcycle, light, solo	249cc	1	4F	
	1939	M21 (K-M21, W-M21)	Motorcycle, heavy, with sidecar/machine-gun sidecar	591cc	1	4F	
	1939	M21 (W-M21)	Motorcycle, heavy, solo	591cc	1	4F	
	1939	M22 (K-M22	Motorcycle, medium, solo	496cc	1	4F	
	1939	Silver Sports M23 (K-M23)	Motorcycle, medium, solo	496cc	1	4F	
	1940	B30-WD	Motorcycle, medium, solo	348cc	1	4F	
	1940	C11 (W-C11)	Motorcycle, light, solo	249cc	1	4F	
	1940	C12 (W-C12)	Motorcycle, medium, solo	348cc	1	4F	
	1940	E15 (WO-E15)	Motorcycle, medium, solo	498cc	2	4F	
	1940	Silver Sports B29 (W-B29)	Motorcycle, medium, solo	348cc	1	4F	
	1959	B15	Motorcycle, medium, solo	498cc	2	4F	
	1961	B40 Star Mk 1	Motorcycle, medium, solo	348cc	1	4F	
	1968	Starfire B25S	Motorcycle, medium, solo	441cc	1	4F	
	1969	B40-WD	Motorcycle, medium, solo; FV2003	348cc	1	4F	
	1970	Victor Special B44S	Motorcycle, medium, solo	441cc	1	4F	
Clyno	1910	5–6hp	Motorcycle, heavy, solo	744cc	V2	3F	
	1913	250	Motorcycle, light, solo	250cc	1	2F	
Clyno/Vickers	1915	5–6hp	Motorcycle, heavy, with machine-gun sidecar	744cc	V2	3F	
	1915	5–6hp	Motorcycle, heavy, light ambulance	744cc	V2	3F	
Despatch Rider	1915	–	Motorcycle, medium, solo	210, 269cc	1	3F	
Douglas	1914	2.75hp Model V military	Motorcycle, medium, solo	348cc	H2	2F, 3F	
	1914	3.5hp Model A	Motorcycle, medium, with sidecar	495cc	H2	2F	
	1914	4hp Models A, B military	Motorcycle, heavy, with sidecar	593cc	H2	3F	
	1929	L29, L29/2, L29/3, etc	Motorcycle, medium, solo	348cc	H2	3F	
	1931	A31	Motorcycle, medium, solo	348cc	H2	3F	trials only
	1934	5Y2 Blue Chief	Motorcycle, medium, solo	500cc	H2	4F	trials only
	1944	DV60	Motorcycle, heavy, solo	602cc	H2	4F	trials only
	1951	Vespa 125	Motor scooter, 2 wheel	125cc	1	3F	licence-built
Excelsior	1942	Universal	Motorcycle, light, solo	122cc	1	3F	
	1942	Welbike Mk I, Mk II	Motorcycle, light, folding, airborne	98cc	1	1F	
Francis Barnett	1928	Military lightweight	Motorcycle, light, solo	172cc	1	3F	
	1929	Model 12	Motorcycle, medium, solo	350cc	1	3F	trials only
	1941	Plover K40/K41	Motorcycle, light, solo	150cc	1	3F	trials only
Greeves	1962	Griffin 24DB	Motorcycle, light, solo	246cc	1	4F	trials only
GHL Defence Prod.	2000	Diablo	ATV quad bike, 4x4	850cc	3	4F	diesel

Make	Date	Model	Description	Engine: capacity	cyls*	Gears	Notes
A W Hall	1906	4hp	Motorcycle, medium, solo	n/a	n/a	n/a	
Hayes/RMCS	2001	M1030M1, M1E	Motorcycle, heavy, solo	580cc	1	6F	diesel
James	1942	K15, K16	Motorcycle, light, solo	150cc	1	3F	
	1942	K17	Motorcycle, light, solo	122cc	1	3F	
	1942	ML	Motorcycle, light, solo, airborne	122cc	1	3F	
	1948	Comet, Comet J10	Motorcycle, light, solo	98cc	1	2F	
Levis	1928	Model M	Motorcycle, light, solo	247cc	1	n/a	trials only
	1928	Six port	Motorcycle, light, solo	247cc	1	n/a	
Matchless	1929	Model T/4	Motorcycle, medium, solo	350cc			trials only
	1930	Silver Arrow	Motorcycle, medium, solo	400cc	V2	3F	
	1935	Model 36, G3	Motorcycle, medium, solo	347cc	1	4F	
	1936	G7	Motorcycle, light, solo	246cc	1	4F	
	1940	G3WO	Motorcycle, medium, solo	347cc	1	4F	
	1940	G8	Motorcycle, medium, solo	500cc	1	4F	
	1940	Military lightweight	Motorcycle, light, solo	245cc	1	4F	trials only
	1940	Model 40, G3/L lightweight	Motorcycle, medium, solo	347cc	1	4F	trials only
	1940	W40, G2M	Motorcycle, light, solo	246cc	1	4F	
	1941	Model 41, G3/L lightweight	Motorcycle, medium, solo	347cc	1	4F	
New Hudson	1929	Model 83E	Motorcycle, medium, solo	350cc	1	3F	trials only
New Imperial	1935	Model 40	Motorcycle, medium, solo	346cc	1	n/a	trials only
	1940	Model 76, 76DL	Motorcycle, medium, solo	500cc	1	n/a	
Norman	1943	Lightweight	Motorcycle, light, solo	125cc	1	n/a	
Norton	1932	16H	Motorcycle, medium, solo	498cc	1	4F	trials only
	1932	Model 18	Motorcycle, medium, solo	498cc	1	4F	
	1932	Model 19	Motorcycle, medium, solo; and with sidecar	498cc	1	4F	trials only
	1936	16H, WD-16H	Motorcycle, medium, solo; and with sidecar	498cc	1	4F	
	1936	16H lightweight	Motorcycle, medium, solo	498cc	1	4F	trials only
	1938	Model 50	Motorcycle, medium, solo	348cc	1	4F	
	1939	633 Big Four Model 1	Motorcycle, heavy, with sidecar, 3x2	633cc	1	4F	
	1939	Military lightweight 350	Motorcycle, medium, solo	348cc	1	4F	trials only
	1939	Model 18	Motorcycle, medium, solo	498cc	1	4F	sprung frame, trials only
	1940	Military lightweight 500	Motorcycle, medium, solo	498cc	1	4F	trials only
	1940	1100 V-twin	Motorcycle, heavy, with sidecar	1096cc	V2	4F	trials only
	1981	Interpol 2, 2A P41	Motorcycle, heavy, solo	588cc	R2	5F	
	1988	Commander P52	Motorcycle, heavy, solo	588cc	R2	5F	
OEC	1928	Caterpillar Tractor	Motorcycle, medium, solo, 3x2	350cc	1	3F	trials only
	1928	Caterpillar Tractor	Motorcycle, light, solo, 3x2	250cc	1	3F	trials only
	1929	Caterpillar Tractor	Motorcycle, medium, solo	350cc	1	3F	trials only
Phelon & Moore (P&M)	1914	3.5hp	Motorcycle, medium, solo; and with sidecar	495cc	1	2F	
	1938	Panther Model 100	Motorcycle, heavy, solo; and with sidecar	598cc	2	4F	
Premier (Coventry-Premier)	1910	–	Motorcycle, heavy, solo; and with sidecar	499cc	1	n/a	
Roush	2006	Arctic Cat diesel	ATV quad bike, 4x4	686cc	2	variable x2	diesel
Rover	1915	3.25hp	Motorcycle, medium, with sidecar	496cc	1	1F	
Royal Enfield	1914	Model 140	Motorcycle, medium, solo; and with sidecar	425cc	V2	2F	
	1917	Model 140	Motorcycle, medium, ammunition carrier	425cc	V2	2F	
	1917	Model 140	Motorcycle, medium, light ambulance	425cc	V2	2F	
	1917	Model 140	Motorcycle, medium, machine gun carrier	425cc	V2	2F	
	1935	Model B	Motorcycle, light, solo	248cc	1	3F	trials only
	1935	Model C	Motorcycle, medium, solo	346cc	1	4F	
	1939	Model D, WD/D	Motorcycle, light, solo	248cc	1	4F	
	1940	Military lightweight 350	Motorcycle, medium, solo	340cc	1	4F	trials only
	1940	Model G, WD/G	Motorcycle, medium, solo	346cc	1	4F	
	1940	Model L	Motorcycle, heavy, solo	570cc	1	4F	trials only
	1940	Model WD/L	Motorcycle, heavy, solo	570cc	1	4F	
	1940	Model WD/C	Motorcycle, medium, solo	346cc	1	4F	
	1940	Model WD/CO, WD/CO/B	Motorcycle, medium, solo	346cc	1	4F	
	1941	Model KX	Motorcycle, heavy, with sidecar	1,140cc	V2	4F	
	1941	Model WD/J2	Motorcycle, medium, solo	499cc	1	4F	
	1942	Flying Flea WD/RE	Motorcycle, light, solo, airborne	126cc	1	3F	

Make	Date	Model	Description	Engine: capacity	cyls*	Gears	Notes
Rudge Whitworth	1912	3.5hp Multi	Motorcycle, medium, solo	499cc	1	variable	
	1936	Rapid	Motorcycle, light, solo	247cc	1	3F	trials only
	1936	Ulster 500	Motorcycle, medium,	500cc	1	4F	trials only
	1938	Military 250	Motorcycle, light, solo	247cc	1	4F	
Scott	1912	3.75hp	Motorcycle, medium, solo	499cc	1	2F	
Scott/Vickers	1914	3.75hp	Motorcycle, medium, with sidecar, machine gun	499cc	1	2F	
Simms/Vickers	1899	Motor scout	Motor quadricycle, machine gun, 4x2	n/a	n/a	n/a	
Sunbeam	1914	3.5hp	Motorcycle, heavy, solo	495cc	1	3F	
	1914	4hp FMM	Motorcycle, heavy, solo; and with sidecar	545cc	1	3F	
	1916	6hp	Motorcycle, medium, solo	398cc	2	3F	
	1916	8hp	Motorcycle, heavy, ambulance	996cc	1	3F	
	1916	8hp	Motorcycle, heavy, machine gun	996cc	1	3F	
	1936	Lion	Motorcycle, medium, solo	500cc	1	4F	trials only
	1941	1000	Motorcycle, heavy, with sidecar	1,000cc	V2	4F	prototype only
Triumph	1913	Model A	Motorcycle, heavy, solo; and with sidecar	549cc	1	3F	
	1913	Model C	Motorcycle, heavy, solo	549cc	1	3F	
	1915	Model H "Trusty"	Motorcycle, heavy, solo; and with sidecar	549cc	1	3F	
	1925	Model P-II	Motorcycle, medium, solo	494cc	1	3F	
	1926	Model P (RASC conversion)	Motorcycle, medium, solo, 3x2	494cc	1	3F	trials only
	1927	Model N, NP	Motorcycle, medium, solo	494cc	1	3F	
	1928	Model ND	Motorcycle, heavy, solo	549cc	1	3F	
	1928	Model NL3	Motorcycle, medium, solo	494cc	1	3F	trials only
	1932	Silent Scout Model B	Motorcycle, medium, solo	493, 550cc	1	4F	
	1935	3/1	Motorcycle, medium, solo	343cc	1	4F	trials only
	1936	3S	Motorcycle, medium, solo	343cc	1	4F	trials only
	1937	3H	Motorcycle, medium, solo	343cc	1	4F	
	1938	3SW	Motorcycle, medium, solo	343cc	1	4F	
	1938	5SW	Motorcycle, medium, solo	498cc	1	4F	
	1939	3TW military lightweight	Motorcycle, medium, solo	343cc	2	4F	trials only
	1939	5T	Motorcycle, medium, solo	498cc	2	4F	trials only
	1940	3H	Motorcycle, medium, solo	343cc	1	4F	
	1940	3TW	Motorcycle, medium, solo	343cc	2	4F	
	1942	3HW	Motorcycle, medium, solo	343cc	1	4F	
	1942	5TW	Motorcycle, medium, solo	498cc	2	4F	
	1948	TRW Mk 1, Mk 2	Motorcycle, medium, solo; FV2001	499cc	2	4F	
	1949	5/3W	Motorcycle, medium, solo	499cc	2	4F	
	1961	Tiger Cub T20T	Motorcycle, light, solo	199cc	1	4F	
	1962	Tiger Cub T20WD, T20MWD	Motorcycle, light, solo	199cc	1	4F	
	1963	3TA Special	Motorcycle, medium, solo	349cc	2	4F	
	1964	TRW Mk 3	Motorcycle, medium, solo; FV2002	499cc	2	4F	
	1966	T50	Motorcycle, medium, solo	490cc	2	4F	trials only
	1978	TR7RV Tiger	Motorcycle, heavy, solo	744cc	2	5F	
Velocette	1939	MAC	Motorcycle, medium, solo	349cc	1	4F	trials only
	1939	MSS	Motorcycle, medium, solo	500cc	1	4F	trials only
	1940	MAC (WD), MDD	Motorcycle, medium, solo	349cc	1	4F	
	1941	MAF	Motorcycle, medium, solo	349cc	1	4F	
Zenith	1908	–	Motorcycle, medium, solo; and with sidecar	500cc	1	variable	stepless

United States of America

Make	Date	Model	Description	Engine: capacity	cyls*	Gears	Notes
Autoped	1915	Ever Ready	Motor scooter	155cc	1	1F	trials only
Cleveland	1915	2.5hp	Motorcycle, light, solo	296cc	1	2F	
Cooper	1944	–	Motor scooter	292cc	1	n/a	
Crosley	1940	–	Motorcycle, heavy, solo	580 cc	H2	3F	trials only
	1940	–	Motor tricycle, 3x2	580cc	H2	3F	trials only
Cushman	1942	32	Motor scooter, with sidecar	246cc	1	2F	
	1942	34	Motor scooter, with sidecar	246cc	1	2F	
	1943	Package Kar 39	Motor scooter, three-wheeled, package delivery	246cc	1	2F	
	1944	Autoglide 53	Motor scooter, two wheeled, airborne	246cc	1	2F	
	1948	67P	Motor scooter, three-wheeled, package delivery	246cc	1	2F	
	1969	Truckster 1002	Motor scooter, three-wheeled, package delivery	n/a	H2	3F1R	
	1974	Truckster 400	Motor scooter, three-wheeled, package delivery	n/a	H2	3F1R	

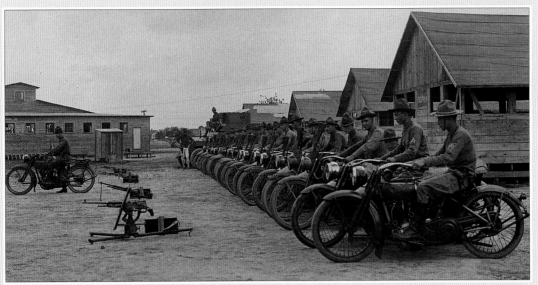

LEFT: **US Motorcycle Corps at Fort Brown, Texas, in May 1918.** Note the long handlebars of the period.

Make	Date	Model	Description	Engine: capacity	cyls*	Gears	Notes
Cushman (continued)	1978	Truckster 434	Motor scooter, three-wheeled, package delivery	n/a	H2	3F1R	
Custer Specialty	1943	Carrier	Motor tricycle, load carrier, 3x1	145cc	1	n/a	
Excelsior Motor Supply	1917	7-10hp	Motorcycle, heavy, solo	997cc	V2	3F	
GM Delco	1938	–	Motor tricycle, 3x2	745cc	H2	4F	trials only
	1939	–	Motorcycle, heavy, solo	745cc	H2	4F	trials only
Harley-Davidson	1912	X-8-A	Motorcycle, medium, solo	492cc	1	1F	
	1915	F, FS, FUS	Motorcycle, heavy, solo; and with sidecar	999cc	V2	3F	
	1916	J	Motorcycle, heavy, solo; and with sidecar	999cc	V2	3F	
	1916	J/AC	Motorcycle, heavy, ammunition carrier	999cc	V2	3F	
	1916	J/GC	Motorcycle, heavy, machine gun	999cc	V2	3F	
	1916	J/SC	Motorcycle, heavy, ambulance	999cc	V2	3F	
	1917	E	Motorcycle, heavy, solo	999cc	V2	1F	
	1924	JD	Motorcycle, heavy, solo	1,213cc	V2	3F	
	1929	C	Motorcycle, heavy, solo	499cc	1	3F	
	1930	VL	Motorcycle, heavy, solo; and with sidecar	1213cc	V2	3F	
	1932	RL	Motorcycle, heavy, solo	737cc	V2	3F	
	1932	VS	Motorcycle, heavy, with sidecar	1,213cc	V2	3F	trials only
	1932	VS/LC (Landsverk 210)	Motorcycle, heavy, with armoured sidecar	1,213cc	V2	3F	
	1934	VDS	Motorcycle, heavy, with sidecar	1,213cc	V2	3F	
	1936	ELC	Motorcycle, heavy, with sidecar	999cc	V2	4F	
	1937	WL	Motorcycle, heavy, solo	737cc	V2	3F	
	1939	ELA	Motorcycle, heavy, with sidecar	987cc	V2	4F	
	1939	UA	Motorcycle, heavy, with sidecar	1,213cc	V2	3F	
	1939	UH	Motorcycle, heavy, solo	1,311cc	V2	3F	
	1939	US/LE	Motorcycle, heavy, with sidecar	1,213cc	V2	4F	
	1939	US/LLE	Motorcycle, heavy, with sidecar	1,213cc	V2	4F	
	1939	WLA "Liberator"	Motorcycle, heavy, solo	737cc	V2	3F	
	1940	Servi-Car GA	Motor tricycle, 3x2	737cc	V2	3F1R	
	1940	Servi-Car GDT	Motor tricycle, 3x2	737cc	V2	3F1R	
	1940	TA field car	Motor tricycle, 3x2	737cc	V2	3F1R	experimental
	1941	FLS	Motorcycle, heavy, with sidecar	1,213cc	V2	4F	
	1941	WLC	Motorcycle, heavy, solo	737cc	V2	3F	
	1942	EL	Motorcycle, heavy, with sidecar	987cc	V2	4F	
	1942	XA	Motorcycle, heavy, solo	737cc	H2	4F	
	1942	XAS	Motorcycle, heavy, with sidecar	737cc	H2	4F	
	1945	WLR	Motorcycle, heavy, solo	737cc	V2	3F	
	1946	WSR	Motorcycle, heavy, with sidecar, 3x2	737cc	V2	3F	
	1948	S	Motorcycle, light, solo	123cc	1	3F	
	1950	M50	Motorcycle, medium, solo	485cc	1	4F	
	1950	Servi-Car G	Motor tricycle, 3x2	737cc	V2	3F1R	
	1953	KA	Motorcycle, heavy, solo	737cc	V2	4F	
	1956	Sport KH	Motorcycle, heavy, solo	901cc	V2	4F	
	1963	Sportster XLA	Motorcycle, heavy, solo	901cc	V2	4F	
	1967	Electra Glide FLH	Motorcycle, heavy, solo	1,213cc	V2	4F	
	1987	MT500	Motorcycle, medium, solo	485cc	1	4F	
	1993	MT350E	Motorcycle, medium, solo	349cc	1	4F	

Make	Date	Model	Description	Engine: capacity	cyls*	Gears	Notes
Hendee Indian	1917	Powerplus	Motorcycle, heavy, solo; and with sidecar	998cc	V2	3F	
	1920	Scout	Motorcycle, heavy, solo	596, 745cc	V2	3F	
	1922	Chief	Motorcycle, heavy, solo	998cc	V2	3F	
	1932	Junior Scout	Motorcycle, medium, solo	493cc	V2	3F	
Indian	1938	Dispatch-Tow	Motor tricycle, 3x2	1,206cc	V2	3F	trials only
	1939	639-B	Motorcycle, heavy, solo	744cc	V2	3F	
	1940	–	Motor tricycle, 3x2	998cc	V2	3F	
	1940	340-B	Motorcycle, heavy, with sidecar	1,206cc	V2	3F	
	1940	640-A, 640-B	Motorcycle, heavy, solo	744cc	V2	3F	
	1940	Chief 340-B	Motorcycle, heavy, with sidecar	1,206cc	V2	3F	
	1940	MTC-18	Motor tricycle, 3x2	1,206cc	V2	3F	
	1941	741-A, 741-B	Motorcycle, medium, solo	493cc	V2	3F	
	1941	841-B	Motorcycle, heavy, solo	744cc	V2	4F	
	1944	Aerocycle 144, 148	Motorcycle, light, solo; M1	221cc	1	4F	
	1944	Chief 344	Motorcycle, heavy, with sidecar	1,206cc	V2	4F	
	1949	Arrow 149M	Motorcycle, light, solo; T3	221cc	1	4F	
Jordan	1951	Jordan Special	Motorcycle, heavy, solo	498cc	1	4F	trials only
Militaire Auto (Militor)	1912	5hp	Motorcycle, medium, solo	480cc	1	3F1R	
	1917	12hp	Motorcycle, heavy, with sidecar	1,306cc	4	3F1R	trials only
Polaris Industries	2004	Sportsman Military	ATV quad bike, 4x4, 6x6	683cc	2	2F1R	diesel; automatic
Rokon	1963	Trail-Breaker	Motorcycle, light, solo, 2x2	134cc	1	1F	other engines also used
Safticycle	1943	–	Motorized bicycle, solo	145cc	1	1F	trials only
Salsbury	1944	–	Motor scooter, three-wheeled, with sidecar	145cc	1	1F	
Simplex	1943	Servi-Cycle GA-1	Motor-driven bicycle, two wheeled	194cc	1	2F	twin pulley drive
J A Strimple	1936	Keen Power Cycle	Motor scooter, three-wheeled, with sidecar	145cc	1	1F	
Thor	1912	7hp Model U	Motorcycle, heavy, solo; and with sidecar	1,000cc	V2	3F	
Whizzer Motorbike Co	1951	Sportsman 300S	Motorized bicycle, solo	145cc	1	2F	trials only

RIGHT: **The Harley-Davidson Model VSC/LC sidecar outfit was supplied to the Swedish Landsverk company for conversion to an armoured machine-gun mount, supplied to the Danish Army.**

Index

ABOVE: **The Honda XR250 was used by US forces in Operation Desert Storm during the first Gulf War.**

ABOVE: **Military re-enactors with their superbly restored Zündapp KS-750.**

Key to flags

For the specification boxes, the national flag that was current at the time of the vehicle's use is shown.

 Austria

 Belgium

 Canada

 China

 Czechoslovakia

 Denmark

 Finland

 France

 Germany 1871–1918

 Germany World War II

 West Germany post-World War II

 East Germany post-World War II

 India

 Italy

 Japan

 Poland

 Soviet Union

 Sweden

 Switzerland

 United Kingdom

 United States of America

Acknowledgements

Picture research for this book was carried out by Pat Ware and Jasper Spencer-Smith, who have selected images from the following sources: JSS Collection, Warehouse, Getty Images, Topfoto, Imperial War Museum, Archives of Canada, BMIH, The Swedish Army Museum and Ullstein Bild.

A special thanks to Emily Fischer of the National Military History Center, Auburn, Indiana.

Much of the colour material has been supplied by the following (l=left, r=right, t=top, b=bottom, m=middle):

Mark Barnes: 152t; 152b.
John Blackman: 15tl; 15ml; 50br; 54tl; 75br; 77t; 77m; 133tl; 133tr; 133b; 139t; 140t; 140b; 145t; 145b; 148tr; 148b; 156t; 156b; 157t; 157b; 178t; 178b; 179m; 179b; 184t; 184b; 185bl; 185br; 194tr; 195tl; 195tr; 200t; 200m; 201t; 201m; 201b; 202tl; 202tr; 202b; 208t; 208b; 209l; 209r; 210t; 210m; 210b; 214t; 214b; 216b; 225b; 235t; 235b.
Club Gnome et Rhône: 116; 117t; 117m; 117b.

Gert Ekberg: 172b.
The Great War Society: 19t; 26b; 32b.
Andrew Morland: 16t; 17tl; 39t; 39b; 86t; 86bl; 87t; 87b; 90t; 90bl; 90br; 91t; 91b; 100br; 134t; 160t; 177t; 194b; 195b; 219t; 222tl; 222tr; 227t; 230t; 230b; 237t; 242.
Phil Royal: 74t; 164t; 194tl; 215b; 224.
Linzi Smart: 175t; 175m; 175b.
Simon Thomson: 46tl; 46tr; 50t; 50bl; 56b; 58t; 58m; 68tl; 68tr; 68b; 69br; 70b; 79t; 89b; 92b; 93tl; 93tr; 93ml; 93b; 94–5; 110b; 129tr; 132t; 132b; 139b; 146; 147t; 147b; 162b; 167t; 179t; 185t; 185m; 186; 199t; 200b; 207t; 215b; 255.
Peter Tipping: 212t; 212b; 213t; 213b.
John Wright: 236t; 237b; 238t; 238b.
Yesterdays.nl: 176ml; 176mr; 188b; 233b; 234tl; 234tr; 234mr; 234b.

Every effort has been made to acknowledge photographs correctly, however, we apologize for any unintentional omissions, which will be corrected in future editions.

ABOVE: German *Kradschützen* move through a Russian village during Operation Barbarossa.